CONTESTING THE NEW SOUTH ORDER

Contesting the
New South

Order

The 1914–1915 Strike at Atlanta's Fulton Mills

The
University
of North
Carolina
Press

Chapel Hill
and London

CLIFFORD M. KUHN

Designed by April Leidig-Higgins
Set in Minion by Keystone Typesetting, Inc.

The paper in this book meets the guidelines for per-
manence and durability of the Committee on Production Guidelines for Book Longevity of the Council on Library Resources.

Library of Congress Cataloging-in-Publication Data
Kuhn, Cliff.   Contesting the new South order :
the 1914–1915 strike at Atlanta's Fulton Mills /
Clifford M. Kuhn.
p. cm.   Includes bibliographical references
and index.
ISBN 0-8078-2644-8 (cloth : alk. paper)
ISBN 0-8078-4973-1 (pbk. : alk. paper)
1. Fulton Bag and Cotton Mills Strike, Atlanta, Ga.,
1914–1915—History. 2. Strikes and lockouts—
Cotton manufacture—Georgia—Atlanta—History.
3. Industrial relations—Southern States—
Case studies. I. Title.
HD5325.T42 1914.A854 2001
331.89'287721'09758231—dc21 2001027123

05 04 03 02 01 5 4 3 2 1

CONTENTS

ILLUSTRATIONS, MAPS, FIGURES, TABLE

MAPS

FIGURES

TABLE

PREFACE

At some level, this work has been over two decades in the making. Over the years, many people have assisted in the effort, and I have long and increasingly looked forward to thanking them. Now is that time.

In the mid-1970s, I wrote a history series for Atlanta's alternative newspaper *The Great Speckled Bird*, addressing various long-suppressed or neglected aspects of the city's past. Three pieces on the 1906 race riot, the Leo Frank case, and the 1916 streetcar strike drew my attention to early-twentieth-century Atlanta, a time and place I quickly realized was much more complex than the conventional historical wisdom would have it. I went to graduate school with the idea of studying the streetcar strike as a lens into the urban South and southern labor history. Eventually I presented a rather grandiose dissertation prospectus on race, labor, politics, and culture in Atlanta from 1880–1920. One of the seven chapters was going to examine three strikes during the 1910s, the streetcar strikes of 1916 and 1918, and the Fulton Bag strike of 1914–15. Now, who knows how many trees worth of paper later, the onetime, would-be third of a chapter has become a book.

One person who helped in this transformation was Jerry Clark of the National Archives, who steered me to the papers of the United States Commission on Industrial Relations. Like many other researchers over the years, I am in his debt. Major thanks are also due Leonard Rapport, who long ago literally rescued the CIR papers from destruction. The records, along with those of the Federal Mediation and Conciliation Service, have proven to be a gold mine of information, belying the claim made by Georgia senator Hoke Smith during the 1915 debate over publication of the CIR material that what the commission produced was "so much junk" that "nobody will read."

Clark and his colleague Jerry Hess are among the many archivists who have been of great assistance over the years. I also wish to thank the archivists at the Southern Labor Archives, Emory University, the Suitland, Maryland, branch of the National Archives, the Atlanta Historical Society, Duke University, the New York Public Library, the State Historical Society of Wisconsin, and the

Baker Library of the Harvard Business School, all of whom have been un-failingly generous and professional. I especially appreciate the work of Peter Roberts of the Special Collections at Georgia State University, whose close examination of the photographs generated during the Fulton strike yielded a great deal about their origins and composition.

Particular mention must be made of the staff at the Georgia Institute of Technology's Archives and Special Collections, a place where I have spent much of the past thirteen years. Ruth Hill, Byron Craig, Michael Branch, Anne Salter, and their associates have answered my every beck and call with good humor and dispatch and have patiently abided my numerous goings-on about the richness of the collection in their care. For the Fulton Bag and Cotton Mills Collection at Georgia Tech is truly extraordinary. In addition to providing arguably the most detailed picture of any early-twentieth-century southern industrial dispute, the collection reveals an enormous amount about working conditions, personnel matters, industrial espionage, management practices, and networks of regional and national manufacturers, among other subjects.

Besides the sheer volume and rich content, several things are remarkable about the collection. First is its very existence. Why did mill management keep such potentially damning documents as spy reports, confidential circulars among mill men, and private correspondence well after the end of the strike and subsequent World War I–era union organizing efforts? The reasons may never be known. One can only speculate that not only did company president Oscar Elsas have a penchant for extensive record keeping, supported by the largest office staff of any southern textile mill of the period, and for vengeance against his perceived enemies, but that his sudden death in 1924 buried the documents until the sale of the mill property in the 1980s.

The diverse documents within the collection complement each other and other sources extraordinarily well. The company payroll books, for instance, offer an opportunity to test the claims of both management and labor con-cerning the impact of the strike. Information in spy reports, internal memos, and presidential correspondence dovetails with oral history interviews and government reports. Documentation of the more than 200 discrete photo-graphic images associated with the strike can be found in a variety of sources. What is most remarkable about the collection, and not a little humbling, is that, despite the fact that historians have been attracted to it for over a decade, much, much more can be gleaned. Indeed, I am confident that historians with a variety of concerns and methodologies will be fruitfully using the Fulton Bag collection for decades to come.

It was Bob McMath who, with customary generosity, first alerted me and other historians to the collection. Over the course of this project, I have become increasingly aware of how history work, for all of its solitary nature, is truly a cooperative venture. I have benefited immensely from the input of a great many people. My dissertation committee—Peter Coclanis, Leon Fink, Jacquelyn Dowd Hall, James Leloudis, and Joel Williamson—all made suggestions that have greatly enhanced the work. I especially wish to thank Leon and Jacquelyn, two friends as well as mentors, who have been models of how to blend collegiality and democratic values with the highest levels of scholarship.

Jacquelyn is just one of a number of historians who have turned their lenses on early-twentieth-century Atlanta in recent years. Others in the informal "Progressive Era Atlanta Club" have included Glenda Gilmore, David Godschalk, Steve Goodson, Georgia Hickey, Tera Hunter, Sarah Judson, Nancy MacLean, Gregory Mixon, and Steve Oney. I deeply appreciate their insights and wisdom, as expressed both in their writings and in numerous conversations over the years. In addition, I have benefited from the comments of Bryant Simon, Bob McMath, and the reviewers for the University of North Carolina Press, as well as from those in attendance at presentations I made at meetings of the Organization of American Historians, Social Science History Association, and the Southern Labor Studies Association. David Perry of the University of North Carolina Press has been an enthusiastic supporter of the project.

Two friends and colleagues warrant particular mention. Gary Fink is one of the most decent human beings I know, a true prince of a man. He has always been supportive and generous in sharing his own research and thoughts about the Fulton strike. Gretchen MacLachlan and I have been talking about working people in turn-of-the-century Atlanta since the early 1990s, when we were both completing our dissertations. Appropriately enough, our most recent conversations have taken place in a restaurant in the neighborhood that once was the Fulton mill district. Over the years, Gretchen has been a critic, a colleague, a springboard, an editor, a prodder, and a good friend. I owe a tremendous personal and intellectual debt to Gretchen, whose own forthcoming book on Atlanta working women will immediately go on the short list of key works on the city's past.

An R. J. Reynolds Dissertation Grant from the University of North Carolina and the William F. Sullivan Fellowship of the Museum of American Textile History helped support the research for this project. A Copen Faculty Grant from the Georgia State University Department of History enabled the production of the maps and the reproduction of the photographs for the book. In addition, the History Department awarded me summer funding and a reduced teaching load to enable me to complete the manuscript. Under the leadership of chairs Gary Fink, Tim Crimmins, and Diane Willen, the department has been a congenial place to work.

William Braverman, Dr. Louis Elsas, Glen Gendzel, Anne Larcom, and P. C. Schroeder all shared materials in their possession with me. Jyostna Vanipalli made sure the notes and bibliography were in order. Elizabeth Adams helped prepare the final version of the manuscript. Jeff McMichael of the Cartography Research Laboratory of Georgia State University produced the two maps in the book. Mary Caviness provided thorough and thoughtful copyediting. To one and all, I am deeply grateful and appreciative.

Last, but certainly not least, I wish to acknowledge three individuals who did not have a great deal to do directly with the making of this work but whose presence was enormous throughout. Kathie Klein and Josh and Gabe Klein-Kuhn have suffused my life with love, richness, support, and never a dull moment. I look forward to spending more time with them.

CONTESTING THE NEW SOUTH ORDER

INTRODUCTION

In his flawed epic *The Mind of the South*, W. J. Cash described how "the Southern mill worker had pretty fair cause for complaint" on the eve of World War I. Moreover, Cash wrote, "Looking casually at the scene, you might easily have concluded, indeed, that he was responding to it directly, vigorously, and with clear eyes. For in 1913 a big strike would break out in Atlanta, and from there spread to other places in Georgia, South Carolina, and Tennessee."[1]

Cash was referring to the strike at Atlanta's Fulton Bag and Cotton Mills (which actually began in 1914), an event at the heart of the American Federation of Labor's first attempt to organize southern workers in over a decade. The year-long strike attracted considerable regional and national attention, from cotton manufacturers to the labor and reform press to a host of federal investigators. As United Textile Workers (UTW) organizer Sara Conboy declared, the Fulton strike "brings before us the whole Southern textile situation." At least in its celebrity, it was the southern counterpart of the contemporaneous industrial conflicts in Paterson, New Jersey; Lawrence, Massachusetts; and Ludlow, Colorado.[2]

Yet Cash also warned that "it is necessary not to read more into this than it contained." As with other previous southern strikes and organizing drives, because it did not bring about lasting modern trade unionism into the textile South, Cash felt that the Fulton strike was "mere foam before passing gusts," a largely spontaneous, ephemeral action of little lasting consequence.

Cash's perspective contained numerous problems. He presented a single, monolithic portrait of Southern mill hands, what might be called "the mind of the male textile South." He narrowly equated "true" class consciousness with the establishment of enduring labor organizations and maintained that southern workers were inherently incapable of attaining either. And he was wrong about the significance of the Fulton strike.

Fulton Bag president Oscar Elsas would have surely disagreed with Cash's assessment of the strike, all of his numerous public pronouncements to minimize its significance to the contrary. For Elsas, the strike certainly mattered, a lot. Because of the incipient union activity at the plant, he hired labor spies to infiltrate the union, the shop floor, and the surrounding community, a practice he would continue into the 1920s. All told, over forty "operatives" filed some 2,700 daily reports to mill management during the six years after the strike's onset. Elsas also launched a vigorous campaign against strike sympathizers that reached high into national financial and corporate circles. He spent a great amount of time preparing for federal investigations of the Fulton situation and the southern textile industry. He drew upon his experiences in the strike to advance unified anti-union employer action at the local, state, regional, and national levels, at the strike's end joining the board of the National Association of Manufacturers (NAM). And he substantially revamped the company's industrial relations policies in the strike's aftermath.

There were other people involved in the matter from different vantage points who also would have taken issue with Cash's assertion that the Fulton strike was ultimately inconsequential. The local branch of the Social Gospel–influenced Men and Religion Forward Movement (MRFM), one of the nation's most active chapters, spent thousands of dollars on newspaper advertisements to draw attention to the matter and linked the Fulton situation to broader concerns of industrial justice and Progressive Era reform. Similarly, UTW and AFL leadership saw the Fulton dispute as central to the southern organizing drive and a key battle in a larger contest for public opinion over the labor question.

Others experienced the strike in more personal ways, no less significant, as the lives of Sallie and Robert Wright illustrate. Sallie Wright, who worked in the printing department of the company's bag mill, was closely monitored by management and then discharged from her job after she expressed interest in the union. Her husband, Robert, who ran a cutting machine in the bag mill, joined the strike after witnessing the wholesale eviction of union members from company housing.[3] One of those evicted was musician "Fiddlin' John" Carson, a weaver at the mill, who would become a pioneering star of country music radio and recording.[4]

Robert Wright quickly became one of the union's most active members. He was a regular speaker at the daily union meetings, touching on a number of concerns and fears of Fulton workers that extended well beyond working conditions alone. In addition, Wright described child labor practices at Fulton

Mills, raising an issue that not only attracted national sympathies but was also at that very moment the focus of a coalition of local Progressives seeking to strengthen Georgia's child labor laws. He denounced the unsanitary conditions in the mill village, the head of the firm's internal security force, and the complicity of the local settlement house with management.[5] Wright also provided testimony about the work rules at Fulton Mills to an investigator for the U.S. Commission on Industrial Relations (CIR) and supervised a picket line to keep newcomers from working at the mill.[6] For his efforts, he was made president of UTW local 886 in August 1914.

Yet Wright soon became disillusioned with the chief union organizers, who became increasingly overwhelmed as the strike dragged on. The union-sponsored commissary was a major problem, since hundreds of people from Atlanta and across the Piedmont flocked to it. Wright claimed that most of those who got food from the commissary were not even Fulton workers but rather "hoboes and bums that blowed in here on a cyclone from everywhere" while "the real strikers fair and square" were shut out. In addition, Wright resented the leadership of the chief local strike organizer O. Delight (Mrs. E. B.) Smith, an active trade unionist who repeatedly challenged and transgressed conventional gender norms. Smith was a particular target for mill management, and she ultimately left town in disgrace as the strike and her marriage fell apart. Yet, over thirty-five years later, she still recalled the strike as the most significant event in her long and illustrious career in the labor movement.[7]

Aiding and abetting Wright in his grievances against union leaders was Harry Greenhough Preston, one of the ablest labor spies employed by the company. In addition to encouraging Wright, Preston became the union song leader and wormed his way into the top levels of the UTW. In contrast to Smith's downward trajectory, he was rewarded for his activities during the strike by being named southern vice president for the Railway Audit and Inspection Company, one of the nation's leading industrial espionage firms.

Until recent years, accounts and memories of the Fulton strike had remained isolated threads of the past, largely buried and not really woven into any larger narrative or analytical fabric. Outside of Cash's passing reference and a few dissertations devoted to other subjects, the strike received scant mention in the historical literature until the 1980s and 1990s.[8] And it was not included in the numerous journalistic treatments of the adjacent neighborhood called Cabbagetown that began to appear in the 1970s.[9] For a long time, it seemed that Cash's interpretation of the event had prevailed.

There are several reasons for this negligence. Cash himself contributed to a historical literature that for decades largely portrayed textile workers in two-dimensional terms, as downtrodden, passive victims of an overarching paternalistic system. Then, too, the relative paucity of available textile industry records mitigated against more nuanced, detailed historical treatments of the southern cotton mill world.

The situation has changed dramatically in recent years. Drawing from larger currents in the history profession as well as from oral and other previously underutilized sources, a burgeoning literature has with great sophistication challenged the previously received historical wisdom on southern textiles. Among others, David Carlton, Allen Tullos, Douglas Flamming, and historians associated with the University of North Carolina's Southern Oral History Program have—often from quite different perspectives—greatly expanded our understanding of workers, managers, and members of mill communities alike.[10]

These studies of southern textiles, along with a larger historical literature exploring the contours of the New South more generally, have helped retrieve the Fulton strike from the dustbin of history in recent years. Even more significant has been the discovery of numerous, illuminating primary sources relating to the strike. In 1983, a staff member at the George Meany Memorial Archives in Silver Spring, Maryland, found a three-volume annotated photo diary of the strike compiled by organizer O. Delight Smith. Around the same time, historians came across the records of the extensive federal investigations of the strike undertaken by the Department of Labor's Division of Conciliation and the Commission on Industrial Relations. These records included affidavits from children and other workers; interviews with mill management, members of the Men and Religion Forward Movement, and others; information on working conditions and management practices; material on worker housing; union publications; and numerous photographs. In all, they comprised arguably the most comprehensive documentation of any southern industrial dispute of the period.

Yet they paled in scope to what was unearthed in 1985, when archivists and historians at the Georgia Institute of Technology obtained what had been left behind in the vaults when the former mill was sold. The Fulton Bag and Cotton Mills collection at Georgia Tech includes architectural blueprints, plate glass negatives, personnel records, accident reports, affidavits, clippings, transcripts of the CIR hearing on the strike, payroll books and ledgers, presidential correspondence, thousands of daily reports from labor spies, and a large volume of internal memos from company informants.

The discovery of these materials has spawned a renewed interest in the Fulton strike, among both historians and the general public. These sources have also contributed to a greatly enhanced appreciation of the strike's significance in southern and labor history. In fact, historian Robert H. Zieger has recently described the Fulton strike as "a critical moment in the history of the New South." We have come a long way from W. J. Cash's description of the event as "mere foam before passing gusts."[11]

This book explores that moment in its complexity. Thus, it differs from an earlier treatment of the Fulton strike by my friend and former colleague Gary Fink. While Fink acknowledged that the strike was "much more than an industrial relations quarrel," entailing "ethnic conflict, gender divisions, social and economic reform, regional and sectional differences, and the textile industry's rendition of the gospel of efficiency," he primarily treated the industrial relations at the firm. Accordingly, the principal strengths of his work are the descriptions of mill management's industrial policies and of the use of spies to help implement and enforce these policies, both during the strike and beyond.[12]

My work departs from Fink's in several ways. The unparalleled documentation of the strike, and of life and labor at Fulton Mills more generally, offers the opportunity to provide a multidimensional portrait of the world of workers and managers in the New South and to test, challenge, and perhaps reshape some of the generalizations about southern textile workers in such synthetic works as *Like a Family*, *Habits of Industry*, and *Plain Folks in the New South*.

I also situate the Fulton Mills community within the larger milieu of the urban South during the Progressive Era. In this regard, I am following up on the admonition by Edward Ayers in *The Promise of the New South* that "[t]he mill people were part of the unstable and rapidly evolving world of the New South, and we should not allow the images conjured up by the phrase 'mill village' to obscure the connections between the operatives and the world beyond."[13] Atlanta during this period was a rapidly growing city that in many ways epitomized the tensions between traditional ways and modern times that marked the New South. Within two years of the Fulton strike, the city experienced animated public debates over child labor and Sunday movies, a successful campaign to clean up the local red-light district, a major streetcar strike, and the Leo Frank case. In one way or another, members of the Fulton Mills community interacted with all of these developments. In other ways, too, Fulton workers related to a broader white working class, black Atlantans, and different constituencies of white middle-class citizens. It is impossible to fully comprehend the strike without an understanding of this larger urban context, a context that, in turn, the strike itself illuminates. As with the historiography on textiles, such a look at Atlanta also tests recent generalizations about the contours of southern Progressivism.

Finally, I explicitly link the Fulton situation to southern industrialization and labor-management relations more generally. At the center of the AFL's first attempt to organize southern textiles in over a decade, the strike drew attention from a wide assortment of parties, from Georgia senator Hoke Smith, to manufacturers throughout the region, to representatives of the National Association of Manufacturers, to congressmen from New England textile districts, to investigators from federal agencies, to trade unions and reform groups across the country. This work sheds light on both the coordination and the divisions among southern textile manufacturers in developing an industrial relations strategy, the fate of the United Textile Workers' southern campaign, and the relationship of textile workers and owners to local, state, and regional politics.

The title of this book, *Contesting the New South Order*, suggests several historiographical debts and debates and some of the book's overarching themes. Robert H. Wiebe's *The Search for Order*, though criticized from various perspectives over the years, continues to offer one of the most useful interpretative frameworks for understanding the Progressive Era.[14] Wiebe's notion of modernization, his concern with the contours of American democracy, and his attentiveness to conflicts in language and communication all have relevance to the Fulton situation.

Certainly nowhere were Americans more concerned with order and disorder than in the New South. In the aftermath of the Civil War and Reconstruction, a new industrial order, a new urban order, a new racial order, and a new sexual order emerged in the region, along with numerous attendant anxieties, fears, and frustrations. Each of the participants in the Fulton strike—from Oscar Elsas to O. Delight Smith, to Harry Preston, to Fiddlin' John Carson, to the Men and Religion Forward Movement members, to people like Robert and Sallie Wright—embodied this tension between traditional ways and modern times, between the nineteenth and twentieth centuries, as it were. This work joins a growing historical literature that explores the nature and degree of change in the New South, its "newness," in other words, along with reaction and resistance to that change.[15]

Despite considerable pressure to conform, the New South was hardly static or monolithic. In Atlanta, as throughout the region, southerners with diverse vantage points, backgrounds, and available resources, who were often in conflict with each other, sought to make sense of and shape their rapidly changing world. The outcomes of southern history were hardly foreordained, though they might have seemed so in hindsight to W. J. Cash and others. The Fulton strike of 1914–15 reveals in high relief many of the complexities and contingencies of the New South.

The first chapter of the book is a nineteenth-century prologue, tracing the evolution of the Fulton firm and its work force through the turn of the century, in order to offer some necessary historical background to the strike. Chapters 2 and 3 provide detailed descriptions of the Fulton community and how this community intersected with broader developments in Atlanta on the eve of the strike. Chapter 4 details the proximate causes of the strike and the evolving strategies and tactics of management and labor at the strike's outset. Chapter 5 explores the activity and attitudes of Fulton workers themselves during the strike, on the picket line, in the community, on the job, and at the union hall. Chapter 6 examines the spirited contest for public opinion through the strike; in particular it looks at the creative use of photographs by both parties in the dispute and the role of the Men and Religion Forward Movement in the matter, along with Oscar Elsas's counter campaign against the MRFM. Chapter 7 illustrates how the strike figured in regional and national labor-related debates and politics, from the halls of Congress, to the CIR, to employer organizations like the NAM, to the labor movement. Finally, the Conclusion details the strike's aftermath and legacy at a variety of levels, showing how the Fulton strike, its context and meanings, were inextricably intertwined with the evolving New South.

CHAPTER 1

The Making of a New South Business, 1868–1900

One mile southeast of downtown Atlanta, across from the former Fulton Bag and Cotton Mills site and the surrounding neighborhood now called Cabbagetown, stands Oakland Cemetery. On a rise in the all-Jewish section of Oakland stands a large mausoleum, with one word on it: ELSAS.[1] It is the burial place of Jacob Elsas, founder of Fulton Bag and Cotton Mills, who even in death looms over the local landscape much as he did in life. As his grandson recalled in 1990, "The old gentleman was the head man on all of this stuff."[2]

The commonly told story of Jacob Elsas is of the penniless, orphaned immigrant, borrowing money for the train fare to Cincinnati, where a relative lived, coming to Georgia with only a pack on his back, and ultimately building up one of the New South's leading industrial empires.[3] As with other tales of self-made Americans, there is some truth to the story; indeed, Elsas came from comparatively humble circumstances to become a millionaire. As with other such Horatio Alger figures, however, a more complicated picture emerges under closer examination. Certainly Elsas often benefited from being in the right place at the right time.

Elsas's ancestors hailed from Alsace before Jacob's grandfather, Isaak Elsass (German for "Alsace"), crossed the Rhine in 1796.[4] Prominent weavers and dyers for generations, the family made the transition from hand production to manufacturing, setting up a small factory in the Wuerttemburg city of Ludwigsburg, where cotton yarn was woven into bed ticking.[5] Isaak's oldest child, Jeanette, bore four children between 1829 and 1842, all apparently out of wedlock. Her first two children died in infancy, and the third, Isaak, emigrated in 1855 to America, where the name became Elsas. Three weeks before her fortieth birthday, Jeanette gave birth to Jacob.[6] One of the first family members to literally grow up under the new industrial order, Jacob worked in the factory to help pay his keep while living with an uncle and sold bed ticking in the surrounding countryside. Facing conscription, at eighteen he departed for America and joined relatives in Cincinnati.[7]

It is hard to imagine a more propitious place for an ambitious youth like Jacob Elsas to begin his career in America. With the completion of the Miami Canal, Cincinnati had become the economic hub of the trans-Allegheny West, its industrial output by 1860 surpassed only by New York and Philadelphia. Though its influence had begun to ebb with the emergence of other railroad centers, Cincinnati remained competitive as the gateway to the South through the establishment of direct rail links to New Orleans and Nashville. Its population had proceeded apace, jumping from 46,000 in 1840 to 161,000 in 1860, becoming the fifth largest city in the United States.[8]

Jacob's uncle provided firsthand evidence of upward mobility, as well as crucial financial resources and business connections. The elder Elsas had come to Cincinnati and started a dry goods store, soon the city's largest establishment of its kind. In 1847, he opened a shoe and boot business, later converting it to a department store. He also became involved in Cincinnati's booming clothing industry, especially the city's ready-to-wear garment trade, by mid-century the largest in the country. Elsas and other merchant-manufacturers used a contracting system that employed thousands of women outworkers to produce ready-to-wear garments. As demand continued, they started up factories that produced goods for their own stores and other retail outlets.[9]

The younger Elsas found work as a packer, then entered the junk trade, doing some selling in Kentucky and neighboring states.[10] In 1864, he found himself in the growing commercial center of Nashville, which at the time was under federal military occupation. Nashville's place as a regional hub had been enhanced by the completion of the L & N Railroad in 1859, and by the Union Army's decision to make the city its primary western headquarters for food, supplies, and ordnance. Like other local businessmen and outside entrepreneurs, Elsas tried to profit from wartime conditions, only to be wiped out by a flood.[11] He was then drafted into the Union Army at Chattanooga and dropped off with the troops protecting General William T. Sherman's supply lines at Cartersville, Georgia, fifty miles northwest of Atlanta.[12] Still in Cartersville at the war's end, Elsas was ordered to return to Nashville, where he prevailed upon friends who knew General George H. Thomas, commander of the Division of Tennessee, to secure a pass that enabled him to travel from Nashville to Chattanooga and Cartersville.

One of the few young men left in town after the war, Elsas quickly purchased a piece of property behind the Cartersville railroad depot. With the labor of a former slave, Mose White, who would work for Elsas for a half century, he then erected a log cabin trading station. He drew upon his connections to build up the business, receiving assistance from his uncle and shipping in merchandise from Nashville and Cincinnati. As his business prospered, he replaced the log cabin with the first brick structure in the area.[13]

By 1868, Elsas had moved to Atlanta, a bustling city that provided fertile soil for his considerable business abilities to flower. Founded as a railroad terminus, the city became a regional commercial and manufacturing center during the Civil War. Atlanta experienced a resurgence after the war, as the railroads quickly were rebuilt and expanded and men on the make came to town from all sections of the country.[14] Changing trade patterns, openness to Northern capital and capitalists, and a comparatively fluid social structure (one that allowed Jews like Elsas to enter the business elite) enabled Atlanta businessmen to tap successfully growing regional demand for consumer and durable goods in the aftermath of slavery and war. Able promoters greased the skids, trumpeting the city across the South. As business boomed, so did Atlanta's population; by 1870, the city numbered 22,000 inhabitants, more than twice its prewar figure; by 1880 its population surpassed 37,000. Reflecting this growth, Atlanta became the state capital in 1868.[15]

Upon arrival in town, Elsas launched three different operations. Reuniting with his brother Isaak, he entered the rag, paper, and hide trade, operating out of a local warehouse. "Here we find," wrote an observer, "old rags, skins, old brass, zinc, loose cotton, bees'-wax, feathers, copper, dried fruits, tallow, scrap iron, lead, old glass, and many other things that are generally thrown away. These find ready sale here."[16] By 1870, the firm was reported to have a stock of about six thousand dollars and to be "doing apparently a brisk business."[17] In addition, with fellow German Jews Morris Adler and Julius Dreyfus, Elsas opened a store selling ready-to-wear jeans, dry goods, and other articles.[18]

Adler and Dreyfus also joined in Elsas's most significant undertaking, a venture that meshed well with the ascendancy of a merchant class in the postbellum South. Since his Cartersville days, Elsas had experienced a shortage of bags and containers for the goods he traded and reasoned that other merchants in the region faced similar difficulties. Stepping into the breach, he and his associates, symbolically breaking from the Old South, bought the former Atlanta slave market house at auction and began the production of both paper and cotton bags for flour, grain, and other commodities.[19]

Elsas quickly brought in machinery that produced 100,000 paper bags a week.[20] Cloth bag production also increased, particularly after the arrival of Isaac May, another German Jewish immigrant from Cincinnati who helped secure a crucial loan of $9,000. By January 1872, the firm had changed its name to Elsas, May and Company.[21] As the firm accumulated enough capital to develop large-scale cotton bag production, the partnership dissolved in 1874, with several associates splitting off to manufacture paper bags, while Elsas and May, the principal partners, launched the Southern Bag Factory.[22]

Credit reports of the R. G. Dun Company provide insight into Elsas and his partners' characters. According to one Dun agent in 1875, the firm's proprietors were "close, prudent and very industrious men." Similar descriptions appeared in other reports: "all Germans, active, energetic shrewd men with undoubted capacity"; "very industrious and prudent"; "men of good character, sober, industrious and economical, manage prudently"; "all Germans who are working harmoniously together and not only bear good characters, but are very careful prudent men addicted to no extravagant habits and have displayed excellent judgment in the management of their affairs."[23]

The Dun reports indicate that Jacob Elsas was the dominant force in the firm. Dun correspondents described Elsas as "an experienced merchant" and "one of the best class of Jews." "The leading partner," wrote one agent, "is Elsas, who is the head and front of the concern [and] to whose capacity and judgment the success of the house can be principally attributed." Another agent enthused that "Elsas the principal partner is a keen shrewd money making man."[24]

Elsas, May continued to expand throughout the 1870s. In 1879, the company conducted trade in some dozen states and grossed $400,000 in sales, leading one agent to call it "undoubtedly the most extensive business of this character in the South." By 1880, the company employed four or five traveling salesmen as well as between 100 and 160 workers, largely women and children, at its complex, which now included a bleachery and print shop as well as the bag mill. The firm was "successful, doing well, making money."[25]

Such success, however, only fueled Jacob Elsas's larger plans. Long concerned about the costs of buying and transporting cloth for bag production from New England, Elsas now sought to establish a cotton mill of his own.[26] This ambition dovetailed with Atlanta's aggressive and capable crusade for local and regional industrial development, epitomized by *Atlanta Constitution* editor Henry W. Grady. In 1874, Grady had coined the phrase "New South" in a column where he called for a man of ability to head up Atlanta's first cotton mill.[27] His choice was Hannibal I. Kimball, arguably Georgia's most controversial Reconstruction figure.[28] Closely aligned with Republican governor Rufus Bullock, the Maine-born Kimball had provided temporary quarters for state legislators, reaped huge profits from railroad bonds issued by the legislature, and used his political leverage to finance construction of the six-story Kimball House, the grandest hotel in the South and a hub of local politics and com-

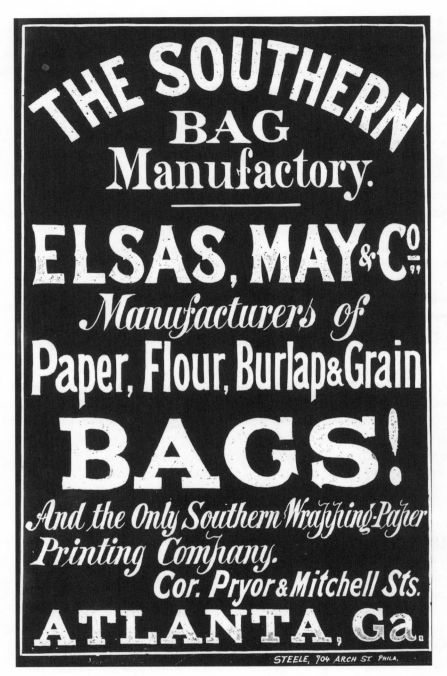

Advertisement for Elsas, May. Special Collections Dept., Robert W. Woodruff Library, Emory University.

merce. Upon the collapse of Republican rule in 1871, Kimball fled the state, only to return to open arms in 1874 and soon afterward spearhead the first local textile campaign, in a striking testament to the ability of Atlanta's business leaders, including ardent Democrat Grady, to let bygones be bygones in pursuit of capital and development.[29]

Kimball sought to finance the new operation locally, issuing 2,500 shares of stock at $100 apiece. Despite the initial enthusiasm, this effort proved to be more difficult than anticipated, as numerous investors failed to pay up on stock that had been subscribed. Ongoing litigation against mill management, difficulty in recruiting labor, and the lingering scent of scandal surrounding Kimball further delayed production. Only when Kimball hired as company treasurer former governor Bullock, now the president of the Atlanta Chamber of Commerce, did the Atlanta Cotton Factory finally get off the ground in June 1879, still plagued by periodic shutdowns and labor shortages.[30]

During the effort to secure capital, Kimball had received a charter from the legislature to launch a second cotton mill, the Fulton Cotton Spinning Company, which had never materialized. He sought to unload this charter just as Jacob Elsas was looking to move into textile production. A frequent visitor at the Kimball House, Elsas learned of the charter's availability and quickly purchased it and its attendant zoning requirements from Kimball for $2,500.[31]

Like Kimball, first-generation New South industrialists of the 1870s and 1880s often had considerable difficulty raising necessary funds to launch factories. In contrast, Elsas and his partners obtained sufficient start-up capital relatively easily, through outside funding instead of local investment. Once more tapping their Cincinnati connections, they appealed to Lewis Seasongood, a prominent German Jewish banker and clothier whom Elsas had known during the war. Seasongood, who would remain on the board of the Atlanta firm until his death in November 1914, arranged an issue of $100,000 in industrial bonds. In addition, the firm received a tax exemption from the Atlanta city council.[32]

Like most of his fellow Atlanta manufacturers in the 1880s, Elsas moved his operation away from the city's center. Mill construction began on a ten-acre tract of land east of downtown alongside the Georgia Railroad. The site possessed several advantages. Because of the railroad, a number of industrial interests had already located in the area, spawning a small but growing nearby working-class neighborhood. For those who lived farther away, a recently built streetcar line extended to the edge of the district. In addition, an underground branch of the Yellow River ran through the section.[33]

Postbellum industrialization in the South has often been described as divorced from any antebellum antecedents. Such was not the case with the Fulton firm. Unlike other first-generation New South industrialists who started out with limited textile and managerial backgrounds, Elsas drew upon the expertise of James Roswell King, perhaps the most experienced mill man in the area, to help him plan and erect the facility. King's grandfather and father had pioneered north Georgia's first textile mills in the late 1830s, founding the community of Roswell. King had supervised production of the "Roswell Grey" cloth used by Confederate officers and had been key in reviving operations after the war. After economic misfortunes, conflict with stockholders, and the death of his first wife, King moved to Atlanta and began work for Elsas, May. He performed the finishing construction on the new factory's smokestack himself and stayed on as superintendent for many years.[34]

In 1881, the Fulton Cotton Spinning Company started production with a few thousand spindles, the same year that Atlanta's heralded International Cotton Exposition opened. The first large-scale industrial fair in the region, the exposition, backed by Grady and the *Constitution* and directed by Kimball, unified the city's corporate elite, drew several hundred thousand visitors, and focused national attention on the "Atlanta Spirit" and the New South crusade. It brought together cotton producers, brokers, and manufacturers; generated great interest in the southern textile industry; and cemented the city's position as the commercial and manufacturing hub of the New South.[35] In its aftermath, the main fair building became Atlanta's third textile mill, the Exposition Cotton Mill, which was organized in 1882 after the city sold the property to a joint stock company of leading businessmen.

During the 1880s, the number of local manufacturing establishments doubled, the value of their products practically tripled, and their capitalization increased nearly fourfold, while Atlanta's population expanded from 37,000 to 55,000.[36] The Fulton Cotton Spinning Company shared in this prosperity, moving quickly toward a fully integrated operation. A new bag factory replacing the downtown plant was added on the site in 1882, with upgraded machinery, machine and carpenter shops, and 5,000 additional spindles following over the next three years.[37]

Jacob Elsas's civic activities grew apace with his industrial fortunes. By the 1880s, he belonged to the inner core of Atlanta's business elite who increasingly set the local agenda for development. More so than in any other major southern city, Atlanta's business leaders recognized the mutuality of their individual interests and those of the larger community, engaged in organized entrepreneurship, and pressed toward a set of common goals, most notably the city's continued growth. Being a recent migrant to Atlanta, even being a Jew, was not a barrier to Elsas's entry into the municipal elite; not a single one of Atlanta's core business leaders of the 1880s had been born in the city.[38]

Elsas worked closely with such prominent Atlantans as Grady, Kimball, cotton broker Samuel M. Inman, industrialist-banker James W. English, and banker Robert J. Lowry on a variety of projects. An active member of the Atlanta Manufacturers Association, in 1883 he chaired the building committee of the newly reorganized Chamber of Commerce.[39] Elsas joined other leading businessmen among the petitioners for the West View Cemetery Company, the stockholders of the Peters Park Development Company, and the founders and officers of the Capital City Bank.[40] He headed the construction committee of the Atlanta Water Works and was the first donor to the Grady Memorial Hospital building fund in 1890, serving also as chair of the hospital building committee.[41]

The development of the Georgia Institute of Technology was one of Elsas's primary concerns. The exposition had shown the link between practical education and industrial growth, and in its wake businessmen across Georgia sought to establish a state technological school. As different sites were being considered, Grady called a meeting of Atlanta business leaders to discuss the matter. It was Elsas who explained the significance of a technological institute to the group in classic New South terms, stating, "We are selling our old raw materials at $5 a ton to states that have trained engineers who fabricate it and sell it back to us at $75 to $100 a ton," and adding that he intended to send his son Oscar to the Massachusetts Institute of Technology. Those present then subscribed $1,000 each to help bring the new school to Atlanta. The Fulton firm quickly became one of the leading customers of the Georgia Tech shops.[42]

In addition to advancing such ventures, which directly served the interests of both the individuals involved and the community as a whole, Elsas and his counterparts in Atlanta increasingly engaged in a variety of cultural and social activities that stamped them as members of the city's emergent elite.[43] Befitting a man of his station, Elsas eventually moved his home away from the center of the city to an exclusive neighborhood at the edge of town, traveled in Europe, and later bought one of the very first gasoline-powered automobiles in the city. Along with others of his class, he helped establish DeGive's Opera House in 1893 and supported other high-culture undertakings. As he became more affluent, Elsas's charitable contributions also increased. He was a major donor to the Hebrew Orphan's Home, which he helped found, and to Grady Hospital.[44]

He also made sure his children got the finest education. In 1870, Elsas had married Clara Stahl, an immigrant from Rheinfalz whom he met in New York.[45] Between 1871 and 1883, Clara bore eight children, six boys and two girls. When his oldest child, Oscar, approached the age of ten, Jacob sent the boy overseas for two years of schooling in Stuttgart, then enrolled him at the prestigious Boston Latin School for his secondary education. While staying in Boston, Oscar boarded with the prominent Ehrlich family, who Jacob had met

Jacob Elsas and children, c. 1910s. Oscar Elsas is second from right. The Ida Pearl and Joseph Cuba Archives of the William Breman Jewish Heritage Museum.

through his business travels. Oscar attended MIT before returning to Atlanta as a junior in Georgia Tech's first class. Oscar's brothers Ben and Louis attended Boston's English High School and Andover Academy respectively before matriculating at Harvard.[46]

For all his civic and business prominence, because of his Jewish background there existed distinct limits to Elsas's assimilation into Atlanta's upper crust. In deference to an unstated dividing line, Elsas and other prosperous Jews settled in a section south of downtown known colloquially as "Seligville" rather than moving onto fashionable Peachtree Street alongside the homes of Kimball, Grady, Inman, and others; it was not until the end of the first decade of the twentieth century that Jews "cracked" Peachtree Street. Similarly, Atlanta Jews could not join the elite social clubs that arose in the late nineteenth century as emblems of the city's well-to-do. And despite his contributions to Georgia Tech, Elsas never was asked to join the institution's board of trustees.

Such exclusion was ironic given Jacob Elsas's only nominal association with religious Judaism. He was a founding member of Atlanta's Reform synagogue, which was overwhelmingly made up of assimilationist German Jews. Even then, he only attended on the High Holidays and expressed reservations about many of the teachings and practices of Judaism, a skepticism he passed on to his family. While he supported certain Jewish causes and organizations, Elsas's Jewish identity was fundamentally cultural rather than religious in nature.[47]

In his relationship to organized religion, support of high culture, personal lifestyle, assimilationism, and expansion of philanthropic activities, Elsas resembled many other successful German American Jews at the turn of the century.[48] As closely intertwined as he was with Atlanta's elite, Elsas was equally at home in the loosely connected national network of prominent German Jewish families. Through his business activities, he soon developed friends and acquaintances in commercial and financial circles across the country.[49] Though he never wavered in his allegiance to Atlanta, Elsas simultaneously moved beyond the city to conduct both his business and personal affairs at a national and even international level.

The Elsas saga was not the only narrative associated with the Fulton firm. The experiences of the people who came to work at the mill stood in stark contrast to the Elsas family's soaring trajectory. The vast majority of first-generation Fulton workers hailed from the Upper Piedmont counties surrounding Atlanta. Like other white Upcountry farming families, they had experienced tremendous upheaval in the years since the Civil War. The war's devastation and subsequent crisis of capital, along with the development of the railroads, helped set into motion the intensification of cotton production, expansion of commercial agriculture, and the emergence of a new, exploitative credit system. Faltering cotton prices and continued high human fertility rates pressured once-independent white farmers into greater debt, tenancy, and ultimately off the land, with little opportunity to move back up the agricultural ladder. As one Fulton worker remarked, farming had become "just nip and tuck like. . . . It had got powerful cheap."[50]

Among the most vulnerable and marginalized of southerners, Confederate widows, other destitute women, and children constituted most of the first workers at Atlanta's three textile mills. In 1879, the superintendent of the Atlanta Cotton Factory pointed out the difficulties many of these people had in adjusting to a new industrial order. Contrasting Atlanta's female operatives with women textile workers in the North more accustomed to an industrial regime, he lamented that "Southern girls think they have no responsibility" and thus were adversely affecting production.[51] In addition, Kimball had located the Atlanta Cotton Factory downtown in part to avoid having to build quarters for workers, and consequently he experienced chronic labor shortages.

Learning from Kimball's example, Jacob Elsas supplied company housing from the Fulton firm's inception. The first Fulton houses consisted of several

Company housing, c. 1881. Special Collections Dept., Robert W. Woodruff Library, Emory University.

rows of modest cottages across the street from the factory. Additional construction of mill housing occurred in 1886 after an expansion of the plant. Yet Fulton's operations regularly expanded at a faster pace than the company could supply housing. In addition, as the industrial east side of town became increasingly congested by the mid-1880s, potential space for company-sponsored housing grew scarcer.[52]

While more dispersed among the general population than their counterparts across the Piedmont, Atlanta textile workers were almost immediately identified and stigmatized as a particularly downtrodden sector of the southern white working class. Despite the city's overall economic growth in the 1880s, periodic downturns, layoffs, and reductions of already low wages plagued the local textile industry for much of the decade. In 1883, a local reporter wrote of the widespread suffering among local mill hands, many of whom were "worthy people but fate has made them destitute."[53] Around 1880, the city's textile districts became some of the first targets for home mission work among middle-class white Atlanta Methodist women.[54] In 1885, in *Working World*, the city's labor publication, a writer described the long hours and paltry wages of mill workers, who then worked on average a seventy-two-hour work week for approximately fifty cents a day, and the "pallid cheeks of women and girls and men and boys as they trudge along in the early morning to their places of punishment."[55]

Passing near the Atlanta Cotton Factory in 1881, one traveler was struck by "the ragged, dirty and seemingly half-starved children, working like the negroes of a Mississippi River plantation did during slavery, for a bare subsistence."[56] For many Atlantans, the plight of white workers in the city's new cotton mills heralded dependency, pauperization, and degradation, conditions commonly identified with African Americans. One speaker at an 1886 workingman's political rally made a reference to the descendants of Ham, who were condemned to be perpetual servants and perceived since slavery by many white southerners as being Negro, and warned that if Atlanta workers "allowed themselves to be trampled on now, their children would be hewers of wood and drawers of water for the next generation."[57]

Such a specter was only one of the ways in which Atlanta's new cotton mills prompted considerable local criticism and discontent in the 1880s, New South pronouncements to the contrary. One particular sore spot was the sale of Oglethorpe Park to the Exposition Cotton Mill. Banker R. M. Richards, a leading investor, justified the sale, asserting that, "Atlanta must commence manufacturing on a large scale if it is to keep up." Similarly, banker and industrialist James English, a close associate of Elsas, declared, "When it comes to fair grounds or factories, I am for factories." In contrast, labor advocates correctly claimed for years that not only had the city sold off one of the few working-class recreational areas in town but had also greatly undersold the property.[58]

On occasion, Atlanta's textile workers themselves openly voiced their discontent with the new regime. In 1883, a burst steam pipe coupled with a wage cut caused "much dissatisfaction" among Exposition workers, many of whom consequently quit. In 1886, sixty-two Fulton workers signed a petition asking for a reduction of the work week from seventy-two to sixty-six hours. When management proposed a compromise of sixty-nine hours, many workers felt it was a "trap" and called an "indignation meeting."[59]

Atlanta's newspapers, the probusiness *Constitution* excepted, frequently carried stories on the poor working conditions, occupational injuries, vulnerability to contagious diseases, periodic unemployment, and widespread suffering of local textile workers, as well as the broadening gap between the city's wealthy and poor residents. "The fires of the well-to-do and rich are lighted," went one typical account, "but within the homes and dingy halls of 'Poverty Flat' the coal bins are still empty."[60] The boosterism of such able New South proponents as Grady certainly had a hypnotic, compelling quality in a city and region recovering from the ravages of civil war. Yet, even in Atlanta, as in countless American municipalities during the Gilded Age, such a vision of industrial progress did not prevail smoothly and without opposition but rather was accompanied by considerable tension, anxiety, and resistance.[61]

Within this setting, the Knights of Labor made substantial headway in Atlanta after 1882, organizing twelve local assemblies with some 4,000 members by March 1886 and becoming a significant force in city politics.[62] By 1885, local Knights membership extended beyond the original core of skilled tradesmen and small businessmen to include railroad workers, carpenters, domestic workers, and factory operatives, along with textile workers.[63]

Workers at the Fulton Cotton Spinning Company were among the founders and members of Local Assembly 4455, organized in 1885. The Fulton plant soon became a center of local labor activity. Some Fulton workers actively supported a local Prohibition initiative. In September 1885, several skilled male Fulton workers were among the seventeen applicants for a charter for the Working World Publishing Company. In July 1886, the executive committee of the Atlanta Knights announced a boycott of the Fulton company because the firm had used convict labor to make the bricks for the new addition to the mill.[64]

In November 1885, fifty Fulton weavers went on strike over a wage dispute, with 150 workers in the plant eventually affected. In addition, some breakage of machinery took place during the two-day strike, one of the rare instances in southern labor history when that ever occurred. The generally cautious Knights disavowed breaking machinery and disapproved also of "the manner of inaugurating the strike." A week after the walkout, the local Knights continued to dissociate themselves from the strike, which the *Atlanta Journal* dismissed as "spontaneous combustion, without form, substance or reason for its ephemeral existence."[65] In 1887, Local Assembly 4455 experienced financial difficulties and was gone from the scene the following year. By the early 1890s, Georgia's textile workers and the Knights of Labor had parted ways.[66] In other ways, too, the 1890s marked a new era in the history of the firm and its workers, the labor movement, and Atlanta.

Because of the mill's expansion and the 1888 death of Isaac May, the firm reorganized in 1889 as the Fulton Bag and Cotton Mills, with capital stock estimated between $250,000 and $600,000 and assets valued at $1,000,000.[67] Despite the national depression, the company's growth continued through the 1890s, as Fulton Bag became one of the country's foremost bag manufacturers and continued to make other textile products.[68] When demand for cloth surpassed the production capability of the initial factory, another cotton mill was constructed at the Atlanta site in 1895, doubling the workforce. Originally designed for 25,000 spindles, the new mill eventually housed over 40,000 spindles, or ten times the spindleage of the original factory. A testament to Elsas's industrial vision and aptitude, one of the largest steam engines in the South drove the plant, fitted with a huge flywheel that in turn transmitted power to shaft lines running the length of each of the building's five stories. The new factory also enabled an expansion of the bleaching and finishing operations. Such success in turn helped propel Fulton Bag beyond its Atlanta base to become a truly national firm. In 1897, the company acquired the New Orleans–based Delta Bag Company, then the next year purchased the Keokuk Bag Company of Keokuk, Iowa, and relocated it to Saint Louis.[69]

Such growth also led to periodic backlogs in orders and a constant demand for labor. By 1896, nearly 700 people worked at the Atlanta complex, making it the city's foremost industrial employer. By August 1897, the figure had reached almost 750 workers, mostly women and children in the production departments. Just how mammoth an industrial operation it seemed to contemporaries is shown by the habitually exaggerated newspaper estimates—between 1,000 and 1,500 people—of the Fulton workforce.[70]

With such growth, stabilizing the labor force became a primary concern for management. Toward that end, around 1890 the company initiated an employment contract with all prospective workers. Under the contract, the company agreed only to employ a worker and did not specify pay rates or the length of employment. The company could fire workers at any time, without having to give notice, provide the reason for dismissal, or follow any established grievance procedure. If discharged, Fulton workers living in company housing had to immediately vacate without further notice and the company could withhold wages "to cover any rent or damage done." The company would not provide any compensation, and could not be held liable, for work time lost due to accidents, disabilities, or other similar causes, no matter who was at fault. If workers felt a pay envelope was short, they had to point it out immediately or automatically lose the difference.[71]

While rarely spelled out in such detail, such practices were common throughout the southern textile industry. In addition to the actual codification of everyday customs, what was unusual about the Fulton contract was the requirement that management had developed to help stem the mill's recurrent high turnover, to keep production running smoothly, and to reduce any "breach of discipline" resulting from workers leaving their employment unannounced: before leaving the company, all Fulton workers had to provide one week's notice, in writing, of their intention to quit. Furthermore, workers were compelled to continue to work for the full period of the notice. To make sure the notice was carried out, the company held back wages when a worker was hired. Meanwhile, the contract left vague management's terms of employment.

From management's perspective the withheld wages constituted a deposit of sorts. For many Fulton workers, however, the contract was unjustified and unjust, coercive and one-sided in favor of the company. On several occasions Fulton workers actually went to court challenging several of the contract's provisions. In 1892, a worker named Wilson contested the clause that exempted the company from any liability due to corporate negligence and sued Fulton Bag for personal injuries sustained from working at a defective machine. Citing previous cases and "the acquiescence of the Legislature" in such matters, the probusiness state supreme court reversed a jury's award to Wilson and ruled in the company's favor, declining to "interfere with the prior law as to other employees or as to employers generally" but instead leaving the burden squarely on the affected individual alone.[72]

Apparently largely because of this decision, the Georgia General Assembly passed legislation voiding any contracts exempting employers from liability due to their negligence.[73] Under this new law, physically injured workers could bring tort action against negligent employers and recover damages encompassing the loss of work time, medical bills, and the cost of permanent disability, as well as for pain and suffering. Yet the only time a Fulton worker ever brought suit against the company under the statute, the Georgia Court of Appeals ruled once more on the mill's behalf, and in every subsequent case contesting the Fulton contract, the courts continued to rule in favor of the company.[74]

To further stabilize the workforce, in 1889 Jacob Elsas announced the construction of a "first class hotel for factory hands" adjacent to the mill, specifically designed to house the many unmarried workers, both male and female, who were "now compelled to put up with poor accommodations in a neighborhood boardinghouse." This ambitious project was to be a sixty-room structure, complete with dining room, ladies parlor, and reading room; "large airy rooms, each to house four occupants"; "furniture of a neat but substantial character"; a kitchen and dining hall to accommodate 200 people; and "a German lady engaged to manage the place." The hotel was intended to make the lot of the operatives more pleasant, give them something better than they ever had, and thus breed contented workers.

In acknowledging the presence of many single people in the workforce, Elsas also pointed out some of what he termed the "drawbacks" associated with hiring mill families, including child care provisions and the preparation of meals. However, in conjunction with plans to run the factory around-the-clock, he also announced his intention to build another hotel just for families, admitting, "We must make our place attractive or we can't get the necessary recruits."[75]

Whereas this second facility never was attempted, the original textile workers hotel eventually did get built. Oscar Elsas later remembered it as "a very modern building at the time," fully equipped with a chef and a full corps of servants. The food, in his opinion, was "high grade," and "practically all the office employees had their lunches with the help there." In August 1897, an *Atlanta Journal* reporter related that about a hundred people—including single workers, married couples, and families—resided in the building. "While it is not so gay and festive as a fashionable seaside resort," the reporter commented, "the inhabitants of the hotel manage to get along very well."[76] Yet, despite being praised by management and the press, by early 1900 the experiment failed, as the hotel residents, exhibiting a recurrent pattern of behavior among Fulton workers, sought to get out from under the company's direct regulation of their personal lives. According to Oscar Elsas, they "gradually drifted from the hotel to boarding houses surrounding the property until the Company found it necessary to discontinue the institution, and converted it to a rooming house where rooms were rented without board."[77]

In addition to the hotel, management periodically constructed new units of company housing, usually in the wake of production increases.[78] Shortly after the 1895 expansion, the company built several blocks of two-story, four-unit tenement-type structures specifically designed to hold the large, extended families of cotton mill workers. These dwellings were located on a triangular tract known as the Factory Lot, situated just south of the mill and the textile workers hotel. The Factory Lot was originally a female stronghold. In 1900, 461 of the 841 residents in the Factory Lot were women. Nearly 30 percent of the 160 Factory Lot households were headed by females. Almost half of the girls and women in the Factory Lot worked for a living outside the home, 90 percent of whom worked at the mill.[79]

In 1899, Fulton Bag built an additional 100 housing units when the mill began a night shift. The timing of this construction, along with the fact that the firm had not yet adopted any corporate welfare practices to speak of, indicates that the company erected housing not out of beneficent concern for the workers but essentially as a means to recruit and maintain labor. The firm also sought to make a profit from the rent paid on company housing.[80]

Despite this additional construction, the mill's burgeoning population extended well beyond the Factory Lot and the textile workers hotel. With the increase of the workforce, housing in both company-owned property and the adjacent white working-class neighborhood filled up to overflowing, causing rents to go up in the community and forcing some workers to walk as much as a mile to work.[81] In addition, many Fulton Bag workers took advantage of living in a city and chose not to live in company housing, despite substantially lower rents, ostensibly better housing stock, and a shorter distance to work. In 1900, 40 percent of Fulton Bag workers lived in outside housing, notwithstanding the recent rent reductions and the fact that many of the newly erected company houses were vacant.[82] The result was that, as a group, they were less under the company's domination than their counterparts in isolated rural mill communities across the Piedmont. More so than in other locales, they had contact with the broader white working class and its institutions, including the city's trade union movement.

In August 1897, white Fulton workers walked off their jobs to protest the company's hiring black women in the bag mill. After five days, the strike ended in management's dismissal of the black women and accession to other worker demands. Historian I. A. Newby has stated, "No other strike of mill workers in the New South had such a successful outcome." Newby and other historians have labeled the 1897 strike a "spontaneous" uprising.[83] Yet such a label hardly does either the strike or the strikers justice. The 1897 strike reflected, and cannot be understood outside of, a convergence of developments in race relations among Atlanta women and within the labor movement.

After the decline of the Knights of Labor, the Atlanta Federation of Trades (AFT) organized in 1890. Affiliated with the American Federation of Labor, the AFT drew principally from skilled white male workers in the building and printing trades, along with the railroad brotherhoods. The local labor movement experienced something of a resurgence in 1896. The Cotton States Exposition of 1895 helped spur union organization, as did the arrival in Georgia of Jerome Jones, who was soon to be business editor of the *Journal of Labor*.[84] The pace accelerated in 1897. In April, the *Atlanta Journal* reported an "upheaval" among the city's labor unions. A strike of local tinners had ripple effects throughout the building trades, while organizing also took place among woodworkers, electrical workers, trunk makers, and butchers.[85]

Amid this activity, organizers for the Socialist Labor Party (SLP) formed an Atlanta chapter, or "section," in July 1897.[86] The historical literature on the SLP has emphasized the antagonistic relationship between SLP leader Daniel DeLeon and AFL president Samuel Gompers.[87] In 1894, socialists helped topple Gompers from the AFL presidency. Upon Gompers's return to office the next year, DeLeon formed the Socialist Trade and Labor Alliance (STLA) as a radical alternative to "pure-and-simple" trade unionism. The split had direct implications for textile organizing in the South. Concerned that the STLA might organize southern mill hands, Gompers in 1895 appointed two part-time southern textile organizers, under the auspices of the National Union of Textile Workers (NUTW). While the union made slow but steady headway in the region during 1896–97, Gompers spent considerable time ridding the NUTW of any socialist influence.[88]

Yet, such bitter national divisions often tended to blur at the local level. In Atlanta, SLP leaders were aware of the importance of the AFT in building any movement; for their part, local trade unionists seemed receptive to whatever allies they could find. Accordingly, the first SLP organizational meeting in Atlanta was held at the Federation hall. The section officers elected at this meeting included SLP organizer and *Atlanta Journal* printer Samuel White, a railroad brakeman, and Fulton workers Nick Ransom and Lou Smith.[89]

From the outset, the Atlanta SLP was interested in organizing local textile workers. At the first meeting, White decried the long hours of the city's cotton mill workers and referred specifically to Fulton's labor contract. The momentum went both ways, too. In addition to reflecting the SLP's special interest in textile workers, the selection of Ransom and Smith demonstrated that some Fulton workers desired to affiliate with possible outside allies.

The local labor movement also reflected the rising tide of white supremacism, at a time when white southerners sought in numerous ways to circumscribe the place of African Americans in the changing New South. In the summer of 1897, prominent Georgia reformer Rebecca Latimer Felton declared in a much-publicized speech, "[I]f it takes lynching to protect woman's dearest possession from drunken, ravening beasts, then I say lynch a thousand a week if it becomes necessary." That summer, Atlanta's newspapers regularly trumpeted accounts of supposed Negro criminality and brutality and praised lynching and other white efforts at retribution.[90]

As Herbert Gutman has pointed out, even during this period of most intense racism, however, there existed occasions when white and black workers united in common purpose.[91] In Atlanta, white and black building tradesmen worked together on selected job sites through the turn of the century, marched together in Labor Day parades, and on occasion expressed class solidarity across racial lines. For instance, roughly half of the bricklayers who struck in 1897 were black, two of the four representatives of the union grievance committee were black, and many black workers continued to actively support the strike until its end.[92]

Yet such episodes of fragile interracial solidarity clearly went against the grain. Reflecting the retreat of the AFL from its original policy of nondiscrimination, in 1895 the International Association of Machinists, founded in Atlanta, became the first international union to receive an AFL charter despite explicitly denying membership to blacks. Racial exclusionism extended to the Boiler Makers, also founded in Atlanta, the railroad brotherhoods, and other craft unions. In May 1896, whites at the Atlanta Machine Works walked off their jobs to protest the placement of a black man on a bolt machine. White workers in Columbus and Rome, Georgia, also struck over the introduction of blacks to jobs seen as traditionally all white.[93]

White efforts to keep African Americans in subservient, circumscribed positions extended beyond the factory floor to all segments of society. In late July 1897, the McKinley administration appointed black Georgia Republican Party leader Henry L. Rucker as Atlanta's new federal tax collector. The Rucker appointment prompted considerable resentment among white Atlantans. The city's newspapers reported the appointment with dismay, predicting that whites in the tax collector's office would soon be replaced by blacks. On 5 August, the day before Rucker assumed his post, six white men in the office resigned, rather than work for a black man.

It was against this volatile backdrop that Jacob Elsas made his decision to hire a dozen or so black women in the largely female bag mill.[94] Elsas maintained that demand for the company's bags had recently soared, making it necessary to increase the number of hands, and that his attempts to secure enough white women were unsuccessful.[95] In hiring the black women, he was not operating in isolation, as the late 1890s marked one of the rare occasions when southern textile manufacturers ever even toyed with the idea of employing black production workers, a development related to the renewed union organization efforts in the region.[96]

On 3 August, Elsas notified the white women in the bag department that the black women would be coming the following day.[97] When the white women and girls of the department arrived in the morning and found the black women had already gone in, they refused to enter. After gathering outside the factory entrance, they returned to the mill district to discuss the situation.[98] Meanwhile, indicating some prior coordination, at dinner time, the other white women in the bag mill and all the white women in the Fulton cotton mill quit their jobs and walked out. By noon, the white male workers had followed suit, and the plant closed down.[99]

Up to this point, women had dominated the strike efforts. At the strikers' meeting that afternoon, one speaker prophesied the strike's success, "because it was started by ladies, and was being directed by ladies."[100] The striking female workers may have been influenced by broader developments among Atlanta women. The Woman's Building at the Cotton States Exposition had both reflected and spurred growing public visibility and organizational efforts of mainly middle-class white women in the city. In 1897, women's organized activity spread to the labor movement with the organization of a United Garment Workers local, Atlanta's first majority female union since the Knights of Labor.[101]

During the strike itself, however, the period of women's visible leadership was short-lived.[102] Once outside the factory gates, male Fulton workers began to assert themselves. Some men began throwing rocks at passersby and at the factory, others clashed with police, while others expressed their hostility toward both black workers and mill management. "We'll fix them niggers when they come out at 7 o'clock," boasted one man. "I wish old Elsas would come out and cross the street," added another. "He's the man responsible for the whole trouble. We'd teach him to respect our wives and daughters." At the meeting held that afternoon in the Federation of Trades hall, two all-male committees were appointed, one to obtain legal counsel for the strikers, and the other to draft a press statement detailing their grievances.

The *Atlanta Journal* described the strikers' declaration issued the next morning as "red hot." Reflecting the influence of SLP member Samuel White, the manifesto stated that the hiring of the black women was "a deliberate attempt to eliminate the white wage-slaves from this avocation, and substitute black wage-slaves because they will work cheaper." The strike did not originate in racial prejudice, it continued, but rather was a protest "against the introduction of cheaper labor; against forcing those people out of work who have held the positions for years, and against the damnable wage-slave system which is building up this cotton mill and the cotton industry of Atlanta on the bodies and souls of the daughters and sons of the fair southland." Daniel DeLeon hailed the declaration as a "strong indictment against capitalism" and reprinted it in the party's national publication.[103]

The statement's authors took pains to openly distance themselves from racial prejudice, yet racial animus, particularly when white women were involved, not only readily galvanized many of the strikers but also drew immediate, widespread support for their cause among a broad cross section of white people in Atlanta and beyond. The local painters union "emphatically condemned" Elsas and suggested that he "be required to do himself what he has endeavored to force white women to do—make social equals of negro women." Added the Columbus, Georgia, *Enquirer-Sun*, hinting at a possible boycott of Fulton Bag and lecturing Elsas on regional folkways, "The sympathy of the white people of the South goes out to the striking women and girls."[104] Indicating that he had learned his lesson in whiteness, Elsas told a local reporter, "I do not mind having my dinner served by a colored cook, but I don't say that they should sit down to my table."[105]

Members of the all-black quarrymen's union of nearby Lithonia had a different perspective, denouncing the strike committee's declaration as "detrimental to the progress of organized labor in the South." In a statement that illustrated the attenuated position of black trade unionists during the period, local president James Weaver said about the white Fulton workers, "It should have been the duty of said employees, if they were going in an organization, to have invited the twenty negro women that were employed . . . to have joined said organization, for the Textile Workers of America are affiliated with the American Federation of Labor, which organization does not discriminate against any one on account of color or previous condition. The resolutions did not say that the colored women were working for less wages or had taken the places of any former employees; therefore we think that said resolutions were very unbecoming for organized workingmen."[106]

On the strike's second day, the strikers sent a committee to ask Elsas to discharge the black women. Revealing his vulnerability on the race issue, Elsas welcomed the strikers and voiced his belief that an "amicable adjustment" could be reached. The head of the delegation then pressed beyond the original request to demand the discharge of nearly all black workers in the plant. Recognizing the strikers' advantage but not willing to concede to their demand or fall behind in production, Elsas parried, "What about extra hours? Will the people be willing to do extra work [if the blacks were fired]?" The committee consented to additional hours if white workers received "proper treatment," and all parties left believing that a settlement was near.

That afternoon, strikers drew up an agreement calling for the immediate removal of all black production workers and stipulating that no strikers be disciplined or discharged for their involvement. When strikers returned to see Elsas, who had just dismissed all the newly hired black women, and pressed him to sign the agreement, he replied that he would not since it did not represent what had been agreed upon.[107] Eventually, Elsas and the committee met in the office of *Atlanta Journal* publisher Hoke Smith to arrive at a settlement. Smith, although by no means a champion of the oppressed, had attracted working-class support for his efforts against the railroads and his comparatively favorable and thorough coverage of Atlanta's workers and their unions. The strike settlement called for the removal of the black women and guaranteed that workers would not suffer for their strike activity. The proposal was ratified, and the mill resumed production.[108]

The strike had several consequences. To many white Atlantans, in its affirmation of whites-only employment the strike's outcome stood in stark contrast to the new situation in the tax collector's office under Henry Rucker. The *Constitution* brought the point home in a racially stereotypical cartoon titled "The Color Line in Georgia Yesterday," showing the two workplaces side by

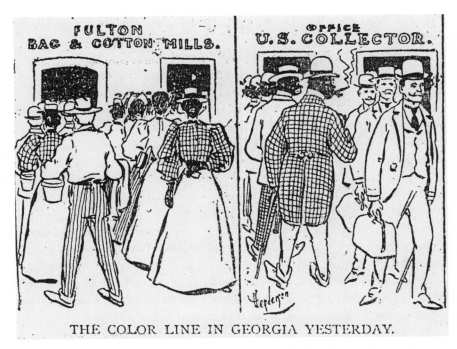

THE COLOR LINE IN GEORGIA YESTERDAY.

Cartoon, "The Color Line in Georgia Yesterday." *Atlanta Constitution*, 10 August 1897.

side, with blacks exiting and whites entering Fulton Bag, and the reverse happening at the tax collector's office.[109] Trade union leaders also drew upon the strike as a lesson in racial exclusionism rather than attempting to organize black textile workers, as the quarrymen had suggested. AFL southern textile organizer W. H. Winn made specific reference to the Fulton situation to bolster his argument for Negro colonization to Cuba, which would ostensibly relieve competition with white workers.[110]

In addition to reaffirming white supremacy in the workplace, the strike galvanized organization among mill hands and other white workers in Atlanta. By the strike's end, workers at the Exposition Cotton Mill had established another NUTW local. As the *Atlanta Journal* reported, "The union sentiment is undoubtedly stronger than ever before in the history of the mills in this city."[111] Reflecting their recent gains and the prominence of their cause, the textile workers led that year's Labor Day parade. The textile workers' delegation contained representatives from each of the departments within Fulton Bag. Leading the way were the women workers, dressed in "light blue shirt waists and snow white skirts," the first time in Atlanta that "women had ever been seen in public parades," another legacy of the strike.[112] The momentum continued through the fall, as organizers reported steady growth among Atlanta workers.[113]

At Fulton Bag itself, it was a different story. By late fall, at least ten people active in the strike had been disciplined by management or no longer worked at the mill, leading many workers to feel that the strike accord had been violated.[114] The situation bubbled over in December after delegations of Fulton workers and from the AFT had been rebuffed by Elsas in their attempts to reinstate a union activist. After some discussion, the union launched another strike on 6 December.

Despite management's attempts to quickly recruit strikebreakers, the walk-out had a significant impact on plant operations. For the week ending 11 December, company payroll was 71.9 percent of what it had been the previous week. The strike's impact was especially felt in the cotton mill production departments, where payroll was only 58.7 percent of what it had been the week before. In the carding and spinning rooms, payroll decreased by roughly a third; among spoolers and weavers, it plunged by close to 50 percent. Only by the week ending 1 January 1898, would the weaving department payroll approach even two-thirds of what it had been before the strike.[115] Unlike in August, it was loom fixers and other male workers who led the December strike.

Yet the near unanimous job action of August was not replicated. Nothing came close to Elsas's hiring of the black women as a rallying point. Placing black and white workers together, particularly when white women were affected, not only galvanized white workers like nothing else but was also perhaps the only action that could have mobilized such widespread white public support for striking textile workers and caused mill management to yield so readily. For many Fulton workers and the press, the issues in December seemed less significant, clear-cut, or imperative. Revealing the shallow roots the union had planted, some female workers "saw no reason why they should be forced to give up their jobs just because somebody else was dissatisfied." Other workers felt the strike issues were not significant enough to make them leave their jobs and lose their pay, especially before Christmas, at the beginning of winter, and in the midst of a national depression in the industry. In addition, the comparatively well paid male weavers who led the December strike evoked less public sympathy than had the impoverished white women of the bag mill.

Without race to contend with, Elsas held the upper hand and could be more aggressive, refusing to meet with delegations from the AFT or other outsiders. When pickets gathered around the factory gates at the noonday dinner hour one day, the company ordered enough provisions to feed 200–300 people inside the plant, giving "such a banquet as has never before been spread within the walls of the big factory." When the picketers outside got boisterous, city police arrived on the scene with a peremptory order banning loitering on nearby streets. When the editor and publisher of the *Tocsin*, the organ of the NUTW local at the Exposition Cotton Mill, tried to persuade women workers at Fulton Bag to stay out, he was arrested for disturbing the peace. Mill management also was able to readily recruit new workers to replace strikers.

Though individual activists clearly were discharged from the mill, Elsas apparently did not engage in a wholesale purge of union members at this time, perhaps because of his concern for uninterrupted production or because he felt that the NUTW presence did not constitute much of a threat. In January 1899, when the mill was about to inaugurate a night shift to catch up with back orders, Fulton management, like other manufacturers in the region, had no qualms about recruiting Augusta mill workers then out on strike. Company vice president Oscar Elsas wrote one of the Augusta strike leaders specifically asking for 50 carders, 180 spinners, and 150 weavers, and some of the Augusta strikers eventually did come.[116]

The night shift experiment was short-lived, however. Oscar Elsas later related,

> The men and boys and some of the women would stay awake all day and could not work at night, and the labor advanced so proportionately to our total poundage that we could not afford to run the mill at night any longer. Although a weaver might get off only a half cut per loom per night, they would still expect the full cut prices when the week came around, claiming it was the greater amount. So as to make the night run a success, we gave in to them for several weeks, hoping to gather a large body of hands so that we could make it go. We found it an utter failure. They loafed or did as they pleased, and the result was that we had to close down the night run.[117]

In addition, aware of mill hands' aversion to night work, other firms successfully recruited workers away from Fulton Bag during the night shift experiment.[118]

After many workers lost their jobs upon the discontinuation of the night shift, they came to the *Journal of Labor* with their grievances, telling of being rendered destitute. They complained that the mill had paid their railroad fare to come to work, then had it deducted from their wages, along with the rent for company housing. They now "were in a very distressed condition . . . left upon their resources without any compensation." *Journal of Labor* personnel in turn raised funds to send some workers back home, and launched an investigation of conditions in the Fulton district and elsewhere. They collected the weekly pay envelopes of Fulton workers to document the meager amounts mill hands received and used that information to advocate strengthened child labor and factory inspection laws. Editor C. C. Houston and business manager Jerome Jones testified about their findings before a congressional committee investigating conditions of capital and labor.

By then, mill management's position toward unions had hardened. Oscar Elsas, also testifying before the congressional committee, declared the company had "nothing against the union" and professed not to know whether a union even still existed at the mill. However, he plainly voiced his belief that unions did "not serve the interests of the employees best." Accordingly, Fulton management no longer met with any labor representatives but now had in place a policy of addressing grievances on a strictly individual basis.[119]

Oscar Elsas also recognized that, for all of management's considerable efforts to regulate and stabilize the workforce, it never was able to attain the control it sought. For instance, absenteeism continued to be a major issue, with some Fulton workers choosing to work five days a week rather than the standard six. "We have a certain element that will not work on Saturday at all," Elsas related. "That seems to be the greatest day to lay off. A certain class of people do that every Saturday." "What is that due to?" inquired a congressman. "Nothing more than they do not want to work," Elsas replied.[120]

Such tensions over the degree and extent of management's control over the workforce were an ongoing fact of life at the mill. They flared up at times when Fulton workers and management directly interacted with broader currents and developments. The late 1890s was one of these times, a period at once marked by escalating racism in the workplace and elsewhere, the increased public prominence of women, who were also entering Atlanta's industrial workforce in unparalleled numbers, an invigorated local labor movement, and a regional textile organizing drive. Another constellation of developments, concerns, tensions, and anxieties marked Atlanta of the early 1910s, the next time that organized labor protest came to Fulton Bag.

CHAPTER 2

Atlanta: Metropolis of the South

In 1914, Tarleton Collier, a reporter for the *Atlanta Georgian*, aroused the ire of Fulton president Oscar Elsas and other textile executives by drawing attention to the plight of child laborers in the region's cotton mills.[1] A generation later, Collier wrote a novel whose protagonist, the daughter of white sharecroppers, moved to Atlanta in the early 1910s.[2] The Atlanta section of the book was aptly titled "Something Old, Something New." For as much as any place in the region, Atlanta at this time epitomized the tensions between traditional ways and modern times, at the cusp of change in the New South, as well as resistance to that change. Fulton workers, managers, and owners were not isolated from these developments but rather participated in and engaged with this larger, dynamic urban world in a variety of ways.

Atlanta's population skyrocketed in the early twentieth century, mushrooming from 89,000 residents in 1900 to over 200,000 by 1920. The city's place as the hub of the regional economy consolidated with the development of a national rail network, the expansion of both the local manufacturing base and service sector, able promotion by a generally cohesive business elite, and Atlanta's emergence as a regional and even national convention center. It was not only economic opportunities that attracted people to Atlanta; by the early teens, the city boasted over a dozen skyscrapers; one of the country's best streetcar systems; drugstores, ice-cream parlors, and nice restaurants; landscaped neighborhoods; a thriving entertainment industry; and numerous other urban amenities. Such development helped Atlanta become not only a regional hub but much more of a "national" city, in ways that could not have happened coming out of Reconstruction. In 1906, the *Brooklyn Daily Eagle* called Atlanta "one of the most American cities in this country," and local elites, Progressive reformers, trade unionists, and other Atlantans moved within national circles and were part of social and cultural currents that extended well beyond the region.[3]

In addition to the attractions of the city, the hardships of an ailing agricultural system—faltering prices, rising tenancy, the crop lien system, soil erosion, and monocrop production—drove thousands of rural southerners into Atlanta. This was especially true for white families from the Georgia Upcountry, who poured into Atlanta at a greater rate than any other segment of the population. Whereas in 1900, African Americans comprised 40 percent of Atlanta's population, by 1910 the black population had dropped to a third of the total. In 1910, white people who had not been on the census rolls in 1900 made up at least a third of the city's population.[4] Atlanta had become, in the words of African American sociologist W. E. B. Du Bois, "the center of the upward striving of the 'poor whites.'"[5]

Atlanta's population explosion had numerous consequences. It further escalated job competition between black and white workers in the building trades, on the railroads, and elsewhere, although not in the city's textile mills after the Fulton race strike of 1897. A 1911 U.S. Senate report described the volatile nature of race relations in the workplaces of the New South's foremost city: "In Atlanta, where the new industrial development of the South is active, where new industrial conditions and relationships are being shaped and where, therefore, the new *post-bellum* relationship between the races is less effective and less understood, the difficulties of the situation are more than usually marked. Though the spectacle is not rare, the position of a white man and a negro working side-by-side at the same or similar occupations is obviously fraught with unpleasant possibilities in the shape of industrial friction."[6] Booker T. Washington similarly pointed out the close and complex relationship between race, class, and employment when he wrote in 1906, "The race question in Atlanta and elsewhere is and will probably continue to be to a great extent a question of labor."[7]

Such "industrial friction" could not be separated from more general white anxieties about the proper place of African Americans in Atlanta and the rapidly changing New South. Racial job competition, along with a lengthy gubernatorial campaign in which the central issue was black disfranchisement, a sensationalist press, and growing white fear about African Americans out of control in the city, in particular the specter of black assaults on white women, all contributed to Atlanta's murderous race riot of 1906. The riot helped cement white supremacy, legal segregation, and political disfranchisement in Atlanta and Georgia, while in its aftermath black Atlantans retrenched and developed their own network of community institutions.[8]

Map 1. Northeast Atlanta, 1914

These developments touched the Fulton community, too. While in 1900, there had existed a smattering of African Americans in the neighborhood surrounding the mill, by 1910 it had become all white, and black Atlantans entered the community at some risk. In 1907, shortly after the riot, the city postmaster was quoted as saying, "If we sent Negro carriers down into the mill district they might get their heads knocked off." "We'd rock them out of there, you know," later recalled Fulton worker Calvin Freeman. "We used to have a time rocking the colored boys back across the railroad tracks towards Edgewood Avenue and over on Decatur Street."[9]

Racial violence occasionally broke out on the shop floor, too. In July 1906, amid the highly charged atmosphere that would lead to the riot, two white women workers assaulted scrubwoman Henrietta Riddle and beat her with a hickory stick. Subsequent years saw the abatement of what Joel Williamson has called "racial radicalism" and the apparently peaceful introduction of black workers into strictly segregated sectors of the Fulton complex, notably the all-female second-hand department of the bag mill, the waste house, and the bleachery, even as the production departments of the cotton mills remained characteristically all white. Yet black workers continued to be vulnerable to verbal and physical abuse. In 1914, for instance, white male card room hands in Mill No. 1 regularly gathered by the elevator and made lewd remarks about the black scrubwomen as they went to the bathroom.[10]

Racial animus extended to owners and managers as well. For instance, in 1914, Fulton president Oscar Elsas appealed to class-based racial prejudice and fear in opposing a compulsory arbitration bill before the state legislature. Noting that the bill might affect any employer of ten or more people, Elsas warned, "Should a farmer employ ten negroes they could lodge complaints and insist upon arbitration, as often as they see fit. . . . [I]n the case of some wealthy families who employed ten servants in their household they could insist on arbitrating their differences with the lady of the house." And mill managers and supervisory personnel routinely employed derogatory epithets and stereotypes to describe African Americans.[11]

The rural origins of so many newcomers provided a country cast to much of urban life, the concerted promotional efforts of the city's elite to portray Atlanta as a sophisticated New South metropolis notwithstanding. "Back in those days, it was country in Atlanta," recalled Rosa Lee Carson Johnson, the daughter of a Fulton weaver who lived in the working-class district adjacent to the mill. "It sure was. Why, you could even raise a cow out there in your yard, and we did have chickens for a long time. And Mama, she'd have her a big garden out there in the backyard, and we'd raise okra and corn and Irish potatoes, tomatoes, onions."[12]

Growing vegetables and raising animals in the shadow of downtown provided food for working-class families in a city with one of the highest costs of living in the country. In a 1911 comparative survey of food prices in American cities, Atlanta ranked sixth highest among the thirty-nine cities examined. A study commissioned for the U.S. Senate reported that food prices paid by working-class families in Atlanta were 9 percent higher than prices in New York City. Even taking into consideration lower costs of housing, rent and food combined still cost more than in New York.[13]

Gardens and livestock also hearkened back to a traditional, familiar rural world. They contrasted sharply with Atlanta's modern emblems, the luxury hotels, skyscrapers, and office buildings that sprang up in the early twentieth century.[14] In numerous other ways, Atlanta of the early 1910s was a city of extremes, of often stark contrasts magnified and intensified by the city's rapid growth and reflecting deep and widening divisions among its population.

Fulton workers and owners manifested these growing disparities and inequalities in numerous ways. In 1914, company president Oscar Elsas moved to Peachtree Street, the city's most fashionable thoroughfare. After graduating from Georgia Tech in 1891, Elsas had become vice president of the firm and had taken on a growing number of responsibilities involving all aspects of plant operations, before assuming the presidency in January 1914. That same month, he and his wife, Emma, whom Oscar had met while boarding with her family in Boston, moved into the new Ponce de Leon Apartments at the corner of Peachtree Street and Ponce de Leon Avenue. In so doing, the Elsases were among the first Jews in the city to have a prestigious Peachtree Street address.[15]

Atlanta's initial modern luxury apartment house built on a grand scale, the Ponce de Leon featured a doorman in maroon livery at the elaborately grilled doors; an ornate lobby with a marble floor, Greek columns, and a Tiffany stained-glass rotunda; a spiral staircase curving upward for all eleven floors; stone lions resembling the gargoyles at Notre Dame at the foot of the twin turrets on the roof; and the city's first penthouse. Residents enjoyed built-in maid quarters attached to the apartments; a dining room serving meals three times a day; ice made daily on the premises and then delivered to every tenant; and grand balls and other gala rooftop parties. Down the hall from the Elsases lived such prominent individuals as the president of the Citizens and Southern Bank and the southern representative for the Draper Loom Company.[16]

The 1911 Senate report explicitly noted that the fashionable residences of Peachtree Street stood "in strong contrast" to the houses in the Fulton district. It singled out the Fulton neighborhood as having "an untidy and depressing appearance; the houses are for the most part poor and often squalid. . . . The cottages are of marked ugliness." In 1907, almost certainly referring to the housing around Fulton Mills, journalist Ray Stannard Baker maintained, albeit with some exaggeration, that there was "little difference in material comfort" between the homes of local mill workers and the slum housing of the city's black residents. And in 1914, an investigator for the U.S. Commission on Industrial Relations (CIR) condemned the area's housing, stating, "With the exception of one Jewish tenement in Chicago, I have never seen anything that equalled in repulsiveness . . . the housing conditions in this district."[17]

Housing was only one expression of the city's increasing social divisions and

Ponce de Leon Apartments. Atlanta Historical Society.

often jarring juxtapositions. The new Municipal Auditorium, erected in 1909, was another. In 1910, amid great local fanfare, the Metropolitan Opera put on five performances at the auditorium, inaugurating an annual practice that would continue for decades. As the only place where the Met performed outside of New York, Atlanta's cultural reputation received a shot in the arm, however well deserved.

Housing in the Fulton mill district, c. 1907. Georgia Institute of Technology Library and Information Center.

The Elsases and other members of the city's German Jewish community and business elite were active enthusiasts of opera. While some patrons supported the opera primarily out of love for classical music, other members of the city's elite saw the Met's visit as a gala social occasion, one of a number of ways in which they publicly marked their position at the top of Atlanta society. Still others saw the opera as a potential economic and public relations bonanza, another opportunity to showcase Atlanta as a national city.[18]

In contrast to the decorum, grandeur, and glitter when the opera came to town in May, the Municipal Auditorium was quite a bit more rambunctious during the annual old-time fiddler's conventions held there beginning in April 1913. Textile workers and other white working-class Atlantans flocked to hear such popular performers as Fiddlin' John Carson, a weaver at Fulton Mills who was widely satirized in the local press for his archaic style and hillbilly ways and who won the best Georgia fiddler award in 1914. The fiddler's conventions were marked by spirited exchanges between performers and audience, widespread high jinks, and general rowdiness that sometimes got out of hand, as Marion "Peanut" Brown, the son of a Fulton worker, recalled: "Them fiddler's conventions, boy, they'd break out in some fights if the thing didn't go the way they wanted it. I've seen a lot of fights up there because they'd give it to one fiddler and another bunch thought the other fiddler got it, and they'd wind up in a big brawl."[19]

One local reporter, appreciative of the growing class distinctions in Atlanta that were illustrated by the diverse musical events held at the auditorium, wrote that the fiddlers at the conventions played songs that "your grandaddies used to dance to in the country cabins before they moved to Atlanta and got rich in real estate and turned into grand opera lovers." Another reporter described how for the many newcomers relocated in an often alien urban environment, the fiddler's conventions offered a haven, a place that was their own that provided a connection to a traditional world now in transition and that evoked "[t]he feel of the old red hills of Georgia and the little old cabin with the golden corn swaying in the wind. . . . Shut your eyes and you forget you are in Atlanta's big Auditorium. You can see the rafters of the old barn and smell the hay up in the mow and 'most hear the lowing of the cattle and the rustle of the hen who complains about her disturbed nest." Similarly, many of the songs that Carson and others sang, drawing largely from a nineteenth-century repertoire, were about rural nostalgia, family, faith, home, and community, comforting themes to many working-class white Atlantans in the rapidly changing New South.[20]

In 1916, Atlanta mayor James G. Woodward, a union printer at the *Atlanta Journal*, lampooned the pretentiousness of the city's grand opera patrons, declaring that Atlantans "don't know B from bull's foot about grand opera, although they go and make a lot of fuss about it."[21] Woodward, elected mayor of Atlanta four times between 1900 and 1914, in many ways epitomized what sociologist Robert Park meant when he wrote in 1906 that "Atlanta is representative of the 'New South,' the South in which the once despised 'poor white' is rapidly becoming a factor. In Atlanta the 'cracker' has come into his own."[22]

Men like Woodward generally prospered from and were identified with the city's sustained growth. By the early 1910s a union printer like Woodward made twice the wages of the most veteran loom fixer at the Fulton Bag and Cotton Mills while working a substantially shorter work week.[23] Such white men—in the printing and building trades, the railroad brotherhoods, and other skilled occupations directly linked with Atlanta's expansion—were at the core of the city's burgeoning trade union movement. In the aftermath of the organizing gains made among white workers following the 1897 Fulton race strike, the percentage of unionized labor in Atlanta's workforce rose from 4 percent in

Atlanta Labor Temple Association members, 1912. Special Collections Dept., Pullen Library, Georgia State University.

1900 to 12.4 percent in 1920, a substantially greater figure than in any other Georgia city and even higher than the national average. The early teens saw the flourishing of the *Journal of Labor*, the local labor newspaper, a new labor temple, the establishment of the Georgia Department of Labor and Commerce, the organization of the Southern Labor Congress, crowds of as many as 50,000 people at the annual Labor Day parades, and a generally invigorated labor movement. "A scrappy activity appears suddenly to have supplanted the accustomed lethargy of organized labor in Atlanta," enthused the *Journal of Labor* in February 1914.[24]

Reflecting the predilections of local labor leaders toward the assertion of citizenship in a respectable manner, their insistence on the ballot as a measure of equality among white men in the aftermath of Populist defeat and African American disfranchisement, and Atlanta's ward-based political structure, organized labor played an active part in early-twentieth-century municipal politics and civic affairs. In the mid-teens trade union members constituted close to half of all the registered voters in the city and held a variety of elected and appointed positions. Even patrician candidates for elected office were compelled to publicly appeal "to all the classes." In addition, trade unionists possessed enough political clout to twice beat back city charter reform attempts in 1911 and 1913, which would have substantially diluted working-class political strength.[25]

As the charter reform movements indicate, working-class influence in local politics did not go uncontested or unchallenged. On the contrary, middle-class reformers and business elites periodically mobilized politically around such issues as the expansion of city services and infrastructure, municipal control of public utilities, taxation, the politics of the police department, vice and corruption, and the purported public drunkenness and immorality of Mayor Woodward himself. Atlanta politics of the era was decidedly turbulent and fractious, with diverse factions and interests regularly contending for and holding power.

Unlike his close associates James W. English and Robert F. Maddox and other members of Atlanta's business elite, Oscar Elsas never got immersed in the hurly-burly of municipal politics. His noninvolvement reflected the growing divisions among the elite that accompanied Atlanta's development. Whereas in the 1880s Jacob Elsas and the other members of the business elite had for the most part acted in a unified fashion, by the 1910s the city's business leadership was diverse, complex, and often factionalized. Atlanta businessmen divided among themselves over issues such as industry's proper relationship to the state and politics, organized employer activity, the commercialization of culture, and trade unionism.

This is not to say Oscar Elsas was apolitical, far from it. Elsas had an abiding interest in state and national politics as it affected industrial relations and the textile industry in particular. In 1900, he had testified before the U.S. Industrial Commission, which was exploring relations of capital and labor. He paid considerable attention to the U.S. Senate's multivolume study of women and child workers published in the early 1910s, cooperating with federal researchers and apparently reading much of the final work. In 1915, Elsas actively opposed pending Senate legislation that ostensibly would have eliminated modern efficiency systems in government employment. That same year, he proudly pointed to his long association with the National Association of Manufacturers, the country's leading open-shop lobbying organization. He also was a political ally and supporter of Joseph M. Brown, governor of Georgia from 1911 to 1913, in large part because of Brown's staunch antilabor position.[26]

But Elsas refrained from such active political involvement at the local level. He certainly was "acceptable to the powers that be," in the words of his son

Norman, and every morning before work he would talk shop with bankers and other prominent businessmen while being shaved in Alonzo Herndon's downtown barber establishment. Yet his relationship with other members of Atlanta's business elite was strained. As a federal investigator stated, "Mr. Elsas . . . is not a man who is popular or well spoken of in a social and civic sense."[27]

Outside of a short stint on a smoke abatement committee, Elsas's activity during the early teens in the Atlanta Chamber of Commerce, a central gathering place for the city's elite, was nominal at best.[28] The two occasions in which Fulton Mills representatives *did* come before the Chamber of Commerce during these years are themselves revealing. In May 1911, Benjamin Elsas and Ben Phillips, Oscar Elsas's brother and brother-in-law and the company second vice president and attorney, respectively, appeared at a joint meeting of the Chamber of Commerce's committees on commerce and cotton to voice their opposition to pending congressional legislation that would enable the admission into the country of free, untariffed burlap products. Benjamin Elsas argued that the free admission of burlaps would significantly displace cotton goods and thus drive down the price of both raw and manufactured cotton. After going into closed session, committee members scoffed at what they perceived as greatly exaggerated estimates of reduced cotton prices and pointed out the advantages of burlap bagging to local fertilizer and cotton oil manufacturers. Later, the Chamber of Commerce wrote Atlanta's congressmen asking them to concur in recent Senate action placing burlaps on the free list.[29]

The only other instance of Fulton representatives coming before the Chamber of Commerce during this period also involved national legislation, and it demonstrated mill management's increasingly hard-line opposition to organized labor. In April 1913, Oscar Elsas wrote the Chamber of Commerce asking that it take action against the pending Sundry Civil Bill, which, in exempting monies appropriated in it from antitrust prosecution against unions, reputedly provided "that government money shall not be used to enforce the law against labor organizations."[30] A week later, Elsas proposed that the Chamber of Commerce immediately wire Georgia senators Hoke Smith and Augustus Bacon with a resolution stating in part that the bill "would deprive the people of the protection of the law of the land when injured in their property and business . . . and would be class legislation of the most dangerous character."[31] Though the Chamber of Commerce directors generally supported Elsas's proposal in principle, they divided on taking any action on the matter, one of the rare times such a split occurred in the body's ranks during this era and suggestive of some dissatisfaction with Elsas's timing and approach, if not his anti-union sentiments. By the early teens, at least some members of

Atlanta's business elite had reached more of an accommodationist approach to organized labor than had Elsas.[32]

Not all Atlantans fared as well as the skilled white craftsmen at the heart of the local labor movement. By the early 1910s, Atlanta's population explosion had put considerable pressure on municipal services and on the city's infrastructure. The police department, for instance, was ill equipped to adequately address crime in a city that had the highest arrest rate in the country, largely for vagrancy, disturbing the peace, and drunkenness. The fire department and Grady Hospital were similarly overwhelmed by the city's burgeoning population. In 1910, only about half of Atlanta's school-age children actually attended school; those who did usually went to overcrowded, dilapidated, and substandard facilities. Likewise, many Atlantans lived without adequate water and sewage facilities, even after a bond referendum to extend the city's overwhelmed sewer and water systems was passed in 1910.[33]

In 1914 a federal investigator observed in the Fulton neighborhood "rows of houses where there is at present only the iron trough sewerage system running through the rows of closets at the back of houses and flushed only two or three times a day." She also described a group of eleven mill houses with only two outside double water closets for the lot of them. "The smell from these toilets was very foul." One mill worker similarly complained about the inadequacy of water closets in the area, stating that the six closets for her row of houses had to do for about seventy-five people, "both men and women." Such an arrangement "did not provide sufficient facilities for a crowd of people, many of whom had to leave for work at the same time and ought to go to the toilet before going to the mill."[34]

Outdoor plumbing and sewage, overcrowded housing, inadequate garbage disposal, and contaminated and stagnant water contributed to the spread of typhoid fever, malaria, diphtheria, tuberculosis, smallpox, influenza, and other infectious and contagious diseases. These occurred at a much higher rate than the national average and often reached near-epidemic proportions, especially in such congested sections as the Fulton district, where residents also suffered from nutritional illnesses and occupational maladies. In 1913, the Russell Sage Foundation issued a devastating report on public health in Atlanta, claiming that up to one-third of the local deaths during the previous year were preventable and pointing to gross inadequacies in the city health department.[35]

The growing population also contributed to a rising incidence of unemployment, low wages, and destitution. In his annual report at the end of 1913, city warden Thomas Evans declared, "Poverty in the city of Atlanta is on the increase." He reported that over 5,000 calls for assistance came to his office the previous year, over 1,000 more than the previous year, almost twice the figure for the year before that, and four times the number when the office was established in 1903. Furthermore, he predicted that the upcoming winter would set a new record for appeals for assistance.[36]

A "large and constantly increasing element" of those charity-case Atlantans, who Evans termed "the really poor and needy, the pathetic poor and needy," were white working women and children, including Fulton workers and their families. "The money they receive is not enough for their support," stated the warden. "They are not able to make ends meet." Evans concluded, "If the city is growing, it is growing on the new system, in which women and children work."

In pointing out the particular circumstances of working women and children, along with their central place in the city's development, Evans drew attention to key Progressive Era issues that not only had a great deal of currency nationwide but were widely discussed and debated within Atlanta. Both the local and national movement to regulate child labor got off the ground at the turn of the twentieth century. In Atlanta, as throughout the United States, a diverse, sometimes fragile coalition of trade unionists, middle-class women, and clergymen developed to push child labor reform, often for quite divergent reasons. For organized labor, child labor embodied the abuses and growing misery of the new regional industrial order, in particular the much ballyhooed southern textile industry, which not only undercut wages of skilled workers but reduced the children of once independent white southerners to a state of subjugation and dependency, comparable to that of African American slaves. In addition, for the skilled white male workers of the Atlanta labor movement, child labor symbolized the real and potential erosion of their own position as breadwinners and patriarchs.[37] For other members of the coalition, child labor reform was an essential part of a larger movement to help regulate and control a segment of the population increasingly seen by the rising southern middle class as disorderly, disruptive, disorganized, and in need of intervention.[38] With the establishment of the National Child Labor Committee (NCLC) in 1904 and the reorganization of the Georgia Child Labor Committee, the coalition, spearheaded by organized labor, launched a successful effort to get a child labor plank into the state Democratic Party platform and to push through Georgia's first child labor law in 1906. The victory had its limits, however, as the original bill was substantially gutted before passage—the result of concerted opposition by many of the state's textile owners.[39]

Unlike many other Georgia mill men, who resented the state interfering with their private affairs, Fulton management did *not* oppose or try to get around the 1906 child labor law. From the Elsases' perspective, grounded in modern principles of scientific management, child labor, however desirable in the short run, was ultimately inefficient. Fulton management kept close records on child employment; cooperated with the women of the neighborhood settlement house to enforce the 1906 law; declined to hire exceptionally young children except under extreme conditions; and screened those young workers who sought work at Fulton Mills, citing extenuating circumstances with a "Minor Employment Contract," signed by their parents or guardians. "Children do not as a rule enter our employ as soon as they are of the legal age," accurately declared Oscar Elsas. By 1914, workers sixteen and younger comprised 12 percent of the mill's labor force, a figure substantially lower than the state average.[40]

In the early teens, as organized labor, middle-class female reformers, and Social Gospel–informed clergy and laity all gathered strength in Atlanta, the issue of child labor reform resurfaced. Public reports helped bring attention to the matter again, as did the social photography of Lewis Hine, who passed through Georgia in 1909 and 1913 on behalf of the NCLC. In 1912 and 1913 alone, the *Journal of Labor* published dozens of articles on the subject, and the *Atlanta Journal* and the Hearst-owned *Atlanta Georgian*, the city's two daily papers most favorably oriented toward the white working class, did likewise. In March 1913, O. Delight (Mrs. E. B.) Smith, a leading activist in the local trade union movement, successfully proposed to the Federation of Trades that a factory inspection committee be established, specifically to monitor child labor abuses. And in 1914, momentum built to pass a stronger child labor law currently before the state legislature.[41]

Like their counterparts elsewhere, many Progressive reformers in Atlanta explicitly linked child labor to the issue of protecting working women, one of the fastest growing segments of the city's population. By 1920, 42 percent of all Atlanta's women sixteen and over worked outside the home, a higher rate of female employment than any other city in the country, outside of a few Massachusetts textile cities and Washington, D.C. Among black women, who overwhelmingly had worked outside the home since Reconstruction, the number of wage earners increased 60 percent from 1900 to 1920. Yet the dynamic growth was among white women, whose workforce participation increased 276 percent, or over twice the city's own rapid growth rate, over the same period. In 1900, white working women had comprised 28 percent of the local female labor force; by 1920, they made up 48 percent of Atlanta women working outside the home, employed in factories as well as in clerical and white-collar positions.[42]

Many Atlantans assumed that black women would work outside the home. The escalating participation of white women in the workforce, though, and the feminization of poverty challenged conventional notions about male authority and the proper place of women in southern society. So did the fact that, like their counterparts elsewhere, white working women in Atlanta increasingly lived away from their families of origin. By 1920, a fifth of the city's working women were such "women adrift," a figure comparable to that of Chicago.[43]

Skilled male trade unionists, female social workers, including those associated with the Fulton neighborhood settlement house, middle-class reformers, clergymen, and the daily press all voiced apprehension that the changed circumstances of Atlanta's white working women upset and threatened traditional family and gender roles. Furthermore, many Atlantans expressed fear that women working and living away from their parents and among strangers, in what often seemed a threatening, volatile urban environment, might be vulnerable to the numerous temptations and hazards of the city, a place seemingly far removed from the close-knit communities of the rural South.[44]

Atlanta did offer many temptations for working-class women and men. Movie theaters, vaudeville and burlesque, pool halls, cheap amusement parks, and dance halls all took root in the first decades of the twentieth century, in conjunction with the commercialization of culture, the emergence of a nationwide entertainment industry, and the city's own sustained economic growth, as well as efforts by local promoters to represent Atlanta as a sophisticated metropolis, in line with national trends and practices. As Mayor Woodward stated in 1913, while defending a proposal to introduce Sunday movies, "We are no longer living in a crossroads village, but in a modern, cosmopolitan city." Yet others dismayed of these developments as signs of rampant commercialism, urban decay, and the erosion of traditional values and norms.[45]

No place more epitomized the availability of and contestation over new forms of public amusements than Decatur Street, which snaked from the edge of the Fulton district into downtown. In many ways Decatur Street was a border zone, where people from different classes, races, and ethnic backgrounds regularly commingled, in contrast to much of the rest of the city, which was becoming increasingly segregated by class and race. In 1913, a local reporter described Decatur Street in colorful and racially stereotypical terms:

> Decatur Street is the home of humanity as it is, where the negro is found in his element of fried fish and gaudy raiment, and characters which might have walked through the pages of Dickens or O. Henry, have their joys and sorrows, and laugh and cry, make love and die, even as their brothers and sisters of Peachtree Street. Here bearded mountaineers from Rabun County

brush shoulders with laborers fresh from the Old Country. Jewish shopkeepers pass the time o' day with the clerk of the Greek ice cream parlor next door. The Yankee spieler cries his wares and the Confederate veteran buys 'em, and through it all negroes, yellow, black and brown, thread their laughing, shiftless way, types of the south which could be seen in no other city in the land in all their native picturesqueness. Decatur Street is the melting pot of Dixie.[46]

Such a diverse, wide-open potpourri of humanity disturbed many middle-class Atlantans, who increasingly sought order in a rapidly changing city, or, as one of their Charlotte counterparts put it, "a place for everything and everything in its place."[47]

Other Atlantans felt morally affronted and threatened by many of the goings-on of Decatur Street. In 1908, Methodist women associated with Wesley House, the settlement house in the Fulton district, deplored the numerous "saloons, low places of amusements, dives of all kinds, [and] houses of ill repute" that dotted Decatur Street and that many Fulton workers frequented. One regular patron was musician Fiddlin' John Carson, who, along with fellow workers and friends from the Fulton district, would often drink and socialize at Bud Johnson's poolroom, a popular Decatur Street hangout and watering hole. As the Wesley House Woman's Club periodically pointed out, the Decatur Street establishments not only attracted a large adult male clientele but also drew small boys from the community who would find and drain off kegs of beer on the sly. For Dorothy Crim, the head resident at Wesley House, Decatur Street was nothing but a den of iniquity. "Numberless are the men and boys who failed to run this gauntlet and preserve their better selves," she lamented.[48]

In the early twentieth century, a furor over the "Decatur Street dives," where working-class whites and—much more alarmingly for white Atlantans—African Americans drank and gathered outside of middle-class view and control, helped lead to the Atlanta race riot and bring about statewide Prohibition in January 1908. Even after Prohibition, though, Carson and other male Fulton workers continued to obtain alcohol from Decatur Street blind tigers, "near beer" joints, and saloons, as well as from moonshine peddlers. In January 1915, a labor spy employed by Fulton Mills reported that one Decatur Street whiskey seller sold fourteen pints to workers in a half hour alone.[49] Liquor continued to be readily accessible from moonshine peddlers in the mill district as well, as resident Peanut Brown recalled: "Yeah, there was half a dozen right around in that neighborhood because when all them mill people got out, man they headed for a bootlegger. They sure did. They wanted to get them a drink when they got out of that dusty cotton mill."[50]

There were numerous other cheap urban amusements available to working-class Atlantans in addition to the Decatur Street establishments. Fulton employees and other white workers attended White City Park, an amusement park a mile south of the mill district, considered off-limits by many middle-class citizens. They also frequented the Star, the Alamo, and other "low-class" movie theaters, which often included vaudeville and burlesque, that clustered in downtown Atlanta after 1907.[51] In 1908, the Methodist Women's Board of City Missions deplored the fact that so many Fulton workers were frequenting "cheap theaters, so hurtful to their morality."[52]

In 1912, the Atlanta Chamber of Commerce explicitly linked textile workers and the movies. Concerned that the city offered "no place for the working classes, such as cotton mill operatives" on Sunday afternoons, the organization appointed a Committee on Public Amusements to furnish leisure activities for "these people" so that they would not get into trouble. Finally the committee, which included *Journal of Labor* editor Jerome Jones, agreed to arrange for local moving picture houses to stay open on Sunday afternoons, but to "show nothing but humorous and educational pictures with no vaudeville."

Before the plan was implemented, however, the committee decided to get the endorsement of the local branch of the Men and Religion Forward Movement.[53] A businessmen's evangelical association affiliated with the Evangelical Ministers Association, an umbrella group of perhaps a hundred of the city's white ministers, the MRFM had organized nationally in 1911 to invigorate male activity in America's Protestant churches. The Atlanta branch quickly became one of the country's most active, targeting a number of perceived symbols of moral decay associated with the city's fast-growing urban-commercial environment.[54]

MRFM president and prominent businessman John J. Eagan and two other members met with police chief James L. Beavers and the Chamber of Commerce committee to discuss moving pictures in such "congested districts" as the Fulton neighborhood. They determined that the larger community would not stand for Sunday movies for profit and that any effort to provide "wholesome amusements to the masses" on Sunday should be completely separated from all commercial interests. This intervention effectively killed the proposal, although the MRFM continued to fight Sunday moving pictures in general and to act as an unofficial local censor, while Fulton workers and other working-class Atlantans continued to go to the movies.[55]

In 1911, the Atlanta Civic League, an organization overlapping with the MRFM, asserted that the "low class moving picture shows down-town," like the Decatur Street dives, spaces outside the view or control of middle-class Atlantans, furnished meeting sites for prostitutes and their dates. While prostitution

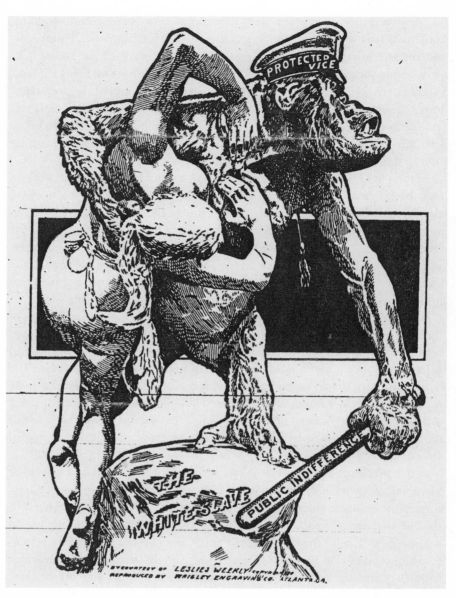

Cartoon from an MRFM bulletin. *Atlanta Georgian*, 24 September 1912.

had existed in Atlanta since before the Civil War, the changed circumstances of the trade, and of the city itself, made prostitution a particular target of local reformers during the 1910s.

Prostitution had become more visible by the teens. Local promoters actually contributed to this enhanced visibility by issuing a pamphlet in 1911 that showed on its cover a picture of Atlanta as a seductive woman luring prospective conventioneers to the city. Like numerous other American cities, Atlanta boasted its own red-light district, and another cluster of brothels just off Decatur Street, which itself was a popular working area for local prostitutes and a target of local reformers. "Here," lamented Dorothy Crim, "many a girl has given up that life which belongs to a pure woman."[56]

In September 1912, the MRFM launched a major campaign to close down the red-light district. Openly appealing to public opinion, the organization issued a series of spectacular page-length "bulletins" in the daily newspapers, bankrolled by John Eagan and authored by attorney Marion M. Jackson, that condemned "The Houses in Our Midst" and successfully put pressure on Chief Beavers to shut down the brothels. The crusade received national acclaim as a model in antiprostitution efforts and consolidated the MRFM's position as the city's leading reform group.[57]

It also led the MRFM to address industrial issues, in particular the position of working women and child laborers. In February 1913, one MRFM leader delivered a well-publicized address titled "A Living Wage in Atlanta," in which he stressed the close connection between prostitution and the lack of a living wage for many women and girls. Later that year, MRFM members and representatives of the Federation of Trades collaborated in forming a commission to examine the treatment of women and child workers.[58]

The MRFM's interest in industrial questions increased in 1914. In January, the Evangelical Ministers Association (EMA) formed a committee to investigate a strike at the *Christian Index*, a local Baptist publication. While they stated they could not take sides in the matter, the EMA members expressed "deepest sympathy with the efforts of laboring men to better their conditions and recognize their wisdom and right in organizing to this end." In the aftermath of this episode, the local Allied Printing Trades Council requested that the MRFM use a union emblem on all its publications. In March, the MRFM executive committee discussed on two occasions the plight of "young women of our city who are receiving inadequate wages to insure [decent] living conditions." In April, the Reverend W. C. Schaeffer, the MRFM's newly appointed representative to the AFT, helped bring the AFT and the EMA "into a more sympathetic relationship." And in May, several of the MRFM bulletins mentioned child labor or other industrial abuses.[59]

Certainly a prostitute could earn considerably more than the women working at Fulton Mills or other Atlanta factories. In 1914, for example, prostitutes at the Empire Hotel made up to three dollars a trick, or nearly half what a Fulton spinner or bag mill worker made in an entire week.[60] MRFM members claimed that 75 percent of the prostitutes apprehended in the cleanup campaign came from the "cotton mill strata," many actually from the Fulton community. A number of "assignation houses" also existed in the mill district itself.[61]

Prostitution was connected to larger tensions and public debate concerning women's changing place in an urban milieu such as Atlanta. Underneath the press's attention to the temptations of the city for white working-class women lay a recognition that many Atlanta women were in fact challenging and transgressing a range of conventional gender norms. The early 1910s saw Atlanta women increasingly take part in organizations and activities outside the home, including the first legislative hearings on woman suffrage in 1914.[62] Along with anxieties about the ramifications of a new urban-industrial order came apprehension about real and potential changing gender roles and sexual practices in the New South.

Some Fulton workers were among those Atlantans who participated in this sexual upheaval. Male and female workers partook in common-law marriages, adulterous and bigamous arrangements, and casual sexual alliances, along with divorce and marital separation.[63] In 1915, one woman in the mill community described another woman as someone who had "done things that are for married women and not single." Dr. W. V. Garrett, a physician who practiced among mill district residents, reported that venereal disease was "exceedingly common" in the neighborhood, as it was in the Exposition Mill community.[64]

"The character of the people at the mill is not good," declared Chief Beavers in 1914. "They are always giving trouble."[65] There certainly existed a grain of truth to Beavers's remarks. Fulton workers, among the most marginalized, impoverished, and transient of the city's white population, got arrested at about twice the rate of other Atlantans. Many workers also exhibited what a local reporter called "a roving disposition," displayed considerable violence and rowdiness, and showed little interest in frugality, regularity, or diligence.[66]

Yet it is important to carefully scrutinize and evaluate Beavers's remark. To begin with, by no means did all Fulton workers get arrested, drink, engage in extramarital sex, or act disorderly. As social worker Emma Burton of Wesley House put it, "a range of morals" existed in the mill community.[67] Furthermore, Beavers's statement has to be understood within a larger context of white middle-class attitudes, language, and behavior concerning the city's textile workers.

In the late nineteenth century, middle-class white southerners had regarded and described mill hands as primarily unfortunate—Confederate widows, for instance—abject, or downtrodden. By the 1910s, because of the growing divisions within southern society, and the turbulence of textile communities and urban life in particular, a broad range of middle-class and upper-class Atlantans, like their counterparts across the urban and industrial South, regularly depicted textile workers as almost inherently ignorant, helpless, suspicious, shiftless, wretched, degenerate, and out of control.[68]

For example, James A. Greer, who left his managerial position at Fulton Mills to become editor of the Charlotte-based *Textile Manufacturer*, described Fulton and other textile workers: "Having come from the farms poor and ignorant, they brought the 'snuff dipping' 'tobacco chewing' and general shiftless habits with them. . . . You can take the man out of the country but you can't take the country out of the man."[69] A doctor associated with the Wesley House clinic branded mill district residents as "those who have reached poverty by their own deliberate transgression of physical and moral laws, they do not seem anxious to do better and are unable to take the initiative to escape from poverty without help."[70] Wesley House staff, while often sympathetic to the plight of mill hands, contended that Fulton workers and their kin suffered from a lack of ambition, were ignorant of any detail of life different from their own, had no ideals of good citizenship, were contented to live in filth and to endure ill health, could not govern themselves, were badly disorganized, and suffered for wholesome social and spiritual expression.[71] The Reverend G. R. Buford of the MRFM stated that Fulton workers and their families had "no social life and no social standard at all, and neither have they any pleasures."[72] Oscar Elsas declared, "The character of the people is such, to a large extent, that they are not interested in their own welfare."[73]

This language, and the attitudes it represented, served to mark Fulton workers and other mill hands as a "fairly distinct element in the population," distanced greatly by habits, values, genetics, and geography from respectable white people.[74] Buttressed by such labeling, a range of middle-class and wealthy southerners concerned about moral, social, and industrial order could routinely assert their own superiority to textile workers, root the source of poverty and degradation in individual rather than systemic causes, and at the same time justify their active intervention in the lives of local mill hands and their families. For example, former Fulton card room superintendent James Greer described such intercession of Elsas and his fellow owners as a public boon. Greer wrote that, like his fellow mill men, Elsas provided a "great civilizing and Christianizing influence" (ironic in light of Elsas's Jewishness) for "mill operatives going through a state of evolution, rising gradually to a higher plane of living."[75]

In addressing such representations in early-twentieth-century Atlanta, Jacquelyn Dowd Hall has written, "Outsiders' labels help create the fund of interpretative possibilities from which identity can be drawn. . . . images help construct relationships of power."[76] No single event of the period had more symbolic resonance than the case of Leo Frank. On Confederate Memorial Day of 1913, Mary Phagan, the thirteen-year-old child of farmers-turned-cotton mill workers, was found murdered at Atlanta's National Pencil Factory, where she worked. Suspicion soon centered around Leo M. Frank, the Jewish, Brooklyn-raised, Cornell-educated superintendent of the firm, who was arrested and then convicted amid a highly charged, frenzied atmosphere. After his appeals in state court were exhausted, Frank's plight drew sympathy and support from across the country, which in turn heightened hostility within Georgia against Frank and his supporters. Following Georgia governor John M. Slaton's commutation of Frank's death sentence to life imprisonment, Frank was taken out of prison and lynched in August 1915, near the grave of Mary Phagan.[77]

For many Atlantans and Georgians, both Mary Phagan and Leo Frank quickly became symbols of much that seemed wrong with the New South, and the case played out at a symbolic level all the way through the lynching. At various times and for various constituencies, Mary Phagan symbolized southern white womanhood deflowered and defiled; the hazards of living in an urban environment among strangers; the diminution of patriarchal authority; and the oppression of women and child workers in Atlanta's factories. Former Populist leader Tom Watson characterized Phagan as "a daughter of the people, of the common clay, of the blouse and the overall, of those who eat bread in the sweat of the face, and who, in so many instances are the chattel slaves of a sordid Commercialism that has no milk of human kindness in its heart of stone."[78] In turn, Leo Frank evoked a history of Yankee oppression of the South and symbolized an exploitative, alien, urban capitalism. As the numerous rumors about Frank's sexuality attest, the case also reflected the anxieties surrounding a new sexual order in the New South. It was precisely the confluence of these various currents and tensions that gave the Frank case its explosiveness.

As might be expected, the Frank case touched the Jewish-owned Fulton Mills. The person perhaps most personally affected was company attorney Ben

Phillips, who in 1913 had joined Frank's attorney Luther Z. Rosser as well as Governor Slaton in one of the city's most prominent law firms. According to one family member, Phillips was "nervous as a cat" throughout the case and feared for his personal safety. Although Oscar Elsas knew Leo Frank, he moved in different social circles and was not so directly impacted as Phillips.[79] Elsas also remained a political ally of Joseph M. Brown despite Brown's public statements against Frank. Yet the case certainly made him quicker to charge anti-Semitism among those who challenged or questioned management's industrial policies.

The Frank case helped widen the already large gulf between Fulton owners and workers and reinforced the alienation that many workers felt. In 1914, one new recruit protested a heavy workload in anti-Semitic terms, stating, "[T]o hell with the G— damn Company and their 32 looms. I never run that many before for anybody, and I won't do it for them, especially a Son-of-a-B— of a Jew."[80] MRFM member G. R. Buford related an apparently widespread belief that Oscar Elsas "would never treat workers of his own race as he treats his Christian employees."[81] Federal investigator Alexander M. Daly also heard of anti-Jewish prejudice among mill hands toward Elsas. Fulton workers joined rallies protesting Frank's commutation, while one resident of the mill district threatened to hang both Slaton and Frank.[82]

The most direct link between Fulton workers and the Frank case came in the person of Fiddlin' John Carson. When he lost his job at the mill in 1914, Carson played for tips before the crowds gathered at the courthouse. He wrote and frequently performed three songs about the case, including "The Ballad of Mary Phagan," which became a southern classic. The lyrics of the songs emphasized Frank's brutishness, Phagan's innocence, the fact that she had passed to a "better world" free of trials and tribulations, and the affinity between Mary Phagan and other hard-pressed white southerners: "Supposing Little Mary belonged to you and me."

Of course, Carson's life itself in its fullness emphatically belied the assertion of the Reverend Buford that Fulton workers had "no social life and no social standard at all, and neither have they any pleasures." Fulton workers and their families were much more complex and less pathetic than either mill owners, social reformers, trade union officials, federal investigators, or middle-class Atlantans almost ever allowed.

CHAPTER 3

A Busy Industrial Community

The roar and throb of machinery" at the Fulton Bag and Cotton Mills, wrote a neighborhood social worker in 1910, "typified the great throbbing heart of an industrial community of more than three thousand people, of all kinds, good, bad, and indifferent."[1] The origins of Fulton workers helped shape the character of their community. Yet these origins were often inaccurately portrayed, in part to fit the perceptions and social agenda of outsiders. In 1915, Oscar Elsas wrote, "The help is drawn largely from the mountain section of Georgia."[2] Others, too, maintained that white Fulton workers hailed from the isolated mountains of southern Appalachia.[3] Labeling workers as mountaineers was one of a number of ways employed by many middle-class Atlantans, like their counterparts across the Piedmont, to depict mill hands as quaint, inferior, disorderly, and in need of intervention.

It is true that some people did come directly to Fulton Mills from such remote mountain areas as White County, Georgia; Marshall County, Alabama; and Copper Hill, Tennessee.[4] Indeed, the mill district's most celebrated resident, Fiddlin' John Carson, reputedly hailed from the community of Blue Ridge, practically a symbol for the farthest reaches of the north Georgia mountains.[5] In addition, many of the workers who moved to Fulton Mills from such hill country mill towns as Gainesville, Canton, Atco, or Cedartown originally came from the southern Appalachians. Yet in the Fulton community of the 1910s, people who hailed from the mountains actually composed a relatively small minority of the total population.[6]

The origins of Fulton workers can be determined in a number of ways. Between March and July 1913, after the mill sent out recruiting circulars and placed an advertisement in the *Atlanta Journal*, the company paymaster re-

Fulton workers. Special Collections Dept., Pullen Library, Georgia State University.

ceived 184 written applications for employment. Of these, 109 came from Georgia, followed by Alabama (27), South Carolina (20), and North Carolina (14). The overwhelming majority of the applicants hailed from other cotton mill communities, paced by Columbus, Georgia (14), and Greenville, South Carolina (8) (see Table 1).[7]

The most comprehensive information about the origins of Fulton workers comes from personnel cards that the company began to compile in 1916. A sampling of 2,500 cards of workers who were at Fulton before 1920 reveals that people came to the mill via several different routes. A smattering of people immigrated from outside the region, principally from the Southwest and Midwest. Others did come from the mountains of southern Appalachia.

A somewhat larger number of workers had been employed elsewhere in the city before moving to Fulton Mills. Most of these had worked in the Exposition Cotton Mill and other area textile factories. Many others, though, had performed a wide range of jobs in Atlanta before entering the mill. Fulton workers had labored at a variety of local industrial concerns, including the Atlanta Hat Factory, Block Candy, Murray Gin, Atlanta Steel Hoop, National Pencil Factory, Southern Spring Bed, Atlanta Paper, and the Empire Sausage Factory.

TABLE 1. Origins of Selected Applicants to Fulton Mills, 1913

City of Previous Employment	Number of Workers	City of Previous Employment	Number of Workers
Columbus, Ga.	14	Huntsville, Ala.	4
Greenville, S.C.	8	Lafayette, Ga.	4
Lanett, Ala.	7	Griffin, Ga.	3
Aragon, Ga.	6	Manchester, Ga.	3
Gainesville/New Holland, Ga.	6	Rome/Atco/Anchor Duck, Ga.	3
Barnesville, Ga.	5	Alabama City, Ala.	2
Lindale, Ga.	5	Anderson, S.C.	2
Macon/East Macon, Ga.	5	Copper Hill, TN	2
Quitman, Ga.	5	Elberton, Ga.	2
Athens, Ga.	4	Knoxville, TN	2
Henderson, N.C.	4	88 other locations	1

State of Previous Employment

Georgia	109	Mississippi	2
Alabama	27	Texas	2
South Carolina	20	Florida	1
North Carolina	14	Kentucky	1
Tennessee	4	Missouri	1
Virginia	3		

Source: "Applications for Employment," Folders 1–5, Fulton Bag and Cotton Mills Collection, Price Gilbert Memorial Library, Archives, Georgia Institute of Technology, Atlanta, Ga.

They had also driven wagons, kept house, peddled produce, swept streets, waitressed, done carpentry and plumbing, butchered, performed odd jobs, and worked on the railroads, at the telephone exchange, for Georgia Railway and Power, and in local pharmacies.

By the 1910s, the great majority of white Fulton workers, however, came from one of two places: either directly off Upcountry farms, or, more commonly, from the numerous mill villages that after 1880 dotted the Piedmont countryside. Some Fulton farmers-turned-mill-hands had tilled the soil in the north Georgia mountains or on farms in middle Georgia and southeast Alabama. But most people who came off the farm to work at Fulton Mills hailed either from Milton, Cobb, Clayton, Gwinnett, and Douglas Counties surrounding Atlanta or from other Upcountry counties in Georgia and Alabama.

A variety of circumstances, from the death or injury of a family member to a poor harvest, could force people to leave farming and seek employment at

Fulton or other Piedmont mills. The story of Polk County native Beatrice Atkinson Dalton was typical: "After Daddy died we didn't have nobody to farm, no boy big enough to plow the land so we had to break up and go to the cotton mill where Mama could work. It was better to work in the mill because the mill was regular and the fields wasn't."[8] Upon leaving the farm, Dalton and her family worked at cotton mills in Aragon, Douglasville, Porterdale, and elsewhere in Georgia before eventually moving to Fulton Mills. In so doing, they were generally characteristic of the mill's labor force. For the greatest number of white people who went to work at Fulton Mills during the 1910s belonged to the first generation that had literally grown up in the textile communities of the Piedmont.[9]

Some Fulton workers migrated from South Carolina's "model factory towns" of Pelzer, Pacolet, and Langley, which were distinguished by large, well-capitalized mills built in previously sparsely inhabited areas. In these locales, mill owners established what David Carlton has termed a "benevolent despotism," providing an elaborate network of company houses, schools, churches, and other services for operatives designed to secure labor and promote industrial efficiency and company loyalty, hand in hand with strict, near-governmental control over workers' lives. A much larger group of Fulton workers hailed from the comparable Alabama "show mill" communities of Avondale, Sylacauga, and Pell City, which were developed by the Comer family.[10] These highly acclaimed developments set the tone for corporate paternalism in the region.

In addition, Fulton workers came from a diversity of other Piedmont mill communities. These included small, comparatively isolated rural mill villages in places like Whitney, South Carolina, or Whitehall, Georgia; Scottdale, Whittier, Piedmont, and other mills on the outskirts of Atlanta; medium-sized industrial towns like LaGrange and Manchester, Georgia; well-established textile centers such as Greenville and Spartanburg, South Carolina; and the large mill communities in Columbus and Georgia's other fall-line cities. Here they had encountered a range of working and living conditions and varying degrees of rural persistence and corporate authority.

Although differences did exist among them, most white Fulton workers shared a common, complex heritage with their counterparts across the textile South. This regional culture included at its core the patriarchal family as a basic institution, source of loyalty, labor system, and metaphor.[11] It also entailed a "touchy independence" intertwined with both patterns of deference and customs of mutuality; a rich musical potpourri of hymns, gospel, ballads, folk airs, minstrel tunes, and popular songs; herbal remedies and other traditional health practices rooted in self-reliance; a penchant for lively oral discourse and occasional violence; an often very personalized Protestant fundamentalism; a legacy of faith and sacrifice, endurance and persistence amid hard times; an occasionally virulent white racism; and work rhythms grounded in subsistence and cotton agriculture, as well as additional links to rural life.[12]

Fulton workers also exhibited another holdover from tenant farming days, what Oscar Elsas labeled "a roving and migratory disposition."[13] In 1914, for instance, one Fulton weaver recalled passing through twenty-eight different mills in Georgia and South Carolina and that "these are not half of the mills I worked in."[14] While probably an extreme case, this example points out the high level of transience among Piedmont mill workers. As Atlanta textile worker Nanny Washburn put it, "Cotton mill people moved very often."[15]

Onlookers from various vantage points explained this restlessness in different ways. Some workers simply sought better pay and working conditions. One Fulton weaver said he changed mills so often because "the work would not run good and then the machinery was poor and some times he couldn't make more than $1.00 or $1.25 a day, or sometimes $1.40 to $1.50."[16] Other Fulton workers also left because of working conditions, complaining, for instance, that the looms were "all buggered up" and "in a hell of a condition," or that it was too hot inside the plant.[17]

Objectionable working conditions extended beyond faulty machines and overheated rooms to management practices. Some workers, like Nanny Washburn's father, left their jobs and moved on to protest what they saw as unfair practices or harassment on the part of supervisors. "He'd get fed up on their tricks," Washburn said of her father. Other Fulton workers left over the poor living conditions in the mill district. Still others migrated from mill to mill on a whim, or to learn new skills, visit friends and relatives, or, in some cases, to avoid being put in jail after altercations with supervisors or other workers.[18]

Oscar Elsas's son Norman later recalled a saying that "cotton mill people hadn't caught up with their moving," implying that mill workers wanted to see the world first before finally settling down.[19] For his part, Oscar Elsas maintained that the principal reason that Fulton workers left was the "solicitation of help by other employers, thereby making them feel independent of retaining present places," along with "rumors of higher wages elsewhere."[20] He accurately suggested that a yearning for independence from corporate control was a primary reason that the children of once self-sufficient yeoman farmers migrated so often.

Even by southern textile industry standards, Fulton workers rambled a great deal. Oscar Elsas reported that the number of discharged workers and those who quit employment at Fulton Bag in 1910 totaled 10,000 people, with the mill then only employing 1,300 hands at any one given time; this number, he professed, was exceptionally high, though, "because in that year great competition existed among mills as to help and factories paid carfare in order to obtain employees."[21] In 1914, however, he told a similar tale of high turnover, stating that Fulton workers averaged merely a month and a half employment before moving on.[22]

On another occasion, Elsas provided a somewhat different story, claiming that the number of workers discharged in 1913 was 536, while those who "left and removed" totaled 3,875. Of this latter group, some 600 people were only hired on a temporary basis to scour machinery and to load and unload cars during the busiest shipping season, leaving a total of roughly 3,300 departing mill hands. A third of these, in turn, were estimated to be "total repeaters," workers who served their notice and drew their withheld back pay on Saturday, then eventually reported back to work at Fulton Bag. Elsas guessed that half of these workers reported back the following Monday, with the other half returning in "from two weeks to six months." In some cases, repeaters came back to the mill "as often as eight and ten times a year." Even discounting the temporary help and the repeaters, Elsas estimated that between 750 and 900 new hands came on the payroll in 1913.[23]

In November 1914, Elsas and general manager Gordon A. Johnstone told yet another story. They related that in the period from 1 November 1913 to 1 November 1914, some 2,469 workers had served their notices, only an estimated 20 percent of whom returned the following Monday.[24] Finally, in 1915, Elsas emphasized the mill's employee stability, asserting that approximately half of Fulton workers had been in the company's service at least five years. This figure was misleading, as it included machinists, carpenters, and office workers in addition to actual production workers. Furthermore, as Cathy McHugh and Douglas Flamming have shown, by the 1910s, stability for a portion of the textile labor force often coexisted alongside widespread worker transience.[25] In any event, worker migration in and out of Fulton Bag was far greater than at neighboring mills.

The concerns that all mill owners had about worker stability, satisfaction, and productivity were thus particularly acute at Fulton Bag, and, like their counterparts across the Piedmont, management adopted a variety of both punitive and attractive measures designed to keep industrial conflict and disturbance to a minimum. These procedures and policies touched various aspects of company operations, from the solicitation of labor, to company housing, to welfare capitalism, to the shop floor itself. While many of these practices resembled developments at cotton mills across the region, others, including some of the more controversial, were unique to Fulton Bag. In any event, whatever the Elsases tried, they never succeeded in obtaining the harmony they sought, as workers periodically exhibited their dissatisfaction in diverse ways.

Like other mill owners, the Elsases favored the family wage system wherever possible. "We prefer families," explained Oscar Elsas. "They are more reliable for continuous service."[26] Fulton Bag kept a standing advertisement for help in the Atlanta papers, promising high wages and steady work and reiterating that the company "can use complete families."[27] Many of these families resided in the tenements of the Factory Lot, just south of the mill, and in other company housing. While not that different from much of the housing available to poor and working-class Atlantans, including that in the surrounding community, mill housing left much to be desired, despite the company's claims to the contrary.[28]

Many workers shared the sentiment of one loom fixer who stated he "didn't have the stomach" to live in company housing.[29] Workers often perceived company housing, in the Factory Lot at least, as something of a stigma, associated with the drudgeries and corporate control of mill life. Social worker Mary Dickinson, who worked and lived in the mill district during the early twentieth century, recalled the great "social distinction" that existed between those workers who lived "on the hill" and those residing "on the lot."[30] For example, a ten-year-old girl from the community who, in the opinion of other mill district residents, had become "mighty uppity" since being sent to the local Home for the Friendless "'lowed she never wanted to see the factory lot again." This gulf was so immense that various church organizations and the mill itself had great difficulty mixing the two groups of workers.[31]

Fulton workers mockingly referred to one especially crowded, bedbug-ridden section of company housing along East Fair Street as "Chinch Row." "Everybody wanted to stay away from Chinch Row," recalled mill worker Calvin Freeman. "Didn't nobody want to live in those houses over there because they were full of chinches." Local trade unionist O. Delight Smith labeled the Chinch Row houses "mockeries of true homes" and "hatching places of crime."[32] Bedbugs were far from the only problem with company housing. Workers also complained about unappealing, shabby dwellings and thin board walls that made it hard to keep warm.[33]

Considerable numbers of Fulton workers chose not to live in company houses. If anything, the proportion of workers living outside of company housing increased over the years. In 1900, Oscar Elsas had estimated that perhaps 40 percent of mill workers lived in outside housing, despite the recent rent reductions and the fact that many of the newly erected company houses were vacant. In 1915, he claimed that "over 50 per cent of the employees do not reside in Company owned houses." And in 1918, he maintained that two-thirds of the Fulton workforce resided in noncompany housing.[34]

There are various reasons why so many Fulton workers lived outside company housing, a number markedly greater than in most Piedmont mill communities. Some workers expressed an aversion to the two-story houses the company had built in the Factory Lot, which were different from any place they had ever resided. "They don't like to live upstairs," Oscar Elsas remarked. In addition, Fulton's operations periodically expanded at a faster pace than the company could supply housing, especially after the development of Mill No. 2, when company housing construction in an increasingly dense area of the city simply could not keep up with the firm's demand for new workers. "The accommodations are wholly inadequate for the number of people," stated a federal investigator in 1914.[35]

Oscar Elsas asserted that this lack of "sufficient facilities" was the sole reason that such a low percentage of workers lived in company housing.[36] But there were other reasons that so many Fulton workers stayed away from company housing. Overcrowded, squalid, unsanitary conditions in the mill district prompted some workers to live elsewhere.[37] Many workers and their families shared the sentiments of Ellen St. John, the wife of an overseer, who longed for "a yard, fruit trees and a garden, such as could be had at Porterdale Mills." St. John believed Fulton Bag paid the best wages of any mill in Georgia, yet she asserted that Fulton workers "would never be satisfied with just good wages— the people wanted good living conditions."[38]

In addition, Fulton workers had a choice of alternative housing available to them in the city of Atlanta, something effectively denied mill workers in most other Piedmont textile communities. Many workers exercised that choice to exert their independence and get out from under company domination, either living in the surrounding white working-class community and other nearby neighborhoods, or taking the streetcar to work.[39] Some workers, mainly the plant's engineers, mechanics, print shop employees, watchmen, and other nonproduction workers, took a further step and moved into home ownership.[40]

The 1911 Senate report on working-class life in American cities stated that in the Fulton district, there existed "few signs of house pride. . . . The furniture is scanty and poor, but even so it is seldom arranged with an eye to securing the best effect."[41] Numerous other middle-class observers commented on the poor upkeep of the company houses by the tenants themselves, in a manner reminiscent of landlords' remarks about allegedly indifferent tenant farmers, and developed various theories for the supposedly low level of worker home maintenance. Social Gospel–influenced individuals like the MRFM's Reverend Buford felt that the small, greatly overcrowded company houses with no living rooms, along with pitiful sanitary conditions and long working hours, naturally "lowered very materially the standard of home life in these homes."[42] In language that resembled late-twentieth-century discussions of "the culture of poverty," others placed the onus for ill-kept homes not on mill management but on ostensibly ingrained characteristics of Fulton workers themselves. The Senate report blamed the mill workers' "vagrant tendency" that remained "deeply rooted despite inducement to remain."[43] Similarly for Oscar Elsas, Fulton workers' seeming disinterest in home upkeep was closely linked to a deeply rooted, near-impenetrable lack of ambition, along with an intense suspicion of mill management in general and the Elsas family in particular. "The people themselves," Elsas declared, "show a lack of interest. They are the ones who should be censured."

On the other hand, he claimed the company was "doing everything possible" to improve living conditions, "in fact, more than can be expected of any landlord."[44] "They don't appreciate it and they don't want anything better," he lamented. "And when we try to help them they think we are trying to make money out of them." Yet, in fact, such a perspective contained more than a grain of truth, as the firm *had* indeed originally tried to make money off of its workers, building company housing with the idea of making a profit, until it was eventually compelled to reduce rents to fill up unoccupied houses.[45]

Worker distrust of management's intentions extended into other arenas of personal life as well. Fulton workers looked upon Dr. Eugene W. Hawkins, who became the company physician in November 1913, "with great suspicion and unfriendliness." No wonder: Hawkins's duties included going through the mill district daily and visiting the home of any worker who had not shown up that morning, then reporting the reasons for absenteeism back to the office. Spooler Margaret Dempsey related, "If you stay home sick they send a man they call a doctor to see you and this fellow just says to you, 'What are you out for' and he never gives you anything . . . just comes to see if you are lying out and if you don't get back to work in five days you don't get a ticket [pay envelope]." "In other words," observed a federal investigator, "it might be said that he exercises a kind of police supervision, rather than that of a careful and well informed physician."[46] Many Fulton workers felt that such monitoring was an unwarranted intrusion into their private lives, a clear violation of their personal autonomy.

Fulton workers generally regarded home life as private, intimate, and off limits to company officials. So, too, were meals, especially the noontime dinner during the work day. After the failure of the textile workers hotel around 1900, management had established a special dining room in a central part of the plant, "so that the help," in the words of Oscar Elsas, "could eat their lunches under proper auspices." Yet after only a month or two, Fulton workers made their own decisions about what was proper and stopped frequenting the dining hall, showing, in Elsas's words, "by their general practice that they preferred eating alone, that is in secluded corners etc."[47]

At the suggestion of the company, the local settlement house then maintained another dining room, furnishing noonday dinners at ten cents a meal. Weaver Jennie Clinton regularly took her meals there, which she described with fondness in 1915: "One day we get stewed beef, Irish potatoes, cake, loaf bread, cheese, coffee with sugar and cream in it just as much as anyone can eat. Then each day it is changed. Next day, beans, potatoes, soup, English peas, cake and coffee."[48] Yet Clinton was much the exception rather than the norm. In great measure, no matter what the menu, the vast majority of Fulton workers stayed clear of this new dining hall as well. According to Oscar Elsas, by the early 1910s, it was rare that over sixty people were present at any given meal, with the average attendance hovering only around forty diners.[49]

Fulton workers often stayed clear of other services provided by mill management that intruded upon personal life, habits, and autonomy. Shortly before the turn of the century, the company began health and child care efforts, along with additional welfare work. (At no time did either Fulton Bag's welfare initiatives or private charity efforts in the adjoining neighborhood extend to the company's black workers.) This was an attempt, in the words of Oscar Elsas, "to build up the moral and physical condition of our employees" and thus contribute to worker stability and productivity. Yet from the outset, Fulton workers often resented such attention and suspected management's designs, causing the company to abandon its welfare activities within a few years.[50]

In 1902, the mill handed over its welfare work to the Woman's Board of City Missions of the Methodist Church, with the company removed from all direct administration but still an interested party.[51] For Oscar Elsas, the transfer of welfare activities to the Methodist women was a welcome relief, given his distinct preference for other corporate operations, his personal detachment from Fulton workers, and the fact that, in his words, "our help" continued to be "rather suspicious of our intentions."[52]

The board converted the entire flea-ridden "Old Hotel" into Atlanta's original full-fledged settlement house, initially called the Methodist Home Settlement, then renamed Wesley House in 1906.[53] At first, the gulf between the Methodist missionary women and the inhabitants of the mill district, along with what workers saw as the motives, shortcomings, and intrusions of earlier company welfare activity, prompted considerable wariness on the part of many

Fulton workers about settlement house efforts. The settlement's initial missionary felt that "the mill people were very hard to reach and were suspecting of all that was done." Dorothy Crim, the head resident at Wesley House, reported that community residents viewed the first settlement house women as "good ladies who came to dole out charity. . . . Some distrusted, some wondered."[54]

After taking over the work, the Methodist women soon upgraded and expanded their activities along more modern social work lines. By the end of its first year, the settlement house had forty volunteers. In 1903, Rosa Lowe, a graduate of Scarrett Training School in Nashville, came to direct the settlement's dispensary, the first such facility outside of Grady Hospital in Atlanta. A doctor attended the sick, and in 1905, reportedly Georgia's first professionally trained public health nurse joined the staff.[55] Later, at the end of 1911, a group of local physicians took charge of the clinic, adding equipment and boosting the staff to twenty-two visiting physicians and dentists by 1916.[56]

In addition to running the dispensary, Lowe organized a night school and assisted in the formation of a boy's club at the settlement. She and fellow social worker Mary Dickinson, director of the settlement's kindergarten, also were among the pioneers of social work in Atlanta that extended beyond missionary efforts. They belonged to the Sociological Society, a newly formed discussion group and club, and were the only women involved in the establishment of the Associated Charities in 1905.[57]

Inspired by Jacob Riis, Charles Stelzle, and other contemporary social reformers, the Wesley House women established a wide range of other activities for members of the mill community. They installed a library and reading room, an auditorium, six "shower baths," and a boxing ring, basketball courts, and other athletic facilities, eventually using forty-seven rooms in all. They organized numerous youth-oriented programs, including boys and girls clubs, athletic teams, cooking classes, games, ice-cream festivals, and Valentine's Day, Halloween, Saint Patrick's Day, and Robert E. Lee's birthday celebrations. They founded a woman's club that in 1910 affiliated with the City Federation of Women's Clubs. They also sponsored quiltings, adult sewing, athletic, and social clubs, Christmas bazaars, programs, lectures, and outings, as well as home visits and religious instruction.[58]

Through these efforts, the settlement house workers and volunteers tried to accomplish a number of objectives. They attempted to inculcate such values as "politeness, cleanliness and independence" and "cooperation, helpfulness and self-control" among what they perceived as "a drifting and unambitious class" that was "badly disorganized." They hoped athletics would foster "ideals of manliness" among the boys in the community. Concerned that many workers only "made the Lord a crutch to help them when disabled, then layed him aside when well," they geared their missionary work toward making religion a "spiritual strength that entered each day" rather than "something to use [only] in case of death."[59]

They also promoted industriousness, thrift, and loyalty to Fulton Mills. In 1908, for example, the day nursery children were introduced to "the story of cotton" through a flour bag "made in our mill."[60] And, although mill management had formally turned over all welfare work to the Methodist women, Oscar Elsas and other company representatives continued to wield considerable influence upon the settlement house. In addition to providing rent, repairs, and fifty dollars a month to Wesley House, Elsas built a fence around the settlement yard, raised the stage in the settlement auditorium, supplied flower garden prizes and seeds, lent an automobile to transport Wesley House Woman's Club members to an exhibit on child welfare, and assisted during a measles epidemic, stating he did not want "our people" to suffer and to depend upon the city for relief.[61] Company dominion extended to other areas of settlement house work as well. The Elsases took an "active interest" in establishing the settlement's kitchen and made known their desire to keep up domestic science work.[62] In 1908, Mathilda Reinhardt Elsas, the wife of Benjamin Elsas and for whom Reinhardt Street in the Factory Lot was named, joined the board of the Wesley House Woman's Club, periodically giving automobile rides for mill children as a reward for good conduct. And Oscar Elsas anonymously donated presents for the Wesley House community Christmas tree.[63]

There were times when the settlement house women, and the workers they associated with, distanced themselves from and even criticized company practices. Dorothy Crim maintained that the "hum drum life and petty movements of the mill" had done much to spiritually impoverish its people, creating a class "always willing to follow the lines of least resistance."[64] Between 1910 and 1912, the Wesley House Woman's Club expressed concerns about poor sanitary conditions in the mill district, petitioning Oscar Elsas for better toilet facilities, uniting with the Third Ward Civic Improvement League, seeking cleaner streets and better sanitary inspection, calling for the removal of sewer pipes from Boulevard (the principal road leading to Fulton Mills from the south), and demanding clean grocery stores and covered garbage cans.[65]

Yet most of the time the settlement house enjoyed what one staff member termed "a hearty cooperation" with mill management. For instance, when twelve boys, all card room and spinning room workers in the mill, got into some mischief at Wesley House one Sunday morning, it was a company supervisor who sprung them from jail so they could be at work Monday morning.

Indeed, the relationship between the settlement house and the company was so close that some workers thought that Fulton Bag actually operated Wesley House.[66]

For their own part, far from being merely passive recipients of settlement house intervention, Fulton workers had a complicated relationship with Wesley House. Depending upon a range of circumstances, at various times workers and their families selectively rejected, criticized, acquiesced in, embraced, transformed, and initiated diverse activities associated with the settlement house.

Particularly in the early years of the settlement, workers tended to be leery of many settlement house initiatives, feeling that these efforts constituted unwarranted and unwelcome encroachments upon traditional values and habits. This was especially true with doctor's examinations and visits, clinics, and vaccinations and other modern medical procedures that felt like invasions of one's privacy and that undermined long-standing health care practices rooted in self-sufficiency and independence. As Fulton worker Effie Dodd Gray recalled, "People didn't run to doctors like they do now. If they had a boil or something, they didn't pick up and run to the doctor. They'd put something on there that'd draw it to a head. They'd give their kids different kinds of remedy medicine."[67]

Workers had similar complaints about the Wesley House nursery. In 1914, for example, Josie Sisk, who at different times worked in both the spinning and weave rooms of Mill No. 1, related she had come across children in the nursery without any cow's milk to drink, forced to stay in the same unchanged diaper all day, and "bruised up very bad." Such claims of neglect were echoed by Sisk's weave room neighbor, Dora Davis, and by Addie Camp, a spooler in Mill No. 2, whose baby died seven weeks after being put in the nursery.[68]

In other instances, Fulton workers saw the settlement house as potentially expanding their horizons, offering an alternative to the tedium of mill life and providing opportunities for personal, family, and community advancement. Many workers raised in impoverished conditions enjoyed such novelties as ice-cream festivals, showers, "tacky [dress-up] parties," and associating with the middle-class missionary women. For example, after a Woman's Club–sponsored picnic in 1908, one worker described a pair of volunteers she had met: "Them two that talked to me was sure nice. I could tell by the way they talked and acted they sure was ladies."[69]

Yet workers' involvement with Wesley House went well beyond simply savoring new favors and tokens. From the time the settlement house was established, boys from the district came by "in numbers" to see whether there was "something doing" there.[70] Young people displayed a "remarkable interest and high attendance" at the Wesley House night school, despite the fact that students were often sleepy after a long workday and that the school only offered the equivalent of a first-grade education.[71] With only meager incomes at their command, mill district residents still raised money themselves for better gymnasium equipment and a piano at the settlement house.[72] In 1906, using Wesley House as a base but apparently to some degree on their own initiative, workers helped organize the Fulton Mutual Aid Society, which offered illness and death benefits in the absence of company-provided assistance. They also formed the Mutual Benefit Association and an additional boys club.[73]

In no area of settlement house work did mill district residents take a more enthusiastic, active involvement than athletics. Baseball and other sports were familiar to people raised in rural areas and Piedmont mill communities and readily transferred to an urban-industrial milieu such as early-twentieth-century Atlanta. Like the fiddler's conventions, sports offered one of the few arenas in the life of a mill hand where hard work and ability *were* recognized and rewarded, where a textile worker was literally on an even playing field with people from other walks of life, where a despised "lint head" could be a big wheel or even a hero. In addition, they provided an opportunity for community members, along with people from other factories and working-class neighborhoods, to gather, socialize, and exchange information in a setting that to a large degree they had made their own. Very tangibly, the community's interest in Wesley House athletics also directly led to better gym equipment, a new playground in the neighborhood, and probably the formation of the company-sponsored baseball team.[74]

The Girls Gymnastic Club, the Wesley House Athletic Club, and boys gymnastics classes, boxing, basketball, and other sports were thus among the most popular settlement house activities. When the Athletic Club and the Wesley House Boys Club played each other in March 1909, the Woman's Club noted the "intense interest in the community." Every public showing of the Wesley House Athletic Club brought forth "royal and enthusiastic support from the neighborhood." Large numbers of community members attended additional sporting events at the Wesley House gymnasium and at other neighborhood parks and playgrounds.[75]

Whatever achievements Fulton workers made in creating something of their own through Wesley House, however, came with a price. Not even baseball was exempt. In 1915, company superintendent E. H. Rogers, revealing the informal communications network that existed among Piedmont mill hands, related that players for opposing teams would openly refer to the company's controversial labor contract in an attempt to rattle the Fulton players and possibly recruit them away, especially at times when labor was relatively scarce: "In beginning ball games at these other mills and in their rooting they would call attention to the contract, and they would say, 'You cannot play baseball over there unless you sign the contract.' That would get to the manager of the teams, and in that way the contract here has gained some notoriety."[76]

Workers often faced condescending attitudes and low expectations on the part of settlement house workers. When local boys tried to organize a Mutual Benefit Association at the settlement house based on principles of self-government, Wesley House workers belittled the notion, highlighting instead the "many tragic and amusing episodes" that accompanied such striving, with "the self governing part allowed to drift into the background."[77] When neighborhood youths formed a boys club with a proposed regulation that nobody who cursed or chewed tobacco could belong, Rosa Lowe felt compelled to intervene and postpone the formulation of any rules whatsoever rather than let the boys decide their differences among themselves.[78] When asked if higher wages would not improve the state of the community, one Wesley House staff member answered in the negative, claiming that if workers had more money, they would just spend it on Coca-Cola and ice cream.[79]

Because of such attitudes, the relationship of the settlement house to the company, and skepticism about settlement house services, despite the popularity of many Wesley House functions, many Fulton workers and their families only occasionally took part in Wesley House activities, if they took part at all.[80] The attractiveness of other urban pursuits and the rigors of work and everyday life also kept families away. Mill district women, for instance, whether or not they worked in the mill, spent a great deal of their time away from the mill attending to their families' welfare: breast-feeding babies, tending the sick, raising livestock and vegetables, gathering salad greens and berries from outlying areas, and preparing meals.[81]

No matter what activities Fulton workers initiated and took part in, they never could fully escape the shadow of the mill. As David Carlton, writing about paternalism in the Piedmont textile industry, has pointed out, "[M]ill and community interpenetrated each other in a seamless web of relationships. . . . The mill . . . was not an irrelevance; it called the community into being, and it sustained the community with the wealth it produced and its intrinsic power over community life."[82] It was also, of course, where people spent most of their waking hours. Just as Fulton workers developed a multifaceted relationship with company welfare activity and with Wesley House, so did they help shape the character of the shop floor itself. Here, too, they were not merely passive recipients of corporate mandates; rather, they participated in an often shifting process of interaction, contestation, and negotiation over

Fulton workers. Georgia Institute of Technology Library and Information Center.

work rules and practices. As with the rest of their lives, depending on the situation, Fulton workers developed and selected a range of individual and collective responses and strategies to address the world of work.

In the late 1970s, two retired Fulton workers, both also longtime residents of the mill district, remembered their complex relationship to textile work. Horace Carson, who went to work at Fulton Bag in 1911 along with four other members of his family, recalled that work in the mill was "dirty, hot, hard, and the hours were long." Furthermore, in his opinion, Fulton "ruled the mill hands and the mill village with the power of a dictator, and the mill hands like citizens of dictatorship remained under the thumbs of oppression." Carson went on to wonder "if the final judgment of history will be whether the children of the cotton mill worker or the children of the blacks were the descendants of slaves . . . in my opinion it will be a moot issue." Yet, at the same time that he issued such harsh convictions, Carson reported quite pleasant memories of Fulton Bag and other mills he worked in. In fact, he took pains to point out what he called "the warmth of the relationship, although not understood by outsiders, between the mill workers and the mill."[83]

Beatrice Atkinson Dalton told a similarly complicated story. She recalled that upon arrival at Fulton Bag, even with several family members working in the mill, "we couldn't hardly make it. It was just almost starvation beside what we had when we lived in the country." Dalton then worked off and on in the spinning room for some sixteen years: "We made yarn to send to the weave shop. I liked it. It was awfully hard but still I liked it. The work run awfully bad, spinning and all, bad to get tangled up. [We had to untangle it] and it was hard to do. It was real hard work."[84] For both Dalton and Carson, as for countless others, work at Fulton was complex and multifaceted.

Working conditions at Fulton Bag were no harsher than at other southern cotton mills in the 1910s. Indeed, the Elsases generally anticipated state hours legislation, employed fewer child laborers than other textile manufacturers, and paid higher than average wages.[85] Yet work still was demanding and onerous. "It was hard to stand on your feet all day," related spinner Blanche Prince. "There was no air, you would almost smother." "When you first open the door into the spinning room," seconded a Fulton weaver, "it sort of takes your breath, like heat from a stove." Along with the heat and lack of ventilation, Fulton workers also endured pervasive cotton lint in the air, along with bleaching dust from the bleachery. "That's why we have to keep chewing something," explained bag mill worker Dorothy Pows. "It makes your nose sore. A lump comes in your throat and you drink and drink water to get it down." Workers in various departments also complained of aching shoulders and arms, sore fingers, catarrh, headaches, and stomach ailments, all ostensibly the result of adverse working conditions.[86]

The hours were long. Each day at 4:30 in the morning, the mill's night watchman rang a bell to rouse workers to get to the job by six o'clock. In conformance with state law, after 1 January 1912, Fulton workers labored sixty hours a week, eleven hours a day during the week, plus a half day on Saturday, with unpaid holidays on Memorial Day, Independence Day, Labor Day, Thanksgiving, and Christmas. The workday also included a forty-five-minute midday dinner break, although some workers maintained they had to be back on the job after only thirty or thirty-five minutes.[87]

The long hours often took their toll, especially on younger workers. The community playground director reported that most neighborhood youth were too tired to play after work or on the weekend. "It is seldom that any of them come to the play grounds to play," she stated. "When they do, they, and even the men, don't feel like playing. They are too tired." Thirteen-year-old Lassie Ward, who worked in the spinning room of Mill No. 1 with her brothers, complained of having to stand on her feet all the time, stating that "it was so long to work every day." Another spinner, twelve-year-old Willie Anne Walker, said, "My legs and back hurt me every night and when I went to bed I just couldn't sleep." Similar sentiments were echoed by many other youthful workers.[88]

Workers sixteen and younger comprised 12 percent of Fulton's labor force in 1914 and were employed chiefly in the card and spinning rooms of the company's two cotton mills, as well as in the bag mill. Fulton Bag actually employed a smaller than average percentage of child workers, as at least 23 percent of the state's textile workers were under eighteen years old. In addition, Oscar Elsas maintained that for child workers at Fulton Bag, though they might labor a full sixty-hour week, work was intermittent and rest periods were permitted.[89]

This may have been true given the comparisons workers made to their work at other textile mills. In testimony gathered by a federal investigator in 1914, young Fulton workers condemned conditions they had experienced in places such as Canton and Roswell and Atlanta's Exposition Cotton Mill, where they often went to work by the age of ten and suffered long, strenuous working hours under bosses who would try to "run over" youthful hands.

Some younger workers *did* experience a comparatively relaxed work environment at Fulton Bag. Thirteen-year-old Bertie May Berry, for instance, who had begged her mother to take her to work because she was tired of school, reported that she and her work mates were able to "talk to each other some" while on the shop floor. They could also send out to a nearby store for food and "play around a while" when "the work run good." Others, however, told a different story of constant work and close supervision. Fourteen-year-old Jason Stephenson lamented that "we didn't have no time to play marbles" while in the mill. For all her self-proclaimed leisurely work pace, even Bertie May Berry complained of sore legs and feet: "I had rheumatism and my legs swelled up." Furthermore, she said that "when the little children got sick and wanted to go home they wouldn't let them; said there [was] nobody to put in their work." Berry maintained that her lunch break was only a half hour instead of the prescribed forty-five minutes, pointed out the sweltering heat in the mill, so hot that she went barefoot at work, and testified that "the lint flies so you have to have something to chew so you can swallow." She also protested the treatment of young workers by some Fulton supervisors: "They would try to run over the little children, they wouldn't say a word to the big ones but they would speak to the little ones as mean as a dog."[90]

For many workers, the family wage system that prevailed at Fulton and elsewhere into the 1910s was more a matter of necessity than choice—in order merely to survive when buffeted by death, disease, or hard times. Nancy Sanders, the mother of several youthful Fulton workers, related, "When I married my husband he had six children and then we had so many children we had to put all of them that could work in the mill to make supportments for the others." Spooler Hattie Peeler, whose two children worked in the spinning room of Mill No. 1, expressed similar sentiments, stating, "I was compelled to place my children in the mill to work, in order that my family could make enough to eat."[91]

By the 1910s the family wage system was beginning to change, however. The percentage of child laborers in southern cotton mills, though still significant and high compared to other industries nationwide, had gradually declined since 1900. In part, this trend illustrated the transitional quality of southern textiles in the 1910s, as cotton manufacturers blended traditional and modern management practices. It also reflected the maturation of the regional textile industry. Adult males who had been reared in a mill environment, who were experienced in various facets of textile work, and who were at least perceived as the most productive workers in the industry increasingly supplanted youthful workers in the region's cotton mills.[92]

Not surprisingly, the efficiency-minded, modern Elsases remained a step ahead of the curve, as the percentage of men at Fulton Bag crept up steadily during the early twentieth century, ahead of the industrywide pace. One indication of this growing male presence was the dramatic increase in the percentage of men who lived in company housing between 1900 and 1910. In 1900, reflecting the central role that women played in the early southern textile industry, there were 100 females for every 82 males residing in the Factory Lot. By 1910, the situation had changed considerably, with 103.6 males in the Factory Lot for every 100 females.[93]

The same trend existed on the shop floor. In mid-May 1914, adult males comprised 53 percent of the 900-plus production workers in the bag mill and the two cotton mills combined. (These figures do not include well over 300 Fulton workers, overwhelmingly male, who worked in the waste house, twine room, cloth room, bleachery, canvas department, press room, shipping department, machine shop, carpentry shop, and office; as yard men and watchmen; and elsewhere on the site.) As the bag mill remained a largely female place of employment, men made up an even higher percentage in Fulton's two cotton mills, numbering 60 percent (444 of 739) of all workers in the card, spinning, and weave rooms of Mill No. 1 and Mill No. 2.

In particular, males at Fulton Bag increasingly dominated the comparatively high paying weave room jobs during the early 1910s. Between 1913 and 1914, the weave room in Mill No. 1 added eighteen male weavers, while the number of female weavers dropped by ten. By May 1914, men accounted for 71 percent (196 of 276) of all weave room positions in the two cotton mills, up from 64 percent (187 of 292) nineteen months before. The relatively high paid and autonomous loom fixers remained, as elsewhere, all male.[94]

The growing preponderance of men at Fulton Bag in the early 1910s was tied to a steady rise in wages, although admittedly only within the limited framework of the southern textile industry. "We insist," declared Oscar Elsas, "that our Mill pays the highest wages of any in the State, or in fact, in the South, on the same character of work."[95] Furthermore, according to mill management, wages had gone up some 30 percent over the previous five years. While wages had not risen quite that much, for the most part the figures confirmed Elsas's claims. In 1914, Fulton carders reportedly averaged $8.59 per week, spinners (mainly women), $6.94, and weavers, $10.01, more than their Georgia counterparts.[96]

Furthermore, to help address its ongoing turnover problem, the company offered a premium for steady work that was unusual in the southern textile industry. For reporting or working daily for three months, Fulton workers received a bonus of 3 percent of their total earnings for that period. After the next three months, they got a 5 percent bonus, with a 7 percent bonus for every subsequent six months of steady work. According to mill management, between 1 January 1913 and 2 May 1914, Fulton workers earned premiums totaling $13,245.05 above their weekly wages. "Ask your friends about the premiums," company notices proclaimed.[97]

Even as the growing presence of male workers helped drive up wages, so did the comparative availability of nontextile jobs for white men in Atlanta. Women who lived in company housing and the surrounding neighborhood had few choices; with few exceptions, they either worked at Fulton Bag or stayed at home. Men, however, had access to quite a number of jobs, in contrast both to women and to their rural counterparts in the textile South. In 1910, 41 percent (73 of 178) of all households in even the Factory Lot, the section of company housing most dominated by the mill, contained a man who worked outside Fulton Bag.[98]

Adult males who lived in company housing as well as men who lived in nearby households in which at least one household member worked at Fulton Bag held a range of different jobs. Many of the men in Fulton households were in the building trades, working as carpenters and house painters in particular, as well as tile layers, cabinetmakers, brick masons, laborers, tinners, and steam fitters. Some men in the mill community drove horse-drawn wagons and other vehicles for nearby woodyards, grocery stores, and slaughterhouses, and for the city of Atlanta. The city parks department, stockade, and sheriff's office provided employment for various mill district residents. Others worked at different railroad jobs and for Atlanta's gas and transit companies. A few made

A store in the Fulton mill district. Georgia Institute of Technology Library and Information Center.

their living on the streets, as fruit or vegetable peddlers, insurance or furniture collectors, or newspaper hawkers, and in one instance, as a "street fiddler." Still other men from Fulton households worked in factories around town, including a paper mill, a tie factory, a steel works, a tile manufacturer, and a candy factory.

A number of men with a household connection to Fulton Bag worked in various local retail establishments as well, including grocery stores, drugstores, and a bicycle shop. The Fulton "extended community" also included grocers and shoemakers; a butcher, a barber, a locksmith, a pool room operator, and a saloon keeper; and others who owned or managed small businesses. There were even a few white-collar male workers in Fulton households, including an architectural draftsman and an office stenographer.

Of course, many of these jobs outside the mill were marginal, arduous, impermanent, or low paying, too. A man who worked as a wagon driver, grocery clerk, or a laborer for the Atlanta Gas Company—all actual occupations of men from Fulton households—made approximately the same wages and worked at least as many hours as a weaver or card grinder in the mill. On the other hand, a carpenter, a house painter, a streetcar motorman, or an electrician could easily earn twice what a textile worker brought home.[99] The essential point is, in the urban environment of Atlanta, male workers from Fulton households—arguably the most sought after and productive members of the mill's labor force—had some choice in where they worked, and frequently exercised that choice. The net result was that they linked themselves and their families, at least to a degree, with a broader white working-class community in the city, they established a certain measure of autonomy from the mill, and they possibly helped push wages of Fulton families above the industry average.

In 1915, Oscar Elsas had compiled figures showing "Average Weekly Earnings of Some Family Groups" of Fulton workers, without identifying the actual families included. Ten of the eleven showcased families purportedly earned between $20.45 and $37.50 per week, with the six working members of the eleventh family making a combined weekly total of $65.00. Yet, such figures did not accurately convey the full picture. The families profiled were hardly representative of the mill community but reflected a comparatively select group of workers. They included the families of G. A. Stalnaker, the section boss of the Mill No. 1 spinning room, and of G. M. Brock, a weaver who proclaimed in a letter he purportedly wrote to the *Atlanta Georgian* that he and his wife had saved $870 in two years while working at Fulton Bag.[100]

Most Fulton families made considerably less money than those spotlighted by Elsas. Such low wages were intrinsically linked to the company's method of payment. As part of its overall efficiency program, Fulton management had adopted a piecework payment system rather than offering a regular hourly wage in both cotton mills and the bag mill to increase production. "We intend to maintain a high wage scale for those who apply themselves," explained Oscar Elsas.[101] Yet, whatever management's goals were for the piecework system, one outcome in practice was huge discrepancies in pay among Fulton workers, even within the same department. For instance, during the week ending 16 May 1914, wages for full-time workers in the spinning room of Mill No. 1 ranged from $4.85 to $9.10 and in Mill No. 1's weave room, from $6.40 to $12.30.[102] No matter what the average wage at Fulton might be, clearly many workers made substantially less than that, despite often working both steadily and hard.

In addition, the piecework system contributed to individual wage instability. The amount a worker got paid often fluctuated considerably from week to week. "A hand never knows what they is going to make until they draw the ticket [pay envelope]," declared spinner Sarah Nations, "because that is a secret of theirs we don't understand."[103] Such variability could, of course, indicate the ebbs and flows of a worker's individual efforts; it could also reflect external factors in productivity such as the condition of mill machinery, atmospheric conditions, or the performance of other workers, as well as the condition of the textile industry.

Moreover, whatever their income, textile workers in Atlanta still were among the lowest paid white workers in the city, working for wages that were only gradually moving much above subsistence farm income levels in the 1910s. For instance, the roughly eight dollars a week that a card room hand at Fulton Bag made in 1914 would translate to approximately a hundred dollars weekly gross pay in 1990 terms.[104] Furthermore, while some mill district residents raised their own livestock and vegetables, as a rule Fulton workers, particularly in the congested Factory Lot, were more dependent than their counterparts across the region on store-bought goods and "city prices," which were among the highest in the country.[105] Even for relatively privileged Fulton workers such as those profiled by Elsas, Atlanta's high cost of living severely eroded real buying power. A federal investigator remarked after visiting the mill district, "The family wage, whatever it actually is, is inadequate." Or, as a bag mill worker put it, things were "mighty near nip and tuck at Fulton Bag and Cotton Mills even with the family working."[106]

Wages were additionally buffeted by an apparently unique system of fines and deductions that the company adopted in the fall of 1911 in the name of efficiency and discipline, hand in glove with the piecework system. "The object of fines," emphasized Oscar Elsas, "is to minimize the defective work, which finally reacts on the earning power of the employees. . . . It is of interest to each operative to have turned over to him for his operation work in good condition."[107] Fulton workers were fined for breaking machinery or equipment, being lax on the job, and, most commonly, for producing a substandard product in management's eyes.

For the period from 1 January 1913 to 2 May 1914, Fulton workers were fined a total of $1,558.99. Of this amount, $871.03 was refunded to workers who had reported the defective work of others, leaving a "net collection" for the period of $687.96. (Of course, such a practice also furthered tensions and divisions among workers.) On various occasions, Elsas wielded these figures as proof that the fines did not in any significant way set back workers financially. He pointed out that the fines were more than offset by the amount returned to workers for reporting defective work, and were far eclipsed by the premiums awarded over the same period. Furthermore, the net collection of fines amounted to only $44.00 a month, which, Elsas stated, "hardly pay clerk hire [office workers] for carrying on the system necessary to keep track of this matter." Figured another way, the net collection fee amounted to only a little over a three-cent fine per worker per month.[108]

At one level, Elsas's assertions and calculations could not be disputed. With figures averaged out in such a manner, the fining system did appear to have a minuscule impact on workers' wages. Yet, in fact, the system was far from benign. Fulton's fining practices actually assumed a much different character than that presented by Oscar Elsas.[109] More telling than the net collection sum, the proportion of the total payroll that fines comprised, or the average fine per worker per week were the frequency, timing, and location of fines. While the actual fines Fulton workers incurred for specific infractions or offenses were generally quite small, the number of fines and of workers affected certainly was not. In just one year, between 1 December 1913 and 28 November 1914, 865 different workers in the card, spinning, and weave rooms of Mill No. 1 and Mill No. 2, or two-thirds of Fulton's total working population at any given moment, were fined a total of 3,745 times. When one figures in the relatives, friends, and neighbors of the people fined, and those workers who reported defective work, it is obvious that the fining system affected a great many workers and their families.

Furthermore, the fines were distributed very unevenly throughout Fulton Mills. By far the fewest fines occurred in the female-dominated spinning rooms. For instance, for the year ending 28 November 1914, only 65 people were fined a total of 92 times in the spinning room of Mill No. 1, which employed an average of 198 workers. In other words, there were fewer than two fines a week in the entire department, and spinners there received full pay over 99 percent of the time. A similar situation existed in the spinning room of Mill No. 2.

In contrast, the card rooms were places of constant fining. For instance, Mill No. 1's card room, which averaged 134 workers, reported 186 people fined a total of 1,269 times during the period. This meant that in an average week, nearly one in five (18.21 percent) card room workers received less than full pay. Moreover, a significant number of carders were fined on numerous occasions. Some forty-four card room hands, or practically a fourth of the average number of workers in the department, were fined ten times or more during the year. The cumulative fines could add up, too. One unfortunate carder was fined forty-four out of fifty-two weeks for a total of $5.71, while another was docked forty-one times for $8.80, or more than an average week's pay.

A similar situation existed in the weave shops. In the weave room in Mill No. 2, which averaged 184 employees, 252 workers were fined a total of 848 times during the period. The fining in the weave rooms also had a particularly irregular quality to it. Some of the best, most experienced weavers got fined comparatively often, while other younger and ostensibly less skilled weavers scarcely got fined at all. A weaver could and often did go many weeks and even months without ever picking up a fine, then get fined for several weeks or more in a row.

In addition, fining in the weave rooms, especially that of Mill No. 2, occurred far more frequently at certain times of the year than at others. For instance, roughly a fourth (209 of 848) of all the fines handed down in Mill No. 2's weave room during the year in question took place during just two three-week periods, the weeks of 6, 13, and 20 December 1913 and 3, 10 and 17 October 1914. If the numbers of fines meted out during these two stretches had continued at the same rate throughout the entire year, there would have been a total of 1,811 fines in the department, or well over twice the number actually registered.

To many Fulton workers, the fining system sometimes seemed capricious, unfair, and unwarranted. "Some weeks you can see why they deduct it," related frame hand Samuel Wilson, "and maybe some weeks you don't see anything why they fine you or dock you. . . . Some[times] they would skip a week and then dock me twice as much as they did the week before."[110] Fulton workers complained of being penalized for mechanical or human failings beyond their control. Loom fixer C. H. Mundy, for instance, resented the fact that, unlike other places where he had worked, Fulton loom fixers got docked 20 percent of the fines weavers received for defective cloth, despite having nothing to do with the weaving. The second hand in charge of the room also got docked at the same time. Furthermore, loom fixers got docked $1.00 for every shuttle that got damaged, regardless of who actually was responsible.[111]

Others felt that certain supervisors unduly asserted their authority by using fines to punish workers for relatively minor offenses. Robert Wright, who worked in the bag mill, reported that women workers got docked twenty-five cents just for going to the dressing room five minutes before closing time. Wright also maintained that "they were even fined twenty-five cents for carrying water to one another at the machines." Spinner Margaret Dempsey similarly claimed that foremen "threaten to take out some of our pay . . . if we stop a minute."

Fining under the piecework system prevented any worker from challenging a supervisor's decision on what constituted unacceptable production. The mother of spinner Eva Stevens claimed, "The hands don't know what they production is. The spoolers are required to make so much and if they don't hear from the bosses—the bosses say, 'If you don't get 24 or 25 checks today [signifying a certain production level] I am going to dock you and take your place from you and put you somewhere else.'" Bag mill worker Alice Carlton lamented, "I was robbed out of a great deal of my money for the forelady would not listen to any explanations which I might make, and would not report the time that I made, and therefore I lost that—and was compelled to take whatever the forelady would put down on the book and be satisfied."

Finally, while the aggregate value of fines might have been minuscule compared to the mill's total payroll, there certainly were individual instances in which fines brought considerable distress to Fulton workers. For example, Nancy Sanders, whose three children and husband worked in the mill, felt that the fines her family incurred forced her to "take in washing together with my house work, to help provide for enough to feed and clothe them." In other words, because of the fines, she had to perform work customarily restricted to black women.[112]

Worker frustration and resentment extended well beyond issues of dollars and cents. Fines were only one facet of an ongoing conflict between Fulton management and workers over the nature, control, and very significance of work itself. Coming from an enormously different vantage point from that of the Elsases, in a variety of ways and situations Fulton workers often questioned, criticized, and challenged management's authority on the shop floor. As superintendent E. H. Rogers related, "There was always more or less complaint all the time."[113]

Traditional work practices and customs of Fulton workers frequently clashed with the practices of mill management. Oscar Elsas took pride in being up to date on the latest technological and engineering developments of the textile industry. He purchased state-of-the-art machinery to help start the textile school at Georgia Tech, reportedly studied contemporary textile processes in Europe, and in 1914 sent his son Norman to study at Cornell, one of the very first electrical engineering schools in the country. As important as his enthusiasm for modern technology was, Oscar Elsas's preoccupation with current scientific management theories and practices, stemming from his days at MIT and Georgia Tech, was at least as great. "I've done quite a lot of it [study of efficiency methods]," he proudly informed a visitor in 1914. When writing about his management philosophy on another occasion, he reiterated his firm belief that "*efficiency counts.*"[114]

The results of such unusual attention to modern efficiency practices could be seen in the premiums, the fining system, and practically every other aspect of company operations. The office staff provided another example, as Elsas explained: "We maintain a very large clerical force to keep records of voluminous reports of all kinds with the object of knowing what is going on. The average cotton mill of this size is content with about three men in the office;

Fulton management personnel, 1910s. Jacob Elsas is at center in the front row. Oscar Elsas is to his left. Special Collections Dept., Robert W. Woodruff Library, Emory University.

and it is natural to suppose that these three men cannot keep as accurate and detailed records that the large number of possibly three times that many can. In fact we have forty people in our offices."[115] Clerical workers at Fulton Bag kept extensive weekly payroll accounts, arranged by department and detailing wages, fines, deductions for rent and sundries, premiums, and money advanced to workers by the company. They also produced elaborate ledger books and, when asked to, provided on short notice lists of fines by department, the "Average Weekly Earnings of Some Family Groups," and surveys of employee home ownership and illiteracy, among other records.

To compensate for the four days of clerical labor it purportedly took to draw up the weekly payroll ledgers, as well as to make sure workers properly served their notices when they were planning to quit according to the Fulton labor contract, the company held back a full week's wages when a worker came on board. From management's perspective the withheld wages constituted a deposit of sorts; if a worker left without giving and completely "serving out" a notice, he or she stood to lose an entire week's pay.

The system could cause considerable hardship and conflict from the very outset of one's employment at Fulton Bag. Many families arrived to work at the mill with no money whatsoever. According to the Reverend G. R. Buford, who had spent several years observing conditions in the mill district, because workers had their first week's wages withheld by the company, they started out "on a credit basis," and thus ended up "hopelessly involved" in debt to the company or other creditors.

The situation was compounded by the fact that when workers got sick—a common occurrence given the unsanitary conditions in the mill district, their poor diet and long hours, and pervasive cotton dust—the company withheld their pay until their illness was verified by a doctor.[116] "If you were sick and didn't have a doctor," explained spinner Blanche Prince, "they held your pay back. . . . I think one of the hardest things for us poor people is having our money held back when we are sick. Suppose you work nine days and fall sick, you can't get your money [until you saw a doctor]."[117] And many workers were not likely to see a doctor. They were accustomed to traditional health care practices rooted in self-sufficiency. They were leery of the Fulton clinic's modern medical procedures that intruded upon personal autonomy, and they distrusted company doctor Hawkins.[118] As a consequence, the process of obtaining one's back pay, only after a physician's validation, could be trying, distressing, and even humiliating.

There were other times, too, where traditional attitudes toward health care combined with confusion over the contract or other company regulations to put workers in the hole. Reverend Buford reported that many workers "were too ignorant to know that by getting a doctor's certificate they would at least not have to forfeit the start they had made toward a premium." Buford also described how one health-related incident ended with a dispute over a Fulton worker's withheld pay. "I had a boy out there who was sick," Buford related, "had quit the mill and wanted to go to the country. The boy said the mill owed him $11.65 back pay but he couldn't get it."[119]

This episode was only one of a number of occasions in which workers and management clashed over the interpretation and implementation of the contract, especially the provisions about giving and serving notice and the company's withholding pay. For example, fourteen-year-old Edgar Gaddis recounted,

In 1912 I put in my notice . . . having 66 hours time in the mill, and drawed 30 cents, [the company] claiming that I had forfeited the balance of the time; by my mother putting in her notice to leave their employment, they said they would have to claim my money as forfeited. This was done in order that they might hold my mother in their employ. After they had called my mother into their private office and told her that they would pay me my entire time, if she would take her notice back and remain in their employ, they paid me my entire wage which amounted to about $2.40. After I received my $2.40, I did not go back into their employ any more.[120]

Fulton's labor contract was only one of a host of company rules and regulations that constantly reminded workers of their subordinate, dependent position. In the weave shops, for instance, the company mounted large posters listing "RULES FOR SECTION MEN IN WEAVE DEPARTMENT." These signs notified the all-male loom fixers, arguably the most independent and skilled members of the workforce, that they were expected to be at their jobs before starting time and that they were not to shut off their machines until the speed slacked at the very end of the workday. Loom fixers had to deposit either one or two dollars to get their straight edges and then use only the kind the department overseer specified. They were informed they would be fined 20 percent of all seconds produced in their section. Furthermore, upon leaving Fulton Bag, whether they served out a notice or were discharged, 25 percent of their time was to be held back pending management's inspection of all the cloth in their section for defects, a process that could take up to two weeks. "This does not cover all the rules for Loom Fixers," warned the notices emphatically, "but is intended to outline some of the most important ones."[121]

Similar rules and regulations extended beyond the weave rooms to the entire plant. Anyone leaving Fulton's employment, "whether on notice or upon being discharged," had to deposit at least a dollar until his or her work had been inspected. Only after company officials had received a postcard with the former worker's new address would they mail a check to cover the amount withheld, "less charges for seconds." Given the transience and illiteracy of many workers, they often never saw their withheld money. While in the mill, workers were only allowed to use the type of matches furnished by the company; if they did not, they were subject to a dollar fine. The company also stipulated that spinning room spoolers had to pay for their own stools if they broke and that nobody could leave the weave department without permission.[122]

Fulton workers often felt the company's regulations to be far out of line, or, in one spinner's words, "just too tight, and that's all there is to it." Bag mill worker Robert Wright claimed that the rules were so numerous "that it was almost impossible to work under them." Other mills frequently seemed—at least in hindsight—more informal, more relaxed, and more personal; one well-traveled weaver spoke for many when he stated, "I have been in a good many mills and the rules in the Fulton Bag and Cotton Mills are worse than in any I have ever seen."[123]

As oppressive and humiliating as the rules could be, though, they were scarcely all that Fulton workers resented. For some people, it was not so much

All operatives must serve ONE WEEK'S NOTICE before quitting.

Machinery MUST NOT be CLEANED while in motion, as same is dangerous.

PAY CHECKS are given out every Saturday morning in the mill an if operative is absent at such time, check can be secured Saturday morning at 11 o'clock at Office of Company, otherwise check can not be had until Monday.

Sulphur matches not allowed---Safety matches furnished without charge.

Payment CAN NOT be made without check.

All complaints or suggestions gladly investigated at the office.

Fulton Bag & Cotton Mills.

An announcement listing some of Fulton's rules and regulations for employees. Special Collections Dept., Pullen Library, Georgia State University.

the company's regulations per se that rankled the most, but rather the behavior and attitudes of foremen and other supervisors. Echoing sentiments common across the textile South, Fulton workers raised a multitude of complaints about their bosses. The most common was that many supervisors were too overbearing and bullying. Nannie May Stevens told of the treatment her sister Eva received in the spinning room of Mill No. 1: "They did treat her mean—they would just rear at her if she did anything they didn't like—they would rear at her." "The thing I wish they could stop in the mills," seconded spooler Margaret Dempsey, "is the unkind talk—they talk to us just as if we was dogs; order us around. . . . They . . . talk to us just awful." In addition, Dempsey and Eva Stevens both complained of supervisors not letting workers leave the job and go home when they felt sick.[124]

Addressing a topic then receiving widespread attention in Atlanta because of the Leo Frank case, Eva Stevens also described what she considered improper conduct toward women, as well as outright sexual harassment that she experienced on the job. "My treatment by the bosses was such that no lady could endure," she stated, "unless forced to take it (as I was) to make a livelihood. John Smith, a second hand, would curse us for not keeping up the work when the machinery would be working badly." Moreover, she related, "One afternoon, P. A. Smith, Overseer, gave me six sides to run, and after I had them all cleaned up and running well, he took two of the sides away from me and gave them to another girl. When I protested, saying that I could not make enough money, by running only four sides, he said he would give me back the six sides if I would let him squeeze me. I gave him a general talking to, and for sometime he would not speak to me, and tried to make my work there as unbearable as possible."[125] Others also had complaints about P. A. Smith. Spinner Sarah Nations reported that Smith "has come to me and asked me to go out with him in the tower. He offered me money if I would go." In November 1914, a labor spy employed by the company reported that Smith was "too intimate with some of the female help" and had been caught "kissing and hugging" with a married woman spinner.[126]

Smith was not the only supervisor who reputedly abused his authority in such a manner. In September 1903, for instance, foreman J. H. Wellaver was placed under arrest for allowing obscene notes to be passed around the shop floor, an episode that, according to the *Atlanta Constitution*, "created a very decided sensation in the district."[127] Eleven years later, bag mill worker Jane Savage related that James I. Brush, the head of the mill's private security force, had been too bold with her and had offered her money to go for a ride. "Brush does too much talking to the girls in the mill," she added, "and he did not care what kind of language he cared to use, even before the young children in the mill."[128]

Such sentiments reflected not only recurrent tensions and anxieties at Fulton Bag but habitual concerns at other New South textile mills and local factories as well. Other worker complaints also extended across the region well beyond the Fulton plant, from supervisors who tried to speed up the work, to aching limbs and bones, to lazy, good-for-nothing fellow workers. Certain grievances, however, were more specific to Fulton Bag. For instance, though in fact only a handful of Germans, both Jews and Gentiles, were employed by the company, primarily in the office, their numbers seemed magnified to the workers who decried the presence of Germans, "dagoes"—an all-purpose word in early-twentieth-century Atlanta describing Jews and Greeks as well as Italians—and other foreigners at Fulton Bag.[129] The company's bag mill also generated its own particular set of grievances. Sack sewer Annie Carlton maintained that the salt put in the bags to make them heavy made one's fingers so sore that she and nearly every other woman in the department "would have to lay off every few days," thus losing their pay.[130]

Company regulations and practices became more strict, and worker resentment intensified, with the arrival in November 1912 of the mill's new general manager, Gordon A. Johnstone. In addition to his overall supervisory duties, Johnstone investigated every case in which a notice to quit work was given, and he took over from Oscar Elsas the task of handling all employee complaints that could not be settled by middle management. He thus played a key role in setting the particular tone of industrial relations at Fulton Mills in the early 1910s.

Johnstone's background differed greatly from the workers he supervised. A self-proclaimed Scotchman, he had grown up in Canada. He then migrated to the United States, applying for work in a Massachusetts carriage shop, where he was told he had to join a union before he could work there. When informed that the union wage scale topped off at $15.00 per week no matter what one's performance was, Johnstone quit, later stating, "I do not believe in my carrying somebody else who wants to work half as hard as I want to work."[131]

Johnstone provided additional insights about his character and attitudes toward work in testimony before the U.S. Commission on Industrial Relations in 1915. When asked about the Fulton contract, he replied approvingly, asserting that, "Any law is a good thing. It is a restraint on those who would otherwise be taking advantage of society." Concerning the rules at the plant, he declared, "Some of the rules are strict. They are good. The rules that are strict are good rules. They make for better discipline, make for better employees and make for a better set of employees after they get over with the first little scare they have, and it is mighty good."[132]

In December 1914, a loom fixer in Mill No. 2 predicted that "some of these days somebody will knock Mr. Johnstone in the head for butting into things even if he is General Manager." Even Oscar Elsas's son Norman concurred. According to Norman Elsas, Johnstone was a hot-tempered man liable to fly off the handle at the drop of a hat, "sort of picayunish" and "very dictatorial." In his opinion, Johnstone's explosive manner lost him "the respect and affection of the people in the plant. . . . He managed to make himself pretty well disliked. . . . A great many of the people disliked him."[133]

Depending on a range of circumstances, Fulton workers interacted with their work situation in a variety of ways. For the most part, whatever their sentiments, they stayed on the job, outwardly at least going along with the company's rules and regulations, and suffering onerous working conditions. Despite the hardships, textile work after all did provide a regular pay envelope (even if one did not know from week to week what that envelope might contain), and for many people it was the only employment they had ever known. In addition to a job, the company furnished affordable housing, athletic teams and—through Wesley House—a night school and other activities. Furthermore, over time many workers developed close personal friendships on and off the shop floor, as well as a loyalty to the company, which helped keep them at the mill. There is no doubt that such corporate paternalism as did exist at Fulton Bag *was* welcomed and appreciated by some workers like Jennie

Clinton, who in 1915 declared, "I have always been treated as if I belong to the mill. I have been treated like a child by this company."[134]

In addition to quitting work and moving out of the community, which was the most prevalent expression of worker discontent, there were ways in which workers to some degree controlled their own lives and expressed their preference for alternatives to the prescribed work regimen at Fulton Bag. On the shop floor itself, some workers helped determine who their work mates and neighbors would be. Others took advantage of slack time, negligent or absent supervisors, or additional circumstances to gather, socialize, trade jokes, and drink or play cards while on the job. Sometimes the jokes were at the expense of other workers; there certainly were times when Fulton workers teased, threatened, and on occasion actually physically attacked one another. Such episodes often stemmed from job-related frustrations. For instance, as in other mills, Fulton loom fixers and weavers frequently were at odds with each other over allegedly shoddy production and work habits.[135]

Absenteeism continued to be perhaps the leading way in which workers exerted some influence over the terms of their employment. Periodically, outside attractions would draw Fulton workers away from work, despite the risk of pay deductions, fines, and even dismissal. In 1904, a woman professing to be "an inspired fortune teller" moved into the mill district, causing "great excitement" as a crowd gathered around her boardinghouse. The *Atlanta Constitution* reported, "When the mill whistle blew, announcing work time, large numbers of these people, men and women, remained around the place and failed to go to work." In 1915, a labor spy reported on one woman who regularly laid out from work after frequenting dance halls the night before.[136] By the early 1910s, Monday had replaced Saturday as the leading day of absenteeism, with summer being the season in which absenteeism was most prevalent.[137]

Whatever form it took, worker resistance to the working conditions at Fulton Bag—as elsewhere in the Piedmont South—was as a rule personal and individualistic, generally spontaneous and unorganized. To a large degree, this reflected the particular culture in which the vast majority of workers were raised, as well as an often hostile anti-union environment. It also represented an accurate appraisal of the enormous inequities of power within the mill, and of the correspondingly limited avenues of redress available to workers. Still, more so than at most cotton mills, throughout the company's history there were occasions when Fulton workers did engage in collective action, affiliating with the local labor movement or initiating strikes and walkouts. The most notable of these times was the strike of 1914–15.

CHAPTER 4

Causes and Commencement

By the late 1970s, there existed very few individuals who recalled the Fulton unionizing effort of the 1910s. One who did was former worker and long-time mill district resident Horace Carson, son of Fiddlin' John. In his memoir, Carson wrote, "In 1913, there was a new word in the mill worker's vocabulary[,] 'Union.' The Company's position was clear . . . 'No Union.' The Company did everything possible to prevent the Union from coming in the mill, many people were fired and forced to move. But, later in 1913, the issue came to a boiling point and the mill workers walked off their jobs on strike."[1] While Carson's chronology was a bit off the mark—the big strike at Fulton Mills originating in 1914 rather than 1913—his depiction was essentially accurate. Even before Fulton workers turned to organized labor, though, they had already initiated a walkout and additional job-related actions in the fall of 1913.

In the year after Gordon Johnstone had come on as general manager, management added and tightened up numerous work rules, causing resentment among many workers. "The rules in force at the mill," in their opinion, "were too strict, almost without exception."[2] In particular, one of the recently adopted regulations raised the number of days' pay held back at the outset of one's employment from five to six. The effect was to make Fulton's already despised labor contract feel yet more oppressive and to suppress the most common form of worker resistance, namely outmigration from the mill.[3]

Other rules specifically targeted the loom fixers and were deeply resented by these comparatively independent male workers. For instance, the company now detailed the amount of work the fixers were expected to perform, subject to daily inspection, at a production level many fixers believed "impossible" to meet. Another new regulation stipulated: "When new shuttles are put in a loom it must be lined up, new pickers put on, power taken off, and the loom put in first-class condition. If on starting up, it be found the loom is not working properly and the shuttles damaged, said loom fixer is subject to a fine of not less than $1.00."[4]

Against this backdrop of increased friction over the new regulations, trouble broke out. Just prior to October 1913, supervisors noticed that the cloth coming out of the weave room in Mill No. 2 was of an inferior, "reedy" grade of production. After investigating the situation, mill management determined that this was not due to any defect in the raw material or the machinery but rather "with the loom fixers [not] keeping the looms in proper repair." Consequently, fines in the Mill No. 2 weave room soared during the first three weeks of October.[5] In addition, company officials insisted the looms be taken down and reset by the nine loom fixers on the floor.

The person overseeing the machine readjustments was Ernest Metzger, the youthful, German-born (though non-Jewish) assistant superintendent for the weave department. Upon the recommendation of Jacob Elsas, Metzger had emigrated from Germany in September 1911 to learn all aspects of the textile business at Fulton Mills. He had worked in various departments before being transferred to the Mill No. 2 weave room, where his presence irritated a number of the loom fixers in particular. In addition to the language barrier, which was "quite a bother," the fixers resented an inexperienced foreigner "learning the American of operating a cotton mill." "According to my knowledge," one loom fixer later declared, "he knowed about as much about a cotton mill as I know about an airship, and we did not feel like taking orders from him. . . . He kind of created disturbance among the loom fixers."[6]

On Saturday, 18 October, when Metzger entered the section of loom fixer William Fowler, sparks flew. According to another fixer, "Fowler asked him to stay off his section. He did not know anything about a loom, whether it was out of order or in order." According to Oscar Elsas, "Fowler told him, in vile language, to leave his section and not to come back there again." According to the *Atlanta Constitution*, Fowler "all but assaulted" Metzger during the confrontation. The company promptly fired Fowler for insolence and insubordination and discharged boss weaver John W. McElhannon for "acting in collusion" with him.[7]

For Elsas, Fowler's swift dismissal was an entirely proper use of management's prerogative under the circumstances. Fowler and his supporters viewed the matter altogether differently. They maintained that the incident was hardly an isolated one but could only be understood within the larger context of increasingly severe company regulations. In addition, Fowler's supporters claimed, the loom fixers had received instructions to receive work orders only from McElhannon. Thus, when Metzger gave Fowler the directive about the looms, he understandably refused. It was Metzger, not Fowler, who then allegedly flew into a rage and "blew his stack." In any event, whatever Fowler did only came after what the *Journal of Labor* termed "a long story of oppression and exploitation"; his dismissal meant that now "a long and enduring patience was exhausted."[8]

Led by the loom fixers, by noon on Monday, 20 October, some 200 mostly male workers at Mill No. 2 walked out. According to the *Journal of Labor*, those who left were not "floaters" but rather longtime employees of the mills, a claim substantiated by payroll records. Protesting the overall strictness of the mill's regulations and declaring that it was Fowler's transgression of an unjust rule that had caused his dismissal, the strikers demanded his reinstatement along with the dismissal of Metzger and Gordon Johnstone.[9]

For his part, Oscar Elsas asserted that the walkout was first confined to the weave department of Mill No. 2, with neither the spinning room nor the card room originally affected. He charged that some of the fixers not only cut off all the looms in the weave room but then ran throughout the plant stopping machinery in other departments and "indiscriminately issuing orders for the help to get out of the Mills, even going so far as to threaten bodily violence if not obeyed."[10]

Elsas quickly called the city police headquarters for assistance.[11] In response, ten mounted officers arrived on the scene. They arrested loom fixers W. E. Fleming and R. L. Wood, weaver James Cantrell, spinner Will Tumlin, and as many as eight other workers for disorderly conduct.[12] For many Fulton workers, as well as members of Atlanta's trade unions, such intervention by the police in a labor dispute was an intimidating show of state force that clearly violated the bounds of acceptable behavior and that set an ominous precedent. On Tuesday, 100 Fulton workers called upon printer-mayor James Woodward to protest the strong police presence during the walkout. Woodward responded that the police had no right to interfere with strikers, as long as they did not break the law.[13]

The *Journal of Labor* also condemned the police action. An editorial posed the question: "Does the position of employer give him the authority to call the police?" The editorial decried the "blunder" at police headquarters in response to mill management's call, compared the "squadron of MPS" at Fulton Mills to Cossack horsemen in Czarist Russia, and denounced such "swashbuckling for private employers." For two more weeks, the *Journal of Labor* addressed the issue, sarcastically proposing that "[w]hen our conservators of the peace are turned into Cossack strike breakers, they should be armed with the knout as an emblem of their new function."[14]

In a testament to the strong union presence in city affairs, as well as the comparative vulnerability of the Atlanta Police Department due to departmental scandals and politics, the public outcry against the police presence had an effect. The *Journal of Labor* reported in late November, "It has been leaked out that Atlanta policemen will never again be used as strikebreakers or strike preventors."[15] In particular, the police would be reluctant to intervene during subsequent labor disputes at Fulton Mills, a stance that would infuriate Elsas.

At the arraignment of the arrested strikers, the courthouse was packed with their supporters. Wood and Fleming were fined $10 and costs, and Tumlin's case was bound over. Cantrell did not appear, having apparently skipped town, and the others received suspended sentences or were acquitted. In the courtroom, Fleming seized the opportunity of a public forum to make an "excited speech" in which he attacked mill management. Other Fulton workers openly condemned Gordon Johnstone, claiming, in an echo of accusations made during the Frank trial, that Johnstone had used "offensive language" toward workers in the mill and that he had carried around a pistol, a charge that he denied.[16]

The strike ended within a few days. On 23 October, a committee of workers met with Elsas and other company representatives to discuss the situation. Management refused to consider the "unrealistic" demands that Fowler and McElhannon be reinstated and that Johnstone and Metzger be discharged. In addition, Elsas stated there would be an internal investigation before Fleming, Wood, and Cantrell could be reinstated. Workers did gain a victory, however: the company agreed to their demand that the rule requiring six days' pay be withheld revert to five. By the end of the week, essentially all Fulton workers had returned to their jobs.[17]

Oscar Elsas later estimated that some 350 of the mill's nearly 1,300 workers had taken part in the walkout.[18] For the week ending 25 October 1913, total payroll for Mill No. 2 was only 67.8 percent of what it had been the previous week ($1,737.15 down from $2,562.45). Payroll in the production departments of Mill No. 1 dropped off at a similar rate, to 70.9 percent of what it had been for the week ending 18 October ($2,189.60 from $3,055.50). In contrast, although it also did decline, payroll in the bag mill dipped only slightly, to 92.6 percent of the previous week's total ($728.25 from $786.40).

More workers took part in the strike from the weave rooms of both cotton mills, and from other departments of Mill No. 2, than elsewhere in the complex. Payroll in the weave department of Mill No. 2 dropped to 65.2 percent of what it had been the week ending 18 October ($876.40 from $1,345.30), and payroll in Mill No. 1's weave department declined even more, to merely 53.9 percent of the previous week ($582.90 from $1,081.60). Payroll in the spinning department of Mill No. 2 fell to 69.1 percent of the previous week's total ($435.45 from 630.40); payroll in the carding department decreased to 72.5 percent ($425.30 from $586.75). In contrast, the card room of Mill No. 1 was the department least affected by the strike, with payroll declining only to 92.7 percent of the previous week's total ($661.60 from $713.60). While male weavers and loom fixers led the walkout, in varying degrees both men and women workers throughout the plant participated.

A week after the strike ended, payroll was back to its prewalkout level, and business as usual seemed to have been restored.[19] But the strike set in motion escalating actions and reactions among both workers and management. On 23 October, walkout leader J. T. Lewis and Harris Gober, a grocer in the mill district, called the *Atlanta Journal* to deny that the strike had been settled, even as that paper was getting ready to announce that the strikers would resume work the next day. They asserted that 300 workers in the card room of Mill No. 1 had gone on a sympathy strike and that 250 bag mill workers would walk out the following day. Though their claims were baseless, the call itself reflected continuing disquiet and the spread of worker insurgency both within and outside the mill.

One week later, eleven section men from the card and picker rooms of both Mill No. 1 and No. 2 petitioned to Oscar Elsas for a wage increase from $1.75 to $2.00 a day. While pronouncing their satisfaction with their jobs and their loyalty to the company, the men stated that "we [feel] that we are entitled to [a raise]," especially, they asserted, since some of them had been at Fulton as long as six years.[20] The overseers of the cording department followed suit a few days later. As with the October walkout, it was veteran workers who initiated these attempts to gain higher wages. Johnstone notified the cording overseers that the company was paying more than other mills already and that, given a "far from satisfactory" business outlook, "[i]t was impossible at this time to consider the proposition."[21]

Mill management quickly took action to monitor and eliminate such incipient worker activism. Before the short-lived October strike was even over, Johnstone sent Oscar Elsas a series of memos that named the workers who had first demanded Fowler's reinstatement; provided details about the arrested strikers and those who swore in court against Johnstone; and reported the abuse purportedly meted out by a second hand in the weave room of Mill No. 1 to a worker who planned to work out his notice rather than join the walkout.[22]

Johnstone also provided Elsas two longer, overlapping rosters of alleged activists. One list named fifty-eight individuals from throughout the plant. The other identified key leaders, department by department, along with the officers and executive committee of the embryonic labor organization then being formed. All told, the two lists included ninety people, a figure that was both an indication of the widespread scope of growing worker insurgency and management's alarm at this development.[23]

Johnstone reported to Elsas that neither Fleming nor Wood were strangers to labor unrest at Fulton Mills. He labeled Fleming "one of the agitators" in some trouble that had gone on at the plant two years earlier. For his part, Wood had once joined loom fixers who refused to work, in solidarity with some men who had left their drawing frames and quit. He had been fired, had laid out a week or ten days, and then was allowed back only when mill management heard that he had been led into his action.[24] This time, however, neither Wood nor Fleming were reinstated.

They were not alone. By the end of October, at least twelve of the individuals on Johnstone's list no longer worked at the plant, although some of them later returned.[25] Though management did not immediately fire all the leaders and participants in the October walkout, they intimidated workers in other ways. In the words of assistant superintendent E. H. Rogers, the company's already strict rules now "had to be enforced more often" to eliminate suspected troublemakers. P. A. Smith, the overseer in the spinning room of Mill No. 1, concurred that top management instructed supervisory personnel to be "more careful" in monitoring and disciplining employees during this period.

The October walkout originated entirely from Fulton workers' own initiative, with no connection at first to any labor union or other outside association. As a minister connected with the Men and Religion Forward Movement stated, the strike leaders "met without any pressure from outside, talked things over and decided they must make certain demands for better conditions."[26] Around the time of the October strike, however, some workers "decided that it was time to perfect an organization for their better protection." Meeting weekly both openly in a hall as well as in secret, they carefully added new participants to the several dozen people originally involved.[27]

Despite their efforts at secrecy, members of this new organization quickly met additional reprisals from management. Rufus Frank Odell, a section hand in the weave room of Mill No. 1, later recounted, "The orders I got was from the overseer in charge of the whole weaving department at No. 1 Mill. He told me the company wanted to get rid of the Union help, but they wanted to get rid of them in a way that would not implicate the company so that they would not say they were discharged on account of the Union. . . . They wanted some excuse, that was all."[28]

One who soon felt the heat was Herbert Newbern Mullinax, a veteran loom fixer in Mill No. 2 and the secretary of the newly formed union.[29] He had taken part in the October strike and had been marked by company officials as one of the leaders in the dispute.[30] He kept his job then, but when he continued to organize among Fulton workers, he felt pressure from management. Mullinax later related,

> The overseer came to see me and talked to me, begging me to take a much more difficult job. I told him that the job was too heavy for me, not being physically able to run it, being a little man. They kept insisting and finally I said that I would take it, if they would give me a raise in pay (I was then getting $2.20 a day, which was the highest pay in the mill for loom fixers). It went on until the following Monday when Mr. Garner, who was then overseer of weaving, came to me and told me to go down and take charge of the basement, and I then said to Garner, "I will go up and talk to the general manager." I went up and talked to Mr. Johnstone. Mr. Johnstone said, "We want you to go as your past record is that you are a cracker-jack loom fixer." I said, "If that is true, I ought to have more money," but I explained to him that I was not physically able to take hold of this heavy job and build it up.

Rather than be fired over this incident, Mullinax chose to quit. By early December, he was gone from the premises.[31]

Another individual targeted was Mullinax's fellow loom fixer F. W. "Fred" Flynn, president of the incipient union.[32] Only two days after the October walkout, Oscar Elsas began a correspondence with B. O. Fussell, a traveling salesman who claimed to have some "goods" on Flynn, specifically that Flynn had once paid him with a bad check. Displaying for the first time his penchant for going to great lengths to ferret out information about those he considered threats or enemies, Elsas invited Fussell to Atlanta, all expenses paid, "to discuss the Flynn matter." The two were to meet in the waiting room of the Terminal Station, where, Elsas wrote, "You will know me by the wearing of a brown Alpine hat, glasses, and dark overcoat." Flynn, when confronted with Fussell's evidence, denied all, causing Elsas to storm, "This party has the most unmitigated nerve of any man we ever came in contact with, and the sooner he can be handled, the better we will like it." Flynn's employment terminated the week ending 10 January 1914, a development Elsas noted in his correspondence to Fussell.[33]

For many Fulton workers these dismissals of union leaders and members exposed the veneer of corporate paternalism and constituted a clear violation of their rights, and they demanded a response. "They roared and pranced about that," recounted loom fixer W. C. Sweatt. "That was a big blow to them." Around Christmas, workers in the weave room of Mill No. 1 "got kind of raw" about the discharge of fellow weaver and union officer James Lewis and stopped production for a short while before being persuaded to go back to work. Throughout the winter, some workers called "all the time" for a strike on the issue.[34]

Other expressions of heightened worker self-activity assumed a more public dimension. The *Journal of Labor*'s 2 January 1914 issue boasted a new name on its masthead: "H. N. Mullinax, subscription solicitor," and editor Jerome Jones wrote a column introducing Mullinax to Atlanta's labor community. In addition to taking this new position, Mullinax initiated a column in the labor paper called "Personals from the Textile Workers."[35]

Patterned after the social columns that appeared in both the daily press and the *Journal of Labor*, "Personals from the Textile Workers" contained the usual news of marriages, vacations, new jobs, visits by out-of-town friends, and the like. Yet, for all its resemblance to other social notes, Mullinax's column had a distinct textile flavor, describing the vicissitudes of a mill worker's life. For instance, one week's column reported the deaths of two young children in the Fulton mill district; a fatal stroke suffered by a woman survived by her husband and nine children; various other illnesses and afflictions; and the news that "Jessey B. Russell who was shot by George Cook some few days past is improving to the delight of his many friends." Another column related the woes of a worker who had had "a very heavy truck [run] over his foot," and yet another announced that weaver J. T. Hendrix was "very painfully" hurt by a brick that had fallen on his head. To put it mildly, this kind of news rarely if ever appeared in the *Journal of Labor*'s personal columns of Atlanta's respectable printing tradesmen and their wives.

Although "Personals" carried news about a broad cross section of Fulton workers, the column devoted a disproportionate amount of attention to the comings and goings of people who had played a leading role in the October walkout. Readers could learn, for instance, that William Fowler's mother was visiting from South Carolina; that weaver R. W. Wiggins and his family were "going to the farm near Toccoa for a year"; that overseer McElhannon was back in town, "shaking hands with friends in the city"; that the child of Fred Flynn was sick; and that both Fleming and Mullinax had moved and were now taking in boarders. In so doing, the column personalized and helped to legitimize identified organizers among Fulton workers and reflected the growing network of overlapping associations, activities, and organizations that workers were developing in the aftermath of the October walkout.

A political advertisement that appeared in the *Journal of Labor* on 20 March 1914 provided another public example of Fulton workers' agency. The ad was placed on behalf of police captain W. M. Mayo, who was then a candidate for Fulton County sheriff. Mayo had been the commanding officer of the mounted police who had come to the mill in October. Discounting charges that Mayo had used excessive force during the episode, sixty-seven petitioners, all purportedly Fulton workers, maintained that Mayo had actually acted in a reasonable manner when he arrived on the scene. According to the ad, Mayo had suggested that the workers try to settle their disagreement with management but was told that they had tried to do so to no avail. The ad also claimed that workers had then told Mayo that if they left their jobs on their own accord to meet with management, they risked losing sixty hours of wages for breaking the labor contract. Accompanying the petition was an affidavit supporting Mayo by Fleming and fellow October walkout leader R. L. Wood.[36]

Counting Fleming and Wood, only fifty of the petitioners can be positively identified as current or former Fulton workers. (Some of those unidentified were likely transient workers, female relatives of mill workers, or people whose names were spelled inconsistently.) The other petitioners included residents of the mill district as well as a brick mason, a clerk, and other white working-class Atlantans. The Fulton workers came from nearly all production departments of the mill. They included loom fixers, weavers, frame hands, spinners, carders, bag mill workers, and at least one doffer, one spooler, and one oiler. Loom fixers were particularly well represented on the list, accounting for at least nine of the names, or roughly half of all the fixers employed at Fulton Mills.

The list also contained a disproportionate number of workers who company officials had identified as leaders in the October walkout. In addition to Fleming and Wood, the petitioners included Fowler, Will Tumlin, and at least ten other workers—and probably some of their relatives as well—whom management claimed had played a leading role in October.[37] Nearly 30 percent (14 of 50) of the Fulton workers who signed the petition were also people the company had identified as active in organizing workers at the plant. Such a correlation was not coincidental; rather, it indicated the growing public activity and outreach of this core group of worker-activists.

The question then is, why did the strike leaders from October also choose to weigh in on behalf of Captain Mayo? After all, Mayo *had* led the mounted police to quell the October disturbance. One likely explanation lies in the involvement in the Leo Frank case by Mayo's political opponent, incumbent sheriff C. W. Mangum. Over the past eleven months, Mangum had frequently drawn fire for allegedly giving Frank preferential treatment in prison, a charge he repeatedly denied.[38] The anti-Semitism and often intense class antagonisms surrounding the Frank affair, and extending to Mangum's treatment of Frank, spilled over to the increasingly organized and outspoken workers at Fulton Mills.[39]

Mullinax's employment at the *Journal of Labor* was only one reflection of a growing connection between Fulton workers and the ranks of organized labor.

In the spring of 1914, Fleming and two other mill workers became the first textile worker delegates in years to attend the Georgia Federation of Labor (GFL) annual convention. At the meeting, Fleming reported a large union membership already enrolled and paying dues and made an "impassioned plea" for delegates to help textile organizing attempts in their own communities.[40]

By this time, what had begun as an independent initiative by Fulton workers had coincided, then dovetailed with the first national campaign to organize southern mill hands in over a decade. Encouraged by the formation of new locals in Virginia and Tennessee, and feeling threatened by the radical Industrial Workers of the World (IWW), in the fall of 1913 southern delegates at the United Textile Workers convention requested that the union launch a new organizing campaign in the region. The appeal corresponded with the ascendance of more aggressive locals within the Fall River, Massachusetts–based UTW and a growth in "high-tax" union membership, which in turn brought a substantial increase in available income for organizing and strike support. The AFL had also recently renewed its commitment to organize the South, which had recently surpassed New England in textile production. The UTW convention approved an assessment of five cents per member for five weeks to carry on "a more aggressive campaign of organization among the textile workers of the country."[41]

At the convention, UTW president John Golden pointed to child labor and the family wage system as the principal motives to organize the South, even as such features of southern textiles were already on the wane. Golden, who was born in Lancashire in 1862, had left England after being blacklisted for his union activities. In the States, he joined the Massachusetts-based mule spinners union, one of several textile organizations that merged to become the United Textile Workers in 1901.[42]

Golden was somewhat familiar with conditions in the South, having toured the region in 1903 and having recently corresponded with South Carolina–born economist Arthur B. Adams about the prospects for southern unionization.[43] Still, he epitomized the New England–based leadership of the UTW. Often of British origin, these men were generally cautious in their outlook and approach. Power in the UTW was highly centralized, with few avenues for input from the rank and file. To maintain a centrally strong union, Golden had actually forced up the per capita tax, even though that meant a number of locals had to drop out of the organization. As historian George Mitchell has written, the UTW's leaders "carried a stout tradition of English craft unionism; with them to retrieve defeat was to cling to organization."[44] Golden and his fellow UTW leaders spent much of their time launching fierce attacks upon the

IWW, especially after clashing with the Wobblies during the 1912 Lawrence, Massachusetts, strike and again in 1913 in Paterson, New Jersey. UTW officials denounced class conflict and expressed "little enthusiasm" for strikes, doing everything they could to avoid them and concentrating their energies instead on financial benefits, uniform wage scales, and proworker legislation. Such a centralized, businesslike approach would not always mesh well with the often marginalized, disorderly world of southern mill hands.[45]

At its convention, the UTW named another Englishman, national organizer Charles A. Miles, to lead the southern campaign. In his eight years of organizing, Miles had been involved with often well-publicized drives in Paterson and Fall River; Utica, Auburn, and Amsterdam, New York; and Springfield and New Bedford, Massachusetts.[46] After the convention, he moved quickly to enlist southern textile workers, beginning in Augusta and other urban areas that had comparatively active local trade union movements.[47] By March 1914, UTW organizing efforts had extended to Knoxville, Tennessee; Columbus and Rome, Georgia; Langley, Bath, and Graniteville, South Carolina; as well as Atlanta, where UTW local 886 was organized.[48]

Around the same time, the IWW also launched a southern campaign that centered around the mills of Greenville, South Carolina. Despite being far smaller in scope than the UTW drive, the effort raised in high relief the specter of the IWW in the South and suffused the entire regional labor picture. Mill men across the region felt that agitation by the UTW and its allies, whatever the UTW's actual stand vis à vis the Wobblies, would in fact create a situation more fertile for exploitation by the IWW. They were quick to assume that UTW organizers might actually be radicals in disguise; any militant prolabor address could thus easily be interpreted as a "radical IWW labor speech."[49]

At Fulton Mills and across the Piedmont, mill management took aggressive steps to quash both the UTW and IWW campaigns. Leading the way was David Clark, founder and editor of the Charlotte-based *Southern Textile Bulletin*.[50] Clark inaugurated a series of occasional dispatches known as "confidential circulars," which he sent out to Oscar Elsas and other mill men across the Piedmont. These "deliberately secret" bulletins detailed incipient union activity, reprinted newspaper articles from affected communities along with correspondence to and from manufacturers, and helped develop a coordinated regional anti-union strategy.[51]

The outlines of this approach, along with the UTW's counterploys, began to emerge at the end of 1913, when a strike broke out at the King Manufacturing Company in Augusta after loom fixers there were discharged for refusing a pay cut. Management turned away a delegation of the loom fixers, spurned Miles's efforts to negotiate what he called an "honorable adjustment" to reinstate the men, stated that there was "no trouble" to arbitrate, and proclaimed that the fixers "could only return upon the company's terms, as individuals."

At that point, workers from throughout the King plant called a strike, insisting upon "the recognition of committees representing the workers, and an opportunity to discuss conditions before accepting any changes in employment." With the aid of local trade unions, the UTW quickly established a commissary "to avoid the extreme suffering which otherwise would have resulted from the strike." After ten weeks, the strike was called off. Although only some of the fired loom fixers had been reinstated, Miles maintained that the strike had spawned an improvement in working conditions at other nearby mills, and had boosted organizing efforts in the region.[52]

The next flare-up in the UTW campaign—and one that management at Fulton Bag and across the Piedmont would watch closely—took place in March at the Anchor Duck Mills in Rome, seventy miles northwest of Atlanta. After workers there had contacted AFL officials, Miles arrived to organize a UTW local, then went to Knoxville, telling union members to make no demands concerning conditions until more workers were signed up.

As Anchor Duck secretary-treasurer C. E. McLin wrote David Clark, who reprinted the letter in a confidential circular, when company officials learned a local had been established at the plant, they quickly summoned the union president and vice president from the weave room. In a manner revealing of the language of Piedmont corporate paternalism and its attendant power relationships, they told the two men that they opposed unionism in the mill because they "did not think it was best for either employer or employee." There had always been a "personal touch" at Anchor Duck, they said; the union leaders were asked not to "set up a condition that would destroy this friendly feeling."[53]

If "this friendly feeling" ever existed, it soon evaporated. When, in the words of C. E. McLin, the two union officers "refused to listen to our suggestion," they were fired on the spot. The company discharged several more men in the next few days and posted a notice, which was later paraphrased in a confidential circular, stating that the mill would run as "an open mill or would not run at all, and we would discharge those who had joined the organization as fast as we found out who they were." Anchor Duck management had infiltrated the union with informants by the time Miles was able to return to town and responded positively to an offer to share information about Miles by the New York–based Fidelity Secret Service Bureau, an industrial espionage agency that had worked to discredit Miles and defeat the UTW during a Utica, New York, strike.[54]

It was only after some forty Anchor Duck workers had been fired, and management had refused all requests for a conference with labor representatives, that Miles called a strike on 20 March 1914 over the issue of union recognition. The UTW sponsored a march through town, with union members holding banners declaring "We are standing for our rights," held two mass meetings at the local court house, and solicited support from the Rome Central Labor Union and the GFL. Yet union efforts were to little avail, as the company quickly evicted strikers from mill-owned housing and recruited new workers, and the Rome strike petered out after a couple of months.[55]

In April, the main UTW action shifted to Atlanta, where Fulton management had continued to intimidate and fire Local 886 members and leaders, in turn fueling worker resentment. In February, "the discharge of members" had become such a sore point among Fulton workers that Miles twice had to go to union meetings and stave off what he called "threatened trouble," or worker-initiated walkouts over the matter.[56] In March, Gordon Johnstone reminded paymaster T. S. Florence to have company doctor Hawkins prepare from his "investigations of lay out's" a list of the hands currently boarding at the homes of Mullinax and union sympathizer Harris Gober. Mullinax later related that his boarders "were given orders to move their boarding place or give up their job"; when they decided to move, he complained, it "busted up my boarding house."[57]

On 25 March, Cleo Breedlove, a bag mill worker who had been labeled in the fall by Johnstone as an activist, wrote mill treasurer August Denk about why she had recently quit work. She had been sick, she said, and when she returned, her supervisor wanted to fire her, "but I insisted upon working out my notice, so he let me." Breedlove had heard she was let go "because I belong to the union." She continued, "I'll admit that I join the union, but only went twice and I wasn't belonging to it when Mr. Baker made me quit." Declaring she was "just a poor working girl" who sought reemployment, she wrote, "I see my mistake in joining the union, for they haven't help me any at all, only helped me to lose my position." The letter eventually came to the attention of Oscar Elsas, who instructed Johnstone to see him about the matter. Breedlove did not return to work at Fulton Mills.[58]

Breedlove's letter reveals the personal ties that many Piedmont mill workers did feel toward their employers, or at least felt obliged to manifest. It shows their naïveté about the possible consequences of joining a union. It indicates the frequently and strongly held belief among mill hands that they had the right to freely attend union meetings without company reprisals. At the same time, it illustrates how many textile workers who not only insisted on their right to attend but often *did* attend union meetings seldom actually signed up as dues-paying members. Breedlove's letter suggests some of the inherent difficulties the labor movement faced in organizing hard-strapped, often desperate southern textile workers. And it shows both Fulton management's awareness of the UTW organizing drive and its concerted efforts to target and fire union members.

One indication of this anti-union crackdown is the fact that identified activists tended to leave Fulton Mills in bunches in the months after October. The first wave of departures occurred immediately after the October walkout. There were other periods, too, when activists left their employment at Fulton Mills en masse. For instance, Cleo Breedlove was not the only worker who concluded her employment the week ending 28 February; six other identified worker-leaders received their last pay envelopes that same week.

Another wave commenced right after the union stepped up its activities in Atlanta. On 20 April, six months to the day after the October walkout, the UTW called a special meeting of Local 886 and signed up a large number of workers.[59] Two days later, office staff member J. H. Baker wrote Johnstone that bag mill workers Fannie May Sisk and Lula Lewis had been identified as union members. By the end of the week, the two women were gone from the mill.[60] Over the next three weeks, eleven identified activists from the fall, including Local 886 treasurer George Christian, left the company's employment. By mid-May, fewer than a fourth of those workers identified by Johnstone as activists after the October walkout still remained at Fulton Mills.

The UTW tried to retaliate and also extended its Atlanta efforts beyond Fulton Mills. Around 1 May, the union issued handbills announcing a meeting of the "Loomfixers, Weavers, Spinners, Carders and other Operatives" of the Exposition Mill. "The time is at hand," the flyers proclaimed, "when the Cotton Mill Operatives must organize, and secure for themselves and families a larger share in the prosperity and progress of the Age." "Ladies" were "Specially Invited to Attend" this meeting, which would be presided over by Miles and Georgia Federation of Labor president Shuford B. Marks.[61]

Marks had been in contact with Fulton workers since the October walkout, after ascertaining they were not connected with the IWW. The upsurge in organization among Georgia mill hands meshed well with his own political orientation. In October 1913, the *Party Builder*, an organ of the Socialist Party, reported that Marks, along with Atlanta Federation of Trades secretary Louie P. Marquardt, had joined the party. In February 1914, Marks had spoken in favor of industrial unionism at an AFT-sponsored conference on "the New Industrialism," declaring, "We have paid too little attention to the unskilled man."[62] His personal involvement in the UTW organizing effort, along with the endorsements of Marquardt and *Journal of Labor* editor Jerome Jones, helped

WORKERS
ATTENTION

A Special Meeting of the Loom-fixers, Weavers, Spinners, Carders and other Operatives of the EXPOSITION MILL will be held

—— IN ——

Chastain's Hall

10th St. and Hemphill Ave., this
FRIDAY EVENING, 8 P. M.

GET TOGETHER!   UNITE!
ORGANIZE!

The time is at hand when the Cotton Mill Operatives must organize, and secure for themselves and families a larger share in the prosperity and progress of the Age.

Speakers, CHAS. A. MILES, Gen. Organizer, and other Prominent Labor Men of Fall River, Mass.

Ladies Specially Invited to Attend

J. A. LaHatte Printing House, ⬗ 10 1-2 South Broad Street

A handbill announcing a UTW union meeting, c. 1 May 1914. Georgia Institute of Technology Library and Information Center.

to legitimize and later provide crucial support among Atlanta trade unionists for Local 886.

Workers from both Exposition and Fulton Mills attended the meeting, along with members of the Brotherhood of Railroad Trainmen, additional representatives of the AFT, and at least one infiltrator, a former Exposition Mill worker whose siblings worked at Fulton. The informant reported to Exposition president Allen F. Johnson, who in turn got in touch with Elsas.[63] The possibility of a strike at Fulton Mills dominated the meeting. Fulton workers asked what sort of support they would receive from organized labor should they go out on strike, prompting one of the railroad unionists present to predict the "non-switching" of railroad cars to the mill in such an eventuality.[64]

As rumors of a strike abounded, the UTW invited only Fulton workers to another meeting on 5 May at the Odd Fellows Hall on Decatur Street, a half mile from the plant. "Get together and unite," union handbills declared. "The time is at hand when the Cotton Mill Operatives must co-operate with each other." The leaflets announced that Miles, Marks, and others were to speak, and—in recognition of the likelihood of a strike, the pinched circumstances of southern mill hands, and the UTW's insistence on dues-paying membership—that the meeting would provide the last chance to enroll in the union at the special reduced initiation fee of sixty cents. At the meeting, workers voted to strike, only to be dissuaded by Miles, who said he needed to meet first with other union officials.[65]

Correctly anticipating that the charge of discrimination would be at the core of whatever collective action Fulton workers might take, the next day management issued a notice, which was posted and publicly read throughout the plant, stating, "This Co. has always been willing to investigate any grievances brought to their attention by *any* employee regarding his or her employment. Rumors or statements indicating any other method of dealing with employees are false, and only made to mislead you. Our motto is: 'JUSTICE TO ALL.' "[66]

In addition, Elsas instructed paymaster Florence to hold onto the lists compiled by the mill's office staff that named those workers who had left the company since the October walkout, the dates they left and were hired, and additional employment information.[67] In subsequent weeks and months, Elsas would periodically draw upon this data to buttress his patently false claims, made both publicly and in private, that the company had *not* discriminated against union members. He maintained that all Fulton workers were hired without regard to union membership. He asserted that during the seven months after the October walkout, "we did not know, and made no effort to know, whether our help was organized or interested in the question of unions."

He said that of the 400 workers discharged during this period, only seventy-five belonged to the union, and, he claimed, workers were not fired merely because they were union members.[68]

In a letter to the *Southern Textile Bulletin*, reprinted as a confidential circular, Elsas revealed his truer feelings concerning union recognition. "We believe," he wrote, "the only method to be pursued is to arbitrarily and absolutely refuse to recognize them [unions]; fight them to a finish, irrespective of cost."[69] Fulton workers also knew better. Throughout the beginning of May, a committee of workers tried to bring up the issue of union-related dismissals with company officials, who "absolutely refused" to meet with them.[70]

By mid-May the situation had reached, in Horace Carson's words, "the boiling point."[71] As in Rome, Miles and other trade union leaders now felt compelled to directly intervene and address the matter, or else risk losing the larger organizing battle before it had hardly been joined. On 15 May, Miles left town to confer with union officials about assistance if a strike broke out, while GFL president Marks advised against calling a strike vote until Miles returned.[72]

On 19 May, Marks sent Oscar Elsas a letter detailing union claims and grievances. Marks asserted that since Fulton workers had begun to organize, eighty-five people who had joined the union had been dismissed. Furthermore, he claimed, with exaggeration, that "not in a single instance have any [of] those not members been discharged." Given that there had been no demands made during this time to improve working conditions, Marks continued, it appeared that those people who had been let go had been dismissed strictly for their union membership. In fact, in several cases Fulton overseers had "unhesitatingly informed parties discharged that it was because they were members of the union." Especially since those dismissed were still unemployed, and since Fulton Mills reportedly could now use additional employees, Marks sought the reinstatement of all the workers recently fired by the company.[73]

Marks's letter was delivered in time for the end of the weekly meeting of the mill's officers. What then transpired was disputed. Oscar Elsas claimed that he was unaware of the letter's existence until after the meeting had adjourned. Furthermore, he did not consider it then because he had to sign his mail and give corrections to the company stenographers before they left work. Trade union officials maintained that Elsas had rebuffed them, but they tried to stave off a strike by seeking another conference.[74]

Many Fulton workers saw the matter differently. In their eyes, once again management had refused to even consider the very basic issue of discrimination, thus transgressing strongly held principles of personal dignity and respect, as well as placing organizing attempts in jeopardy. It was the straw that broke the camel's back; as W. E. Fleming, who had succeeded Fred Flynn as local president, stated, "We could no longer tolerate it without a protest."[75]

At a meeting that night presided over by Marks, Fulton workers heatedly discussed the situation. During the meeting, a telegram from Charles Miles was read, which said, "to the effect," according to Marks, "that they [the UTW] could not guarantee the regular strike benefit to all of those affected, if a strike was called, but would give all the support morally and financially that they could give but they would not bind themselves to anything definite." Despite such cautionary words, after some debate members of Local 886 then cast a secret strike ballot, with approximately 350 in favor of striking and only three opposed.[76] The strike was on.

Around 9:00 on the morning of Wednesday, 20 May, workers from throughout Fulton Mills walked off their jobs over the issues of union recognition and nondiscrimination.[77] Company officials notified the police, and Captain Mayo and two other officers arrived on the scene. Rather than arrest people this time, however, the police simply informed the strikers that they could not congregate on the street. The crowd withdrew to Harris Gober's grocery store, then reconvened in a mass meeting at the union hall on Decatur Street.

Estimates of how many people actually took part varied widely depending on one's vantage point. Strike leaders maintained that as many as 500–600 of the mill's 1,300 workers went on strike that first day, while Oscar Elsas publicly asserted that only 78 people walked out. In addition, in an attempt to further minimize the impact of the strike, he claimed that most of those who walked out were women and children. Elsas asserted that he did not even know what the trouble was about, since none of the strikers had been to see him, but he felt certain it was the result of "outside agitation" that had started the previous October when Fowler had been discharged. In any event, he stated that the disturbance was "very slight" and publicly predicted most strikers would be back at work within a day or two.[78]

Elsas was correct when he said that only a relatively small percentage of all Fulton workers actually struck that first day. During the week ending 23 May, the total number of production workers employed in both cotton mills and the bag mill actually rose slightly from the previous week (945 up from 937), as did the production payroll. In fact, the female-dominated bag mill and the bleachery were only minimally affected throughout the strike.[79]

In contrast, the impact in the Fulton weave rooms was hardly "very slight." The total number of looms run in the plant dropped over 25 percent the first day of the strike, from 1,860 looms on 19 May to 1,365 on 20 May. By the next day, production had fallen to 1,134 looms. The situation was particularly acute in Mill No. 1, where the number of looms in operation dropped by over 50 percent in the strike's first two days (757 to 367 looms).[80]

Contrary to Elsas's forecast, the strike did not last only a day or so but rather continued in one form or another for practically a year. Yet in many ways, its contours and dimensions were established within its first few weeks. For all his public claims of the strike's negligible effect upon production, Elsas swiftly put into action a multifaceted anti-union campaign that revealed extensive planning and coordination. It also signified his recognition of the considerable and varied resources that striking Fulton workers had at their own disposal.

On the strike's first day, Local 886 president Fleming, a vociferous spokesperson for the strikers, told the press of the unprecedented financial support already mobilized or pledged by local trade unionists, the UTW, and the AFL, declaring that the strikers had "enough money to fight it out." A few days later, Fleming gave a preview of two other interrelated aspects of the strikers' effort, both of which evoked the Leo Frank case: an emphasis on the particular tribulations of women workers at Fulton Mills and the amassing of affidavits with an eye to public opinion. "Women past middle age who had worked in the mill since they were eleven were discharged for no other offense than joining the union," Fleming asserted. "Affidavits can be produced showing where overseers have heaped indignities upon and insulted women in their departments. We are prepared to present facts that will startle the people of Atlanta, and in a few days will do so unless the matter is adjusted."[81]

Despite Fleming's claims, up until this point the strike efforts had met with only partial success. But momentum began to build during the second week. On Monday morning, 25 May, Fleming and other workers gathered around a switching engine bringing boxcars of supplies into the Fulton yard. Several people in the crowd began to hurl rocks at the train. Fleming, another striker, and a former Fulton worker were arrested for rioting and were subsequently fined heavily, with their cases bound over to state court.[82] Strikers also started picketing outside the plant gates and other sites near the mill, as well as at the Terminal Station, where they met potential strikebreakers arriving by train. Many of the pickets were women, who made a special point of targeting the female workers still employed at Fulton Mills. In addition, the strikers visited the homes of people who had remained at work, trying to convince them to join the strike.[83]

At the same time that Fulton workers themselves initiated and carried out such activities, local and national labor leaders contributed their own complementary abilities to the cause. As early as 21 May, O. Delight Smith, one of the city's most prominent and capable trade unionists, began to document poor working and living conditions at Fulton Mills.[84] On 26 May, UTW organizer Charles Miles returned to Atlanta to coordinate strike efforts along with Smith.[85]

Smith and Miles quickly moved on a variety of fronts. They placed an ad in the *Atlanta Journal* warning workers to stay away from Atlanta and presided over the increasingly well attended daily strike meetings at the Odd Fellows Hall on Decatur Street. Along with Fleming, they made a successful appeal for funds from the Federation of Trades, obtaining a pledge of fifteen cents a week in strike support from each local trade unionist. While Smith supervised relief efforts, Miles met with people at City Hall, approached leaders of the Men and Religion Forward Movement (MRFM), and solicited donations from the AFL. By the end of the week, support had come as well from Atlanta streetcar conductors, electricians, wagon drivers at the city stockade, and union musicians.[86] These combined efforts began to pay off. While the bag mill remained more or less unaffected, for the week ending 30 May, the number of production workers in the two Fulton cotton mills dropped nearly 20 percent from what it had been the week before the strike (624 from 757). The number of looms operating was barely two-thirds of the prestrike figure (1,293 from 1,860), with Mill No. 1 especially hard hit. (See Chapter 5, figures 1 and 2.)[87]

Responding to this stepped-up union activity, on Friday, 29 May, Oscar Elsas gave or had delivered what he called an "appreciation" speech to the employees still working at the mill. The speech revealed and anticipated many of management's anti-union themes and statements and drew upon a venerable regional tradition labeling any disorder as the work of outside agitators. The ringleaders of the strike, Elsas claimed, were either "outsiders," bad characters, or individuals who had just commenced working at Fulton Mills. Many of the "troublemakers" did not even work at the plant. They were led by a "Yankee outsider" (a reference to Miles) who allegedly got a percentage of the union dues he raised. These dues, he asserted, would amount to forty cents a week, or fully twenty-one dollars per year, a significant cut out of a mill hand's wages. Furthermore, union representatives had promised workers money, had made other promises, and had "*not kept a d— one.*" The strike was, in Elsas's opinion, "poor business"; the union preferred to shut down the plant rather than care for the workers. Finally, he gave the employees advice in how to comport themselves over the weekend.[88]

Management was only partially successful in turning workers away from the union. On Sunday, 31 May, the UTW sponsored a mass meeting at White City, a popular working-class amusement park south of the mill district. In a tribute to the organizing ability and efforts of both the strikers and strike leaders, as many as a thousand workers and their families attended the gathering, along with "a number of prominent citizens." The *Constitution* commented on "the pentup natures" of those assembled, reporting that "men, women and children crowded eagerly" to hear the speakers.[89] Miles, Smith, and S. B. Marks addressed the crowd, pointing out both the perceived abuses at Fulton Mills and the resources of the union. In particular, they described the high walls surrounding the mill, with broken glass scattered on the top, and the company's fining system. One speaker claimed that a company official stated that it was the fining system that had built Fulton Mills "from a small shop to one of the greatest of cotton mills."

Directly addressing the concerns of workers afraid of losing their jobs and anxious to be provided for, and trying to bolster the UTW's credibility, the speakers announced that a union commissary was opening that afternoon in the mill district, with "everything the strikers need . . . free of charge." With the establishment of the commissary, union leaders anticipated that the number of strikers would increase significantly. The union had also rented transfer wagons and its own boardinghouses for workers who might be evicted from company housing.

In addition, Miles declared, in a reference to the ties being cultivated with the MRFM and the Evangelical Ministers Association, the "largest churches in Atlanta" had tendered support for the strikers. He also said that 5,000 local trade unionists and an estimated two million nationwide were prepared to back the strike financially. Miles avowed that the UTW was ready to camp in Atlanta "until Gabriel blows his trumpet." The Fulton strike, he announced, would ultimately affect "every mill in Atlanta, the state and the southeast."[90]

Fulton workers were not the only ones who paid close heed to Miles's remarks. The following day, Oscar Elsas arranged a meeting with his counterparts at the five other Atlanta-area mills. "It is a matter of great importance to the Cotton Mill interests," he wrote to them.[91] After this meeting, Elsas sent a letter to all Georgia cotton manufacturers. In a direct reference to Miles's speech, Elsas wrote, "Miles has stated that if he succeeds in organizing Fulton Bag and Cotton Mills, he intends to organize each and every mill in Georgia." Accordingly, Elsas appealed for assistance from his fellow manufacturers, more specifically asking for the loan of "30–40 weavers accustomed to Draper looms running on plain sheeting," which would enable the mill to resume full production. He wrote, "Your interest, as well as the interest of every Mill in Georgia, is such that you could well afford to send us a couple or more of competent weavers who could be depended on to be faithful and not join the strikers—even though this might shut down a couple of sets of looms for you."

Lest his request be interpreted as a self-interested attempt to resume full production, Elsas claimed that "[w]e are not asking this for our own benefit, but for the benefit of all the mills in Georgia." Furthermore, in an appeal to sectional pride and identity as well as employer solidarity, he predicted that "[i]f we succeed in whipping out this fight, we have reasonable assurance that Mr. Miles will go back North where he came from, and let Georgia and the South alone. If we do not whip it now, your time will come sooner or later. We shall, therefore, have to band together for our mutual protection."[92]

Elsas's subsequent correspondence with his fellow manufacturers accentuated his often prickly relationship with them. While a few mill men responded positively to his request, most declined, usually stating that they had few or no workers on hand familiar with Draper looms. Elsas seemed skeptical of such claims. He did not accept at face value the replies from other manufacturers but rather challenged them. "Surely you have some weavers who have had some experience on Draper looms," he replied to various owners who had originally denied his request, and he expressed his disappointment at others who did not respond. He assumed that any mills that had not yet come to Fulton's assistance "undoubtedly consider our request for help a selfish one" and warned that "if they do not help us, it will be their turn next."[93]

Elsas did more than appeal for recruits from his fellow manufacturers to help break the union. Building upon what he had developed since the October walkout, he also set into motion a massive surveillance operation with inside informants and outside agents. One barometer of this effort was the increase in the company's "store and watchmen" department, or private security force. During the week before the strike, management paid thirteen people in this department a total of $122.95. By the week ending 6 June, both the number of people employed and the department payroll had doubled (27 people receiving $244.10) to a level that would continue through August.[94]

Heading the department was James I. Brush, a former member of the Atlanta Federation of Musicians.[95] Brush was at the center of an extensive network of Fulton employees who provided written information about the strike to Elsas, Johnstone, and other company officials. The informants included members of the mill's regular security force, additional security personnel hired during the strike, section hands and supervisors, the store room attendant, company doctor Hawkins, office staff, and other workers scattered throughout the plant, numbering at least forty-two people during the course of the strike.[96] They sent literally hundreds of reports and affidavits to management; between the strike's outset and 6 June, no fewer than twelve company informants wrote at least fifty-four dispatches. Reflecting Elsas's militarylike perception of the whole affair, these reports, handwritten on often little more than scraps of paper, were filed under the heading "Our Forces."

Since Brush personally carried out and epitomized many of management's anti-union initiatives, a detailed look at his activities during the strike's first few weeks sheds light on both the tone and scope of these strategies and tactics, as well as those of the strikers and their allies. Well before the 20 May walkout, Brush had already been centrally involved in the company's internal surveillance of incipient union activity.[97] As soon as the strike broke out, and suggesting some prior planning on the part of management, he made use of his license as a notary public to gather the company's own affidavits from Fulton workers and others, a practice he would continue for months.

The depositions Brush collected fell into several categories. Many individuals testified about the strikers' threats, taunts, and general carrying-on. For instance, Sarah Nix told Brush that striker Will Norris had stopped her fifteen-year-old daughter after lunch on the strike's first day, threatened retaliation if she went back into the mill, and forced her to attend the afternoon union meeting against her wishes. Others told of vile language employed by the strikers ("I could not tell all the words they said," declared one woman) and of being annoyed by strikers and their supporters "congregating, shouting and singing until late every night."[98] In addition to chronicling the strikers' harassment of other workers, these depositions also buttressed management's case for improved police protection.

On 22 May, Brush gathered two affidavits from worker Lonnie Middlebrooks. Middlebrooks testified that he was approached by striker Si Prater, who declared that if Middlebrooks stayed in the mill, he "was not as good as the damned Jews." Middlebrooks also said he had overheard a city police officer, himself a former Fulton worker, say that he had been posted near the mill "to keep these damned Jews from getting killed."[99] While the similarity of Middlebrooks's language in the two affidavits leaves some question as to their authenticity, worker anti-Semitism at the time of the Frank case may have been a particular facet of the strike that Brush sought to document.

Middlebrooks's testimony was hardly the only critical remark made to Brush about the Atlanta police. Especially after it became apparent that the strike was not going to end soon, Elsas increasingly perceived police indifference toward the strikers' threats and intimidation, and even what he considered their collusion with the strikers, as a major part of his problems. As part of management's concerted effort to draw attention to police behavior, Brush gathered several affidavits describing officers consorting and making jokes with strikers, being lax on the job, and harassing members of the mill's private security force.[100]

Through the affidavits he gathered, Brush targeted individuals considered to be particularly troublesome by management. For instance, worker Lillie Priest testified to Brush that physician W. V. Garrett had asked her to draw two other employees off the job. Garrett had attended to strikers' families and authored articles documenting cases of pellagra and condemning poor sanitary conditions in the Fulton district. Similarly, on another occasion, Brush and company doctor E. W. Hawkins provided affidavits about the prostitution at the Empire Hotel, an establishment that apparently had connections to strikers or their allies.[101]

Brush did much more than collect affidavits during the strike's first weeks. He also supervised the escorting of nonstrikers to work and commanded the operations of other members of the company's security force.[102] He monitored striker and potential striker activity in the mill district, on the picket line, in court, and on the shop floor, and he regularly wrote detailed memos to management describing various facets of the strike effort. Between 23 May and 5 June, Brush wrote a total of twenty such reports.

On 28 May, Brush began filing reports detailing the strikers' picket activities near the mill, making sure to identify the various pickets involved. In these dispatches, he singled out the activities of women pickets, who transgressed his idea of proper female behavior. Brush wrote that striker Eva Daniel "has been vicious in her statements and she and the Lewis girls most active in stopping people." He described as a "very annoying pair" the "female pickets Josie Sisk and Dora Davis who either stopped or walked with every woman or girl who passed them."[103]

Brush was especially busy on 2 June, filing five memos in all. He portrayed strikers Margaret Dempsey and Alice Carlton as "very active and offensive pickets," stating that Dempsey had grabbed a bag mill worker around the waist and did not let loose until the woman agreed to join the union. He related that two other strikers were beginning a house-to-house canvass of the mill district to convince people to stay out. From Bernard Kane, another member of the mill's security force, he learned of the efforts of Miles, Fleming, and Mullinax to secure support from local grocers for the union commissary. Kane also reported to Brush that a neighbor of Gober had stated that it would "take powder and lead to stop this mill."[104]

Brush's lengthiest memo that day detailed his conversation with mill district resident Emily Addison, who gave Brush the names of four people who had drawn rations from the union commissary. She told him that strike sympathizer Andrew Clark, a neighborhood painter, was picketing "all available new help." Clark and another man had been assigned to trail company doctor Hawkins to spot any potential new workers the doctor might recruit. Their message to these would-be workers was threefold: that the strike was on, with nearly everybody in the mill out; that the union was providing commissary and board free; and that the trouble at Fulton was only the beginning of the trouble to come throughout the southern textile industry. Clark also asserted that three members of the mill's office staff, including one person "mighty close" to Elsas and Johnstone, had joined the union.[105]

Finally, Clark told Addison about an incipient attempt to organize the black workers at Fulton Mills. Leading this effort was M. C. Parker from Rome, Georgia, an organizer with the Hod Carriers Union. As with many unsung southerners of the period, little is known about him. Parker had been a leader in Georgia's black community since at least 1897, when he was one of the featured speakers at a July 4th rally at Atlanta's Lincoln Park and was introduced to the crowd as "the Eagle Rock of the Mountains." By 1899 Parker had become one of Georgia's few black attorneys, and he later obtained a position in the Post Office. By the fall of 1913, he had shifted his energies to the labor movement, organizing a local of the Hod Carriers at Stone Mountain.[106]

The circumstances of the strike opened the door, if only a crack, for a black man to speak at the otherwise all-white union meeting and to organize black workers. Tellingly, however, the UTW decided not to issue commissary rations to African Americans. Parker's efforts alarmed Elsas, who quickly took steps to counter them. He had a black informant, John Craig, an overseer in the bleachery department, monitor Parker's activities and file reports back to "Mr. Oscar." Elsas also investigated Parker's background. Upon discovering that Parker had once been convicted for embezzlement, he repeatedly sought to get him disbarred. In addition, Elsas wrote about Parker to former governor Joseph M. Brown, a rabid opponent of organized labor, especially among black workers. Parker continued his efforts well into July but apparently to little effect.[107]

For the most part, the reports of other company informants paralleled the information provided by Brush: they documented threats and intimidation; identified and described the activities of strikers, strike leaders, and supporters; chronicled police indifference; and the like. But a couple of reports and affidavits during the strike's early weeks reveal additional facets of the strike and of management's response. For example, Dr. Hawkins relayed a complaint that spinner Augusta Mullinax (no relation to H. N. Mullinax) had been conducting an "assignation house," or house of prostitution, out of her company home. After checking out the story, Hawkins reported back to paymaster Florence, who instructed Hawkins to notify Mullinax to vacate immediately. In addition, he reported, striker Annie Green was arrested at Mullinax's house on a charge of immoral conduct.[108]

This was one of the first times, but by no means the last, that management attempted to link strikers and strike leaders to morally questionable or illegal practices. Mullinax was hardly an arbitrary target, either; she was the mother of Milton Nunnally, a boy whose photograph the union sent across the country as a compelling symbol of child labor in the southern mills.[109] (For more on the use of photographs during the strike, see Chapter 6.) By thus associating strikers and their leaders with morally questionable practices, at a time of great anxiety about the erosion of traditional values in an urban milieu, management sought to denigrate, discredit, deflect, and ultimately derail the strike efforts.

On 3 June, a company informant reported that strikers and their supporters were changing the lyrics of traditional and popular songs to advance the union cause. This use of music went well beyond the live accordion, banjo, and fiddle tunes, phonograph music, religious songs, and dancing that comprised an integral aspect of the daily union meetings.[110] For instance, to the tune of "Battle Hymn of the Republic," the strikers sang, "We'll hang old Johnstone to some apple tree," also substituting the name of "Jake Elsas." To the tune of "How Dry I Am," one newly invented verse went:

I'll pawn my hat
I'll pawn my shoes
Before I'll work for a crowd of Jews

with an alternative version substituting for the last line:

Before I'll drink old Elsas' soup.

Their opponents were quick to reply, singing back to the same tune a refrain about the recently established UTW commissary:

I'd pawn my ring
I'll pawn my shoes
Before I'd go to the Union Store,

as well as an apparent reference to Miles or one of the other union organizers:

How dry I am
How dry I am
I've never been led by a wall-eyed man.[111]

The topical singing grew to such proportions that it drew the attention of company secretary-treasurer Louis J. Elsas, Oscar's brother. In a memo to Gordon Johnstone, Louis Elsas remarked on the popularity of the pro-union verses in the mill district, observing that "[e]ven the friendly [to management] children are singing." Declaring that "[t]hey might as well be singing something to create friendly sentiment," he tried his own hand at song writing, proposing additional lyrics to "How Dry I Am" that referred to the hangers-on that the strike and the commissary attracted, and the relative respectability of those still at work:

So get a job
You stranger bums
Lord only knows from where you come

and:

We want to work
And draw our pay
And spend it right next Saturday.

He urged Johnstone to "please take up" the matter of the songs with Oscar Elsas.[112]

It is unclear whether either Oscar Elsas or Johnstone ever adopted Louis Elsas's suggestion, although two spinners and a bag mill worker did come up with additional anti-union verses to the tune of "Yankee Doodle" as well as "How Dry I Am."[113] It is also difficult to ascertain what impact the songs had during the strike. What the songs do illustrate, however, is that almost at the outset of the matter, all parties involved recognized at some level that the contestation, manipulation, and appropriation of a diversity of cultural forms and symbols would be central to how the strike developed.

As extensive as the company's network of internal informants was, Oscar Elsas drew upon yet another resource to monitor the strikers' activities—labor spies. Aware of the tinderbox atmosphere at Fulton Mills through his company's existing forays into Georgia, on 13 May, H. N. Brown, the vice president and general manager of the Philadelphia-based Railway Audit and Inspection Company, one of the nation's largest labor espionage outfits, wrote Elsas promoting and detailing the work of his firm. It was not the first time that Brown had contacted Elsas; he had made another overture in October during the earlier disturbance at the plant.[114]

In subsequent correspondence, Brown arranged a meeting between Elsas and Railway Audit district manager E. G. Myers, indicated that he had two agents available who were experienced weavers, and provided references in Augusta and West Point, Georgia, as well as in Atlanta.[115] Driving a hard bargain, Elsas at first refused the offer, complaining to Brown about the cost and stating that Fulton had had an "unsatisfactory experience" with two other espionage agencies in the past. Even as he said this, he and Exposition Mill president Allen Johnson were apparently already employing a spy, almost certainly a Pinkerton agent, who was identified only as "#40," to, among other activities, investigate O. Delight Smith's background.[116] Nevertheless, after checking Railway Audit's references, and in light of the fact that the strike had already broken out, in late May Elsas signed on with the espionage firm.[117]

The first four Railway Audit agents, known as "operatives," arrived in Atlanta over the weekend of 30–31 May, each ready to perform his particular specialty. One of these men was J. W. Williams, who obtained a room at the Terminal Hotel next to that of Charles Miles and began tailing Miles as he went about his business. Williams shared his hotel room with A. E. Winyard, who was an authority in the electronic surveillance of the day, or, as Oscar Elsas put it, an "expert wireman." Reflecting Railway Audit's already considerable reach into southern textiles, this first group of operatives also included the firm's two "experienced weavers": Henry J. Day, an Englishman from Whitmire, South Carolina, who went by the name of George Thompson; and Harry A. Hughes, an Irishman from Burlington, North Carolina. At the end of each lengthy working day, all of the operatives wrote detailed, typewritten reports that went to Elsas.[118]

Hughes and Day quickly found lodging in the mill district, began fraternizing with workers, pretended to look for work at Fulton Mills, where they were turned away by pickets, and then signed up with the union, soon taking an active role in its affairs. Hughes was particularly energetic in this regard. By 5 June he had kept attendance at one union meeting and at a UTW-sponsored parade, had been made an assistant to O. Delight Smith in looking after the possessions of those evicted from company housing, had gone along with Smith to ask a worker to join the union, had worked as one of Smith's bodyguards, and had been named secretary to the committee calling on people still working at the mill.[119]

The daily reports that Hughes and Day filed clearly showed that the strike was gaining steam in its third week. The spies reported that nearly 100 workers joined the union between 2 and 5 June and that attendance at the packed daily union meetings hovered between 250 and 300 people. Day wrote on 4 June, "I could not find one single man who was willing to give up the fight, and the ladies seem to think in about 3 weeks they will have the Mill owners come to them for the people to go back to work on their own terms."[120]

That same day, 4 June, also marked the pivotal moment of the strike's first weeks, when the entire tenor of the dispute was transformed. O. Delight Smith aptly called it "the day of days, and one that would be well remembered."[121] On that morning, Marshal O. E. Puckett arrived in the mill district along with his assistants, some of whom were mounted on horseback, several black laborers, and company security personnel. They began evicting strikers and union members living in company housing, entering the homes and putting both workers and their belongings out on the street. In so doing, mill management followed the March example of Rome's Anchor Duck Mill, where evictions of strikers from company housing had appreciably helped to break the union organizing effort.

The evictions, along with another wave on 8 June and smaller scale evictions later in the summer, undoubtedly dealt the UTW a major blow. By 13 June fifty-five strikers and union members, not counting their family members, had been evicted. A federal investigator later estimated that 218 men, women, and children in all were ousted from their houses (contradicting Oscar Elsas's claim that only seventy-eight people went out on strike).[122] The evictions dislocated workers, diverted organizing efforts, and added considerably to the strike's financial burden. As one informant reported, Charles Miles was "very much shot up and had a bad case of blues" over them.[123]

Yet union organizers recognized that the evictions also provided a ready-made opportunity for compelling visual documentation, a potential public relations bonanza in a contest for public opinion that spread far beyond Atlanta's boundaries. Smith in particular understood how photographs and movies of the evictions could advance the union's cause. Furthermore, rather than squashing pro-union sentiment, the manner in which mill management handled the evictions rubbed many workers the wrong way, including people who up until then had been loyal to the company, and actually boosted the number of strikers.[124]

Certainly the strike continued to grow. During the week of 8 June, the number of production workers in the two cotton mills dropped to three-fourths what it had been before the strike (580 from 757). The decline was particularly marked in the spinning room of Mill No. 1, which fell from 199 to 135 workers. In addition, the number of looms in operation remained at roughly 70 percent of the prestrike level for the first two weeks of June, then dropped to 62 percent for the week of 15 June. Mill No. 1 continued to be the most severely affected.[125]

In addition to worker resentment over the evictions, the ability of union organizers to attract a broad base of support for the commissary and other strike activities was crucial to the strike's building momentum during its third week. The Atlanta trade union movement accounted for much of this aid, with local typographers, coat makers, carpenters, bricklayers, painters, and machinists, as well as the Atlanta Labor Temple Association, the Federation of Trades, and members of various ladies auxiliaries all making donations. Support came from a wide range of other sources in the Atlanta community as well, including the owner of a woodyard, a man who hauled a load of furniture to a union-sponsored hotel for evicted workers, the "Women's League of Atlanta," grocery stores, a Decatur Street pool hall, the local Socialist Party, and even farmers who distributed potatoes and other food to strikers. Finally, the UTW and the AFL, along with individual trade unions outside of Atlanta, made major contributions. In all, the strikers received approximately a thousand dollars in support during the week, a level that remained constant well into the summer.[126]

A number of these supporters, including representatives from the painters union and the Brotherhood of Locomotive Engineers, other trade unionists, and out-of-town organizers such as Max Wilk, secretary of the Socialist Party in Georgia, also spoke at the daily union meetings.[127] One particularly prominent strike supporter was G. W. Lindsay, a former Fulton worker and now a freight brakeman for the Southern Railroad and a member of the Brotherhood of Railroad Trainmen. Lindsay, who had taken part in the organizing at both Fulton and Exposition Mills and now helped Miles secure groceries for the commissary, appeared on behalf of the strikers before local Socialists, suffragists, and other groups and made numerous speeches at the union meetings. On one occasion, he boasted of having won strikes at other places; on another, he vowed he would give up his job and sell his property, if necessary, for the good of the strike; on a third, he fanned class and perhaps anti-Semitic antagonisms when he made a long speech about the "$10,000,000 plant earning $6 million profit a year to be used to purchase a Lord or European Baron for some of the daughters" of the Elsas family.[128]

Such activities soon caught the attention of Oscar Elsas, who, characteristically, went after Lindsay with a vengeance. By 5 June, at Elsas's behest, Lindsay had already been called before his superintendent over his strike support. On 8 June Elsas had a phone conversation about Lindsay with H. W. Miller, assistant to the president of the Southern Railroad. A railroad official then spoke to Lindsay, who purportedly promised to quit his strike support activity. Yet that same day, Lindsay defiantly addressed the daily strike meeting as well as a Socialist gathering, prompting Elsas to write Miller the next day that Lindsay's "method of exciting our help by his talks is becoming very obnoxious and, in our opinion, dangerous. Won't you haul him over the coals again, and kindly consider this matter confidential."[129]

Strike leaders Smith and Miles were key in shaping and building the strike during its third week. They spent considerable time procuring tangible goods and services for the strikers: soliciting strike support, buying groceries for the commissary, renting a large building to hold evicted workers, and so forth. Such actions not only provided much-needed supplies for the strikers; they also served to bolster the credibility of Smith and Miles and, by extension, the UTW. On 8 June, Miles stopped a weaver outside the plant and told him, "You need sunshine and fresh air." Promising "a good home and three good meals a day," he asserted that the union had "plenty of money and will give you a good vacation." For at least some workers accustomed to onerous working conditions, job uncertainty, and a paternalistic milieu, such promises of protection—and their fulfillment—helped them choose to join the strike, as much as any particular grievance, previous union exposure, or commitment to unionism.[130]

Aware of this appeal, Miles and especially Smith played up their own roles as benefactors to the Fulton strikers, using a language that in many ways evoked mill owner paternalism. Smith announced at the 3 June union meeting, "We can and will take care of you." On another occasion, she referred to a group of about a hundred workers at the union commissary as "a few of my family." Furthermore, she underscored the reciprocal aspect of this relationship in an attempt to exhort workers and advance strike efforts. "I have been working for you night and day for ten days," she proclaimed at one meeting, "and I want to know how many of you will do something for me."[131]

On numerous occasions, too, Smith and Miles issued warnings and admonishments to the strikers that resembled parental reprimands against disorderliness. Strikers were told to clean up their rooms for the Board of Health inspectors who would be visiting and to be as neat and careful in the union hall as they would be in their own homes. They were not to congregate in bunches on the street, as it "doesn't look good," nor do anything "unladylike" or "ungentlemanly." At the 6 June meeting, Smith announced that any worker who brought a whiskey bottle to the meeting would be fined fifty cents.[132]

Yet it would be a mistake to say that Smith and Miles replicated the paternalism of Elsas and his counterparts. While they clearly were in command of the strike, they did encourage the involvement of workers at a more thorough and egalitarian level than mill owners ever did. Unlike Elsas, they did not blame workers for their own condition or engage in psychological theorizing about the mill population. And, of course, the organizers were involved in an enterprise that in many ways fundamentally challenged rather than perpetuated existing power relationships in southern textiles.

In addition, their warnings and desire to maintain control were informed by a setting that was riddled with labor spies and other informants, a situation of which Smith, Miles, and other strike leaders were well aware. As early as 2 June, Miles reported that "two sneaking detectives" had taken the hotel room next to his own, a reference to spies Williams and Winyard. At the meeting the next day, Smith told of people snooping around her house and cautioned the strikers not to reveal the goings-on inside the union hall to anyone on the street. On 4 June, Miles warned, "Be very careful what you say and who you say it to; do not tell anyone on the street what happens in this hall." At the

A crowd outside the union commissary. O. Delight Smith and Charles Miles are at front, center. Special Collections Dept., Pullen Library, Georgia State University.

5 June meeting, he counseled, "Remember they are watching you. I know that there is some gentleman in this room with his book," and another speaker related that there was "agitation" in the police department over the presence of the labor spies.[133]

Smith and Miles themselves were at the heart of management's surveillance attempts. On 9 June, Elsas sent instructions to have H. A. Hughes get Smith's address "and try to — her." Since Hughes had to suddenly leave town shortly afterward, he was not able to carry out the assignment.[134] Elsas was not deterred. He wrote C. E. McLin of the Anchor Duck Mills, inquiring into Miles's personal behavior while the organizer had been in Rome, explicitly seeking information that would show Miles not to be a "very religious man," as he had presented himself before the MRFM. "Anything you can say," Elsas wrote, "will help us in our scheme of fighting him."[135]

With his response, McLin attached a letter he had received in April from the New York–based Fidelity Secret Service Bureau, a private detective agency. The Fidelity representative claimed to have dealt with Miles during a strike in Utica, New York, and to have placed Miles in such a position that he had to leave town. More specifically, he asserted that Miles had been bought off by the Utica Employers Association and that there was documentation available should McLin want it. Upon receipt of McLin's letter, Elsas wrote Exposition

Mill's Allen Johnson, suggesting that he and Johnson go in together to obtain this information and to "run Miles out of town." He also asked Johnson to follow up a lead that a superintendent in the Martell Mills, located outside Atlanta, knew about Miles's Utica experience, and he tried unsuccessfully himself to gather this information.[136] In addition, he communicated about Miles with the district superintendent for another New York–based detective agency, the International Auxiliary Company.[137]

Day and Hughes were not the only Railway Audit spies to monitor and report back on the daily union meetings at the Odd Fellows hall. On 1 June, operatives Williams and Winyard met with Elsas, who had obtained a key to the meeting room. The two spies then rented rooms across Decatur Street from the hall, purchased wire and other supplies, then, pretending to be electric repairmen, installed in the hall a Detecto dictograph surveillance device, which was apparently a cross between telephone and primitive radio technology. Despite occasional glitches, they were able to listen in on the union meetings from their vantage point across the street and provide verbatim accounts of the proceedings.[138]

On 9 June, however, the surveillance ended. That day, someone at the union meeting heard a whining noise, looked up, and discovered the dictograph. Williams and Winyard quickly left their hideout, checked out of their hotel, and took a train to Cartersville, after feeling that their original destination of Marietta was still too close for comfort. Winyard departed for good, although Williams did go back to Atlanta and spy for a while longer. The incident caused a sensation in the Fulton district; in its aftermath, spy Henry Day also found it prudent to return to Philadelphia. Railway Audit sent Oscar Elsas a bill for the rental of the Detecto and continued to send spies to Atlanta.[139]

Smith declared at the meeting the next day that "the Jews were sweating blood, and are worried, or [they] would not have put in [the] dictograph." It was hardly the only time that Smith and Miles appealed to workers' anti-Semitism to advance the union's cause. At another meeting, Miles pronounced, "These Jews are worried." He also explicitly linked the strike to the Frank case, as Hughes, paraphrasing Miles's speech, reported: "[H]e [Miles] did not expect anything from a Jew. That Jew of the National Pencil Company did not surprise him, and nothing the Fulton Bag and Cotton Mill Company will do would surprise him either." At the same meeting, Smith called upon workers to bring up their pay envelopes, "so I can show these Jews how we can show them up as liars," and made other anti-Semitic remarks. The following day, Miles declared, "Why, even some of the Jews around told me that the victory is ours."[140] When it suited their needs, Miles and Smith appealed to white supremacy as well.[141]

Other rhetorical devices that Smith and Miles employed to reach workers and keep up the strike's momentum had a more positive cast. Building upon a theme he had introduced at the 31 May rally, Miles in particular tried to raise the stakes for those involved by accurately declaring that the Fulton strike was of concern and significance to other people in Atlanta, across the region, and even throughout the nation. At one union meeting, he exclaimed, "We will have your pictures taken and we will send them broadcast from East to West in the United States, so that everybody will see them." He also stated that he had drawn up a document about the Fulton situation to be read in Congress and that he was a personal friend of U.S. secretary of labor William B. Wilson.[142] Such attention was rare for a southern mill hand and was designed to strengthen commitment to the strike; it also tended to enhance the perceived resources and dedication of the strike organizers. Mindful of his evolving relationship with the MRFM, Miles evoked religious metaphors and images in a similar vein, in effect providing biblical sanctions and comparisons for the strike.[143]

In addition, Smith and Miles documented company abuses in a manner resembling management's solicitation of antistriker affidavits. They gathered pay envelopes and other information to challenge company claims about wages, the fining system, and child labor. They also obtained their own depositions from Fulton workers, in particular women and children who were especially likely to evoke public sympathy. At the 2 June meeting, Smith called upon the women in attendance to provide her with testimony about sexual harassment, "for the purpose of showing the public how you have been treated in this mill in the past." Appealing to female solidarity, she said, "I want you to come and tell me what you cannot tell the men, for the Company will have affidavits too, and I want yours to fight them with, and I want it in black and white, or it won't be any good."[144] The weapons in Miles and Smith's documentary arsenal also extended beyond the spoken or written word to photographs and even movies.

All the tactics that Smith and Miles developed at this time were directed toward two complementary strategic objectives: to galvanize, mobilize, and sustain striking workers so as to significantly affect production at Fulton Mills for a prolonged period of time; and to bring outside pressure to bear upon the situation. They were not alone in their activity. Though often shut out from the UTW's decision-making process, and frequently misrepresented in the public discourse surrounding the strike, Fulton workers drew upon their own distinct resources to influence the strike as it unfolded.

CHAPTER 5

We Thought We Knew Our Help

In the spring of 1914, precisely at the time of the Fulton strike, Norman Elsas, Oscar Elsas's son, graduated from Phillips Andover Academy, then worked at the plant before going off to Cornell that fall to study in one of the country's pioneering electrical engineering programs. Later, he would himself head up Fulton Mills, sell the company in the 1950s, and pursue a subsequent career as an inventor and businessman well into his nineties.

During several interviews conducted between 1988 and 1991, Norman Elsas provided his memories of what he called the "so-called strike." On one occasion, he related that "there were men picketing, but not much"; on another, he stated, "I don't recall any picketing at all during 1914." Concerning the evictions of strikers from company housing, he acknowledged "some friction in there" but believed only "some of the families" were affected. "There was really nothing to it," he summed up. "There never was any shutdown in the mill at all."[1]

In minimizing the strike, Norman Elsas echoed his father's pronouncements from three-quarters of a century earlier. In particular, his narrow equation of a strike with a complete stoppage of production closely resembled Oscar Elsas's assertion, made on the strike's first day, that the strikers included only the seventy-eight people who walked out on the morning of 20 May.[2] With slight variations, Elsas repeated the seventy-eight figure on numerous occasions into the spring of 1915 to advance management's position: in the newspaper advertisement the company took out on June 3; before the Atlanta Chamber of Commerce; to federal conciliators; to the superintendent of the *Atlanta Journal* compositors room; and in correspondence to Mayor James G. Woodward, Georgia commissioner of labor H. M. Stanley, Congressman William Schley Howard, New York bankers and industrialists, and Justice M. C.

Sloss of the California Supreme Court, among others.[3] In not acknowledging as strikers either those workers who had quit or had been discharged for union membership before the morning of 20 May, or those who joined the strike afterward, Elsas misrepresented the situation.

Union appeals were equally misleading and extreme. Strike leaders publicly estimated that more than 500 workers had walked off their jobs on 20 May, with the figure climbing to well over 700 by the end of the strike's first week. By mid-July, a union publication claimed that 1,050 Fulton workers were on strike, and the UTW issued flyers and statements throughout the summer and fall asserting that 1,200 people had struck. Such erroneous figures were repeated without challenge in labor and reform periodicals, by Congressman William S. Greene of Fall River, Massachusetts, and in the report of two federal conciliators.[4] Given the disparities between labor's and management's accounts, and the refusal of Elsas to turn over payroll records, it is small wonder that one observer wrote, "It has been a very difficult proposition here to ascertain actually how many were on strike."[5]

It certainly was not the first time that outsiders misrepresented those actually involved, either. Mill management, UTW officials, strike organizers, MRFM members, and federal investigators all tended to employ inadequate, misleading, or two-dimensional terms whenever they described Fulton workers, whether "thoroughly contented" (Oscar Elsas) or "sacrificed to the cotton juggernaut, crushed and broken in mind and body" (the UTW).

Fulton workers' actual attitudes regarding and behavior toward the strike and the union were quite complex and went considerably beyond either a simple endorsement or rejection of unionism per se. Financial concerns, personal relationships, work situations, perceptions of management and the union, pressure, intimidation, and other contingencies all informed individual workers' decisions to quit or stay. Such considerations were variable over time as well, evolving with the ebb and flow of the strike. Even Oscar Elsas, for all his seeming command of the situation, candidly admitted to his father, Jacob, that "those who we least expected to go out left us, and those who we really expected to go, stayed with us."[6]

Belying his public pronouncements about the inconsequential impact of the strike, Elsas quickly took steps to recruit workers from across the Piedmont. In addition to asking his fellow Georgia cotton manufacturers for labor, he placed notices seeking help in Atlanta newspapers and in other papers around the region.[7] He also sent company agents to Columbus, Athens, and other Georgia mill communities to solicit and report back on potential recruits, some of whom previously had worked at Fulton Mills. In particular, the agents sought weavers and loom fixers, along with families who could provide more than one worker.[8]

Reflecting the peripatetic life of Piedmont mill hands, many of the specific people the agents sought were no longer at their last known place of employment. One Columbus man had died, and another was now working in a dairy. A father and son had gone to South Carolina for a week's visit. Quite a few people had migrated to other textile communities, and others simply could not be located. One agent reported that the entire mill at Barnesville, Georgia, had shut down because of the current slump in the industry.

Many potential recruits and their employers expressed reservations about workers going to Atlanta. One agent reported that the parent of a Columbus youth "does not want him to leave home as he is only [a] young boy." The president of a Moultrie, Georgia, mill wrote Elsas that "[t]he men I had expected to send have never traveled much. . . . It will be a hard matter to get them off." Similarly, a textile executive from Thomaston, Georgia, stated, "Our weavers are all country people and we do not think it advisable to attempt to send any of them away to the city," to which Elsas replied, "[O]ur experience has been that some of the staunchest help we have is the very country help you talk about and they stand no foolishness from the pickets." As news of the strike spread quickly across the regionwide informal communications network of Piedmont mill hands, other workers chose not to go because of the particular circumstances at Fulton Mills. The manager of a Thomson, Georgia, mill wrote Elsas that weavers there "do not want to go to Atlanta as there have been some rather wild reports to reach them from Atlanta of personal violence to the strikebreakers and it was impossible to convince them of their safety in coming."[9]

On 3 June, Oscar Elsas sent a letter to a weaver in Easley, South Carolina, whom he understood was coming to work at the mill. "We shall be glad for you to say to any of your friends that want to come with you that we can take care of them and can give them regular work," Elsas assured. "Our weavers make the highest wages of any *white* weaving jobs in the South, and our work runs good. We pay off every Saturday." However, instead of the anticipated weaver, the letter itself came back to Elsas, with "WE DON'T SCAB" handwritten around its margins. The author also wrote on the letter: "We understand that a man has to sign his life away to get a job in your penitentiary," in a reference to Fulton's labor contract.[10]

New recruits coming in by rail faced being confronted by designated union pickets who regularly gathered at Atlanta's two downtown train stations. Adopting what Oscar Elsas accurately termed "aggressive" behavior, the pickets were successful in turning away some of the newcomers. On 7 June, for in-

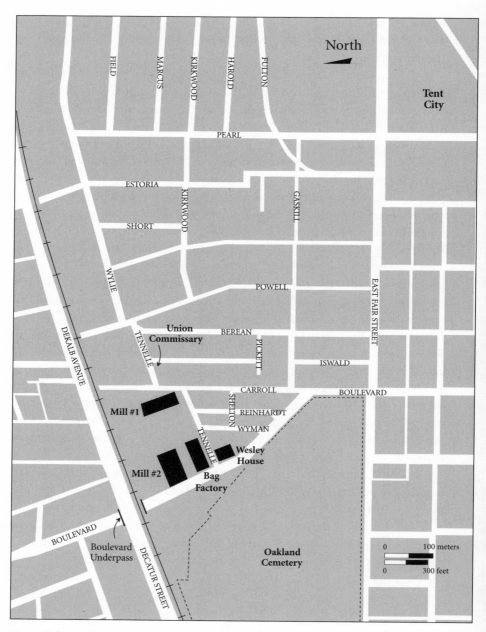

Map 2. Fulton Mill District, 1914

stance, the pickets persuaded three new arrivals from Columbus not to work at Fulton Mills.[11] Another dissuaded Columbus recruit, a former Fulton worker, later described his experience in a letter to Oscar Elsas. "I came back here to go to work," he wrote, "but I was met at the train by a crowd of strikers." The only one in the group he recognized was Cliff Stevens, who, with his family, had been evicted from company housing. Stevens, he stated, "told me all kinds of things about you [Elsas] and your mill and kept me under gard [sic] just like I [was] a [prisoner] and threatened violence." According to this recruit, Stevens also made threats against those still in the mill. "I have worked for you before 5 or 6 years ago," concluded the author, who signed only his initials for fear of reprisals from strikers. "Your company treated me right and I don't feel right to go back with[out] explaining [sic] to you for I don't want to work hard [all day] and be bothered at night with them strikers."[12]

Elsas quickly moved to address the situation. On 9 June, he sent a memo to Charles A. Wickersham of Atlanta's Terminal Station, stating that he would help station officers locate pickets so they could be removed from the premises. On 22 June, he wrote another letter to R. T. Pace, the superintendent of the station. In it, he alluded to a conversation with Wickersham about the pickets, mentioned that mill representatives recently had seen pickets around the depot, and attempted to clarify Wickersham's order to keep pickets off the Terminal grounds. In response, Pace pledged his support to prevent pickets from congregating at the station.[13]

Union pickets and strike supporters attempted to turn back would-be workers at other sites, too. For instance, on the evening of 12 June, at the Boulevard underpass leading to Fulton Mills, seven or eight men stopped a driver from the Atlanta Baggage and Cab Company carrying four recruits from the Terminal Station. They turned his horse around, ordered him to get away as fast as he could, and told him in no uncertain terms not to bring any more fares to the mill.[14]

These efforts to turn away strikebreakers often involved prior coordination. A labor spy reported that there were pickets at every entrance into town, with each suspicious arrival phoned into the union commissary. The Boulevard underpass was not an arbitrary meeting place. It was used because it was well concealed, near Decatur Street and a streetcar line, and situated on the only route into the mill from the north. Therefore, it was one of several strategic locations where strikers and their supporters regularly congregated to head off new recruits as well as others still working in the mill.[15]

Another site for pickets was outside Harris Gober's grocery store at 24 Carroll Street, directly across from the rear entrance into the plant adjoining the mill district, and just around the corner from the union commissary on

Tennelle Street.[16] Not only was the store already strategically located, but pro-strike forces also blocked an alley leading onto Carroll Street farther south, thus funneling many people walking to work right in front of Gober's store and the commissary.[17] Gober had been a staunch supporter of Fulton workers in their protests at least since the walkout of October 1913, and by March, as union organizing progressed, he and his boarders had been targeted by management as potential troublemakers. On the first day of the strike, when police asked the strikers not to congregate on the street, it was to Gober's store that they withdrew. Gober reportedly was also a member of the crowd who stoned the switching train on 25 May. He also cut off the credit of one worker who did not go out on strike, joined picket teams, and provided his car for union organizers.[18] His store, which was literally in the shadow of the mill, thus offered a safe haven and rallying place for the strikers and their supporters.

Members of the mill's internal surveillance network closely monitored the goings-on around Gober's store. Company informants reported nearby altercations, efforts to turn workers away and get them to join the union, and the friendly relationship between Gober and strike leaders and supporters.[19] They also described the store as a regular hangout for Atlanta policemen who were supposedly on duty patrolling the mill district but actually, according to informants, asleep, fondling women, or idling inside or near Gober's store.[20]

For Oscar Elsas, such behavior was emblematic not only of mere indifference or dereliction of duty on the part of the police but also of their sympathies with the strikers. Charles Miles, O. Delight Smith, W. E. Fleming, and other strike leaders openly boasted of their friendship with the police, who on numerous occasions were seen fraternizing with strikers and their supporters.[21] In addition to sympathizing with people from their own class, the police displayed a particular animus toward the company's security personnel and the labor spies, who they viewed as rivals treading on their turf.[22]

Elsas felt the police inaction undermined the authority that he merited after building up a model New South firm. He believed that a double standard existed, whereby the police cracked down on the company's security forces yet allowed strikers and their supporters, including "people never in our employ, some of whom are not even citizens of Atlanta," to interfere with Fulton employees and operations. In his opinion, the police, with a few notable exceptions, openly condoned the harassment of those people trying to work, and even winked at acts of outright lawlessness. For instance, on one night, according to a company informant, a "big mob" gathered on East Fair Street. Both men and women in the group reportedly were "very abusive and did lots of mean talking, calling our crowd names too bad for repeating." Yet the two police who passed by only "saluted them [the mob] politely."[23]

East Fair Street was not a random spot, either, but rather constituted the third strategic site near the mill where union pickets regularly assembled. Located at the edge of the mill district and on an east-west streetcar line, it also traversed Boulevard, the principal road leading to Fulton Mills from the south. Large crowds could gather on a nearby vacant lot. In addition, new recruits were put up in several large East Fair boardinghouses, which became particular targets of strikers and their supporters.[24]

According to an internal report of P. A. Smith, a spinning room overseer in Mill No. 1, not all the newcomers were dissuaded or intimidated by the strikers' actions. Smith described the arrival of the Miller family, who came to work at Fulton Mills and moved into company housing with the assistance of two of the company's watchmen. As soon as they moved in, four women, including one still-working spooler, came by and informed them not to pay any attention to the union people. In particular, the Millers were told "to run anyone off that came talking union." Mrs. Miller assured the women that she "was able to keep them [the strikers] from disturbing them—as she had a gun and knew how to use it."[25]

Not only new recruits were targeted. Prostrike advocates made a concerted, often vociferous effort to convince the many still-working residents of the mill district to quit their jobs and join the strike. Much of this activity was carefully coordinated, or, as Oscar Elsas, with his appreciation for modern management methods, put it, "systematized." Strike organizers quickly established a "visiting committee" and drew up the names of those workers to be seen. For instance, strikers compiled a list of fifty-five people supposed to be working in the mill on 8 June to be visited by the committee. At the 9 June union meeting, committee members reported that they had approached half of the people on the list.[26]

In addition to the visiting committee's efforts, numerous strikers and their supporters addressed still-working mill district residents on their own. Much of this activity took place on the shop floor itself, since many workers sympathetic to the union chose to put off giving their notice to quit in order to receive their withheld back pay. In the meantime, they could try to convince other workers to give notice as well.[27]

The impact, however, was mixed. On the one hand, waiting until they served their notice did give workers an opportunity to join the strike with a little cash on hand, without overtly revealing their intentions to management. On the other hand, aided by internal surveillance reports, management then attempted to persuade people who had given notices to reconsider and remain at work. In addition, no matter how people tried to get around it, the notice/ back pay provision of the labor contract essentially served as a deterrent for workers who had very little financial means to join the strike. Oscar Elsas certainly recognized this fact and later asserted that the contract was crucial in keeping people on the job during the strike. "There was no other way," he claimed, "which would have compelled them to stay at work than the strict terms of that contract, for they knew that if they quit work they would forfeit their whole week's pay."[28]

Encounters between strikers, nonstrikers, and their respective supporters went on beyond the shop floor as well. Out of necessity, such confrontations generally occurred at night, on the weekends, or as people were going to and from work in the mill. Throughout the month of June and beyond, "loud and boisterous" exchanges in the mill district between still-working employees and strikers and their supporters punctuated practically every night.

Compared to those that took place in other American industrial disputes, such encounters were comparatively mild. Yet at times they did have an assaultive, even menacing quality. Some village residents, already working long hours at the mill, simply resented the lack of sleep caused by the "intolerable" nightly din in the streets.[29] For others, the situation went beyond annoyance to harassment and intimidation. An overseer in Mill No. 1 described a woman on East Fair Street "doing a lot of talking and calling us people that is at work all kind of names." Matters could easily go beyond name-calling, too. Company informants described strikers and their allies forcibly entering the houses of Fulton workers and jostling or "rolling" strikebreakers on the street.[30]

These practices were mild compared to what was sometimes threatened in the heat of the moment. Security head James Brush gathered affidavits from four members of one family who testified that striker G. N. Ogle had warned them that if they did not leave the mill now, the strikers "were going into the mill with guns even if they had to take them out through blood." A newcomer from Cedartown related being told by five union people in front of a Decatur Street saloon that if he entered the mill, "they would raise more knots on my head than I could count in a hundred years." Others threatened to dynamite the mill if workers did not come out.[31]

A few people who persisted in working at the mill received handwritten threats from strikers or supporters. One of these was Walter Burdett, who got this warning:

WALTER BURDETT
IF U GO TO WORK IN THE FULTON MILL ANY MORE IT WILL BE AT YOUR OWN
RISK SO TAKE WARNING AN DONT GO IN THE MILL NO MORE
A STRIKER

Burdett received another note that warned, "you must stop work in the fulton and your children or you will be in trouble." Other workers got similar threats.[32]

Sporadic incidents of violence initiated by strikers or their supporters did occur. Several episodes took place over the weekend of 13–14 June. In one case, a group of strikers and supporters who were gathered in a Decatur Street saloon called frame hand Bud Fuller "a son-of-a-bitch of a scab." When he took offense, Rob Raines, a structural iron worker who was in town to work on the new county courthouse, knocked him through a window. Fuller was arrested for disorderly conduct, and Raines eventually was charged for making an insulting remark. In another case, J. A. Cain, a driver for the Armour Packing Company and the husband of a striker, hit overseer J. W. McCuen in the eye and knocked him into a post. In a third incident, strikers R. F. Odell and Jim Rice attacked a worker as he entered a local barber shop.[33]

Such episodes should not be discounted or ignored. Yet, it is also important to remember that the extent and nature of violence, intimidation, and harassment was to a large degree in the eye of the beholder. From his vantage point, Oscar Elsas sought to emphasize threats and lawlessness by the strikers and their supporters in order to discredit the strike, secure support for his position, and more generally advance law and order. Many of the altercations documented by Elsas, however, seemed little different from the Saturday night fights that regularly occurred in the mill district anyway.

Indeed, other observers with more comparative experience and less vested interest than Elsas in highlighting the violent aspects of the strike saw the matter differently. A police captain told a federal investigator, "This strike has been very peaceful." In his annual report for 1914, police chief James Beavers stated that the strike "had no incidents of a serious nature, and we have had only minor offenses to deal with in this connection." Federal investigator Alexander Daly similarly pointed to the "exceedingly small" level of violence "as compared with the conditions and with the number of people involved." And, naturally, strike organizers stressed the peaceful nature of union pickets.

Rough words and intimidation were not the sole province of strikers and strike supporters either. For instance, Fulton worker J. A. Morrison, who had been detailed by Brush to escort operatives to work, was arraigned and fined for using abusive language in the presence of a female striker. Strike organizers complained as well of the treatment they and various strikers received at the hands of company security forces.[34]

On 13 June, G. A. Stalnaker and Homer L. Sargent, two overseers in the spinning room of Mill No. 1 and members of the company's internal surveillance network, reported hearing striker Mose Barton boast "a right smart" that the strikers had been successful in getting all new recruits either to join the union or to get a railroad pass out of town. Barton maintained that the union was enlisting or turning away between twenty-five and seventy-five people a day.[35] Such claims were obviously exaggerated, designed to impress people with the strikers' success and bring them over to the union side. Yet on a number of occasions pro-union forces did succeed in winning over or dissuading new recruits. It would be a mistake, however, to assume this success was solely due to harassment or intimidation. Workers had a wide range of reasons for both leaving and staying on at Fulton Mills that went considerably beyond simple endorsement or rejection of unionism or pressure by pro- or antistrike forces.

For some workers, the strike dovetailed with, highlighted, and reinforced existing grievances, dissatisfaction, or alienation. Thus, one weaver in Mill No. 1 announced he was quitting on account of a second hand he did not like. Other workers complained of being put on jobs in which they could not make a living, in particular where the looms were in poor condition and badly maintained. "That Son-of-a-B— of a loom fixer don't know how to fix anything," exclaimed one weaver. "He just holds me up all the time. I guess I'd be better off if I had just went on strike." One new recruit protested having to run thirty-two looms and complained in class-conscious terms that Oscar Elsas rode around "in a damn machine [automobile] while we all worked our life out, in that mill, making him richer."[36]

Nothing enraged and aroused workers more, including many people who up until then had been loyal to the company, than the wholesale evictions of strikers from company housing beginning 4 June. The evictions provided a reminder of the subordinate, dependent position of cotton mill workers, and the manner in which mill management carried out the evictions further evoked feelings of humiliation and shame. For many people, the forcible entry into workers' homes—in at least one case, with even the horses of the assistant marshals entering a company house—constituted an abusive violation of personal dignity, respect, and honor. The fact that it was black men who actually removed workers' personal belongings onto the street added fuel to the fire, symbolizing the degradation of the descendants of once independent white farmers.

Many Fulton workers responded quickly and intensely to the evictions. A weaver named O'Kelly protested to paymaster T. S. Florence about evicting people without thirty days' notice. When Florence candidly replied, "I know but we are blowing them [off]. They don't know any better," O'Kelly responded, "It ain't right and it ain't law." Another man, who had been compara-

An evicted family of Fulton strikers. Special Collections Dept., Pullen Library, Georgia State University.

tively quiet until this point, now declared that the evictions "were too much for a white man to stand." A bag mill worker related, "That got more people out there from the mill than anything else, seeing these people thrown out."[37]

Robert H. Wright, who worked in the stockroom of the bag mill, was one person moved to action by the evictions. As his wife, Sallie, who had been discharged for sympathizing with the union after the October walkout, related, "My husband did not pay any attention to it [the strike] until he seen so many people thrown out there. . . . And he began to sympathize with the people then and come home every day at dinner and go on about it and most every day he would see somebody that had been out of a house. . . . He didn't think it was just right."

Once his sentiments about the evictions became known, Wright was approached by W. E. Fleming, H. N. Mullinax, and Harris Gober, who tried hard to persuade him to join the strikers. Charles Miles and O. Delight Smith also contacted Wright, promising him rent and groceries if he went out. They were particularly interested in recruiting Wright since he was an "exhorter" in his church, a talent that could also be used in the service of the union.[38]

Once Wright decided to come out, he quickly became one of Local 886's most active members. "I went into the fight with my coat off and my sleeves rolled up," he later related. "I was making my speeches up there [at the union hall] as spicy as I could." Over the next month, Wright spoke perhaps a dozen times at the daily union meetings. His speeches, usually delivered in a "religious strain," tapped into a variety of anxieties held by Fulton workers that extended well beyond the particular issues of the strike. In one speech, he equated the dependency of the workers at Fulton Mills to that of "antebellum slaves." On another occasion, addressing widespread concerns about a new sexual order associated with industrialization, concerns that had particular resonance in Atlanta at the time of the Frank case, he claimed that the heads of several departments in the mill flirted with female operatives. In a similar vein, he denounced "spies and young men who failed to protect the good name of a sister."

Furthermore, Wright asserted that the company sponsored a "Tango Dance" at noon every day, "which would make the lowest nigger of Decatur Street blush with shame." Though there was absolutely no basis in fact for this claim, Wright's accusation revealed the connection between the Fulton strike and larger tensions and anxieties workers experienced in the urban New South. Wright also condemned child labor practices and onerous work rules at Fulton Mills, the unsanitary conditions in the mill district, and the complicity of the Wesley House with management, whom he branded "the blackest Liars from the smoke of hell."[39]

Wright was not the only individual whose abilities or position were of particular interest to strike leaders as they sought to bring workers out. Another was Will C. Sweatt, a former loom fixer and now a member of the company's private security force and a man who Charles Miles stated had "good influence" among Fulton workers. In addition, Sweatt had already actively expressed pro-union sympathies before he actually left his job. Two days after quitting, Sweatt met with Miles at the union hall and told him he would have to find another job, as he had a young son and his wife had diabetes and had to eat special food. According to Sweatt, Miles replied, "Well, we would take care of you and your little wife, we will lay out the expenses of everything." Miles and other strike organizers then agreed to install Sweatt as president of the local, a position he assumed on 23 June, and to pay him four dollars a week above his own expenses.[40]

Sallie Wright later stated, "My husband and I came very near to separating" because of differences of opinion over the strike. This was only one of a number of occasions when families themselves divided over the strike, which often raised in high relief already existing domestic tensions.[41] Informant P. A. Smith reported several such complex family divisions in a memo to Gordon

Johnstone. Two girls in one family were convinced by overseers Sargent and Stalnaker to withdraw their notices to quit, while their father cursed the company and said he "couldn't work anymore for these — Jews." Homer Sargent himself got into an argument about the strike with *his* father, who became active in turning people away from the mill. One of the people the elder Sargent was after was M. D. Young, a member of the company security force, whose family was on its way from Canton, Georgia, to work in Fulton Mills, even as Young himself was "on the fence" about staying. Smith also heard about an evicted striker who was trying to convince her still-working son-in-law to get her former company house and let her stay on with him.[42]

Some workers, however, remained on the job only because of family considerations, like the man who asserted, "I'm not going along Damn, and if I had no one but myself, I wld leave this G— Damn place right now, for I ain't making no money." Family ties could pull someone off the job as well; upon receiving a letter from his wife to come home, one recently recruited weaver handed in his notice to quit.[43] It seems that for the most part families acted together, either staying on with the company or joining the strike as a group. Certainly for its part, the company discharged many people simply because they had family members who were strikers.[44]

Some workers who continued with the company occasionally felt ambivalent, let down, or alienated. One worker complained about working through the strike and then being put on a job where he could not make a living. Even one member of the company's intelligence network, an overseer in Mill No. 1, declared, "I expect I'll join the union. I may as well do that as be in this damn place, working my life out."[45]

For many people, the union and its provisions—food from the commissary, perhaps room, board, a few dollars, tobacco, or a rail pass out of town— seemed an alluring alternative to the hardships and incessant nature of textile work.[46] "I will go in the Union and lay for awhile," announced one worker. "They give you three or four dollars a week, and if you want to leave the city, they give you a pass." Claiming that the union had promised board, a train pass, and tobacco, another worker asked, "What in the h— more does a man want than that, when he don't have to work?" Echoed a weaver in Mill No. 1, "Those Union men sure do help you up. They give you house rent free and all you want to eat and a few dollars a week, you wouldn't want any more than that, would you?" Such aid was particularly welcome during a record-breaking heat wave, as another worker observed: "The Union will keep you and take care of you, so what the h— is the use in you working in this hot weather[?]"[47] "Why the H— don't you join the Union and loaf awhile if you don't feel good?"

a weaver asked labor spy G. J. Manuel, who himself had a hard time adjusting to the work regimen at Fulton Mills as well as boardinghouse food. "It will do you a sight of good to have a rest at their expense."[48]

Such statements indicate that for many people, the union and the strike represented little more than a temporary relief from the normal alienating drudgery of cotton mill work, a small and rare opportunity for respite. They also reveal the deep cynicism that some workers felt about both the company and the UTW. A new recruit in Mill No. 1 spoke for many when he declared that "he was going to get all he could out of the Company, then live on the Union for awhile, or until the strike was over, then they could all go to H—."[49] Others, however, clearly placed more hope in the union and its possibilities. Card room hand A. J. Watts, for instance, predicted, "When the union wins we won't have none of the overseers that the company has got now. We are going to have our own overseers, men who will look out for the union instead of the company." Similarly, Sam Bryant, who worked in the drawing room of Mill No. 2, declared, "The union is striking for our rights."[50]

In short, the reasons for quitting work and joining the union, as well as for staying on the job, were extremely varied and complicated. No neat dichotomy separated strikers and strikebreakers, pro- and anti-union forces. The complexity of the entire situation for the people actually in the middle of it is illuminated by a detailed look at the experience of some recruits from the Boston-owned Massachusetts Mills of Georgia, located in the community of Lindale, seventy miles northwest of Atlanta near Rome, and one of the largest textile plants in the state.

Two days after Elsas's 3 June appeal to his fellow Georgia cotton manufacturers, Massachusetts Mills agent H. P. Meikleham committed ten or twelve weavers to Fulton Mills, a decision made easier by the fact that the Lindale plant was shutting down a thousand looms anyway during the industrywide lull. On 11 June, Fulton assistant superintendent E. H. Rogers traveled to Lindale to meet with prospective recruits, who were promised nearly double their normal wages for twenty days if they came to Fulton Mills. Oscar Elsas notified Meikleham, "We shall prepare to receive them, treat them properly, and return them to you when you say the word."[51] On or about 12 June, between nine and eleven weavers from Lindale arrived in town, accompanied by the Lindale boss weaver, their train fare to Atlanta paid by Fulton Mills. A second round of recruits followed a few days later.

Most of the Lindale recruits were put up in a large boardinghouse on East Fair Street. Operating the house was Viola Granger, who also worked as a weaver in Mill No. 1. Granger had run the boardinghouse only for a week or so. Prior to then, she had operated another establishment with only two boarders.

On 3 June, she had provided details about two strike sympathizers to Brush and at the same time made it clear she wanted more lodgers. For her efforts, she was rewarded with the larger boardinghouse, and she and her husband continued to supply information useful to the company.[52]

Another resident of the boardinghouse was G. J. Manuel, a recently arrived labor spy who had been assigned to infiltrate Mill No. 1, where the Lindale workers were concentrated. Mill No. 1 was the most severely affected by the strike at this point; for the week of 15 June, the number of looms run there only amounted to 60 percent of the prestrike total.[53] On Saturday, 13 June, Manuel reported that some of the Lindale recruits frequented a total of seven nearby saloons. On Sunday, one of the Lindale men also visited a friend, a sergeant at police headquarters, where he learned that strikebreaker Bud Fuller, an acquaintance of his, was in jail for fighting with a union man. Fuller declared that he had been arrested before and so didn't really mind being locked up.[54]

Over the weekend, mill management tried to please the Lindale workers on hand in order to keep them around. At management's expense, both the mill watchman and the second hand in the Mill No. 1 weave room treated the newcomers to automobile and streetcar rides, moving picture shows, and other favors. For all management's efforts, however, they met with only mixed results, since such modern treats were perhaps less novel to Piedmont textile workers than management had realized. "Hell," exclaimed Lindale weaver Sam Womack, well aware of the recruits' bargaining power during the strike, "we can ride a Damn old street car any time. They have to show us boys a better time than that or we are going back to Lindale."[55]

In addition, the Lindale recruits complained about the filth at the boardinghouse, along with food "not fit for a dog." Perhaps because of such conditions, three of the men returned to Lindale on 13 June, "with the intention of telling the others not to come here." Another Lindale recruit joined the union and expressed optimism that the strikers would soon get the other Lindale hands out.[56]

At the same time, the company attempted to import additional hands from Lindale. In recognition of the union's growing appeal, Oscar Elsas told Meikleham that he only wanted men who could "Stand the Gaff." "There is no use in sending any weak-kneed brothers here," Elsas wrote, "as it simply means they will join the strikers, and although it puts them [the union] to extra expense in supporting these people, still it makes both you and our Mill lose them for the time being."[57]

Very early Monday morning, a crowd of strike supporters went to have words with the Lindale men, some of whom stated that they had a three-week contract with Fulton Mills at forty-five dollars each, and that after that time they would join the union. The same day, Manuel reported that one of the Lindale recruits, J. A. McCauley, was disgusted with the way he had been treated, receiving no sleep because of the strikers coming by and getting nothing for breakfast at the boardinghouse. McCauley also indicated that he was having some problems with his machinery in the weave room.[58]

That night, a crowd of strike supporters gathered around the boardinghouse, "making it very unpleasant" for the boarders, in the words of Oscar Elsas. In the meantime, weaver Sam Womack had brought in five more recruits from Lindale, three of whom had immediately gone out with union men and gotten drunk. Womack, whom the company had been treating as a middle man to avoid dealing directly with all the Lindale men, also complained of losing money to some of his fellow recruits and about the boardinghouse food.[59]

On 17 June, McCauley had a conversation with a local railroad unionist, who condemned Oscar Elsas. He urged McCauley not to be "a G— D— Sucker for that Son-of-a-Bitch that walks around dressed up with a barrel of money in his possession, taking life easy while you toil your life out for him." Shortly afterward, McCauley became the first of the Lindale recruits to join the strikers. The following day, he made a speech at the union meeting to great acclaim, in which he asked for volunteers to call on the rest of the Lindale men that night. For the remainder of the week, he and additional strikers endeavored to bring the other Lindale men out, despite the company's employment of a special watchman on the boardinghouse porch all night long to "prevent unduly annoyance."

But perhaps the straw that broke the camel's back for the Lindale recruits came on the night of 20 June, when boardinghouse keeper Viola Granger and her drunken husband got into a loud, five-hour domestic fight over her refusal to turn over half of the boardinghouse money to him. As Oscar Elsas delicately put it in a letter to Meikleham, "the husband of the boarding house keeper . . . became intoxicated, and undoubtedly made plenty of noise for most of Saturday night."[60]

By Sunday, 21 June, almost all the Lindale men had announced their intention to quit and join the union. One of them, revealing a class consciousness common among Piedmont mill hands, said: "If we were to stay until after this strike was over, the G— damn company would not notice us on the street, but now they will do anything for us, because we are nothing but damn suckers for them, and have been ever since we came here."

Lindale recruit Cliff Lanham nearly joined the others in leaving but ultimately was one of the few Lindale men who chose to remain. His decision to stay was not primarily based in anti-unionism per se but rather in his disgust at how the Fulton strike was being handled. As he emphatically told Manuel, he "didn't see a D— thing to it, that this thing they call a Union here, wasn't anything but a lot of bull s—, and he was a Union man himself and wouldn't scab on anybody."[61]

The Lindale men collectively concocted stories to tell to company officials on Monday morning in order to get out of their obligations. Through Manuel, however, Elsas was alerted of their plans, and he "promptly told them we were on to the game, and that we were not going to allow them to work us in any such way." At the union meeting that afternoon, nine Lindale men came to the front and declared that they had come under a "misrepresentation" and would stay to help the strike. Indeed, several Lindale recruits continued to be active strikers for months to come.[62]

After the men had quit, Elsas wrote Meikleham his account of the Lindale episode. In hindsight, he criticized giving the Lindale recruits so many favors. "The Writer presumes things were going so easy with them," Elsas conjectured, "that they thought they could have their way in everything." He therefore suggested that if future Lindale workers were sent to Fulton Mills, they should come on their own resources and be reimbursed for railroad fare only after they had worked a few weeks. "Under such an arrangement," Elsas predicted, "they will not be so independent."[63]

The Lindale incident both reflected and influenced the progress of the strike at its high tide. For the week of 15 June, the total number of looms running in the plant dropped 10 percent from the previous week. The number of production workers in the two cotton mills also declined slightly, to roughly three-fourths of the figure before the strike. And attendance continued to be high at union meetings.

In addition, on 18 June, veteran UTW organizers Sara Conboy and Mary Kelleher arrived in Atlanta to help with the strike effort. Conboy, a Boston native and former carpet worker, had directed the UTW relief operations during the 1912 Lawrence, Massachusetts, strike; in 1915 she would become the UTW's secretary-treasurer and thus the highest ranking woman official in the American trade union movement. Most recently, both women had been involved with organizing drives in the Pennsylvania silk districts. As was his wont, Elsas immediately began to seek information on Conboy and Kelleher that might discredit them, with no success.[64]

At the same time, however, there were clear signs that the bloom was beginning to wear off the union rose, as the strike moved beyond its first few weeks and the UTW resources became increasingly taxed after the evictions. Certainly some of those evicted were soon able to find jobs elsewhere. For instance, after being evicted, musician Fiddlin' John Carson, a weaver in Mill No. 1, sold hot dogs in a Decatur Street pool room and played his fiddle on the streets for money, often for the crowds gathered for the Frank trial, and members of his

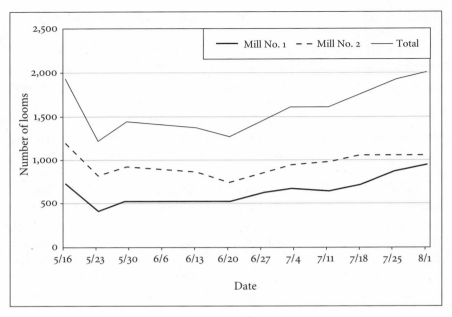

Figure 1. Number of Looms Run, Mill No. 1 and Mill No. 2, 16 May–1 August 1914
Source: "Number of Looms Run—5-14-14 to 9-3-14," Folder 20, Box 1, Strike Records,
Fulton Bag and Cotton Mills Collection, Price Gilbert Memorial Library, Archives,
Georgia Institute of Technology, Atlanta, Ga.

family scraped floors and hawked newspapers. Other Fulton workers who had
quit or were discharged or evicted also found new employment. Some women
strikers, for example, obtained positions in local stores or factories. Often
aided by a union-supplied rail pass, some strikers found work out of town as
well; a number of people, including several weavers, joined the Kansas wheat
harvest. Still others got by through the assistance of relatives or friends. R. H.
Wright, for instance, was helped by his son-in-law, who worked for the gas
company and who "volunteered to see that I didn't suffer."[65]

At least one evicted family, the Wards, attempted to get relief from the city's
Associated Charities. After a query to the mill about the Wards from the
Reverend C. B. Wilmer of the MRFM and an article in the *Atlanta Georgian* on
child labor that mentioned them, mill management, concerned about a precedent being established, contested their effort. Paymaster Florence first detailed
the family's work history and its earning potential in an internal report, even
providing a chart of the Wardses' earnings. Company secretary-treasurer Louis
Elsas then presented Florence's findings to social worker Joseph C. Logan

of the Associated Charities in an attempt to remove the Wards from the charity rolls.[66]

But many of the people who quit or were discharged or evicted remained in Atlanta at the union's expense, living in housing that the UTW or the Atlanta Federation of Trades furnished or, more commonly, continuing to draw from the union commissary. Originally, the commissary was well stocked. On 6 June, for instance, one striker filled an order for flour, coffee, potatoes, sugar, rice, cabbage, corn, tomatoes, and meat. Yet the provisions quickly dwindled. On 12 June, a labor spy related that the commissary was running short of supplies; on 17 June, another spy reported that there was little but flour left. Despite additional infusions of money and food, shortages persisted.[67]

The problems with the commissary were greatly compounded by the fact that, in addition to strikers and their families, the commissary fed a growing number of people who had not recently worked at Fulton Mills, if they ever had done so, as organizers tried to keep them from entering the mill. Oscar Elsas was quick to point this out, asserting that the great majority of individuals associated with the strike were "strangers" and thus had no justification to get involved. Similarly, a labor spy estimated on 26 June that fewer than a fourth of those attending union meetings and drawing from the commissary had actually ever worked in the mill.[68]

In fact, the situation was somewhat more complicated than mill management's portrayal of it. Some of these individuals had been attracted to the strike out of common cause with Fulton workers. This support came not only from local trade unionists but also from others in the city's white working class who often knew Fulton workers personally. For instance, Luther Twedell, a former Fulton worker who had been discharged in the spring, quit his new job with the Southern Spring Bed Company "so that he might be out here 'with the boys during their trouble' and was aiding them in every way he could."[69] During the week of 8 June alone, switchmen, brakemen, and members of various other railroad brotherhoods, workers at the nearby city stockade, painters, brick layers, structural iron workers, and others all joined with the strikers at union meetings, in the mill district, in saloons, and at other gathering points.[70] Those who flocked to the union and the commissary included residents of the mill district, relatives and friends of Fulton workers, and former Fulton hands themselves, including many who had quit or had been discharged in the months just prior to the start of the strike.[71] Others came from the swelling ranks of Atlanta's many unemployed and poor.[72]

Not only local people were attracted to the commissary and other union-provided goods and services, though. A member of the mill's security force reported meeting a group of newly arrived men from South Carolina who stated that since it was too hot to work in the summer, they had come to join the union. The newcomers then asked if the union paid anything or supplied free rations.[73] They were hardly alone. In a testament to the pinched circumstances, marginality, and transient lives of many working-class white southerners, as well as to the informal communication network that spread across the region's mill communities, literally hundreds of people from across the Piedmont partook of the union's offerings at one time or another. As R. H. Wright put it, the newcomers "blowed in here on a cyclone from everywhere."[74]

As early as 7 June, a spooler in Mill No. 1 declared that "the Union is only starving a lot of them damn fools half to death, and I'm sure I ain't going to be hungry as long as I can work and make a living." Others spoke with anger and resentment of unfulfilled promises that strike organizers purportedly had made. For instance, informants Stalnaker and Sargent reported that members of one family who had gone out on strike now cursed strike leader H. N. Mullinax "about some talk about not furnishing people groceries any longer." The family matriarch related that Mullinax had "begged her children into that Damn Union and now he could go to Hell for her part."[75]

Similarly, former worker Lola Petty, a widow with a small child, wrote Oscar Elsas in July that "I am absolutely done sick and tired with the union." In Petty's opinion, the union had gotten her to join under false pretenses. She had ostensibly been promised four dollars a week, "and if they have ever given me one penny I am a rich woman." Instead, Petty maintained, she had only received "a little of the ruffest kind of groceries." Twice she had gone to organizer Charles Miles to settle her board bill and to transport her out of town, and twice she had been turned down. "Now this is as true a statement as the stars is to heaven," she concluded.[76]

Many still-employed Fulton workers developed a low opinion of the commissary's offerings, and by extension the union and its ability to deliver the goods, figuring they would fare better by remaining at work. Perhaps at management's suggestion, two sisters, both still-working spinners in Mill No. 2, made up derisive verses to the tune of "Yankee Doodle." Fannie Beavers composed:

> The strikers will soon be starving now
> Before they can get back
> Running around with a railroad man
> With a tater in a sack
>
> (Chorus) Go to work and pay your debts
> And don't be called a debtor

Your grocery man will keep you up
And you'll be a hearty eater

I saw one going home last night
With a tater and an onion
But course thats best they can afford
Since they have joined the Union

Her sister, Jennie Bell Beavers, made up another verse:

As we went long on Tennelle St
We spied their Commissary
It looks just like a Weiner stand
And smells just like a Garbage Can.[77]

In contrast to the union, in what Oscar Elsas claimed was a measure to protect workers from confrontations at the plant gates but was also an effort to reinforce management's role as benefactor, the company provided free daily meals at Wesley House for hundreds of workers from the first day of the strike into mid-August.[78]

The increasing scarcity of union supplies almost inherently fostered a fertile situation for charges of favoritism and mismanagement. R. H. Wright, for instance, claimed that commissary orders were inexplicably lost. He also maintained that sides of meat and other provisions "that should have been on the strikers' tables" ended up in the store of commissary clerk Ollie Simpkins's father instead. Wright later related, "[O]ne time there was a lady passed by my home . . . and she was almost crying. She says, 'I am going to the commissary again to make another effort to get some bacon. This is the third time that I have been down there and have not been able to get any.' . . . I told her, 'I will go with you to the commissary and get some bacon. I am pretty sure there is some there.' When I got there I found a couple of large middlings ready and I asked why it was they said they did not have any. Ollie Simpkins, one of the head clerks, said it was special instructions from Mrs. Smith."[79]

Much of the resentment over the commissary and the strike's direction more generally centered around organizers Smith and Miles, who became increasingly vulnerable to a variety of attacks as the situation deteriorated. W. C. Sweatt, who briefly served as union local president, denounced the autocratism of Smith and Miles, a condemnation with which Wright concurred. "Miles was the boss man," Sweatt later related. "The man acting President up there wasn't nothing at all."[80] For Sweatt, Wright, and others, this attitude on the part of the strike organizers evoked long-standing practices in which mill hands were ignored or discounted. There certainly was some truth in such

H. N. Mullinax, Charles Miles, and O. Delight Smith in front of the union commissary. Special Collections Dept., Pullen Library, Georgia State University.

accusations. Miles and Smith usually played things close to the vest and excluded strikers from union decision making, especially as the strike wore on. Yet their exclusivity was at least partially informed by the presence of labor spies, who spread and embellished charges against the two organizers, whether substantiated or not.

A key player in this regard was Harry G. Preston, one of the most capable of the Railway Audit labor spies.[81] An Englishman like Miles, John Golden, and fellow spy H. A. Hughes, Preston posed as an out-of-work singer from Philadelphia who had come south in mid-June to cure bronchial problems, then joined the union after seeking work at Fulton Mills. After his arrival, Preston, who reported to Oscar Elsas as Operative No. 115 and publicly went by the name of Harry Greenhough, monitored union meetings, picket activity, and the commissary situation; stole copies of the meeting attendance book; entered the confidence of UTW organizer Sara Conboy; and became the union's music director. He also used his musical abilities to help gain access to the MRFM.[82]

Preston did whatever he could to disparage the leadership of Miles and Smith, for whom he had a particular animus. Through his friendship with Conboy, he helped widen an already existing rift of indeterminate origins between Conboy and Smith and Miles. By the time Conboy and fellow UTW organizer Mary Kelleher left Atlanta in late July, Preston described them as being "in open rupture" with Miles and Smith. In addition, when he could do so without being detected, he conveyed his opinions to strikers and other workers as well, in particular to coveted union recruits like Sweatt and Wright, who Preston also carefully cultivated.[83]

Even workers with pro-union sympathies began to have misgivings about the strike's direction. For instance, a weaver in Mill No. 1 related, "[T]his union is a H— of a good thing, but these men don't work it right, and that is the reason that I don't join them." Another weaver related that he was a union man himself but did not think the strike would amount to much since there was no money in the treasury. And a card room hand in Mill No. 2 stated that he had thought about joining the union but was glad he didn't because it had taken in "all these damn bums and hoboes."[84]

Especially after the latter part of June, many of the workers who had walked out trickled back into the mill, provided they were permitted to do so by management. For some, it was dissatisfaction with the union that brought them back. The members of one family, for instance, stated they wanted to return to work because they "had enough of that union bunch." For others, it was an inability to make a comparable or adequate living outside the mill. For instance, one bleachery worker wished to return because he was tired of working for a dollar a day on the outside; a female striker made only thirty cents for a day's labor at a local pants factory.[85]

Even so, some people decided to return only under duress, but without forsaking their antipathy for the company. On 14 July, a company informant reported that Edith McMurtry and Alma Collins, two spinners who had been "very active on the streets for a while," were now talking about coming back to work "but just hate to do so." Walt Abernathy, another onetime "active picket," expressed his desire to return but also promised "to make it hot for some who are now working if he does get back." Management did not rehire him.[86]

Along with a growing strain on the commissary and a gradual migration back into the mill, strike organizers also had to reckon with a waning in picket interest and activity. As early as 9 June, strike organizers had trouble sustaining the picketing. On that date, strike leaders told those present at the union meeting that they would have to cut off negligent pickets from their rations. On 25 June, Smith advised pickets to do their job better. On 29 June, Mary Kelleher warned that strike organizers might fine workers for missing picket duty, a development that mill management found ironic in light of the union having targeted the company's fining system. And on 4 July, Conboy berated strikers for their lack of interest in picketing.[87] In a manner that in some ways paralleled the situation of the Lindale recruits, many of the newcomers to the union, once having been fed at the commissary, felt little or no obligation or

The union commissary. Sara Conboy is on the far right. Special Collections Dept., Pullen Library, Georgia State University.

commitment to picket. They had never attended union meetings, indeed had never worked at Fulton Mills. In addition, outside of Fleming, Mullinax, and perhaps several dozen other staunch unionists, most strikers eventually tired of the rigors of constant picketing.

The same was also true of some of the company's watchmen who monitored the pickets. In mid-June, one of the watchmen expressed a desire to resign *his* picket duty, declaring it was "too hard on him to stay up at night." Later that month, another member of the company security force, A. J. Gibbs, revealed that he hoped the strike would soon be over, as he was "just tired of street walking." Unlike some of his peers, however, Gibbs said he "wouldn't kick to the Co. because they had promised him another job in the fall of the year, and he would stick it out now."[88]

On 25 June, Harry Preston accurately stated that the influx of newcomers, the overstretched commissary, and the decline of picketing together posed a "complex problem" for strike organizers, who tried to address it in several ways. They established a "trial board," ostensibly to check the credentials of those who joined the union and partook of the commissary. However, on only one recorded occasion was anyone brought before the board. Organizers adopted new methods to screen the growing numbers of what Preston termed "undesirables" and announced that strikers would be punished for not picket-

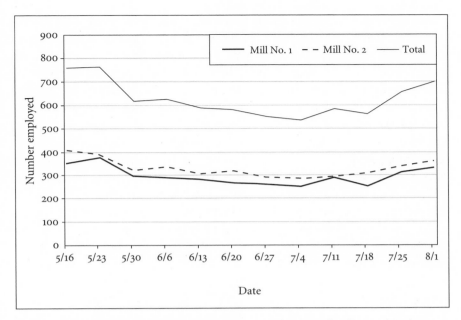

Figure 2. Employment in Production Departments, Mill No. 1 and Mill No. 2 (Card Room, Spinning Room, and Weave Room), 16 May–1 August 1914
Source: Payroll Book, 1913–15, Fulton Bag and Cotton Mills Collection, Price Gilbert Memorial Library, Archives, Georgia Institute of Technology, Atlanta, Ga.

ing. On 17 July, three people were expelled from the union for selling off their commissary tickets to others. And on 25 July, organizers began to require strikers to sign for their commissary rations in person.[89]

Yet whatever strike organizers, strikers, and their supporters tried, they failed to prevent the company from moving back to full production. During the week of 22 June, the average number of looms in operation rose to 70 percent of the prestrike figure; during the following week, it climbed to 79 percent of what it had been before the strike, and it steadily rose each week until production reached the prestrike level in late July. The number of people employed similarly crept upward, as management did ultimately recruit replacement workers. (See figures 1 and 2.) "I am sure from a careful investigation," wrote an observer on 31 July, "that the Mills are now running with a full force."[90]

By this time, mill management felt that it had beaten back the strike. On Friday, 24 July, the company posted large notices around the outside of the plant, announcing that all former employees could apply to return to work if they so desired, up until the following Monday. After that, according to general manager Gordon Johnstone, "if they failed to ask for reinstatement we would not consider their applications."[91] By the end of July, Oscar Elsas felt comfortable enough with the situation to leave town and to take a vacation, leaving plant operations to his father, Jacob, for a while. The temporary turnover to Jacob heartened a number of the remaining strikers, who felt they might get a fairer shake with the elder Elsas than with his son. Such hopes proved unfounded, though, as Jacob Elsas did little during his brief stint back at the helm but build upon the anti-union tactics that Oscar had already initiated. In fact, if anything, Jacob, perhaps because of his better relationship with various influential Atlantans, proved more successful than Oscar in neutralizing the police and undermining the MRFM, which had become involved in the strike.[92] Yet management's confidence that the matter was over was premature. For the strike had moved well beyond the original issues and the actions of Fulton workers themselves to a fiercely fought contest for public opinion that had a forceful momentum of its own.

CHAPTER 6

To Present to the Public a True Picture

Three-quarters of a century after the Fulton strike, Norman Elsas, Oscar Elsas's son, described the origins of the affair. "They had gotten some union agitators in here to work with these people," he stated. The "they" he referred to were the members of the local Men and Religion Forward Movement, who, in Elsas's opinion, were actually the ones responsible for initiating the strike, exploiting anti-Semitism at the time of the Frank case. "They picked up this strike, as an anti-Semitic thing," he asserted. "They started a strike at Fulton Bag and Cotton Mill because it was Jewish owned."[1]

Actually, the MRFM members did *not* launch the strike at Fulton Mills, nor did they get involved principally because of anti-Semitism, if they did so at all. To locate the cause of the strike in the anti-Semitism of outsiders served in memory, as it did in 1914, to remove the company, its policies, and its practices from any responsibility in the matter. Elsas's strong though inaccurate memories reflect the charged environment in which the strike took place. They also may have been informed by the fact that once it was engaged, the MRFM *did* play a leading, perhaps even the dominant, role in successfully publicizing the strike, both in Atlanta and elsewhere, and accordingly evoked an especially vehement response from Oscar Elsas. The MRFM, however, was only one of a widening circle of parties privately and publicly interested in the dispute, which quickly moved beyond simply a contest between Fulton workers and management alone.

In mid-June 1914, Atlanta Federation of Trades officer Louie P. Marquardt wrote an article in the *Journal of Labor* in which he listed what he called the "munitions of war" the strikers needed in what was the opening salvo in the southern textile organizing campaign and what was evidently going to be a protracted fight. "First," Marquardt said, "they need money," recognizing that the strike's financial requirements had increased significantly with the wholesale eviction of strikers from company housing and the establishment of the union commissary.

Marquardt also mentioned a second, interrelated need: "Next to funds is publicity. Let every union man and woman keep constantly before the public the fact that the textile workers are on strike and what they are striking for. The daily press cannot find in this struggle of dollars against women and innocent children anything of interest to the public to print. So the fact of spreading before the world the great injustice perpetuated upon a helpless and unfortunate people depends upon the activity of organized labor and its friends. Publicity will win the battle."[2]

Marquardt's statement reveals strike leaders' fear of not getting publicity and their attendant need to actively join the battle for public opinion. In their appeal to public opinion, trade unionists adopted conventional, two-dimensional images of textile workers. Marquardt described the strikers as "women and innocent children," despite the fact that men constituted a higher than average and growing percentage of the workforce at Fulton Mills, that the Elsases observed state child labor laws, and that the all-male loom fixers had been at the core of worker insurgency. Such a description cast upon the strikers engendered characteristics of weakness, frailty, and defenselessness, thus portraying them principally as objects of pity rather than as actors in their own right, and reinforced the stereotypes of southern mill hands as downtrodden and childlike. Marquardt's depiction of Fulton workers as a "helpless and unfortunate people" had a similar effect.[3]

This language also explicitly linked the Fulton strike to the widespread debates then going on in Atlanta and elsewhere about working women and, in particular, child laborers. Like other reformers, strike leaders were keenly aware of the propaganda value of children as the blameless victims of social circumstance.[4] As early as 3 June, organizer Charles Miles asked the children in attendance at the daily union meeting to leave their names so that strike leaders could begin to document and present evidence of child labor at Fulton Mills. Public strike demands quickly expanded from the original worker-generated issues of reinstatement and union recognition to include the elimination from the mill of all children under fourteen years old and a reduced work week for women and minors, as well as a pay increase. And the UTW released flyers across the country stating that most of the striking Fulton workers were "sad eyed, overworked women and children."[5]

At a meeting largely devoted to the issue of child labor and reported on at length by all the Atlanta daily newspapers, Miles described how child laborers kept wages down, since they were easy to control and did not protest their conditions. He also directly linked the Fulton strike with the concurrent campaign to get a strengthened state child labor law passed in the Georgia legislature, stating that it was "the first time in the history of the South that cotton mill operatives favored such legislation," a claim repeated on other occasions. Strike organizers continued to openly support the proposed legislation; for instance, at the June 24 union meeting, O. Delight Smith announced her plans to gather a group of small children and bring them to the state capitol.[6] The reason to make such connections between the strike and child labor reform was tactically obvious. As a result, women's groups, social gospel reformers, the Hearst-owned *Atlanta Georgian*, organized labor, and other advocates of the proposed legislation could and did point to Fulton child workers as an example of oppressive conditions and the need for change; in addition, in publicly pointing out the supposed plight of child laborers at Fulton Mills, strike leaders attracted attention, sympathy, and support from a variety of quarters.

In other ways, too, strike organizers tried to keep children, as well as women workers, squarely in the public eye. For example, children and women were prominently featured in union-sponsored parades downtown. On 19 June, a labor spy reported that Smith and Miles "intend to use small children" in the next day's parade "to get the sympathy and support of the church people in particular." According to Oscar Elsas, who had mill supervisory personnel monitor the event after receiving the spy's report, the parade included a "wagon load of children, none of whom worked at Fulton Mills." Similarly, on 24 June, Smith announced her plans for the strikers to march to a mass meeting "with women with babies, barefooted children, etc."[7]

In addition, the strike organizers, and especially Smith, utilized photographs depicting child labor at Fulton Mills to draw attention and support to their cause. Appreciative of the potential of the camera as an organizing device ever since the strike's outbreak, Smith, with the backing of Georgia Federation of Labor president S. B. Marks, had already personally taken dozens of pictures with her Kodak, capturing some of the more squalid and miserable aspects of cotton mill life. Many of these early photos, often out of focus and poorly composed, documented the crowded housing, outdoor plumbing, and open sewage dumps in the Fulton mill district. They complemented the union's ultimately successful appeal to the Board of Health for an investigation of mill district sanitary conditions, a reflection of organized labor's political clout in the city.[8]

Smith also no doubt was familiar with the work of other reform photogra-

Child laborers at Fulton Mills. Special Collections Dept., Pullen Library, Georgia State University.

phers, especially Lewis Hine, who had traveled through Georgia the previous year on assignment for the National Child Labor Committee. Certainly, the pictures of child laborers at Fulton Mills she took or commissioned drew from familiar, conventional pictorial iconography and imagery of the day.[9] The children portrayed were usually formally, stiffly posed, invariably barefoot and grimy. Like Hines's work, many of the Fulton child labor photographs included captions, often written directly on the negative, which detailed the age and weekly wages of the subjects or emphasized the tragedy of wasted lives in the mill.

In addition, Smith and Miles effectively disseminated the child labor photographs in Atlanta and elsewhere. The 17 June issue of the *Atlanta Journal* included photographs of Fulton child workers, a fact remarked upon by both the strikers and labor spy J. W. Williams.[10] The *Atlanta Georgian* and its *Sunday-*

American also published some of the photographs, in conjunction with its crusade for the new child labor law.[11]

In addition, as had recently been done with the miners in Ludlow, Colorado, the UTW adopted a popular form of communication to its own ends, captioning some of the Fulton child labor photographs and converting them into postcards, which were sent across the country for publicity and support. Eventually, the postcards also entered the reports of investigators from the Commission on Industrial Relations and the Division of Conciliation in the Department of Labor (DOL).[12]

The most widely circulated child labor image during the strike was that of Milton Nunnally (or Nunley, to which he was often referred in captions), who, according to the captions that frequently accompanied his picture, purportedly was ten years old and had received a total of sixty-four cents for two weeks work at Fulton Mills. Nunnally postcards were spotted in Sanford, Florida, and San Antonio, Texas. Nunnally's picture was reprinted in the *Atlanta Sunday-American* during the debate over proposed child labor legislation, as well as in the *Columbus (Ohio) Citizen*, the *Fort Smith (Arkansas) Southwest American*, and various labor journals as a symbol of the oppression of the southern mills. UTW president John Golden included a picture of the boy in an appeal to Secretary of Labor William B. Wilson for federal intervention in the strike. An aide to Wilson reported seeing the Nunnally postcard in the hands of a northern congressman. At the AFL annual convention that fall, UTW organizer Sara Conboy told a heart-rending story using Nunnally as an example of the "grey, colorless lives" of "kiddies of the mills."[13]

However symbolic, Milton Nunnally was an extreme case, and *not* fully representative of child workers at Fulton Mills. Furthermore, as his Fulton minor contract of employment showed, he actually was twelve rather than ten and had entered the plant only with the written permission of his mother. In addition, he apparently had done very little work during his brief stint in the mill; according to a supervisor's report, Nunnally was "always into some kind of mischief."[14] A federal investigator later expressed skepticism about Nunnally's representation, stating, "All the records of the mills show that this boy was absolutely worthless, refusing to work, idling away his time and in a few days was discharged for these reasons. The people who are against child labor used this as an instance of [Elsas's] utter disregard of the rights of the child in paying such poor wages, etc., and heralded this all over the country by post cards, newspapers, etc. Your investigator believes in this particular case that Mr. Elsas was in the right and that all the facts were not known by the persons who made the charges in reference to this child."[15]

This increased emphasis on child labor was only one strategy strike leaders

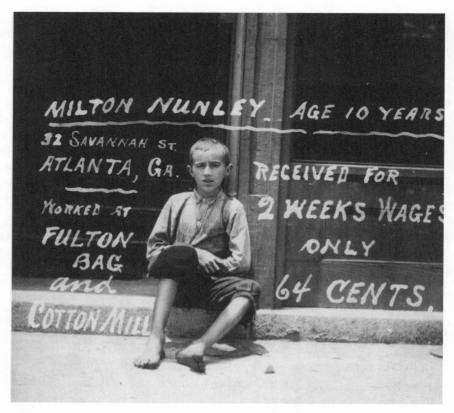

Milton Nunnally. Special Collections Dept., Pullen Library, Georgia State University.

developed to counter what they saw as unfavorable press coverage or, worse yet, little or no coverage at all. Their frustration increased after Fulton Mills placed a quarter-page advertisement in the 3 June edition of the *Atlanta Constitution* addressed "TO THE PUBLIC." Countering what it termed "unwarranted" statements about the situation, management maintained in the ad that only seventy-eight people, or about 5 percent of Fulton's workforce, had actually gone out on strike on 20 May. Furthermore, the ad pointed out, the company, which had been in continuous operation since 1881, paid comparatively high wages, had always anticipated legislation pertaining to hours and age of employment, strictly complied with child labor laws, and paid its workers in cash. It had never operated a commissary, and its fines accounted for only a tiny fraction of the weekly payroll. In an appeal to hostility against outsiders, the ad stated, "The striking employees . . . are misled by persons who are not employees, and some of these strangers have never been in our employment, and are not citizens of this State." Finally, it concluded, "We do not believe this community can be benefited by having mis-statements spread broadcast, hence we furnish the facts."[16]

At that afternoon's union meeting, Charles Miles condemned the ad, claiming Fulton officials "were doing all in their power to get the public on their side." Strike leaders quickly assembled a parade of strikers to pass by the offices of the *Constitution* and Atlanta's other daily newspapers "to show the public the truth and prove the report of '78 on strike' a lie." According to a labor spy, at least 420 people took part in the march; the *Georgian*, the only daily newspaper in town to cover the event, reported 252.[17] Complaints about local press coverage persisted. An aide to Smith on the recently formed union publicity committee related that "they could not get a newspaper to publish any of their news, and that would considerably hamper them in letting the public know the true condition of the mill." And Miles told the strikers they were not getting much publicity because "the big papers would not publicize their news for fear of losing the advertisements" from large mill owners.[18]

Along with increasingly emphasizing the plight of children and women workers, strike organizers developed several approaches to counter this perceived lack of publicity. In particular, they extended the use of photographs, as well as moving pictures, to publicize issues other than child labor. As Maren Stange has pointed out, in its "uniquely documentary and mass reproducible" nature, photography was an especially well suited vehicle of reform, a fact that Smith and Miles, like many of their Progressive Era counterparts, keenly appreciated. By this time, photography was also quite well established and popular in Atlanta. In fact, that very month of June 1914, the city hosted the annual convention of the Photographers Association of America. This was the first time the national meeting had been held south of the Mason-Dixon line and was reflective of Atlanta's growing stature as a convention center.[19]

Smith and Miles's photographic strategy began to unfold at the morning union meeting on Wednesday, 3 June. Smith notified those in attendance to return to the union hall prior to the march that afternoon, as a photographer would be there to take their pictures. Concerned that workers might want to get dressed up before the camera, and thus convey the wrong image or be unfit to perform other strike-related tasks later, she advised the strikers to wear their regular clothes, stating, "[D]on't come all dolled up in high collars and silks and satins. . . . [C]ome up just as you are." In addition to photographing the strikers outside the union hall, the unidentified photographer Smith recruited also took pictures of the march.[20]

At the same meeting, Smith announced plans to photograph the wholesale evictions of strikers from company housing that management had scheduled

A parade of strikers, June 1914. Special Collections Dept., Pullen Library, Georgia State University.

for the following day.[21] While the evictions would greatly disrupt the strike, Smith recognized that they also might provide a weapon in the battle for public opinion. At the meeting, she exhorted workers not simply to vacate their houses when company agents came. Rather, Smith urged, "Make them drive you out. We will have a moving picture machine on the ground, and it would make some nice pictures. . . . We are going to make [the marshal] earn his pay, so good people make him drive you out."[22]

Early on Thursday morning, right after the marshal and his assistants, black laborers, and members of the company security force arrived in the mill district to carry out the evictions, Smith and Miles appeared, accompanied by local commercial photographer Duane A. Russell. Russell had been in Atlanta since at least 1905, when he documented the construction of the prestigious Ansley Park neighborhood. He had also taken portraits of the extended family of former governor Joseph M. Brown.[23] Russell's presence signaled a growing awareness on the part of Smith and Miles of the potential value of photos in the strike effort. The photos he took were superior in quality to those taken by Smith; they were crisper, clearer images and better composed to more dramatically tell a story. According to spy Henry Day, Smith and Miles declared that the eviction scene was "just what they wanted." They then directed Russell to "take the picture of the goods in the street, and got some children to stand to be taken with them." Over the next few hours, Russell took a number of other shots as well, while Smith also took various photographs with her Kodak.[24]

The picture taking did not go unnoticed or unchallenged. The marshal and several Fulton office men tried to stop Smith from employing Russell's services, but, according to spy H. A. Hughes, "Mr. Miles came and told them he would have them arrested if they did not let her alone, as she was acting peacefully." A. J. Gibbs, the keeper of the company storeroom and also a member of the mill's private security force, attempted physically to block Smith's camera, only to be photographed himself.[25]

Later that day, Miles approached an Atlanta police officer, pointed out Gibbs, and called for his arrest, saying that police chief Beavers wanted to know what the officer would do about the situation. No action was taken, since the incident had occurred on private property. At the union meeting the next day, Smith referred to both the episode and Chief Beavers. "I got a picture of the thug who tried to stop me from taking pictures," she announced. She added, "The police are with us, all but two, and I am going to see Chief Beavers and see if they can't be taken away. Chief Beavers is my friend and has been, all of my life. I was on my way to Union meeting, and Chief Beavers saw me and hollers, 'Say, Smithy, come here.' And I pointed my camera at him, but he dodged behind a pole and said, 'Is that the machine that caused all the trouble yesterday?' "[26]

This statement reveals Smith's feistiness and flamboyant style, as well as her transgression of traditional gender roles. It shows how she and Miles viewed and often successfully tried to keep the police as allies rather than antagonists during the strike. It indicates how strike organizers played up to the strikers their contacts with people in prominent places, thereby enhancing both their own credibility and the significance of the strike itself. And it illustrates how the camera was increasingly seen by a variety of parties as a key weapon in the dispute.

From the outset, strike leaders had a clear idea about how they would use the eviction photographs. On the day of the evictions, Smith indicated that the pictures that had been taken would be enlarged and placed in the display windows of downtown stores. Henry Day also reported that the photos would be put "in prominent places in town." This news was of such significance to Oscar Elsas that he underscored the mention of the photos in Day's report and wrote a follow-up inquiry about them.[27]

At the 5 June union meeting, Miles reiterated that the photographs would be placed "in the windows of the principal stores." True to his word, that night he and Smith worked until eleven o'clock mounting the newly developed and captioned photos onto cardboard backing. By the next afternoon, they had put at least one display of eighteen four-by-six-inch photographs in a major downtown drugstore window. In so doing, they drew upon a common practice among Atlanta publicists; for instance, photos of the visiting Metropolitan Opera stars who came to town in the spring also were featured in downtown drugstores.[28]

In addition, as with the child labor pictures, the UTW made plans to disseminate the eviction photos well beyond Atlanta. At the 5 June meeting, Miles vowed to send the pictures to "all parts, far and wide over the United States and Canada, to let the people know the conditions of the Cotton Mills of the South. . . . We will send them broadcast from East to West in the United States, so that everybody will see them. . . . We will make copies and send them from one end of the country to the other; far and wide."[29]

The strike leaders had another targeted audience as well: the Fulton workers themselves. Organizers believed that for often despised mill hands, seeing photos of themselves in "prominent places" or "the principal stores" (just like the opera stars) would be a rare validating and authenticating experience. Likewise, the knowledge that the strike was not merely a local disturbance but was of concern and significance to others in Atlanta, the region, and even the nation, could enhance workers' self-esteem and commitment to the cause.

Strike organizers employed motion pictures in a similar fashion. The UTW hired the local branch of the New York–based Sphinx Film Company to film evictions and other strike scenes. In addition, a representative of the Hearst-Selig News Pictorial outfit filmed the union's 6 June parade. Smith and Miles then showed the parade footage at the downtown Atlanta Theater, admitting all union members free, thus providing workers with the unusual and no doubt affirming experience of seeing themselves in the movies.[30]

On Monday, 8 June, the Sphinx crew was back in the mill district, filming a second wave of evictions. An operator from the Hearst-owned Pathe Weekly newsreel was also in attendance. When Smith and Miles arrived, they staged a scene involving evicted spooler Margaret Dempsey, a fifty-four-year-old widow. According to her testimony during the strike, Dempsey had worked in cotton mills about eighteen years; other union accounts stated that she "had slaved 37 years" and that she "was fired after 39 years service." In any event, she seemed a fitting subject to evoke sympathy for the strikers' cause.[31]

After the belongings of Dempsey and her son Clarence were put out on the street, a spy reported, "It was arranged for her to make a speech and throw her arms up and the son to go to his mother and try and comfort her and she to push him away. While this was in progress, the [motion picture] operator and

The eviction of Margaret Dempsey. Special Collections Dept., Pullen Library, Georgia State University.

the man who was with him were giving instructions, and told her to drop into a seat, then fall over as if exhausted. This was all carried out fine, and Mr. Miles said to me and Mrs. Smith, 'see, that woman could make a good living, acting for moving pictures.'"[32]

A representative of Sphinx Film wrote Oscar Elsas that afternoon. Maintaining that "it is not our intention to present this matter to the world in an unfair manner," the letter's author asked Elsas if he would not like to have included in the footage to be sent up to New York "a scene taken at the lunch hour Tuesday showing you feeding the vast number of satisfied and contented workers." Furthermore, even though the eviction footage accounted for over 100 feet of the 150 feet of finished picture the New York office expected, the Sphinx representative proposed that this footage could be reduced so that mill management "can get equal representation." "The New York office seems to have an inflated idea of the size of this strike," the author wrote, "but we do not expect any more calls after they receive this print." No record exists as to how or whether Elsas responded.[33]

In addition to being filmed, Margaret Dempsey was also photographed with her arms akimbo and in other poses that paralleled the staged motion pictures of her. She was then described in the various captions that accompanied her photos as "Old Ma'am Dempsey," "Mother Dempsey," and "An Ancient Victim." Dempsey was hardly alone in this type of representation. As with the child labor images and the other photographs taken by Smith, the eviction pictures contained a pronounced theme of victimization. Widows and children were prominently featured in the photos, which also detailed the meager belongings of the Fulton strikers out on the street. Captions like "The Homeless Strikers" further emphasized the workers' plight.

In other ways, too, the eviction photographs were often quite carefully arranged, even staged, with an eye to public relations. For instance, one of the families evicted was that of Fiddlin' John Carson, a striking Fulton Mills weaver. Photographer Russell drew upon a common Atlanta convention concerning Fiddlin' John, making sure to capture Carson with his famous fiddle, large family, and ever-present hound dog.[34]

Not all the eviction photographs were so well composed or crafted, however; they also included their occasional comic moments. Accompanying Smith, Miles, Russell, and the motion picture crew on their rounds through the mill district was none other than spy H. A. Hughes. As Hughes related in his report that night, "The photographer had to go away and Smith asked me to take pictures of the household goods, so I had to do so"—which perhaps accounts for the poor visual quality of certain eviction photos. Furthermore, Hughes's partner in espionage, Henry Day, received a "used roll of films" from Smith and reported that "when I had the chance, I exposed them to the light to try and spoil them."[35]

Notwithstanding such episodes, for the most part strike organizers consciously framed the eviction photographs, as well as other union-commissioned pictures, to advance several themes. In addition to portraying forlorn, downtrodden workers, the photos publicized the dastardly deeds of the company and its agents. They included images of hired thugs ostensibly trying to goad strikers into retaliation, of mill officers supervising the evictions, of deputies and company doctor E. W. Hawkins—considered little more than a spy himself by many workers—on hand, and of mounted police officers and marshals putting workers' belongings out on the street.

One activity that strike organizers and UTW officials frequently publicized to various audiences was the employment of black laborers in the evictions. At the meeting at which Miles announced plans to place the eviction photos in downtown stores, he declared, "We are going to . . . show the people of Atlanta how you people were put out of your homes, by niggers." According to Smith,

"FIDLING" JOHN ABOUT TO BE EVICTED

Russell

Fiddlin' John Carson. Special Collections Dept., Pullen Library, Georgia State University.

black labor was used because "no white man would *stoop* to help" the marshal in putting the strikers out on the street; she said even the blacks hired to assist in the evictions were "ashamed" of what they had done. To bring the point home, captions on the eviction photos described "Negro's Employed By the Mill" and "Negro's Evicting Whites." For many Fulton workers, indeed for many white people more generally, such images evoked humiliation, degradation, and outrage.[36]

Reflecting the degree to which white supremacism was national and not merely regional in scope, union-sponsored appeals to racial prejudice and anxieties extended well beyond the boundaries of Atlanta and the South. The Massachusetts-based UTW openly exploited racism to gain support for the strikers' cause. In flyers distributed across the country the union pointed out how the "white slaves of the mill" had been evicted by "burly Negroes hired for

An evicted striker; the racial epithet was added to the photograph by a strike organizer. Special Collections Dept., Pullen Library, Georgia State University.

the purpose." (In so doing, the UTW also evoked "white slavery," or prostitution, another central Progressive Era concern.) In a typical appeal, UTW president John Golden wrote, "Just imagine white southern Americans, mothers with little babies in their arms, little white children taken from the little beds and thrown out on the street by negroes in this twentieth century. . . . Sick women were thrown homeless into the street . . . by the hired niggers."[37]

The eviction photographs and other pictures taken around the same time also emphasized the good character of the strikers and the services provided by the union and its leaders. The images and associated captions portrayed peaceful, well-dressed pickets; "cool headed" strikers resisting the disruptive efforts of company-hired thugs; mill district residents "still defiant" and denouncing the evictions; and union members quietly parading behind a large American flag. The eviction photos also showed strikers and their belongings being transported by "union transfer" trucks to a "textile workers hotel," a large local boardinghouse provided by the UTW. Workers were also shown carrying goods from the union-sponsored commissary. The extent and concrete nature of union support, along with the perceived resources and commitment of the strike organizers, was underscored by a posed picture taken by Russell showing perhaps a hundred workers, along with Miles and Smith, in front of the commissary. Another commissary shot, simply labeled "strike leaders," accentuated the importance of Smith, Miles, and Local 886 officer H. N. Mullinax.

Strike organizers employed photographs in other ways as well. On 17 July, a labor spy reported that the strikers were starting up their own newspaper, "since they couldn't get publicity." The following day, the first and apparently only issue of the *Strikers' Journal* came out, complete with photographs of Fiddlin' John Carson and other evicted strikers, as well as the union commissary. Copies of the paper were hawked on streetcars and elsewhere, with the proceeds used to replenish the commissary.[38]

In addition, the organizers contemplated using photographs to unmask the spies within the union's midst. On the same day that the Detecto machine was discovered in the union hall, Smith told spies Day and Hughes that she had obtained part of a daily report filed by a private detective (probably Hughes or Day) who had been tailing her. "Now boys, get busy and find this man," Smith told the spies. "I expect to have a copy of a full report, also the man's name; his photo and who he works for, tonight." She also assured them that an unidentified third party would soon get the "skunk's" picture. By the following day, Smith had clearly established a link between Hughes, probably Day as well, and the two Detecto operators. In Chief Beavers's presence, she openly hinted at taking pictures of Day, who was standing nearby. Day quickly left the scene and along with Hughes soon departed Atlanta for good.[39]

Fulton management took their cue from the union and also engaged in the photograph war. During the last week of June, Oscar Elsas learned that strike leader W. E. Fleming was about to leave the presidency of the local and travel across Georgia to organize workers at other mills. "A photograph, or good description of him," Elsas wrote Exposition Mill's Allen Johnson, "would undoubtedly put the mill people on their guard, so that whenever he reached their village they could take the necessary steps to block him."[40] Although there exists no evidence that such a picture of Fleming ever was taken or disseminated, by 29 June Elsas had set into motion his own photographic campaign against other perceived company adversaries.

Most of Elsas's efforts during the last three weeks of June, however, centered around the documentation of perceived abuses by strikers and their allies, and the attendant complicity of the Atlanta police. On 9 June, he wrote *Southern Textile Bulletin* editor David Clark that "[t]he great trouble we are experiencing now is the indifference on the part of the police force. If they handled the situation with the firmness and fairness that the case warrants, the trouble would be very short-lived, but they seem to be sympathetic, taking no steps to keep our property free from aggressive picketing, both night and day, with the result that our help is being harassed unnecessarily. We hope in the next day or two to have these conditions ended. If not, we shall probably have to seek some other method."[41]

Elsas adopted several interrelated tactics to address the situation. For a while, despite his leeriness of media publicity, he actually considered using force to break the strike and rout the outsiders from the mill district. This possibility reached the attention of Jacob Elsas, Oscar's father and the founder of Fulton Mills, who was on company business in New York City. Alarmed by the potential effects of such an approach, including the adverse publicity that might arise, Jacob Elsas actively intervened in the Atlanta plant's operation for the first time during the course of the strike, promptly sending Oscar a telegram and a follow-up letter of fatherly advice.

"I am opposed to any harsher measure than an attempt to work Mills," Jacob wrote, "but not getting entangled further." He added, "We must make up our minds that we cannot get all we want, but we may get more than we want by using force. A force that will perhaps be worse than combating present idlers. I am opposed to hiring detectives [to break the strike] and since we know the sympathy of the police and the Mayor, let us do [the] best we can, unless we conclude that we get worse off all the time. Don't use the newspapers if avoidable, but state our side to people of influence."[42]

Having already arrived at the same conclusion, Oscar Elsas followed his father's advice to reach influential people out of public view. He contacted a railroad representative and the head of the city stockade to inform them of their employees' involvement with the strikers.[43] In addition, he wrote Atlanta mayor James Woodward about the situation. In his letter, Elsas maintained that mill management was willing and ready to meet about grievances, re-employment, or other matters with any individual current or recent employee, outside of those who insulted female workers "or those who have threatened, intimidated or assaulted any of our employees." Elsas also laid out what he termed "certain facts" for Woodward's information. These included the by-now familiar assertions that since only about 75 of the 400 Fulton workers discharged since October belonged to the union, "there has been no discrimination against Union members"; that Fulton Mills paid the highest wages in the region; and that only 78 workers "have seen fit to indulge in the so-called strike" (the same phrase that his son Norman used seventy-five years later).

He also drew upon a central tenet of the ideology of New South manufacturers, that because they had provided industry and jobs to an impoverished region, they merited special authority and consideration within the community. Elsas reminded Woodward of the company's role in the development of

Atlanta and the New South, declaring, "[Fulton Bag] is a distinct Atlanta enterprise; it was initiated and built up by Atlanta men and energy. It is the largest enterprise of its kind in the South, and has had no little to do with the building up of this City. Its officers have not interfered with politics, nor sought to evade the laws of the State. It has never attempted to impede legislation toward the betterment of manufacturing conditions, but, on the contrary, has, during its whole history, moved in advance of legislation upon those lines." While denying he sought any favors, Elsas maintained that the firm's "history and efforts have been such that it is entitled to fair protection from the City Authorities." Finally, he extended an invitation for the mayor to visit the mill, to no avail.[44]

Three days later, Elsas wrote a letter to acting chief of police E. L. Jett. After claiming that not more than twenty-five of the people "who are interfering with our operations" were former Fulton employees, Elsas gave his account of several altercations and acts of violence that had taken place during the strike. Stating that the employees still working at the mill ought to be protected "in their desire to keep and carry out their contracts with us," Elsas requested that the police keep nonworkers away from the Fulton premises and that Fulton workers be accorded the same protection given people elsewhere in the city. Finally, he offered to pay the costs of police supernumeraries to patrol Fulton property at night. Copies of the letter were sent to the members of the police committee of the Board of Alderman and to Mell W. Wilkinson, president of the Chamber of Commerce.[45]

In his response, Jett pointed out that in each episode Elsas described, cases had been made against the accused offender. He also maintained that there existed adequate police presence around the Fulton property and rejected Elsas's offer to pay for supernumeraries during the strike, "as it is the duty of this department . . . to furnish necessary police protection without expense to private individuals." Elsas wrote back that the cited incidents represented only the tip of the iceberg concerning disturbances around the mill, and he informed Jett of additional anticipated altercations about which the company had learned through its intelligence network.[46]

At Wilkinson's suggestion, Elsas got onto the agenda of the Chamber of Commerce directors' meeting on 19 June, and he invited Exposition Mills's Johnson to the meeting as well. Apparently making reference to another episode involving perceived lack of support for local textile manufacturers from Atlanta's business community, Elsas asked Johnson to "explain the final conclusion of your Board of Directors as to not building a 30,000 spindle mill." Johnson agreed to attend.[47]

At the meeting, what he later called the "first public attempt made by us to set our case before the business men,"[48] Elsas itemized in New South terms the contributions of Fulton Mills to the Atlanta economy, pointing out the size of the plant, its large payroll, its comparatively high wages, and the "fact" that it was developed with local capital. He stressed once more that only 78 people had originally walked out, leaving, in contrast, some 1,300 contented employees. He mentioned the original strike demands and how they had gradually changed. Distributing the letter he had written to Jett and the police commissioners, he described the picketing, insults, and threats that had gone on and the accompanying police indifference. He brought up the MRFM's recent involvement in the strike and hinted that various unspecified "plans for future improvement" had been or might be "abandoned." And he invited the Chamber of Commerce to appoint a committee "to look us over" and to use its influence "to stop attacks on capital and give same proper protection."[49]

While the Chamber of Commerce decided not to take action at the time, Elsas continued to write letters to Wilkinson, Mayor Woodward, and the police department documenting perceived abuses by the union force, along with police negligence. By mid-July, the Chamber of Commerce agreed to appoint a committee, headed by Trust Company Bank vice president John Murphy, to investigate the situation. By late July, the Chamber of Commerce was putting pressure on the MRFM not to support the U.S. Commission on Industrial Relations hearings in Atlanta. And Murphy, if not the entire Chamber of Commerce committee, was apparently in on behind-the-scenes machinations against O. Delight Smith or Charles Miles.[50]

Elsas was not the only one upset by the boisterous goings-on in the mill district; Smith and Miles were concerned as well about both the presence and appearance of strike-related disorderliness. At the 6 June union meeting, Smith and Miles told those assembled not to congregate in bunches on the street, because "it doesn't look good," and warned that there would be a fine for anyone bringing a whiskey bottle to the meeting hall. On 8 June, Miles asked the strikers, with the exception of those who had been designated as pickets, to stay away from the plant gates and to keep the union hall neat. On 9 June, strikers were explicitly informed that there was to be no throwing of bricks or stones. And on 22 June, a labor spy reported to Elsas that the organizers "are taking great pains to warn your people against all disorder."[51] Such warnings reflected the organizers' concerns about controlling a rapidly growing and often unruly population, comprised of both Fulton workers and others, as the UTW sought to attract favorable publicity and funds for the strike. As Miles confidentially remarked to H. N. Mullinax, "They [the strikers] won't do what [they] are told."[52]

In particular, strike organizers feared that disorderliness might offset their budding attempts to bring into the matter Atlanta's active and well-subsidized Men and Religion Forward Movement. By the end of May, Miles had made contact with MRFM leader Marion M. Jackson, an attorney and the district manager for the American Surety Company. Knowing little of the matter beforehand, Jackson attended a Federation of Trades meeting devoted to the strike. At the meeting, he was apprised of Fulton's labor contract, its fining system, and the unsanitary conditions in the mill district. Jackson was also "struck by the fact that the original trouble was the discharge of workers for joining the union." As a result of this meeting, Jackson "decided that the Fulton Bag and Cotton Mills should be willing to do what their laborers were requesting, that is to consent to an investigation of their difficulties and arbitrate."[53]

On 1 June, Jackson reported back to the MRFM executive committee that "this Committee has an opportunity to exert an influence to satisfactorily settle this difficulty."[54] Over the next few days, members of the MRFM publicity committee obtained information about the textile industry, communicated with Miles, and observed firsthand such events as the eviction of strikers from company housing and one of the union's downtown parades. For his part, Miles made sure to employ various religious references in his addresses to the strikers.

On the morning of 5 June, Miles fretted that the expected contributions from the MRFM had somehow not yet come through.[55] That support finally did arrive that afternoon and the next morning in the form of "Men and Religion Bulletin No. 119," which was placed in all the city's daily newspapers.[56] Coming only two days after the company's own ad, the bulletin foreshadowed in style, tone, and content subsequent MRFM bulletins about the strike. Under the heading "LET US HAVE JUSTICE," in three-quarter-inch-high capital letters, appeared the biblical citation: "But let Justice roll down as waters, and righteousness as a mighty stream." Then followed a brief account of two men who "DIED ON THE ALTAR OF ALCOHOL AND GREED IN ATLANTA." "Their search for happiness here is over," the bulletin read, "Their bodies cry out for justice for those who live. Who next?" The next section described others in search of happiness, namely the peaceful Fulton strikers recently on parade. "Look to the east!" the bulletin continued. "There on the city's edge, three smokestacks tower above massive buildings; a great wall surrounds them; glass and barbed wire run along the top. Above it one sees a gaunt black bridge; over it goes a group of children as the morning whistle blows; a little girl not over twelve, her pink dress fluttering against the grime, runs through a forbidding door to work. SHE AND THEY SHOULD BE AT PLAY."

Facing Oakland Cemetery, the bulletin went on, the company houses in the

Factory Lot constituted "graves of the living." Here lived laborers who, against a backdrop of many complaints, had gone out on strike over the dismissal of union members. "This the mill owners deny," reported the bulletin. "But why do they refuse to have an impartial board investigate and dispose of these complaints? The strikers are willing." A reference to the evictions followed: "YESTERDAY MARSHALLS OF OUR COURTS WERE PUTTING HOUSEHOLD GOODS INTO THE STREETS. THE STRIKERS MUST MOVE ON. THE MILLS MUST HAVE THEIR HOUSES. GOD PITY AND PROTECT THEM AND THEIR KIND!"

After alluding to the recent labor-related massacre in Ludlow, Colorado, the bulletin cited a *New York Times* editorial opposing what it called the employers' "closed shop," that is, "closed against the unions." In contrast, it continued, the *Times* had approved of "the Protocol of Peace" in New York's garment district, under which over 7,000 grievances had been settled since 1911.[57] In addition, the bulletin referred to federal reports that indicated the income a family of five needed to earn to maintain a minimal "fair standard of living," a sum far beyond the average wages of a worker at Fulton Mills, not counting fines and penalties. "Think!" it continued,

> And you will see that the presence of children, who should be in school and at play, working their lives away in mills is not wholly due to shiftless fathers, who will not work, but to the grave necessity for supporting the family life— THE LACK OF A LIVING WAGE. THERE ARE NO PROBLEMS IN THE GRAVEYARD OVER WHICH THE THREE STACKS BELCH THEIR SMOKE, BUT THERE ARE QUESTIONS BENEATH THEIR MOVING SHADOWS WHICH GOD WILL HAVE YOU ANSWER. The liquor problem, the question of brothels, the handling of prisoners and the living wage are all part of the same great question. The spirit of God is abroad in the world. And men are crying for justice. In the end they will have it.

The bulletin introduced for the first time what would be a recurrent request on the part of strike leaders and supporters: an independent investigation of the situation. This appeal reflected an appreciation of the implacability and considerable resources of mill management and the difficulty of sustaining a prolonged strike effort. Tellingly, although the MRFM's first and subsequent bulletins clearly were sympathetic to the strikers, the MRFM did not ever actually endorse either the union or the strike, never going farther than an appeal for mediation or arbitration.

Bulletin No. 119 also reinforced and perpetuated stereotypical, two-dimensional images of downtrodden southern textile workers, images that were at odds with the complex realities of Fulton workers' lives. For instance, perhaps the majority of Fulton workers did *not* in fact reside in company housing, or what the MRFM called the "graves of the living." Even when they did, they were likely to live in a household in which at least one person worked outside the mill and in a neighborhood that featured a bustling commercial district, access to downtown, and occupational diversity within a white working-class context. The bulletin's stark portrait of the mill and its emphasis on child labor conveyed a similar message of downtroddenness. In addition, the bulletin explicitly linked conditions at Fulton Mills to other symbols of urban decay.

In its imagery, the bulletin reflected the direct influence of Smith and Miles upon the MRFM. For instance, the bulletin almost precisely replicated the language that Smith used in some of her early photograph captions: a photo of a street in the mill district was labeled "the burial ground of living bodies"; another picture with an arrow drawn on it to highlight the mill's three smoke stacks had the caption, "the towering smoke stacks could tell tales of misery." The bulletin's description of the glass and barbed wire on top of the wall surrounding the mill evoked Miles's mention of the same subject at the 31 May strike rally. In fact, Miles told the clerk at his hotel that he had personally written part of the bulletin and was helping prepare another one.[58]

Miles and Smith were elated by the MRFM's involvement. On 5 June, Miles spread out the *Atlanta Journal* in his hotel and declared to two visitors, "I guess we will win now." The next day, he read from the bulletin at the union meeting, stating he was glad to see the MRFM behind the strikers, who now "would have a better chance than ever. . . . Never have I seen such a nice article written up as that, and I have been in this business for a long time." And on 7 June, Smith told a rally that the strikers now had "86 ministers who were going to back them up."[59]

On 8 June, the second strike-related bulletin appeared. At the MRFM executive committee meeting that day, Jackson reported that "conditions apparently were unchanged among the textile workers" and that the publicity campaign would continue. To avoid an anti-outsider backlash, Jackson advised that the bulletins not present the issues at hand as being merely local or sectional in nature. In addition, the executive committee planned to meet with the county association of cotton manufacturers "in the hope that some amicable adjustment be affected."[60]

This was wishful thinking, given the position of strength and the anti-union attitude of management at Fulton Mills and other nearby cotton mills. Soon after the MRFM got involved, Fulton general manager Gordon Johnstone paid a visit to Jackson, stating that the Evangelical Ministers Association was making "a great mistake" and presenting management's side of the matter. When Jackson asked him if the company then would accept an impartial investigation into working conditions and the causes of the strike, conducted by "the leading men of the city of Atlanta, whose standing and position could not be questioned," Johnstone replied that he was "not in a position to accept this proposition." Shortly thereafter, Jackson met with Ben Phillips, Oscar Elsas's brother-in-law and attorney for the mill, and repeated his call for an investigation to "quiet the situation and remove the difficulties." Jackson's proposal to Phillips that Rabbi David Marx of the Temple, the Reform synagogue where the Elsases were congregants, be appointed one of the investigators fell on deaf ears.[61]

At the 15 June meeting of the MRFM executive committee, Jackson reported on a conference he had held with Sam Carter of the Gate City Mills, who had informed him that "all the operators discourage organization among the employees." An interview Jackson had the following week with Exposition Mills's Johnson, the president of the state cotton manufacturers association, produced a similar result; as the executive committee minutes recorded, no doubt with some understatement, Johnson "stated plainly and unequivocally that the association stands opposed to the unionization of textile workers."[62]

By this time, Oscar Elsas had already begun to counter what he termed the "uncalled-for attack" by the MRFM. He asked former governor Joseph M. Brown to get in touch with MRFM leader Reverend John E. White. Brown, who always had been hostile to organized labor, had stepped up his antilabor rhetoric that summer during his campaign for the U.S. Senate seat of his longtime political rival Hoke Smith. During his campaign, Brown linked organized labor to "anarchistic practices" and direly predicted what might happen if the "hordes of negroes" in Georgia were unionized. In Brown, Elsas recognized a staunchly antilabor kindred spirit.[63] At Elsas's behest, Brown advised White "to go slow in condoning or excusing a movement characterized by stone-throwing and stabbing." In addition, at his appearance before the Chamber of Commerce, Elsas maintained that the MRFM had unfairly singled out Fulton Mills and had misrepresented the earnings of the company's workers.[64]

Undaunted, the MRFM continued running its bulletins in the papers twice weekly. Its activities prompted Herschel Jones of the *Atlanta Georgian* and the National Child Labor Committee to address the MRFM executive committee on 22 June to seek help with the pending state child labor legislation. At the same meeting, a letter from Miles on behalf of the strikers was read, requesting the MRFM's services as arbiters in the Fulton dispute. Miles wrote: "Realizing that your Movement, representing, as it does, the spirit of the Churches of the City, and aiming to apply the teachings of Christianity to the practical affairs of life, we are willing to permit you to be our judge and jury. We are willing to submit the whole matter at issue to a committee appointed by you, with the understanding that both sides may present their evidence to the committee, who shall arbitrate their differences; their findings shall be handed down in writing, and be final and binding upon both parties directly involved in the strike."[65]

Miles's letter, reprinted in the *Journal of Labor*, was an indication of the increasing difficulty UTW organizers were facing in sustaining the strike. Miles's willingness to appoint the MRFM as "judge and jury" also helped remove control of the strike yet further from the Fulton workers involved, even as it boosted the MRFM's sense of self-importance. However, his call for arbitration, along with a similar appeal in the *Journal of Labor*, also had the effect of subtly but significantly shifting the MRFM discussion about strike options from impartial investigation to arbitration or mediation, a development that Oscar Elsas immediately recognized.[66]

In the words of MRFM president John Eagan, when labor representatives asked the MRFM to be judge and jury "in the controversy now on between capital and labor," they "laid upon the representatives of the church the responsibility of seeing that this controversy received a fair, impartial hearing." Accordingly, the MRFM began to plan a mass meeting, titled "Capital, Labor, Christ," to be held at the Grand Opera House on Sunday, 28 June. The MRFM publicity committee issued tickets in advance of the event to ensure a full house, and Jackson himself spoke to the strikers about the meeting.[67]

The public nature of the meeting, as well as its potential size, promised to significantly alter the discourse surrounding the Fulton strike, a fact Oscar Elsas realized well. The meeting could help legitimize the strikers' cause in the eyes of a wide range of Atlantans, publicly offer a challenge to the authority and claims of mill management, undermine Elsas's attempts to minimize the matter and keep it out of the press, and set a dangerous precedent for future industrial disputes and other local conflicts. Elsas wrote Brown again about John White, one of the three scheduled speakers at the meeting, suggesting that Brown could be quite beneficial in exerting his personal influence to prevent White from "adding his strength to such an irresponsible movement." He maintained that he had tried to refrain from public statements about the strike, "feeling that justice would prevail sooner or later," but that "for these gentlemen [the MRFM] to attack us in an open meeting hardly seems fair." "If, therefore," he wrote, "you are in a position to prevent this, we would certainly appreciate it."[68]

White, however, did give his speech at the packed 28 June mass meeting, attended by some 2,000 persons, and likely the largest public forum held in Atlanta in decades.[69] Reflecting the MRFM's recent shift in emphasis, White spoke on the subject of "Mediation." Mediation, White opened, "is a word that fits well the lips of [C]hristian ministers in talking anywhere and under any conditions." Expressing sympathy for both capital and labor and acknowledging that industrial disputes and controversies were perhaps inevitable, White deplored the resolution of such conflict through strikes and lock-outs, or what he called "industrial war." As had been shown on numerous occasions, he asserted, this approach damaged not only labor and capital but also the general public. Mediation provided an alternative to such disorder.

The central obstacle to mediation, White said, was the lingering idea that "the employer is the superior, and the working man the inferior." It was critical to recognize "the equality between the dollar and the man—an equality between capitalists and laborers." In White's opinion, when capitalists finally realize "that there is no question of superiority or inferiority, but that equality is given to the situation, then mediation will have no difficulty in its path whatsoever." White closed by stating that in the democratic, homogeneous, and, in particular, Christian South, there was the opportunity to avoid the conflict that had marked the North and Europe and to chart a new course in industrial matters.

The next speaker was the Reverend C. B. Wilmer, who discussed child labor, followed by Marion Jackson, speaking on "the coming of the kingdom of God." Jackson opened his speech by denouncing widespread accounts of anti-Semitism in Atlanta at the time of the Frank case. "I revolt at that from the bottom of my soul," he exclaimed, "and deny from the bottom of my soul that . . . such prejudice exists in the city of Atlanta. It does not exist in the state of Georgia, and it is a lie that has been sent to the four corners of the earth."

Jackson continued, "It is not true that I think of the Jews simply as Shylocks and characters of that sort, but I think of them as people to whom the world owes much." He recounted some of the contributions made by the Jewish people, from Moses, "the first great Hebrew who ever led a labor strike," to Jacob and Joseph, to Jesus himself. "The Jews," Jackson proclaimed, "are the most wonderful nation the world has ever seen." He then said he wanted "to come down to a few facts of our day," adding, "What the Jew needs and what the Christian needs . . . is to come down and see what the Jew and what the Christian are doing in this day and time with regard to our fellow-man."

Jackson's first exhibit in this regard was the Fulton labor contract, which he denounced for "[forgetting] entirely the interests of the laboring man." He criticized the one-sided clause in the contract that absolved the employer from having to pay for lost time resulting from accident or disability, while workers had to reimburse the company for any damage caused by their negligence. He cited another clause in the contract that provided a ready means for management to fire someone simply for belonging to a union. To add insult to injury, those dismissed for unionism would also lose a week's withheld wages. "Is that right?" Jackson asked to applause and cries of "No!" "Is it just? Ought such a thing to be permitted in civilized communities?"

He then brought up the reference in the bulletin to mill houses as the "grave yards of the living." "I am frank to say," Jackson declared, "and you can publish this abroad, that I would prefer my grave to living in one of them." "It is murder," he said, to herd people together in such crowded, unsanitary conditions; small wonder workers turned to a union. "When I look at the faces of those women and children," he said, "they tell a pathetic story." He went on to support the pending child labor bill, stating that "the man who is willing to fatten on the life-blood of women and children by selling them liquor, is willing in identically the same way to fatten on the life-blood of women and children by working them in their mills."

Jackson then returned to the subject of the Jews, who had been in Georgia since its colonial beginnings "and became good American citizens." In Atlanta, too, "the Jew has shown himself to be a good American citizen. He is living in a Christian country to-day, and to-day in Christ's name and in the name of the Christian city and in the name of the Christian church and Christian people, we ask him to do justice to this workingman." By justice, Jackson meant consent to an impartial arbitration of the differences between management and labor. "Is there anything unreasonable in that?" he queried. "Can anything be fairer? Can Mr. Elsas object to that?"

In summation, Jackson offered a resolution:

> Whereas, the strikers at the Fulton Bag and Cotton Mills have signified their willingness to have the differences between them and the mill arbitrated; and, whereas, for the protection of women and children and the health of the community the public is very vitally interested in reconciling the points of difference between both strikers and mill owners; Be it resolved that we, the citizens of Atlanta, Fulton County, in mass meeting assembled, do urge upon the Fulton Bag & Cotton Mills the necessity of meeting the offer in the same spirit of fairness as it is made, and that an arbitration be made between the strikers and the mill in a manner and form to be determined by them.

The vast majority of those present then rose in favor of the resolution, with nobody standing in opposition, and the meeting adjourned.

The meeting, widely reported in the press, brought various reactions from different quarters. A labor spy reported Miles to be "in ecstasies." Local trade unionists were also jubilant about the gathering. The *Journal of Labor* hailed the meeting as "historic," and a representative of the Atlanta Typographical Union approached John Eagan to ask the MRFM to sponsor similar mass meetings on a regular basis in the future. Indeed, the MRFM made plans for a subsequent mass meeting on 12 July.[70]

Bolstered by the meeting, the MRFM naively continued to push for arbitration. At the 29 June executive committee meeting, Marion Jackson proposed that MRFM representatives attempt to meet with Oscar Elsas, carrying with them the original letter from Miles concerning arbitration and a copy of the mass meeting resolutions. In addition, the Evangelical Ministers Association passed a resolution commending "to both parties in the controversy at the Fulton Bag and Cotton Mills the duty of arbitrating their difficulties and tender to this and the good offices of this association in any way which may be deemed useful." Along with supporting the child labor measure, the MRFM now helped introduce a compulsory arbitration bill in the state legislature. Finally, the MRFM sent telegrams to Washington requesting the presence of federal mediators on the scene.[71]

Not all the MRFM members were so inclined, however. At the executive committee meeting on 6 July, it was reported that wholesale grocer H. Y. McCord had resigned, "basing his action upon the attitude of this committee relative to the present industrial situation." Despite entreaties from other MRFM members, McCord refused to withdraw his resignation.[72] Not all members of Atlanta's religious community agreed with the MRFM position, either. Reverend Alvan F. Sherrill, dean of the Atlanta Theological Seminary, wrote Elsas that the MRFM mass meeting "may not assume to represent all the religion or all the wisdom of Atlanta." Sherrill also had harsh words about Marion Jackson and John White. "We can regard the former," he wrote, "a bundle of inflammations, and the best to say of the latter is we are still 'pulling him green.' "[73]

In addition, Sherrill commended Elsas for the official company response to the mass meeting. Management had publicly announced: "After carefully considering the suggestion that we arbitrate our business affairs, we have decided, in view of the fact that we have at the present time about 1,200 satisfied employees at work, and less than 85 now out, there is nothing to arbitrate." According to a labor spy, the strikers were "crestfallen and downcast" upon hearing Elsas's reply. C. E. McLin of Rome's Anchor Duck Mills, on the other hand, sent congratulations to Elsas for taking a firm stand against the MRFM.[74]

A great deal more was going on behind the scenes. Already angry with the MRFM's involvement, feeling it constituted unwarranted, irresponsible meddling on his terrain, Elsas became incensed after learning what had transpired at the mass meeting. He was particularly irked by the speech of Marion Jackson, which he felt exuded anti-Semitism. His sentiments were shared by his brother Louis, the company secretary-treasurer. Jackson's speech, Louis Elsas wrote, "clearly indicated his bias. Though the subtlety of his forensic was worthy of a Marc Antony, he hardly made an attempt to conceal his dastardly purpose of stirring up religious prejudice. His words speak for themselves, irrespective of his introductory disclaimer."[75]

Whatever Jackson's intents or sentiments were, it is easy to see how from Elsas's perspective the speech was suffused with anti-Semitism. Jackson not only unnecessarily brought up Elsas's religion and mentioned the name of Shylock, but even when he discussed the deeds of such Jewish heroes as Jacob and Joseph, he resorted to anti-Semitic stereotypes, portraying Jacob as a wily businessman, cutting a deal with God at favorable interest rates, while Joseph amassed huge profits from hungry people after cornering the world's grain market at a time of famine.[76]

Even Jackson's praise of the Jews and disavowal of prejudice had a kind of "some of my best friends are Jews" quality. It evoked the closing argument made by solicitor general Hugh M. Dorsey in the Frank case, in which Dorsey praised the contributions of the Jews and denied being anti-Semitic himself, then went on to list the deeds of various Jewish fiends and criminals in history. "They [Jews] rise to heights sublime, but they also sink to the lowest depths of degradation," Dorsey had said.[77] Furthermore, as Elsas pointed out, religion had no bearing whatsoever on the matters at hand but was only publicly brought to light because Elsas was a Jew; had he been a Methodist, for instance, his faith would never have been an issue.

Indeed, though Elsas may not have been aware of it, this was not the first time that the MRFM had displayed such insensitivity. Just a month before, the MRFM had issued a bulletin in the Atlanta papers that included a reference to Anniston, Alabama's "gallant Chief of Police, the Jew, Shiretzki [sic]," who had recently died in the line of duty. Atlantan Morris Benjamin, the slain police chief's uncle, promptly contacted the MRFM and the Atlanta Journal in response. "Permit me to suggest," Benjamin wrote, "It was not the Jew Shiritzki, but the man who sacrificed his life. Why comment on his religion? His being a Jew was utterly apart from the office he held. . . . We are not ashamed of being Jews, on the contrary will proudly acclaim the fact when the occasion requires, but we do not parade our religion any more than our other personal feelings when utterly irrelevant, as in this case."[78]

It was this sort of insensitivity, on top of the MRFM's already unwelcome involvement in the strike, that led Elsas to increasingly target the MRFM. When Reverend Wilmer approached him about arbitration, Elsas responded that "the mill had received incalculable injury at the hands of this committee" and doubted "that any good could come out of such a conference at such a late date." On the day after the 12 July meeting, Elsas sent another communication to the MRFM executive committee, explaining at "considerable length" why he would not meet and attacking the MRFM for singling out Fulton Mills. And in early August, Jacob Elsas wrote a letter to John Eagan, stating that the facts in the bulletins were wrong and serving formal notice that the MRFM would be held responsible for the damage done to Fulton's business by the ads.[79]

In addition to such direct communication, Oscar Elsas launched a behind-the-scenes campaign against MRFM leaders Jackson and Eagan that drew upon his family's far-flung contacts in the top ranks of regional and national corporate circles. On 2 July, he wrote a letter devoted to Jackson to James A. Emery of the National Council for Industrial Defense (NCID), a spin-off of the militantly anti-union National Association of Manufacturers, for which Emery also served as counsel and chief lobbyist.[80] Emery and Elsas, a longtime member of the NAM, had crossed paths as recently as May, when Emery had addressed the Georgia Cotton Manufacturers Association (GCMA).

Reiterating the false claim that Fulton management had not selectively discharged union members, Elsas told Emery that the mill had gradually gained back its workforce since the strike began, with only forty weavers away from being at full capacity. (In fact, though it was on the increase, the number of looms running for the week of 29 June was still only 79 percent of full capacity.)[81] Then he got to his main point. In his opinion, the continued circulation of the MRFM bulletins would "only produce greater friction between capital and labor." Therefore, to make Marion Jackson understand that "his methods of attacking industries without proper investigation" were damaging not only to textiles but to other industries as well, he thought that "the National Association of Manufacturers could bring pressure on the directors and managers of American Surety." Elsas then asked Emery to get the NAM to take up the matter "along their usual aggressive lines." He asked that Emery not present the situation as Fulton's fight alone "but along the broader lines of mutual protection of manufacturers against outside assault."[82]

Elsas followed up with a second letter to Emery, enclosing a copy of the MRFM bulletins and Jackson's speech at the 28 June mass meeting. "The first bulletin is incendiary enough," Elsas wrote, "but the others gradually build up a sentiment that breeds antagonism, and can have no other result. Such work is damaging to the whole structure of co-operation between employer and employee, and certainly should be discouraged on the most positive terms by any who have influence in this direction."[83]

Elsas wrote a third letter to Emery a few days later. In it, he enclosed a recent front-page article from the *Cincinnati Post* describing conditions at Fulton Mills. Elsas was sure that Jackson was a party to this additional publicity, "and we do not know but what he has tried to get it in other papers." Elsas also explicitly associated Jackson's efforts with the IWW's southern organizing drive, writing, "We heard this morning that the Monaghan Mills, of Greenville, S.C., have gone on a strike, and it is self-evident that this is the beginning of more trouble among the mills if such agitators as Jackson are not stopped in their unreasonable work." Emery replied that he had taken up the matter with the NAM's manager, "who believes he is in a position to do something in the premises immediately."[84]

This was not the only time that Elsas and his associates in their intense anti-unionism raised the specter of the radical IWW, despite the fact that strike leaders and sympathizers clearly tried to distance the UTW effort from the IWW. O. Delight Smith publicly maintained that the Fulton strike could be conducted "decently and sanely without the wild methods of IWW agitators or the desperate bitterness of the Lawrence struggles." Similarly, the MRFM told regional cotton manufacturers that they would eventually have to make a choice between the respectable AFL and the subversive IWW. Nevertheless, the district superintendent of the International Auxiliary Company, a New York–based labor espionage firm seeking Fulton's business, sent Elsas an IWW publication, stating that "the IWW . . . was attracted to the cotton district through the A.F. of L.'s efforts in your plant."[85]

Indeed, for a while Elsas was ready to believe that UTW organizers Sara Conboy and Mary Kelleher had IWW connections. Elsas wrote Franklin W. Hobbs, president of Boston's Arlington Mills and an officer in the National Cotton Manufacturers Association, for information about Conboy and Kelleher. Hobbs wrote back, improbably stating that "Mrs. Kelliher and Mrs. Conboy were both connected with the 'I.W.W.' and have been interested in radical labor movements in the North." Eager to follow up, Elsas wired Hobbs asking for details about Conboy in particular, who was "posing as an exceptional woman" and had gained the full confidence of the MRFM. No such details were forthcoming, though, as Hobbs admitted that not only had his informant "never heard any hint of moral laxness" about Conboy but that "she is an ardent Roman Catholic and that devotion to her church has made her a consistent and bitter opponent of the I.W.W. and its leaders." An officer of the Roxbury Carpet Company wrote a similar letter about Conboy to Gordon Johnstone.[86]

Meanwhile, other members of the Elsas family also joined the campaign against Marion Jackson, building upon their extensive connections with regional and national elites. Fulton vice president Benjamin Elsas sent letters, along with copies of the MRFM bulletins and Jackson's 28 June speech, to James S. Alexander, president of New York's National Bank of Commerce, and Charles E. Perkins, head of a Brooklyn textile firm and an investor in Fulton Mills. In the letters, Benjamin Elsas repeated the by-now-familiar management themes of high wages and good conditions at Fulton Mills, a largely contented workforce that was now almost at full capacity, and outside interference in the so-called strike, especially on the part of Jackson and the MRFM. Wishing to avoid "newspaper controversy" since "every statement that we make is merely distorted by the other side, who are willing to twist facts to make their own point," he then asked whether Perkins and Alexander could give the MRFM bulletins and Jackson's speech to officers or directors of American Surety. This, he wrote, "will do us and business interests generally some good." However, Elsas cautioned against letting American Surety personnel know that Fulton management was making this request, lest it "bring about even more vicious attacks on the part of Mr. Jackson."[87]

Both individuals quickly responded. Alexander turned over the enclosures of Elsas's letter to "a close business and personal friend who is a prominent director of the Surety Company," who in turn relayed the information about Jackson to company president F. W. Lafrentz. "You may rest assured," Alexander wrote back to Benjamin Elsas, "that the American Surety Company does not approve or sanction such writings by their agents."[88] Perkins went even further. After talking over the situation with another Elsas brother, Adolph, who was then residing in New York, he wrote a letter to Lafrentz, comparing Marion Jackson to muckraker Upton Sinclair and enclosing Jackson's speech. "I think the time has come," Perkins added, "when sober minded men should endeavor to calm public sentiment, rather than encourage fiery agitation."[89]

Lafrentz replied that Jackson represented no one but himself in making his remarks "and does in no sense reflect the opinion of others connected with this corporation." He acknowledged that it would be difficult for company officials to interfere with Jackson, who might well say his affairs were none of their business. However, Lafrentz noted, "I have taken cognizance of what is going on and the matter will have due consideration at our hands."[90]

Upon reviewing this correspondence, Benjamin Elsas sent Perkins another copy of the MRFM bulletins and Jackson's 28 June speech, as well as a clipping detailing Jackson's speech at the 12 July mass meeting. In addition, he suggested Perkins contact textile magnate Seth M. Milliken about the matter. As Milliken was in bad health, Perkins chose to write prominent LaGrange, Georgia, cotton manufacturer Fuller E. Callaway instead. He also announced his intention to take up the subject again with Lafrentz and suggested Elsas get in touch with William Donald of the Hanover National Bank in New York, with whom the Fulton firm did business.[91] Elsas's subsequent letter to Donald, complete with enclosures, resembled his earlier letters in its presentation of "the facts" of the Fulton situation, its reminder of secrecy to avoid adverse publicity, and its account of Jackson's and the MRFM's activities. In Elsas's opinion, the MRFM's goal "has been merely to gain more notoriety and power, and the effect is to probably foment discord between employer and employee."[92]

Benjamin Elsas wrote Donald that, despite the fact that many Atlanta businessmen and some MRFM members themselves disapproved of the MRFM bulletins, "none of it seems to have any effect" upon Jackson. He therefore suggested that Donald, like Alexander and Perkins, place the bulletins and Jackson's 28 June speech before the officers and directors of American Surety, in particular one Walter Johnston.[93] In addition, Benjamin Elsas sent copies of his correspondence, along with his clippings, to his brothers Adolph and Louis, and to Oscar Elsas's Boston-based brother-in-law Adolph Ehrlich. To each of them, the message was the same: while keeping Fulton management's involvement out of the picture, get as many "prominent people" and acquaintances as possible to "protest to the American Surety Co. against their Agent interfering in this matter." In particular, because of the MRFM's supposed exploitation of anti-Semitism, it was suggested that Louis Elsas, then visiting Chicago, contact prominent Chicago Jews Julius Rosenwald and Albert D. Lasker, both of whom had been actively involved in the defense of Leo Frank.[94] "We want to work this to the limit," Benjamin Elsas declared. "If we can oust Mr. Jackson, we think it would be the best answer to his anarchistic talk."[95]

Oscar Elsas also vigorously opposed the compulsory arbitration bill that Jackson was then pushing in the state legislature, a measure that to Elsas was "of a very radical character, and to our mind would prevent any Manufacturer from successfully conducting his business." He wrote Allen Johnson, Mell Wilkinson, and J. T. Rose of the Atlanta Builders Association in opposition to the bill. Appealing to racial prejudice as well as class solidarity, he argued that the bill's effects would be far-reaching, potentially affecting any employer of ten or more people, and enabling black sharecroppers and maids to "lodge complaints and insist upon arbitration, as often as they see fit," on an equal footing with their employers. Elsas also proposed that the various employers associations across the state, along with local Chambers of Commerce, employ a lobbyist "to handle the matter vigorously," and he also suggested the formation of a local employers group.[96]

Fulton management adopted a different strategy against John Eagan. The day after the 28 June mass meeting, Benjamin Elsas contacted Oscar Mayer, an acquaintance in Birmingham, Alabama, and asked him to inspect Eagan's American Cast Iron and Pipe Company property there. The next day, Mayer reported back that the ACIPCO surroundings were filthy—covered up with weeds and stagnant water holes, and that there was no sign of any disinfectant. "[The] General upkeep of the place," Mayer wrote, "is absolutely rotten." The ACIPCO company houses, "if you can call them same," rented for four to six dollars a month; Mayer related that "a darkey" told him he would not live in one if he could live there for free.[97]

Intrigued by this information, Oscar Elsas drew upon a regional network of contacts to get additional goods on Eagan. On 7 July, he met with James W. Conway, the southern manager of the General Fire Extinguisher Company and a neighbor of Elsas in the Ponce de Leon Apartments, who in turn had phoned J. M. Broome of the Greenville Iron Works in Greenville, South Carolina. Broome had formerly worked at a Birmingham plant and was "fully conversant with foundry and pipe work, also with the conditions in and around Birmingham." The following evening, Oscar Elsas and Conway met with Broome at the Georgian Terrace Hotel, across the street from Elsas's residence, and arranged for Broome "to go to Birmingham for the specific purpose of getting up the data."[98]

The "data" came back a few days later. In addition to expanding on the previous account of unsanitary living quarters, it described child labor at ACIPCO, poor ventilation amid intense heat and dust, filthy bathing facilities, and other "almost unbearable" working conditions, as well as the markups charged at the company commissary. Broome also specifically mentioned that inside the foundry "both blacks and whites alike" drank from the same vessel and that outside the plant a white boy carried water to "both the whites and blacks."[99]

In addition, he mentioned various photographs that had been commissioned by Oscar Elsas to reveal "the general conditions and character" of the ACIPCO living quarters, similar to the photos gathered by O. Delight Smith of the Fulton mill district. The parallels continued, too, as Elsas sought in particular to document *Eagan's* use of child labor and questionable racial practices. He wrote to the Birmingham commercial photographer involved requesting an additional picture, specifically "the photograph of a white boy, nine or ten years old, who carries water for the outside employees, both whites and blacks." Eager to get such documentation, Elsas permitted the photographer to pay the boy a dollar to pose for the picture, as Margaret Dempsey had posed for Smith and Miles.[100] The water boy's picture and the other ACIPCO photographs commissioned by Elsas were mounted on canvas with a perforated edge, then placed in an album.[101]

What then transpired is sketchy. At some point on or soon after 4 August, Fulton management prepared a statement titled "THE MOTE IN YOUR NEIGHBOR'S EYE, THE BEAM IN YOUR OWN."[102] The statement first condemned the "unfair and unjust" attacks in the MRFM bulletins and the fact that, in conjunction with the pending child labor bill, the MRFM executive committee had specifically called attention to Fulton Mills, inviting people to "go out and take a look." After affirming that the company in fact observed and had no objection to child labor laws and offering an invitation for state representatives to visit the mill themselves, the statement cut to the chase:

> Since the Executive Committee of the Men and Religion Forward Movement has taken on itself to ask that our plant be looked over, we desire to call attention to a certain plant in the City of Birmingham, the principal stockholder of which is John J. Eagan, as we are informed.
>
> It is the plant of American Cast Iron Pipe Co.
>
> We have had a number of photographs taken of this plant, including its dilapidated houses for employees, surface closets and stagnant water pools, and invite any person interested to "take a look."
>
> We are certain that after an inspection of these pictures the thought will naturally occur that perhaps Mr. Eagan could employ his talents, as well as his money, in sweeping the dirt from his own door.
>
> This rule of conduct might also be observed by others besides Mr. John Eagan.

In addition, mill management prepared an accompanying statement, addressed "to the public."[103] The statement first declared, "We have patiently and silently suffered unjust and untruthful attacks against this company. Only because we believe that the interests of the people of this State are involved, as well as our own, do we now make this statement." Then followed a brief description of the current dire state of the cotton industry with the drying up of foreign consumption and an appeal to "all good citizens" to support the industry. "We are endeavoring to do our part," the statement read. "This company could have, with profit, shut down its mills and disposed of its raw cotton weeks ago. It preferred not to do this, but to continue to afford employment for those who desired to work for it and to comply with its contracts."

Despite this service, the statement continued, a "self-constituted body of censors [the MRFM] has continued to abuse and malign this company," even though Fulton Mills paid relatively high wages and conducted its business in strict accordance with the law. The statement concluded,

> We have been furnished much scripture, and we will also invoke scripture. "Let him who is without sin cast the first stone." May we ask if *all* the members of this Committee are free from error? Have they entirely corrected the evils which are within their own affairs? Does Mr. Eagan, whom we are informed is the chief stock-holder in an industrial plant in Birmingham, pretend that this industry is a model one? We have photographs of this industry, which will satisfy anyone that there is a great deal of work that this censorious person might undertake, with profit to his own preaching.

Seventy-five years later, Norman Elsas recalled the Birmingham photographs and described a dramatic incident that took place in the offices of Atlanta clothing store owner George Muse, who was an MRFM member and a director and stockholder of ACIPCO:[104]

My father sent a photographer over there who took photographs of that steel mill village. And he got affidavits from the employees regarding what they earned, living conditions, and so forth. And he had all of this in triplicate form, the originals in the bank vault. He then told George Muse that if he didn't call a meeting of these men [the MRFM] to talk to him, he was going to publish [the affidavits] in the Atlanta papers. And if the Atlanta papers didn't take it, Mr. Anderson, who ran the *Macon Telegraph*, would do it. And the Elsas family had enough money to send up plenty of editions of the *Macon Telegraph*. So George Muse called a meeting of these men, and Dad threw out these copies of affidavits and photographs of the steel mill village. . . .

Now, when Dad got through telling them about this and they got through reading the affidavits and they saw the photographs, Dad said, "I don't want anything published regarding the Fulton Mill, or I'll move [from Atlanta]." And one of the men said something, and Dad pulled a gun out of his pocket and laid it on the table. . . . And he said, "I'm going to leave this room—or some of you are going to leave with me, dead." And then he said, "I want no more advertisements from the Men and Religion Forward Movement telling lies about the Elsas family and the Fulton Bag and Cotton Mill."

And the *Journal* came out that night with a blank space, that they [the MRFM] had paid for—and they pulled it. And that was the end of the Men and Religion Forward Movement.[105]

He also recalled that his father had hired Pinkerton detectives to take pictures of two MRFM members in bed with prostitutes at a downtown Atlanta hotel.[106]

However compelling, Norman Elsas's recollections were a bit embellished. For instance, while MRFM strike-related bulletins did cease after mid-August, the MRFM never substituted a blank space in the newspapers for a bulletin. Furthermore, the MRFM continued to be a presence in Atlanta well into 1916. Nevertheless, it is clear that Elsas's surveillance of ACIPCO and subsequent encounter with the MRFM roughly corresponded with a waning of the MRFM's involvement in the Fulton strike. On 27 July, the MRFM refused an appeal by the strikers to replenish the depleted commissary fund. In addition, outside of one brief mention, the MRFM executive committee did not bring up the Fulton strike after 10 August, as the organization shifted its primary emphasis from industrial concerns to movie censorship. By early September, a labor spy reported that there existed "no hope for any further help" from the MRFM.[107]

Along with Elsas's campaign against Eagan and Jackson, there were other reasons why the MRFM backed off its strike-related activities when it did. For instance, labor spy Harry Preston repeatedly tried to influence MRFM members against the strikers and their leaders.[108] In addition, production at the mill had gradually moved back to full capacity by the end of July, likely signaling to the MRFM that the strike was over for all intents and purposes.[109] It is also possible that the MRFM members felt that they had largely accomplished what they set out to do. The child labor and arbitration bills, though considerably watered down, had moved through the state legislature. And, through the MRFM's intervention, in mid-July two representatives of the U.S. Department of Labor's Division of Conciliation had arrived to investigate the Fulton situation, as did other federal conciliators and investigators from the U.S. Commission on Industrial Relations. Their presence inaugurated a new phase in the matter, in which the federal government would become increasingly important. In one form or another the strike did continue into 1915, with ripple effects in Atlanta, throughout Georgia, across the textile South, and even nationwide, as well as among Fulton workers themselves.

CHAPTER 7

The Fight Will Be Centered There

I n 1920, Mary Anderson, director of the U.S. Department of Labor Women's Bureau, wrote Samuel J. Gompers Jr., son of the AFL president and chief clerk of the Department of Labor, concerning a Women's Bureau investigation then being conducted on women in Atlanta's industries. Anderson recalled that "during the War Labor Board's existence the women investigators for the Board were sent to Atlanta to investigate the Fulton Bag Company and that a report by these investigators was rendered."[1]

Anderson's memories were blurred. The National War Labor Board did conduct hearings in Atlanta in 1918 but primarily about the wages and working conditions of the city's streetcar men.[2] More likely, Anderson was referring either to the several Fulton Mills–related visits to Atlanta by representatives of the DOL's Division of Conciliation or to the various reports spawned by the Fulton strike for the U.S. Commission on Industrial Relations.[3] Though these federal investigations into the Fulton situation were hazy in Anderson's memory and were not consulted by any historians until the mid-1980s, at the time they seemed important to all parties involved. The strike both highlighted and figured in a variety of national and intersectional labor-related debates, initiatives, and networks as the dispute moved yet further beyond the scope of managers and workers alone.

In early July 1914, the Evangelical Ministers Association, the MRFM, and the Atlanta Federation of Trades sent telegrams to U.S. secretary of labor William B. Wilson, Atlanta congressman William Schley Howard, Georgia senator Hoke Smith, and President Woodrow Wilson, requesting that the Commission on Industrial Relations investigate the Fulton situation and the condition of southern textile workers more generally. The CIR had been established in 1912 in the aftermath of the celebrated McNamara brothers' bombing of the *Los Angeles Times*. Its purpose was to explore industrial relations and the roots of industrial unrest through a combination of research and highly publicized open investigations, with the intent of informing public debate and policy.[4] The telegrams to Washington were widely reported in the Atlanta press; *Southern Textile Bulletin* editor David Clark also mentioned them in one of his "confidential circulars" to southern cotton manufacturers.

The telegram to Hoke Smith was not without its ironies. In the past, Smith had endorsed measures such as child labor laws and strengthened workmen's compensation legislation, and he was currently under attack by Joseph M. Brown, his opponent in the U.S. Senate race, precisely for his reputed ties to organized labor. Yet Smith had begun to soften his prolabor position and more actively defend southern industrialists. That very week, in fact, Smith led the cry among southern Democrats in the Senate to slash appropriations for the CIR, claiming that various federal departments were better equipped to address industrial issues and that some of the testimony the CIR had already gathered, especially on the issue of child labor, was "ludicrous." He continued his opposition throughout the CIR's existence, becoming, in historian Graham Adams's words, its "*bête noire*."[5]

In addition, on 1 July, Secretary of Labor Wilson met with Schley Howard to discuss the strike. Wilson offered to send federal mediators to Atlanta to "amicably adjust differences" in the affair. Recognizing labor's clout in local politics, Howard relayed this news to trade union leaders in Atlanta, who in turn commended him for his involvement. Oscar Elsas protested to Howard that "the suggested mediation is really unnecessary," repeating his claim that "not over 85 have quit" and that the vast majority of Fulton workers were "thoroughly contented with their wages and conditions." Nevertheless, Wilson appointed outside conciliators W. W. Husband and Herman Robinson to go to Atlanta.[6]

Given the gradual attrition of union forces and the problems with the commissary, the strikers and their leaders eagerly awaited the arrival of the federal labor representatives. Far from being considered neutral or antagonistic, they were seen as potential allies in the strike. Like the National Industrial Recovery Act of 1933, which would guarantee workers the right to organize, the CIR symbolized to many Fulton workers the federal government's recognition, if not outright endorsement, of their cause. At the 2 July union meeting it was reported that "Uncle Sam" was now taking a hand in the matter. The next day, Charles Miles boasted of his personal influence on Secretary Wilson, and rumors spread that the federal investigators would shut the mill down.[7]

Husband and Robinson arrived in Atlanta on 12 July. As a labor spy reported, 13 July was "a big day for the strikers, with their men from Washington." The two conciliators spent practically all day at the union hall with the strikers. Buoyed by Husband and Robinson's arrival, Miles expressed his optimism that evening. Both the *Atlanta Journal* and the *Atlanta Georgian* featured articles that week on the conciliators, who also spent considerable time with members of the MRFM.[8]

O. Delight Smith reiterated to the strikers the crucial need to impress the visiting investigators. Oscar Elsas, believing himself to be firmly in command of the situation, did not feel quite the same need, although he certainly made sure he presented a favorable picture to the conciliators. After Husband and Robinson met with him and company attorney Benjamin Phillips, Elsas wrote, "We told them, plainly, that we did not intend to arbitrate or mediate the conditions existing here, as we were in as good shape now as we have been most Summer months." In addition to having a "lengthy talk" with the conciliators, Elsas and Phillips took them around the plant, "and they undoubtedly were impressed with the general conditions." He concluded, "We do not think we will hear much more from them, as our answer was very positive—that we would not mediate or arbitrate." He and Fulton general manager Gordon Johnstone reiterated this message to the conciliators.[9]

Husband and Robinson reported, "This decision on the part of Mr. Elsas was repeatedly stated, and he was particularly emphatic in this regard in replying to our suggestion that after a careful study of the situation we were convinced that the actual differences between the contending parties were not great and could be adjusted with little difficulty." Despite his apparent confidence, such suggestions contributed to Elsas's apprehension about the consequences of the conciliators' trip to Atlanta. While he believed that Husband had "capitalistic tendencies," Robinson seemed to be "a rank labor man." By the time of their second visit to his office, he was "getting irritable" with them. Furthermore, it appeared suspicious that Husband and Robinson departed Atlanta on the same train as UTW organizers Sara Conboy and Mary Kelleher.[10]

Elsas also was not sure of the precise powers of the conciliation service, or, for that matter, the recently formed DOL itself. He also believed that sustained federal interest in the strike, Fulton Mills, and the southern textile industry might cause nothing but needless problems, especially since the mill was essentially back at full production. He therefore wrote Claude N. Bennett, manager of the Congressional Information Bureau in Washington. Bennett had known the Elsas family for some time, perhaps since his prior employment as secretary to Hoke Smith.[11] Elsas asked Bennett to stay in touch with the DOL concerning Husband and Robinson.[12]

On 26 July, Bennett, who would play an active role on behalf of mill management well into 1915, caught up with Husband and discussed the Fulton situation with him, taking the opportunity to speak on Elsas's behalf. Bennett then wrote Elsas, assuring him that since the mill was running full time and Elsas had rejected any arbitration effort, in light of the limited powers of the conciliators, "there really was nothing that they could do." In addition, he related, "It is not expected that the report will be published or that anything further will be done about the matter in question." However, Bennett did caution that Secretary Wilson was a "pro-Labor man and it is of course possible that his view may not be as liberal as Mr. Husband's."[13] Indeed, three weeks later, Bennett reported back that Wilson, after reading the Husband-Robinson report, did *not* deem the matter closed but was considering sending additional conciliators back to Atlanta, despite Bennett's efforts to influence Wilson's office "in a diplomatic way" on behalf of Fulton management. Union publicity efforts had paid off: Wilson's staff perceived the strike as being intermingled with the broader issue of child labor in the southern mills.

This news prompted company patriarch Jacob Elsas, at the helm during Oscar's vacation, to write Georgia senator William S. West in an attempt to obtain the report. Jacob Elsas played down and distorted what had occurred, referring to the strike as merely "a little disturbance we have had in our mills." Yet when West made inquiries, a DOL representative informed him that not only was the report unavailable but "the matter has not been finally disposed of, and it is likely that negotiations will be reopened at an early date." For months, mill management attempted to secure the report, without success, while the Division of Conciliation's involvement in the Fulton situation continued.[14]

By this time, in response to the appeals by the MRFM and the Federation of Trades, two investigators from the Commission on Industrial Relations also had arrived in Atlanta, despite a plea from Oscar Elsas to Hoke Smith to "use your good offices to prevent any further interference from outsiders." The first to come, on 21 July, was Alexander M. Daly, a labor lawyer from Dover, Delaware, who had most recently conducted studies for the CIR of the textile industry in Philadelphia, Massachusetts, and Rhode Island, as well as of Ohio's bituminous coal fields.[15] Upon arrival in Atlanta, he interviewed the secretary of the Chamber of Commerce and sought an audience with Oscar Elsas.

When they met, Daly reported, Elsas "treated me with great courtesy and seemed very willing to give me any information that I might desire." In this regard, Elsas resembled the NAM's James A. Emery, Walter Drew of the National Erectors Association, and other nationally prominent militant anti-unionists who, despite their original antagonism to the CIR, once it was a fait accompli, used it as a vehicle to promote their positions and thwart the opposition.[16] However, Elsas refused to provide Daly access to the company payroll and balked at supplying information about withheld wages and money that was never turned over to workers who had left the employ of Fulton Mills.[17]

Along with conferring with Elsas, Daly spoke with Husband and Robinson, and conferred with MRFM members, Exposition Cotton Mill president Johnson and other manufacturers, Charles Miles, state labor leaders, Chief Beavers, and others. He visited the Fulton district, went to see mills at Gainesville, Georgia, and attended a union meeting. As with Husband and Robinson, he found the strikers eager to see him, hopeful that the CIR "will do something for them, and that I will be able also to help." In addition, in anticipation of a possible hearing on conditions in the southern textile industry, which was already targeted by the CIR as a leading area of industrial abuse, Daly developed a questionnaire and submitted it to Elsas and fifteen additional Georgia cotton manufacturers.

Daly also met with labor spy Harry Preston. Before leaving town on another assignment, Preston spent nearly eight hours with Daly, providing him, in Preston's words, "a complete history of [the] strike as I saw it." Preston estimated that the "legitimate strikers" numbered fewer than a hundred and described the opening up of the commissary to "every 'Rag Tag' and 'Bobtail' that applied." He expressed his contempt for the personal habits of the strikers and those who came to the commissary. In addition, he spent considerable time disparaging the strike leadership. According to Preston, Smith and Miles misled and manipulated workers, secretly advocated violence, and otherwise "ran the strike as they pleased, making their plans in secret, and just having [the] Union as a figure head." He also mentioned the rift between Conboy and Smith.

After Daly left town to investigate conditions in the southern iron and steel industry (including the ACIPCO plant owned by MRFM member John Eagan), Elsas wrote to David Clark that the investigation had amounted to nothing and had no direct bearing upon the strike.[18] In his summary to CIR research director Charles McCarthy, Daly stated he merely had supplied "a bald description" of the facts in the matter and was "leaving it up to the other person to develop."[19]

That person was Inis Weed, who also arrived in Atlanta on 21 July. Before working as a CIR investigator, Weed had been a freelance journalist concentrating on industrial issues. In November 1913, she had authored an article in *The Masses* drawing from a lengthy interview she had conducted with a fifteen-year-old Paterson, New Jersey, silk worker who had toiled in a situation similar to that of Fulton Mills, marked by numerous fines and a "vicious" labor contract under which workers' wages were withheld. She had also favorably covered the "Protocol of Peace" in New York's garment trades.[20]

With the assistance of Smith, Miles, Federation of Trades official Louie P. Marquardt, and H. G. Jones of the National Child Labor Committee and the *Atlanta Georgian*, Weed gathered testimony of child laborers and other workers at Fulton Mills, documenting a range of industrial abuses. She toured the mill district with MRFM member G. R. Buford and prepared a map of sanitary conditions in the neighborhood. In addition to assisting Daly in developing the questionnaire for Elsas and other manufacturers, she also evaluated the newly passed state child labor law and the Georgia Department of Commerce and Labor. She examined the working conditions of women in local factories and department stores as well and traveled to other textile communities. From her investigations she drew up the first of several reports she would compile on the Fulton situation and other Georgia textile communities.

She also talked with Oscar Elsas. Posing as a magazine writer for unspecified reasons, Weed conducted an interview with Elsas on 24 July. Elsas, preferring to talk only with the government representatives and not knowing Weed's identity, was reluctant to talk with her. What Elsas did relate, though, was revealing. First, showing the lesson he had learned after the company's 3 June newspaper advertisement and the union's subsequent reaction, he reiterated his aversion to any sort of publicity about the strike in the press. "My theory," he stated, "is that the less this trouble is talked about, the better. . . . That's my policy, starve 'em out by giving them absolutely no statements to feed on." Along with sharing his fear that strike organizers and sympathizers would exploit his remarks, Elsas expressed cynicism about popular opinion. "Oh, the public doesn't want the facts," he told Weed.

Showing a keen sense of who ultimately held the upper hand during the strike, he also candidly conveyed his situational approach toward arbitration, which contrasted with the approach he advocated in his private correspondence and public pronouncements. "I'm like the workers," he confided. "When they can't win, they're for arbitration. When I can't win I'll be for arbitration." In addition, Elsas condemned the MRFM as "a lot of fanatics" and expressed his desire that the government handle the IWW as Pancho Villa had dealt with "*his* enemies." In response to a question about how to break strikes, he bluntly declared that to defeat a strike in an "acute situation" with only men involved, he'd "just as soon get guns and mow 'em down as not."

Weed described Elsas as looking "hard and injured" as he spoke. Indeed, more than on any other recorded occasion, Elsas revealed the extent of the personal toll the strike had taken on him. "It's all I can do to hold in," he related, getting ready to take a vacation after the ordeal. "This getting up at five o'clock every morning for ten weeks and the constant strain is enough for one man." Despite the posters that had gone up that morning announcing that no former workers would be taken back after 27 July and that the company had returned to full production, Elsas speculated that the matter might drag on in some form for quite a while.[21]

Elsas was accurate in his prediction. In early August the strikers received another blow when the Atlanta Federation of Trades withdrew its financial support. O. Delight Smith and AFT officer Marquardt appealed to AFL national leadership for emergency assistance but were informed by Gompers that the organization had no funds available that could be used for this purpose.[22] Yet later that month, Smith and Miles, under the direct supervision of UTW president John Golden himself, developed another tactic that would keep the strike—now seen as crucial to the UTW's entire southern campaign—alive until the following year.

On 28 August, the strike leaders announced plans to close down the union commissary and establish a tent colony for strikers a half mile southeast of the plant. The idea was to eliminate the costs associated with housing strikers, winnow out the stragglers who had flocked to the commissary, and thus try to regain control over a rapidly unraveling situation. In deciding to move to the tents, the organizers also were well aware of the recent national public outpouring of sympathy for the tent colony of displaced miners and their families in Ludlow, Colorado.[23] They knew that the placement of Fulton workers in tents could reap a publicity bonanza and invigorate union efforts.

Indeed, that very day, an article about the situation caught the eye of DOL conciliation commissioners Robert M. McWade and John B. Colpoys, who were in Atlanta on other business. McWade and Colpoys met with Gordon Johnstone, who provided an account of the trouble, including the familiar points that only seventy-eight employees had walked out, that "not over ½ of 1%" of those drawing rations from the commissary had ever worked at Fulton Mills, and that the plant had been back at full production for some time. Whereas McWade, a former manufacturer from Philadelphia, seemed satisfied by Johnstone's remarks, the prolabor Colpoys asked further questions about the reasons for the strike, in particular the issue of anti-union discrimination.[24]

The move to the tents set off a two-front war in which management and labor engaged throughout the fall, not only renewing interest in the strike beyond the city's boundaries but having implications for the people most directly involved. Although some strikers were attracted by the "novelty" of living in tents, others expressed "considerable dissatisfaction" with and even "open rebellion" toward the prospect. Many workers vowed they would return to Fulton Mills before living in tents; others feared that the organizers would get them in tents and then abandon them. Such misgivings certainly intensified during the first rain-filled days of the colony's existence, when many of the tents, mainly Georgia National Guard rejects, got drenched and collapsed.[25]

Labor spy Harry Preston, who returned to town just as the move to the tents was initiated, offered a scathing critique of the new habitat, in a manner that resembled criticism of the living conditions in the Fulton mill district and other industrial communities. "The tent colony is really a joke as it stands now," he reported on 2 September. "There are absolutely no proper sanitary conditions, and the place must certainly be condemned by the health authorities. They have no water, there are no toilet accommodations, the garbage is thrown around everywhere, and the way meals are cooked as I saw them today, was filthy beyond description."[26]

Preston's remarks reflected his middle-class biases, his desire to see and present the strike's demise, his personal contempt for the strikers and their leaders, and his consistent underestimation of their resources. They also were made when the tent colony was first established, before the situation had stabilized somewhat. Yet other observers also described sometimes miserable camp conditions. A spy reported that a cold spell was "making things very disagreeable" for the residents. When another round of heavy rains flooded the camp site, even the dyed-in-the-wool strike leader W. E. Fleming allowed that "things are a little wet." Later in the fall, unusually cold weather, gale-force winds, and even a snowfall buffeted the tent colony.[27]

Not only bad weather and poor sanitary conditions alienated many onetime strikers from the camp and the union leadership. In an increasingly chaotic, attenuated environment, marked by pinched resources and the continued presence on the scene of many people with no connection to Fulton Mills, Smith and Miles introduced various control measures that further disaffected some strikers and supporters. On 27 August, the roll was called at the union meeting in order to cut off provisions to those who did not attend regularly. On 1 September, Miles announced that supplies would be provided to residents of the tent colony only and that campers would eat together in a mess tent rather than receive individual disbursements.[28]

With this announcement, Miles "created quite a sensation," especially among those in attendance who did not want to move into the tents. One of these was Robert Wright, who had been designated Local 886 president by late August and who served as a spokesmen for workers increasingly at odds with the strike's direction. As a consequence of the union's decision to cut off aid to people who did not move to the camp, Wright wrote, many "real strikers of the better class" were going hungry and about to be evicted from wherever they were living. This included some of the people who had first walked out and who were now "really suffering," like one widow who had come out on strike with her children and had been calling on the city for relief.

To counter such sentiments and win over workers to the tent colony, Smith and Miles, sounding much like Theodore Roosevelt or other proponents of vigorous outdoor activity, extolled the "beauties and healthfulness of camp life." Union publications struck a similar tone. For instance, an article in the *Textile Worker* emphasized the "healthy, orderly and comfortable manner" in which the camp was ostensibly conducted. The article maintained that "the strikers say they have never felt better in their lives than they do now that their existence is pitched in the open air with wholesome food and healthful work." In a *Journal of Labor* column Smith authored throughout the fall, Smith portrayed camp life in the same vein.[29] More pragmatically, to ensure the camp's success and to ward off charges and the reality of disarray, Smith, Miles, and other strike organizers also set up hospital and meeting tents, as well as a mess tent to replace the commissary, supervised the digging of trenches for sanitation and drainage purposes, and eventually established rules for the camp, with a police force of strikers, headed by former second hand R. F. Odell, to help maintain order.

Their efforts temporarily paid off. After a shaky start, the tent colony got off the ground and would remain in existence in some form until May 1915. The establishment of the camp enabled organizers to revive picketing for a while, too. By 11 September, regular picketing had resumed outside the mill; by 19 September, there were twenty-eight union pickets outside the plant gates; by 22 September, informant James I. Brush counted forty-one pickets.[30] Moreover, despite all the tribulations of camp life and the strike more generally, some workers remained committed to the principles that had brought them out in the first place. One of these was Annie Carlton, an original striker. "She is very bitter in the strike," Preston reported, "and said that she would rather be in a strike like this than eat."[31]

Yet union organizers faced an uphill battle in sustaining local support. Robert Wright and others felt that most of the tent colony residents, like the patrons of the commissary, were "hoboes and tramps" who had never worked a day at Fulton Mills. These were the individuals, Wright maintained, who were "reaping the benefit of what is being spent on the strike." In addition, Wright accused the strike leaders of favoritism, alleging that they continued to supply provisions to some people who had not even gone out to the tents, while others went hungry.[32]

Such purported partiality at the expense of "real strikers of the better class" offended the religious Wright's sense of personal morality. Adding to his growing disaffection, and that of others, were the reports of questionable moral behavior in the strikers' camp. On 2 September, one of the tent colony residents stabbed Pat Calahan, a union sheet metal worker who had been active in strike support since the summer.[33] From the time the camp was set up, accounts abounded of prostitutes and other sexually active women living in the camp, venereal disease, and almost nightly drunkenness. Referring to an unmarried woman who bore a child in the camp, even union stalwart H. N. Mullinax acknowledged that "there have been some things in it [the tent colony] that don't bear a good reputation." Wright later exclaimed, "This has been an immoral strike from start to finish."[34]

Actively aiding in tracking down, spreading, and embellishing rumors of immorality was Harry Preston. In early September, Preston reported that Local 886 secretary D. L. Miller was "afflicted with a loathsome, transmittable disease, and . . . had caused several girls to be afflicted with the same disease. It is also reported that there are a number of loose women who are at the camp." Two weeks later, he wrote, "[I]t is being openly said that camp and some tents is nothing but a collection of 'Bawdy Houses.'"

In pointing out such reputed immorality, Preston specifically targeted Robert Wright, who had already manifested a deep personal moral conservatism that could now be tapped against the strike. In late July, Preston had scoffed at the "religious strain" of Wright's speeches at the union hall, calling one address "the usual tirade of oppression, justice, etc.," but now he appealed precisely to Wright's religious and moral sensibilities to help win him over in opposition to the strike's leadership.[35] He encouraged Wright to document that the two organizers had run the commissary in a corrupt and slipshod fashion, kept no records of the money received for union dues, and otherwise personally profited from the strike. He also helped Wright draw up and circulate a petition critical of Miles and Smith's leadership, which was eventually signed by forty-five strikers.[36]

In June, Smith and Miles were able to deliver on many of their promises, but by the fall their claims about the strike sounded false to more and more people; their desperate circumstances, in turn, prompted them to make additional assertions and forecasts that to many did not ring true. "When they begin lying like they did to others, then their faults will come to light," Wright wrote about Miles and Smith to his newfound friend and confidant Harry Preston. "God says, 'Be sure your sins will find you out.'" Or, as the more secular Preston put it, "Miles is rapidly digging his own grave."[37]

As a woman who frequently, publicly, and assertively crossed conventional gender boundaries, Smith drew particular heat for her perceived moral transgressions. Wright and Preston charged that Smith had openly drunk beer in the vicinity of the commissary and that on one occasion she became so intoxicated that she had to be taken away at 2:00 A.M. from the German Cafe by strike supporter Harris Gober. Wright also alleged that Smith had received a rake-off on the grocery bill for the commissary and that she used it to help pay for her home. "Mrs. Smith was not a fit woman to lead the strike," he later declared.[38]

Smith's reputation took a decided turn for the worse after she befriended and took into her home Pat Calahan, the strike supporter who had been stabbed at the camp, over the objection of her husband, Edgar. After Calahan's wound had healed, Edgar Smith told him he would have to find a job because Edgar was no longer willing to support him. When Calahan objected, Edgar went to O. Delight, who backed up Calahan in the matter. Edgar, in turn, ordered her out of the house and left town himself. Preston reported a change in O. Delight Smith after the separation: "the 'cockey' walk, and actions she used to have, are all gone, and she goes around like a smacked 'a—,' now, (excuse expression, it fits so perfectly)."

Smith's fortunes continued to spiral downward. Later in the fall, Edgar filed for divorce. The December divorce trial raised in high relief the anxieties that Atlantans felt about the changing place of women in the urban New South; indeed, divorce itself was a concern of the MRFM and others who sought to strengthen Georgia's existing divorce law that very year by making divorce more difficult to obtain. At the trial, Edgar Smith testified he had come home once to find his wife, drunk and "about half dressed," in Calahan's company. He also charged that in her union activities she had "mapped out a line of conduct for herself entirely at variance with the duties of a good wife." On the stand, among other things, O. Delight Smith admitted that she had had several abortions. In mid-December, she left town in disgrace with Calahan.[39]

Smith's downward trajectory corresponded with a gradual dwindling of tent colony residents throughout the fall into the winter. As early as mid-September, H. N. Mullinax and other strike leaders were "begging and pleading" people to go to the camp, to replace others who had departed. For a while at least, these recruiting efforts were successful. In early December, a labor spy reported some 250 people living in the camp, most of whom had never worked at Fulton Mills. But by January, Oscar Elsas, who had a good idea of the camp's population from spies and informants, estimated that the tent colony residents numbered only thirty adults and thirty-five children. By March, just a few dozen people—mainly hard-core unionists such as Fleming, Mullinax, and Odell—remained in the camp.[40]

By spreading and embellishing accounts of immorality, Preston and other spies did more than appeal to the anxieties of workers and foster doubts about the strike and its leadership. They also provided fodder for Oscar Elsas in his efforts to dismiss the strike as an misguided venture entirely without cause, led and embraced by people who were little better than disorderly rabble. And by discrediting the strike leadership, the spies sought to put "into the minds of as many as possible," as Preston expressed it, additional reservations about the strike by erstwhile allies, most notably the MRFM and the local labor movement.[41]

On 13 September, after a visit to several MRFM members, Preston reported that "Smith and Miles have lost all respect and all confidence from this quarter." Later, he reiterated that "the 'Men and Religion' people are thoroughly disgusted with the way their confidence was abused."[42] The same was true with organized labor. On 6 September, Preston noted that union carpenters, Atlanta Typographical Union 48, and various railroad brotherhoods had all withdrawn strike support. Relations had become so strained that Miles and Smith stayed away from the local Labor Day parade, though some of the strikers themselves participated. In two visits with mill management, William S. Weir of the printers union related what he had heard about the unsanitary and immoral conditions in the camp and admitted that he "dislike[d] Miles and Mrs. Smith very much."[43] In addition, after accruing substantial unpaid debts from the organizers, even onetime staunch strike supporter Harris Gober had become disaffected.

Realizing that only the AFL and the UTW were now funding the strikers, in mid-September Preston, with management's backing, embarked upon a plan to alienate these last two sources of support and thus end the whole affair.[44] The scheme entailed widening the already existing schism between Sara Conboy and Smith and Miles, then, with Conboy's assistance, presenting evidence about the strike's mismanagement to the UTW executive board and eventually the AFL. Though Preston successfully carried out the various tactics associated with his plan, the larger strategy backfired, as the UTW and the AFL reaffirmed support for the Fulton effort and the southern organizing campaign.

On 12 September, Preston sent the first of many letters he would write to Conboy throughout the fall, "giving her all the knowledge that I had concerning Miles and Smith." On 19 September, he left Atlanta to meet with Conboy in Paterson, New Jersey, only to find she had returned to Boston. On 23 September, he made contact with Conboy, who arranged a meeting that evening between her, Preston, Golden, and UTW secretary-treasurer Albert Hibbert. That day, Preston also met at the Boston train station with Gordon Johnstone to talk over the unfolding events.[45]

At the two-hour meeting with the UTW leaders and in a subsequent conversation with Golden, Preston laid out the charges of mismanagement, favoritism, and immorality against Smith and Miles and recommended that the strike be discontinued. In response, Golden called a special meeting of the UTW executive board for 25 September in Fall River to discuss the Atlanta situation with Preston. Yet he also indicated, in what came as a surprise to Preston, that the UTW and AFL intended to thoroughly and indefinitely support the Fulton strike, because to pull out "would destroy the prestige" of the entire AFL southern organizing drive.[46]

Before going to the executive board meeting, Preston met again at the train station with Johnstone to review the matter. He also attended the annual convention of the Massachusetts Federation of Labor, at which, reflecting the significance of the Fulton strike and the southern campaign for New England trade unionists and textile workers, he was introduced as an honored guest and seated as a delegate. At the Fall River meeting, he provided the board "a full history of the strike as I saw it," detailed the allegations against Smith and Miles, described the sorry conditions at the tent colony and the withdrawal of local support, and advised calling off the strike.

Preston reported that "I readily met every question promptly, and gave them every detail on every subject required. . . . In fact, I missed nothing, being supplied with notes previously made." He described the board as "both amazed and indignant" at the actions of Smith and Miles and forecast that, as a result of his work, Smith would be soon "fired bodily out; and without ceremony" and that Miles, too, would be dismissed or, at least, "very shortly be removed from the south in disgrace." After the meeting, Preston returned to Philadelphia for several weeks, all the while keeping up a correspondence with both Wright and Conboy.[47]

Preston was both on and off the mark in his predictions. The discreditation campaign certainly contributed to both Miles and Smith eventually departing Atlanta and the strike. But where Preston erred, having been overly influenced by his personal dislike for Miles and especially Smith, was in his assumption that the removal of the two organizers would automatically lead to the strike's demise, and in his only gradual realization of its importance, however ill conceived or carried out, to the UTW's and the AFL's overall southern strategy.

Indeed, immediately after Preston's report to the UTW executive board, Golden informed him that the union "intended to organize the entire south, and would keep up this strike at all cost." Golden himself went to Atlanta in early October to personally monitor and direct the situation. There, he ousted Miles after "an awful row" and sent him to Nashville, where Miles took part in an organizing effort at the Morgan and Hamilton bag factory. Oscar Elsas quickly wrote mill treasurer Joseph Morgan that he could provide "some pointers on how to handle the situation" and recommended that Morgan try out the Railway Audit and Inspection Company. A few days later, Morgan wrote back that Miles had "failed ignominiously" in his organizing attempt, which prompted Elsas to suggest the two manufacturers compare union-busting notes.[48]

While in Atlanta, Golden also got printer William Weir from the *Atlanta Journal* to meet with Oscar Elsas and try to effect a settlement, not surprisingly with no success whatsoever. In addition, during his Atlanta stay, Golden organized and spoke at a mass meeting, reinstituted the practice of holding week-end rallies, and heard the complaints of Wright and others about the local strike leadership, as well as the counterclaims of tent colony residents. He probably also commissioned photographs of the camp then. In mid-October, Golden left to go to the UTW annual convention in Scranton, Pennsylvania.[49]

Also arriving in Scranton was Preston, now more reporting on the UTW than directly trying to influence its actions regarding the Fulton situation. Preston noted that a representative of the Atlanta Federation of Trades spoke before the convention. The speaker described the large debt that body had incurred on account of the strike, claimed that Miles had misled the AFT, and now sought reimbursement. Miles, Preston reported, was now "condemned on all sides." When Miles tried to present his side of the story, Golden cut him off; the UTW executive committee made him "look like a whipped dog." Smith, for her part, was "given no consideration whatever" by the delegates.

Despite Smith and Miles's fall from grace, however, the UTW showed no signs of abandoning either the Fulton strike or the southern campaign. Quite the contrary: "the agitation was to continue at all costs." Preston reported, "In regard to Fulton Bag, there is not the slightest doubt but that the fight will be centered there, as they realize that if they lose that, they may as well give up the South altogether." Moreover, it was obvious that the AFL would continue to back up the UTW in the effort. Based on what he heard at the convention, Preston speculated that this continued resolve to organize the South stemmed in part from the fear that the IWW would soon make headway among the approximately 100,000 textile workers (and potential dues-paying members of the UTW) in the region.[50]

Preston also reported that Luther Monday, an organizer from Knoxville who had shown success in organizing mill hands there, would play a leading role in the southern campaign, which prompted Elsas to immediately initiate surveillance of Monday through a Tennessee contact.[51] Preston also heard that Conboy and Mary Kelleher were to be reassigned to Atlanta. This news, along with Smith and Miles's downfall, caused him to once more reassess his relationship with Conboy. As he had with Wright, in the summer he had mocked Conboy's emotional speeches at the union hall. Later, as he had begun to discredit Miles and Smith, he joined with Conboy as a potential ally against them. In contrast to Smith and Miles, Conboy seemed dedicated and honest, and Preston praised her abilities repeatedly in his reports. It got to the point where he momentarily lost sight of the larger picture and Gordon Johnstone actually had to intervene and remind Preston that if Conboy were in fact so effective, then *she* should be targeted, too. Now, hoping to maintain his position and keep tabs on the Fulton situation and the southern campaign, Preston concurred with Johnstone that it was indeed Conboy who was the most dangerous organizer.[52]

At the UTW convention, Smith and Miles openly displayed hostility to Preston, which was not especially surprising to him, since he knew that they were aware that he had pressed charges against them. What was more disturbing was Conboy's apparent "coolness" toward him as well. Trying to figure out what was going on, after the convention Preston wrote Conboy, who responded in a polite but noncommittal manner.

Preston's cover had been blown. In November, strike leaders tried his unwitting accomplice Wright for treason, later reducing the charges to creating "a division of the union" and being misled by "Mr. Greenoff" (Harry Greenhough, Preston's alias). They ousted Wright from the local presidency and ultimately expelled him from the union. Strike leaders like Mullinax, Fleming, and Odell openly labeled Preston a spy, and soon his true identity was known to all parties, including CIR investigator Alexander Daly. While he did continue to correspond with Wright for a while, and came south again in late 1914 on another espionage assignment in North Carolina, Preston did not return to Atlanta for the duration of the strike.[53] His work there was through.

With the high stakes involved, Golden, on the other hand, visited Atlanta throughout the fall. Immediately following the UTW convention he returned to the city and delivered an address at a union rally in which he emphasized his own working-class background and associated the recent death of a child in the tent colony with the tyranny of Fulton Mills. Later in the fall, he took steps to clean up the camp, warning that any tent colony resident who got drunk or who otherwise did not follow the rules recently established by AFL organizer B. F. McIntyre would have to leave. He also bought everyone in the camp a new pair of shoes, in an attempt to shore up the union's reputation as a benefactor.[54]

In addition to his work on the scene, Golden launched a national publicity campaign using the Fulton strike as a symbol of the oppressive southern mills and of the UTW's challenge. With some accuracy, given the way the strike had gone and the realities of organizing in the South, the UTW leadership viewed

A family in a tent colony. Special Collections Dept., Pullen Library, Georgia State University.

this renewed publicity initiative as being of crucial importance, not only to continued support of the Fulton strike itself but, more significantly, to keeping the entire southern organizing drive alive.

As it did earlier to document child labor and evictions, the union commissioned a local commercial photographer, Will F. Nelson, to take and caption pictures of the tent city. In their themes, captions, and composition, Nelson's photos, many of which were reproduced in postcard form and distributed across the country, and other tent colony pictures evoked familiar themes used by the strike's publicists. They highlighted women, children, invalids, and downtrodden workers; the indomitability, patriotism, clean habits, and industriousness of the strikers; and the prominence of Golden and other leaders. In addition, in their often near-Arcadian presentation, the tent colony photos reinforced the organizers' claims about "the beauties and healthfulness of camp life," an image somewhat at odds with the leaky tents and other harsh realities of the colony.[55]

The photographs also misrepresented the number of people residing in the camp. At least one picture, a panorama of the colony and its residents, was actually a composite of two separate photographs, designed to make the strikers in the tent colony seem twice as numerous as they actually were. Another panoramic image was in fact a collage of three different photos discretely cobbled together.[56] Union statements and publications similarly exaggerated the tent colony population. In a speech before the AFL convention in Novem-

Panorama of tent colony. John Golden and O. Delight Smith are in front, center. Various individuals appear in both halves of the photo, reflecting its composite nature. Special Collections Dept., Pullen Library, Georgia State University.

ber, Conboy asserted that 1,400 people had been evicted from company housing, all purportedly now in the tent colony. In January 1915, an article in the *Textile Worker* alleged that some 300 adults and 60 to 75 children were dwelling in the tent community, all "cheerful and confident."[57]

In addition to disseminating the new photographs of the camp, the UTW resurrected the photographs that had been taken at the height of the strike, circulating them in Atlanta and around the country. In November, union members displayed some of the eviction pictures at the Good Roads Congress then convening in Atlanta. Postcards of Fulton child laborer Milton Nunnally began cropping up again across the United States.[58] The UTW was also behind the appearance of Nunnally's image in an article about the tent colony, and the photo was reprinted in the *Fort Smith (Ark.) Southwest American*, the *Columbus (Ohio) Citizen*, and other newspapers. The union also placed articles about the strike in the *Fall River Daily Globe* and the *Fall River Daily News*, and in additional newspapers in Massachusetts textile communities where feeling about the industry's migration southward ran high.[59]

The actual visual images used in the UTW's publicity campaign complemented what the union called "word-pictures" of the strike. At the UTW convention, Harry Preston wrote that Conboy, Golden, and others "painted a picture of conditions" that were calculated to arouse the sympathy and gain the support of the delegates; they were "picturing the 'horrible' conditions of the mill workers of the South, and they are getting all the money that they can."[60] Similarly, at the AFL convention in November, Conboy, seeking financial assistance, "painted the picture and other delegates added details to make it complete" of "little children driven into the mills sapped of their life-blood," "the dreaded disease, pellagra," "tiny company shacks," and other stereotypical images associated with oppressed southern workers. According to the *Textile Worker*, evoking Civil War imagery, this depiction "brought tears to many and . . . fixed in the hearts of delegates a resolve to send the emancipating hosts of organization marching through the Sunny South." The AFL executive council consequently voted to make Fulton strike support one of only three beneficiaries of the federation's national appeal for financial aid.[61]

On at least one occasion, however, Oscar Elsas, drawing upon his far-flung influential contacts, proved successful in nipping in the bud what he called "grossly exaggerated pictures" of the strike and Fulton Mills. At the instigation of the Philadelphia *North American* and an affiliated newspaper syndicate, freelance writer A. St. George Joyce came to Atlanta in December to do a series of articles on the Fulton situation. Joyce first met with tent colony residents and labor leaders, including Golden, then sought an interview with Elsas.

When Joyce got in touch with Elsas, he stated he had been instructed to write a story describing what Elsas labeled "Pitiful Working Conditions" or "Sob Stuff." Reluctant to get involved with the press yet apprehensive about the tone this article might take, Elsas personally escorted Joyce around the plant, making sure to show him "some of our satisfactory [*sic*] help," talked with him for another hour or so, and handed out a lengthy prepared statement presenting management's public viewpoint of the strike.

According to Elsas, when Joyce got ready to leave the plant, he stated, "The props have been knocked out from under me, and I do not see how I can get up an article for my paper that will fill the bill." "Naturally," Elsas related, "we felt encouraged." Yet the next day, Joyce sent to Elsas a draft version of the article that was sympathetic toward the strikers. The article described, with considerable hyperbole, the tribulations of life in the tent colony, the adamant stand of mill management against any sort of mediation or arbitration, working conditions that compared unfavorably to slavery, child labor (including a reference to Milton Nunnally), the employment contract and fining system, and the evictions from company housing.

Elsas termed the article "the vilest misrepresentations we have read since we had the labor troubles." He immediately wrote back a five-page letter to Joyce refuting point by point the article's allegations and tone and praising the company's performance record. In addition, he personally visited Joyce's hotel room that night "and let him understand that his article was thoroughly unfair and untrue." After about an hour of this, Joyce finally tore up the article and said he would not send it forward. He also wired the *North American* stating that there was no story and offered to write an article for *American Industries*, the organ of the National Association of Manufacturers, drawing upon the information Elsas supplied.

Despite Joyce's actions, Elsas, feeling he had been duped once and not wishing to be misled again, took additional steps to ensure that the article never saw the light of day. He twice wrote the *North American* providing his account of the situation. He also asked a Philadelphia acquaintance, manufacturer H. W. Butterworth, to intercede. Butterworth immediately contacted Samuel Steel of the *Textile Manufacturers Journal*, who had a relative at the *North American*, and got him to take action. Butterfield also got in touch with the *Public Ledger*, another Philadelphia paper for which Joyce had written, and reported back to Elsas that he was "arranging matters satisfactorily." In addition, Elsas asked his brother Adolph at the company's New York branch to get *New York Times* publisher Adolph Ochs to exert his influence in killing the article. Finally, he wrote James A. Emery about the matter.

When Joyce found out that complaints had been registered with the *North American* and *Public Ledger*, even after he had promised to pull the article, he became incensed. He claimed that Elsas was cutting him out of his livelihood, that what transpired between him and Elsas was a private matter, not to be disclosed to newspapers or other potential employers, and that as a reward for his "squareness" with Elsas, he had been treated unfairly. Elsas put up a front, alleging that he had tried to stop his original letter to the *North American* from going out after his conversation with Joyce in the hotel, but to no avail, as it had already been sent. In his correspondence with Emery, however, he candidly admitted to taking measures behind Joyce's back to nip the article in the bud.[62]

Along with the renewed publicity campaign, Golden worked to maintain ongoing federal involvement in the Fulton situation. In mid-October, he requested that the DOL again send conciliators to Atlanta to try to effect a settlement, whereupon Secretary Wilson appointed to the case John Colpoys and Robert McWade, the two conciliation commissioners who had passed through town in August. In November, they visited Oscar Elsas, stating to him that the earlier report of Husband and Robinson had been inconclusive and did not sufficiently cover the details of the strike. They also refused to let Elsas see the Husband-Robinson report, stating he would have to petition the DOL. For his part, Elsas said the mill was now "overrun with help" and declared that under no circumstances would the company reemploy the people now in the tent colony.[63]

On Colpoys and McWade's next visit, Elsas provided them with substantially the same statement that he presented Joyce. He also declared that he would never alter the contract in any way. In addition to reducing labor turnover in general, Elsas asserted, the contract had been of crucial importance in keeping people from leaving their jobs during the first days of the strike. He told McWade and Colpoys, "I have made my mind up on that subject and I will not change that contract system until Hell freezes over. I would sooner shut down these mills and keep them so until moss and any other kind of vegetation would grow over their windows than agree to change my attitude on that question. If the Courts decide . . . that it is illegal, we will sell out our interests at 50 cents on the dollar rather than operate without a contract." Elsas also claimed that the MRFM had attacked Fulton Bag strictly out of "religious prejudice and racial hatred" and that "all of the mill-owners are against me for the same reason."[64]

Colpoys and McWade continued to monitor the Fulton situation, as well as organizing efforts in other southern communities, until the summer of 1915.[65] Their final report clearly reflected the input of the UTW leadership. They condemned the "odious and tyrannical Brutality of the Mill Bosses" and accepted uncritically the claims that 92 percent of Fulton workers had gone out by the end of the first week of the strike and that over 2,000 people had been fed daily at the commissary. They also attached to the report numerous UTW-commissioned photographs of child laborers, the evictions, peaceful picketers, and the tent colony.

Colpoys and McWade did criticize what they called Miles and Smith's "rather loose and reprehensible methods" of conducting the commissary and the camp. "Outside of profligate expenditures," they reported, Smith and Miles "were and are openly accused of gross immorality and undoubted unfaithfulness to the trust reposed in them." They also described with some distaste the snuff-dipping habits of Fulton workers and their aversion to food to which they were not accustomed. In the end, the two conciliators "regretted that they were unable to effect a settlement of the trouble," an outcome that was assured from the beginning given Elsas's resistance and the fact that the plant was running at full capacity.

The Conciliation Service was only one of several federal avenues that Golden pursued. He got Fall River congressman William S. Greene to introduce a resolution on 15 September calling for a congressional investigation of the textile industry in Atlanta, similar to the well-publicized recent hearings on the Lawrence strike. In bringing up the bill, Greene quoted Golden about conditions in Atlanta. He also explicitly raised sectional differences. The UTW, Greene declared, "is planning to emancipate the textile workers of the South. . . . "[T]he inhuman and uncivilized conditions surrounding these people . . . would not be tolerated a minute in the cotton mill sections of Massachusetts."[66]

The resolution immediately attracted the attention of various interested parties. The Atlanta Federation of Trades, despite whatever misgivings members may have had about how the strike was conducted, passed a resolution praising Greene for his action. In addition, the AFT criticized Congressman William Schley Howard's seeming inactivity on the matter and wrote Howard a letter asking whether his position regarding organized labor had changed. Oscar Elsas also took quick action. Before the day was out, he had contacted Claude Bennett of the Congressional Information Bureau, asking him to promptly bring up the matter to Georgia's congressional delegation "and tell them that it is time to quit agitating this subject." On his own accord, Bennett notified Elsas about the resolution, offering his assistance in the matter.

Elsas also wrote Howard, stating that Greene was resurrecting "the old fight of the Eastern mills against the Southern mills." Even though Elsas himself had many close ties to New England textile manufacturers, he sounded the theme of sectional colonialism to Howard, lamenting the efforts of northern textile interests to subordinate the southern mills through legislation "and every other conceivable way." Elsas even suggested that northern mills were behind "the organization of the Southern labor." In concluding, he urged upon Howard "the importance of killing off any further agitation on this subject, as it can only engender unnecessary hard feelings between employer and employee."[67]

On 16 September, Bennett wrote Elsas that the resolution had been referred to the House Rules Committee, where, he predicted, it would not be reported out of committee. He later elaborated that the committee had consistently turned down similar requests for investigations, and that it included a number of southern Democrats, such as Georgia's Thomas W. Hardwick, who would keep it from ever reaching the House floor. Howard also informed Elsas that the resolution was dead in the water, being "nothing in the world but political buncombe" on the eve of Greene's own re-election bid. In addition, Howard wrote the AFT that Greene was merely pandering to the manufacturing interests of his district to gain campaign support and was engaging in "pure, unadulterated demagogy" with no hope of actually having the measure passed.[68]

James Emery also quickly spotted the Greene resolution and concurred that it would go nowhere, although fundamentally for reasons of partisan politics rather than sectionalism or constitutional questions. He believed that the Democrats in Congress were tiring of investigations and in particular of "the constant effort to drag the Democratic party into the help of some strike effort." In addition, Emery suggested that Elsas contact Georgia senator Hoke Smith, who chaired the Senate Committee on Education and Labor, before which the resolution would come if it ever reached the Senate. Even if the House did appoint its own committee to investigate the matter, Emery felt that Smith's influence would override any such action.[69]

In voicing this opinion, Emery showed an up-to-the-minute appreciation of Smith's recent support of southern industrialists. Elsas was not so sure of Smith's leanings. He wrote Emery that "confidentially, Senator Hoke Smith has always shown inclinations toward labor." Elsas told Emery he was going to refrain from bringing up the matter directly with Smith, unless it reached the point where the resolution actually reached the Senate, in which case, "we would commence taking steps to use his influence in our favor." Nevertheless, Elsas did contact Claude Bennett, Smith's former personal secretary, and asked him to talk with Smith on the company's behalf. Bennett assured Elsas that he would get in touch with Smith "and endeavor to enlist his sympathies."[70]

After another article about the Greene resolution appeared in the *Atlanta Georgian* and other Hearst newspapers, Elsas tried to influence Rules Committee member Thomas Hardwick through Judge John S. Candler, his neighbor at the Ponce de Leon Apartments and the brother of Coca-Cola magnate Asa Candler. Elsas had learned John Candler had recently had a conversation with Hardwick about the Greene resolution and asked Candler to write a follow-up letter to Hardwick to ensure that the resolution did not leave committee. In his letter to Hardwick, Candler praised the welfare work of Fulton Mills and stated that the proposed investigation was not needed, especially since the DOL had "ample machinery for investigation."[71]

The issue died down until after the elections and the reconvening of Congress late in the year. On 8 December, Golden asked Greene to resurrect the matter. In so doing, he appealed to Greene's pride, stating that both Elsas and Howard had dismissed Greene as merely "playing cheap politics" in an election year; now that the election was over, Greene could prove them wrong. Golden also reiterated the importance of the Fulton strike to the entire trade union movement.[72] In addition, Golden got the AFT to write Howard another appeal for a congressional investigation. Although he responded courteously, Howard conveyed doubts that such an investigation would ever be held, since it would be outside the constitutional bounds of Congress. He pointed out that Congress had "absolutely refused" to investigate the Lawrence strike, "the most horrible industrial upheaval in the textile industry that we have had in this country for years."[73]

Oscar Elsas also tried to get in touch with Howard about the Greene resolution. After failing to meet the congressman in person when he visited Atlanta, Elsas wrote a letter to Howard emphasizing the threat that any "agitation" posed to the southern economy, especially at a time of regional economic depression. "The one essential point to bear in mind," Elsas wrote, "is that the South is so closely allied to the future in the cotton goods industry and everything relating to cotton, that we can ill afford to do anything that would engender or encourage additional strife," as the Greene resolution threatened to do.[74]

In February 1915, Greene made a speech about the Fulton situation before the entire House. He included in his remarks a reading of the company's labor contract in its entirety, as well as the rules for operatives. He also quoted a UTW-planted article in the *Fall River Daily Globe* titled "Deplorable Textile Conditions," along with correspondence from Golden, Howard, and the AFT.

His address sparked a heated exchange on the floor between northern and southern congressmen. One representative from Tennessee interrupted Greene to point out that two years earlier, the House Rules Committee had looked into a similar situation in Massachusetts, referring to the Lawrence strike, and had come to the conclusion that Congress had no authority to call a major investigation. His remarks were echoed by fellow Tennessean Finis J. Garrett, a member of the Rules Committee, who maintained there existed no federal question involved that would permit Congress to launch an investigation. Garrett, who admitted he knew nothing about Fulton Mills, also erroneously speculated that "the majority of the stock of that particular factory, like the majority of the stock of a great many other southern manufactories, is owned not in the South but in the North." Greene, in turn, asserted that several members of the Rules Committee had promised a hearing to him, if not a full-fledged investigation.

On 2 March, Congressman Howard addressed the House on a point of personal privilege to respond to Greene's remarks. Howard claimed that Greene knew from the beginning that the resolution wouldn't pass yet had misled Golden to the contrary. In addition, he alleged that Greene had not protested the mistreatment of workers during the Lawrence strike and had voted against labor on various occasions. Howard also took the opportunity to defend southern mill hands in nativist terms, stating that "as pure Anglo-Saxon blood as flows in the veins of any citizenry of America flows in the veins of Georgia textile workers." Conversely, he associated many of the wretched conditions in the Massachusetts mills with the large foreign-born population there.[75]

Underlying the discussion of the Greene resolution from start to finish was the possibility of a full-scale CIR public investigation into the southern textile industry. As early as 16 September, Bennett wrote Elsas that Greene predicted the resolution would go nowhere in Congress, with the expectation that he would then take steps to initiate a CIR investigation. Anticipating such a likelihood, Bennett assured Elsas that his office "will diplomatically sound the Commission on the subject as soon as possible." He also told Elsas that any danger resulting from a CIR investigation was quite remote, with the only potential problems being unfavorable publicity and renewed "agitation."[76]

A week later, Bennett sent a copy of the legislation that had created the CIR to Elsas, who had not been sure of its exact powers. In addition, Bennett indicated he had been afraid to ask high-ranking CIR officials directly about an investigation lest he arouse suspicion or reveal uneasiness. However, he had consulted with an anonymous individual, whom Bennett identified only as "one of our friends," who was also "one of the special experts of the Commission" as well as a southern Democrat. This person had related that the CIR was for the most part sticking to its established investigation schedule and that it had already made its investigation of the textile industry. He therefore felt that it was unlikely the CIR would follow up on Greene's activity, although he did not rule out the possibility altogether. Indeed, in November, word spread that the CIR intended to conduct hearings in Atlanta.[77]

For his part, Elsas expressed no apprehension about a possible investigation, once he understood that all the CIR was empowered to do was investigate and make recommendations, and he notified James Emery that he would be glad to tell his side of the story at any CIR southern investigation. Emery himself had participated in CIR hearings, and with the formation of the CIR had helped create the Joint Committee of Associated Employers, consisting of what Joint Committee counsel Walter Drew called "the radical, aggressive open shop employers of the country," to work with the commission. "We have nothing to hide," Elsas told Emery, a theme he echoed to others as well.[78]

On 6 February 1915, CIR director Frank P. Walsh announced that the commission *would* conduct hearings in Atlanta the following month. In anticipation of the hearings, Elsas immediately took a variety of steps. He asked Bennett for background information about the nine CIR commissioners, including "their personal inclinations, that is, either for labor or for capital." Upon receiving the list, he realized that, through his connections in national German Jewish circles, he and commissioner Harris Weinstock, a department store owner from Sacramento and a leading California Progressive, almost certainly had an acquaintance in common, California Supreme Court justice M. C. Sloss. Elsas then provided Sloss his version of the strike, including his claim that only seventy-eight people had ever taken part. He also asked Sloss to put in a good word for Fulton management to Weinstock, about whom he had doubts, given Weinstock's positions on arbitration and other labor-related matters. Sloss replied that he would do all that he could to influence Weinstock without violating the proprieties of the commissioner's position.[79]

Elsas also read newspaper accounts of the CIR hearings on the New York garment industry and sought to get transcripts of the recent hearings in Denver, which focused on the Ludlow massacre. Unable to obtain either transcripts or digests of the hearings through Bennett, he asked an Atlanta acquaintance on business in Denver to secure copies of the *Denver Post* for the relevant period. He also contacted his brother David at the firm's Dallas factory about the CIR's hearings in the Southwest.[80]

In addition, making full use of the extensive company office staff, he began preparing a raft of exhibits for submission to the CIR. These exhibits were of several types. Many contained detailed information on working conditions at Fulton Mills, including the fining system, child labor, the employment contract, labor turnover, the impact of the strike upon production, and the weekly wages of "representative family groups," which actually represented the high end of the Fulton wage scale.

Elsas also prepared a report for the CIR on the incidence of home ownership among Fulton workers. As with family wages, he misrepresented the situation, neglecting to say that probably the majority of employee-owned homes belonged to nonproduction workers. To advance the company's position, he also included photographs of some of the nicest worker-owned houses, juxtaposed with pictures he had specifically commissioned of "the dilapidated, or the worst features" of mill district housing not owned by Fulton Mills.[81]

Yet another group of exhibits developed for the CIR attempted to discredit perceived antagonists of the company. Toward this end, Elsas supplied a list of all the purported assaults by strikers and their allies during the course of the strike. He also provided a complete set of the MRFM strike-related bulletins, as well as correspondence with MRFM member C. B. Wilmer. In addition to compiling exhibits, Elsas wrote numerous drafts of his answers to the questionnaire drawn up by investigators Daly and Weed.

One of the most significant steps Elsas took was to contact James Emery for assistance with the CIR. Emery, in turn, put Elsas in touch with National Erectors Association president Walter Drew, who was representing the Joint Committee of Associated Employers before the commission.[82] Drew, a militant open-shop advocate, had long been a leading force in the NAM and other employers organizations. According to Emery, he had been "the chief factor" in securing the arrest and conviction of the McNamara brothers. In his capacity as counsel to the Joint Committee, he had attended all the CIR hearings, providing assistance to local manufacturers in selecting witnesses and preparing testimony.[83]

In Emery and Drew's opinion, such assistance was of critical importance in ensuring the proper presentation of management's position before the CIR and to counterbalance the testimony from organized labor, as well as the commission's own prolabor prejudices. As Drew wrote to the Fulton attorneys, "It has seemed best to us to do what we could to get the real facts concerning industry into the record, rather than to stand aloof and permit a one-sided case to be made. Should the employers refuse to deal with the Commission, it would only serve the purposes of those who wish to make out a case against the employing interests, for it would be said, and generally believed, that an employer's refusal to submit facts and to cooperate with the Commission was because of his fear that the truth would come out."[84]

Oscar Elsas readily concurred in this assessment. He had considerable difficulty, however, in getting the Georgia Cotton Manufacturers Association to extend a formal invitation to Drew, as recommended by Emery. Elsas had to resort to "some strenuous talk" to get Exposition Mill's Allen Johnson, the president of the GCMA, to agree to write a letter to Drew. Even then, Johnson sent the letter off only after Elsas became "insistent," impressing upon him the urgency of the matter.[85] The reasons for this aversion to hire Drew were complicated. Johnson and other GCMA members were reluctant to make a potentially hefty contribution for Drew's services, especially given the distinct possibility that the CIR hearings were only going to focus on Fulton Mills. Indeed, given reports of the CIR's attenuated financial circumstances and political difficulties, it was a legitimate question as to whether there would be any Atlanta hearings at all.

Yet, there were other reasons for the GCMA's reticence. No doubt, some Georgia mill men did not share Elsas's enthusiasm for unified action among employers, particularly at the legislative level. For the most part, they had a more regional focus than Elsas, and were not as tied in as he was to the NAM and its related organizations and networks. In addition, it seems probable that, given the labor agitation and intense scrutiny and widespread publicity that Fulton Mills had already attracted and was likely to draw through the CIR hearings, many Georgia cotton manufacturers sought to distance themselves as much as possible from the company and its practices. Even Exposition's Johnson, who shared information about labor spies and otherwise kept in touch and cooperated with Elsas throughout the strike, criticized Fulton's contract, fining system, and high turnover rate in his remarks to federal investigators.[86]

Elsas's often prickly relationship with his fellow manufacturers certainly contributed to this coolness as well. Elsas maintained that he was being made a scapegoat by the other cotton manufacturers in the state. He complained to Drew that "the investigation of the cotton mill situation ought not, properly, to fall on us merely because we were brave enough to take care of our interests without calling for help from our brother manufacturers." Throughout the strike, he also claimed that the purported lack of cooperation he received from his counterparts was in large part due to anti-Semitism at the time of the Frank case.[87]

Like Elsas, both Drew and Emery felt that the foot dragging by the GCMA was "extremely imprudent and short-sighted." Emery believed that, even though Fulton Mills would undoubtedly be one of the principal subjects of any investigation, a CIR hearing in Atlanta would certainly treat "the entire textile situation." Given what had happened at other CIR hearings, Emery predicted that "[e]very endeavor will be made to assist trade unions in presenting as extreme an attack as can be made upon the textile industry. Every isolated and exceptional case will be brought to the attention of the Commission and exaggerated into prominence as though it were typical and generally illustrative of the condition prevailing in the industry."

In particular, Emery feared that "the usual child labor attack will be strongly pressed" at any CIR hearing in Atlanta. For Emery and Drew, the consequences of such an attack could easily extend beyond the South to affect all American industry. From their national perspective, they felt that an emphasis on child labor at the Atlanta hearing would provide ammunition for the supporters of pending congressional legislation limiting the shipment in interstate commerce of commodities produced by children. In turn, agitation around the interstate commerce bill would lead to additional unwarranted federal regulation of industry; in Drew's words, it was "merely the first step in an extensive movement to secure Federal control of conditions of production under the guise of regulating commerce."[88]

Despite the GCMA's continued reluctance to contribute to Drew's funding, Drew offered his services anyway to Elsas, who offered a contribution from Fulton Mills to the Joint Committee of Associated Employers whether the GCMA paid or not. Drew stated he could probably not make it to Atlanta for more than a day or two himself, but he did send his assistant, John Macintyre, who arrived in town on 15 March to help management in its preparation for the CIR hearings, to be overseen by Alexander Daly.[89]

On 17 March, Macintyre was conferring with Oscar Elsas when a telegram came from Drew announcing that a full-scale public hearing in Atlanta had been called off. Daly instead had been instructed only to gather testimony in closed session from both parties in the dispute, along with related exhibits pertaining to the Fulton situation alone. The news came as a surprise to Daly, who had recently written Elsas that he thought the Atlanta hearing would extend to the textile industry throughout Georgia. "I am unable to say what the reasons were which prompted the Commission to take this course," Daly wrote Elsas.[90]

The cancellation of the public hearing disappointed the Federation of Trades, which called for an investigation into the matter. The standard account of the CIR indicates that opposition from Hoke Smith and other southern Democrats in the Senate, who were afraid of the "violent senatorial repercussions" of a public examination of labor in the South, proved crucial in preventing CIR hearings in Atlanta and elsewhere in the region. In addition, by early 1915, the CIR faced major budget difficulties and internal problems, which contributed to a substantial reduction of its activities in its final months.[91] Yet, at least in the Atlanta case, the active intervention of Drew and other militant pro-employer spokesmen may also have helped curtail CIR involvement.

Oscar Elsas certainly implied as much in his letters to other Georgia textile manufacturers after the hearing. He wrote F. B. Gordon of Columbus that the Joint Committee of Associated Employers had been "instrumental" in preventing a public hearing. He similarly asserted to H. P. Meikleham of Lindale,

> It was due to the strong efforts of this Joint Employers Association that the public Hearing was prevented in Atlanta. I think, from the developments, that it is exceedingly fortunate that no public Hearing was held. It would have been the beginning of undue agitation and notoriety in the papers, resulting in unduly exciting the help, and the probable result of more organization among them than now exists. No matter what showing would have been made by the mills themselves, the labor element would have predominated, and so framed the questions that only the bad spots would have been picked out by them for investigation; while we, on the other hand, would have found it more difficult to present the good spots.[92]

The nearly sixty witnesses who appeared before Daly in the closed hearing constituted a veritable Who's Who of people associated with the strike, outside of the departed Smith and Miles. Witnesses for management included not only Elsas, Gordon Johnstone, and other supervisory personnel but also Wesley House workers and physicians connected with the clinic; company doctor Hawkins; loyal employees; Meikleham; disillusioned strikers and one-time strike supporters; and the plumber who had installed individual toilets to replace the latrines in the mill district after the union's agitation over the matter. In turn, the UTW put up on the stand strike leaders Mullinax, Fleming, and Odell; MRFM members, local trade unionists, and sympathetic physician

W. V. Garrett; evicted strikers; recruits from Lindale; and residents of the tent colony.

To a large degree, the testimony followed familiar lines. Mullinax and other workers described Fulton Mills's system of fines and deductions, the employment contract, and other onerous working conditions, inadequate medical care as epitomized by Dr. Hawkins, and squalid conditions in the mill district. Along with local trade unionists Louie P. Marquardt and S. B. Marks, they recounted the causes of the October walkout, subsequent unrest and organization among Fulton workers, the company's harassment of identified union leaders, the origins of the strike itself, evictions from company housing, the dictograph incident, and blacklisting of known Fulton strikers by other mills. They and witnesses like the MRFM's Marion Jackson also emphasized the strikers' peacefulness and good conduct throughout the dispute.[93]

Witnesses for management provided essentially two different sorts of testimony. Elsas, Johnstone, and other supervisory personnel and Wesley House workers described and defended the company's employment practices, rules, and labor turnover rate, as well as the settlement house work. Elsas and Johnstone in particular also denied keeping track of whether workers had joined the union before the strike and elaborated on how they came to the conclusion that only seventy-eight workers had struck. In addition, Elsas took issue with the union's version of the strike's origins, maintained that few of the pickets had ever worked at Fulton Mills, emphasized that in contrast most workers had been contented and loyal throughout the strike, reiterated management's refusal to negotiate with any outside party, condemned the MRFM, and specifically refuted various claims by Golden and others about the strike and the company's conduct.[94]

Other management witnesses testified primarily about the unsavory character and conduct of the strikers and their leaders, particularly O. Delight Smith and Charles Miles. Two key individuals in this regard were disillusioned former Local 886 presidents W. C. Sweatt and Robert Wright, both of whom described their recruitment into the strike and their installation into a position of supposed leadership without, in Sweatt's words, "no say so over nothing." They also recounted the proliferation of individuals on the scene not having any prior connection to Fulton Mills; the abuses associated with the commissary; and Smith and Miles's broken promises and other questionable moral behavior.[95]

On several occasions, Daly raised the issue of labor spies, a major concern of the CIR more generally. Daly also asked both labor and management witnesses about the company's purported surveillance and harassment of union activists in the months before the strike. Contradicting the testimony of Elsas and

Johnstone, paymaster T. S. Florence and Superintendent E. H. Rogers acknowledged that indeed the company *had* singled out union members. Rogers testified first, stating that once an organization had been formed, he kept tabs on it by asking questions "of some of our people I knew I could get information from." He then, he recounted, reported the names of union members to his superior and to Johnstone, who discharged "quite a number." During the following day's testimony, upon persistent questioning by Daly, Florence reluctantly concurred with Rogers's account.[96]

This was hardly the only time during the hearing that even company witnesses provided testimony that challenged top management's version of the strike and conditions at Fulton Mills. Rogers, for instance, admitted that the firm's employment contract was notorious throughout the Piedmont. Other management witnesses, including R. H. Wright's wife, Sallie, condemned the contract as well. In addition, Sallie Wright described some of the tensions surrounding the October walkout and revealed how unpopular the evictions were among many Fulton workers. Even bag mill worker A. S. Guffin, who in July had written a letter to the newspaper expressing his loyalty to mill management, testified about the difficulties of making a living at Fulton Mills.[97]

Alexander Daly placed his stamp on the entire proceeding. He devoted much of his questioning to the contract, fining system, and sanitary conditions in the mill district, as well as the proximate causes of the strike. What was not discussed was equally revealing. By and large, Daly skirted the issue of child labor, which he correctly felt really did not apply to Fulton Mills. He also generally avoided such favorite management themes as the strike-related incidents of violence and the purported anti-Semitism of the MRFM. When he finally read the testimony, Oscar Elsas felt sufficiently dismayed by Daly's performance that he wrote Walter Drew expressing his disappointment, stating that "Daly's *peculiar* method of questioning" had led the witnesses "unreasonably."[98]

Elsas also submitted a thirty-four-page brief to CIR director Walsh, elaborating on points that had not been addressed to his satisfaction at the hearing. In addition to refuting charges that had been leveled against the firm and providing additional documentation about conditions at Fulton Mills and the southern textile industry more generally, Elsas addressed what he called "the whole crux of this situation," meaning "the proper comprehension and understanding of this particular element of labor with which the Southern manufacturer is confronted."

In no other instance did he present his personal perceptions of the people who worked at Fulton Mills in such an analytical and revealing manner. Elsas first traced many of the characteristics, "both desirable and undesirable," of southern mill workers back to colonial days and to Great Britain. Among these "hereditary traits" were pride and independence of spirit, resentment of outside interference, a strongly held concept of personal liberty and equality, suspicion of the motives and intents of others, a religious traditionalism, and an indifference "as to the manner of living and as to general appearance." Such a constellation of attributes caused inherent difficulties for southern manufacturers, he maintained. "All of these peculiar characteristics," stated Elsas, "make the handling of these people an exceedingly vexatious daily problem," which the strike had illustrated in high relief.

A few weeks after Elsas wrote his brief to Walsh, Congress voted not to print the testimony gathered by the CIR, restricting publication of CIR material only to the commission's final report. Paced by Georgia's Hoke Smith, southern Democrats led the fight against the printing appropriation. "I have not the slightest respect for anything the Commission did," Smith declared on the Senate floor. "I regard it simply as so much junk." Smith decried the "utter lack of reliability" of much CIR testimony, which, he predicted, if printed, "nobody will read and to which nobody will give shelf space." Despite efforts by organized labor over the next year to have the entire CIR proceedings printed, only the final report was ever published.

The winnowing down of the Atlanta hearing to a closed session involving Fulton Mills alone, and its subsequent nonpublication, was in some ways a metaphor for the entire Fulton strike, which was officially called off, one year after it began, in May 1915.[99] Yet the strike not only had a significant and lasting impact on all directly involved parties and their associates but also revealed in high relief many of the dynamics, tensions, and characteristics of Atlanta and the New South.

CONCLUSION

The Strike's Legacy and Place in Southern History

Like wars, natural disasters, and other major upheavals, strikes potentially offer a glimpse at many aspects of a society that normally are concealed or overlooked. The disruption of business as usual can lay bare attitudes, dynamics, tensions, etiquette, and power relationships that customarily go unrecorded. Tumultuous events often attract exceptional attention and generate an uncommon amount of documentation, as in the case of the Fulton strike; without this evidence, our understanding of such events is likely to be substantially reduced. Such documentation also frequently extends beyond the specifics of the matter at hand to the larger historical setting. In addition to having a significant impact on southern labor relations and on the people directly involved, the Fulton strike reveals a great deal about the urban-industrial New South.

The reasons that the strike ultimately failed, in a seeming best-case scenario, have been recounted elsewhere, most notably by Gary Fink. Fink points to such factors as the availability of cheap labor, the implacability of management, the transience of the workforce, the shortcomings and miscalculations of union organizers, and the active intervention of labor spies.[1] These factors are indeed important. Yet the strike offers a great deal more than just another lesson of failure in the history of southern labor unions.

The story of the Fulton strike is at once an Atlanta story, a regional story, and a national story. Obviously, Atlanta was not a typical isolated southern mill community but rather by the teens served as the provincial capital of the South. As such, it functioned as a border zone mediating between the region and the rest of the nation, between traditionalism and modern times, at the cusp in some sense between the nineteenth and twentieth centuries. The city included among its rapidly growing population a wide range of social types who really did not exist in the post-Reconstruction South, many of whom had some direct connection to Fulton Mills and to the strike: professional social workers, trade unionists, middle-class reformers, women like O. Delight Smith who were increasingly active in public life, Socialist Party members, purveyors and consumers of cheap amusements along Decatur Street and elsewhere, luxury apartment dwellers, patrons of Grand Opera and fiddler's conventions, labor spies, practitioners of scientific management, female factory workers and "women adrift," and third-generation cotton mill workers, as well as affluent, educated, and criminal African Americans, white-collar and service workers, eastern European Jewish immigrants, club women, and others. In essence, by the mid-teens there existed many different Atlantas.

This splintering of Atlanta's population had important consequences. In many ways, the city's diverse residents were increasingly unable to effectively understand, appreciate, or communicate with one another. They frequently lacked a common language, a common background, a common etiquette, a common vision, a common set of shared values and assumptions, or common arenas for public discourse. The cultural gulf between the Elsas family and the people who worked at Fulton Mills was as great as any divide in the city (at least among white people), but numerous other chasms existed as well. For instance, Oscar Elsas and the MRFM members operated on vastly different planes; there was no way they could ever come to terms around such issues as arbitration or workers' rights. The MRFM members dismissed out of hand the activity of the Wesley House women as something that was properly "red-blooded men's work."[2] For many Atlantans, both O. Delight Smith's union activities and her personal behavior flew in the face of what was familiar, appropriate, or acceptable. And the respectable Atlanta trade unionists, the UTW leadership, and the MRFM members could hardly comprehend the world of Fulton workers.

Indeed, among the few things that united middle- and upper-class white Atlantans, along with their counterparts elsewhere in the region, was a near-universal low regard for mill hands and their depiction of textile workers in two-dimensional, stereotypical terms. These portrayals took several forms. Mill workers were often described as almost innately childlike, incapable of self-governance or making informed decisions on their own. Alternately, they were labeled inherently suspicious, touchy, or fiercely independent, to a degree out of proportion to what was warranted. Finally, they seemed threatening to New South advancement in their lack of ambition, questionable moral behavior, and general unruliness.

Among other consequences, such stigmatization of mill workers severely limited the realization of any sort of collective action, regardless of other circumstances. During the strike, Fulton workers were for the most part described by union partisans not as active agents working on their own behalf but as utterly oppressed and downtrodden, "sacrificed to the cotton juggernaut, crushed and broken in mind and body." Despite the fact that skilled male workers were at the core of the insurgency, strike organizers, MRFM members, and trade unionists all depicted the strike as being mainly made up of women and children, thus ascribing to it engendered attributes of frailty, weakness, and victimization. And the various presidents of Local 886 were essentially figureheads, cut off from any meaningful input into union strategies and tactics. Union democracy, whatever that might have meant, almost inevitably went by the wayside before it ever even had a chance.

Many middle-class white southerners both feared and despised "lint heads," even as the New South depended on their labor. Of course, the same was true, to a far greater degree, for African Americans. Mill owners, workers, and managers, members of Atlanta's business elite and white working class, labor spies, and UTW leaders and strike organizers all reflexively exploited racism or used racial stereotypes during the course of the strike, in a reminder that, even in a dispute largely among white people, race and white supremacism were never far from the surface in the early-twentieth-century South.

Labor spies, while employing racial stereotypes themselves, reported how black scrubwomen at Fulton Mills received derogatory comments from white workers on the shop floor. When Robert Wright tried to condemn the company in the strongest words he could find, he claimed that the mill sponsored a daily "Tango Dance," "which would make the lowest nigger of Decatur Street blush with shame."[3] One of the most galvanizing events for white Fulton workers was the eviction of strikers from company housing by black laborers. In addition to the humiliation of company agents entering their private homes, the fact that it was black workers who did the dirty work added to the sense of violation. O. Delight Smith, Charles Miles, and the UTW national leadership quickly recognized the potential for white outrage and openly appealed to it at union meetings, with the captioned photographs of blacks carrying out the evictions displayed prominently in downtown Atlanta and on broadsides and postcards distributed across the United States.

Management's white supremacism and exploitation of race was at least as pronounced. Gordon Johnstone and other associates of Oscar Elsas routinely called African Americans "nigger" and "darkey." When black organizer M. C. Parker of the Hod Carriers tried to recruit and bring out the firm's black workers, he was at least allowed to speak to white strikers at the union hall,

Cartoon that appeared in the June 1918 issue of the employee newsletter, *The Fulton*. Special Collections Dept., Robert W. Woodruff Library, Emory University.

even if the UTW did not extend commissary benefits to black workers; in contrast, Parker's presence sent chills up the spine of Oscar Elsas, who immediately communicated about Parker with race-baiting politician Joseph M. Brown. When Elsas sought to get damaging photographs of MRFM leader John Eagan's Birmingham factory, he was particularly interested in getting an image of the boy who ladled out water from the same dipper "to both whites and blacks." He opposed the arbitration bill pending before the state legislature in racial terms, warning that black maids and sharecroppers might meet as equals with their employers or landlords. In 1918, when the company sought to promote its new welfare capitalism initiatives in the employee newsletter (benefits that were never extended to the black workers at Fulton Mills), it did so in a racially stereotypical cartoon.

In distinct though interrelated ways, both African Americans and white textile workers embodied many of the apprehensions that numerous Atlantans and other southerners felt at a time of sweeping change in the city and region. A mill hand's life was frequently disorderly, if not marginal in its transience; weekly lack of certainty about work and pay; susceptibility to disease, debt, and injury; and general rambunctiousness. A tramp weaver, a resident of the mill district who drank too much or who carried on an adulterous affair, or a striking worker all challenged attempts to establish or maintain order in what was at its heart a volatile, anxious, fear-ridden environment, all the New South and Atlanta boosterism aside.

The very size, growth, and anonymity of the city meant that every day one was in close physical proximity with strangers, perhaps people different from and threatening to oneself, in a way that marked a clear departure from the comparatively close-knit locales of the rural South. Within this setting, suspicion ran rampant. This climate of distrust and fear helped fuel the widespread propagation of misinformation that characterized Atlanta in the 1910s. During the Leo Frank case, for instance, newspapers routinely concocted stories, witnesses lied on the stand and in affidavits, and rumors abounded concerning Frank's sexuality and other matters.

Similarly, all parties in the Fulton strike, hardly thinking about it, lied and exaggerated to advance their case. Oscar Elsas repeatedly declared that only seventy-eight people had gone out on strike, maintained that the company had not discriminated against union members, and presented misleading statistics concerning average wages and home ownership. However, while Elsas consistently downplayed the significance and extent of the strike, he and other cotton manufacturers were quick to magnify the threat of labor organization in the region after the UTW and especially the IWW embarked on their southern campaigns. Anyone critical of management was labeled a "trouble maker"; anyone who attended a meeting was a union member or warranted watching; anyone who made a speech was a rabble rouser; any union organizer or sympathizer might be a wild-eyed radical in disguise. In some respects, the reaction in management circles to the organizing drives of the teens resembled the near-hysteria that had swept the South in the aftermath of the John Brown raid.

UTW leaders and strike organizers concerned about the fate of the southern campaign, in turn, exaggerated the number of workers out on strike, over-stated the presence of child laborers at Fulton Mills, embellished the attributes of life in the tent colony, and staged and falsified photographs. The MRFM and some of the federal investigators presented hyperbolic descriptions of the strike that were at considerable odds with the realities of the situation. (CIR investigator Alexander Daly was a notable exception.) And, of course, the spies and company informants were in the very business of deception and misinformation.

Interestingly, much of the strike-related falsification came via modern emblems of authentication and verification that were so much a part of the Progressive Era. The affidavit, the statistical study, the photograph, the official report, the newsreel, the interview, the dictograph, the investigative journalism piece, the hearing, and even the typewriter itself all constituted emergent means by which early-twentieth-century Americans ostensibly sought to gather and present the facts in support of their arguments, to scientifically and objectively muster evidence. Yet in the case of the Fulton strike, each one of these devices also became a vehicle for manipulation and misrepresentation.

In addition to all parties' creative employment of new media and technology, the Fulton dispute was a modern strike in other ways, most notably concerning the involvement of the federal government and the contest for public opinion. The very concept of public opinion, along with the related fields of advertising and social psychology, was in some sense a new creation of the Progressive Era, and certainly a central theme of the period.[4] Given the obstacles to organizing presented by the structure and depressed condition of the southern textile industry and the intransigence and dominant position of cotton manufacturers, Smith, Miles, and the UTW leadership knew that the Fulton strike, and the southern campaign more generally, had to extend beyond a battle between workers and managers alone if it had a chance to succeed. Similarly, Oscar Elsas's discrediting efforts were aimed not only at alienating workers and strikers but at influencing various other interested constituencies as well.

The establishment in the early 1910s of the Commission on Industrial Relations, the U.S. Department of Labor's Division of Conciliation, and the DOL itself, as well as the Georgia Department of Commerce and Labor, all represented

Progressive Era efforts to involve the state in a remedial way to address the "labor question." Not surprisingly, the strike organizers, UTW leadership, and the MRFM actively cultivated government intervention. Yet even the strikers themselves, arguably among the most localistic of Americans, welcomed federal involvement in the matter. Belying the reputed antigovernment hostility of many southern mill men, Oscar Elsas also fundamentally cooperated with the federal investigators, although he certainly did not welcome them.

Much of the strike's modern character stemmed from its Atlanta setting and the particular circumstances of Fulton Mills. By this time, Atlanta attracted a great deal of regional and even national attention. In the early teens, the city hosted the annual conventions of numerous organizations, from the International Typographical Union to the Photographers Association of America. Conversely, Atlantans such as O. Delight Smith, *Journal of Labor* editor Jerome Jones, and MRFM members John Eagan and John White were regular fixtures at labor and reform conferences outside the city and region. The MRFM's campaign to clean up the red-light district had drawn widespread publicity across the United States. In addition, Atlanta's cotton mills had already come under scrutiny by northern journalists and in a federal investigation of women and child workers.[5] Miserable working conditions, child labor, the wholesale firing of union members, and evictions of strikers from company housing were commonplace in southern labor disputes; undoubtedly what helped bring these issues to national attention in the Fulton strike was their Atlanta setting.

And as Atlanta paced the urban South, so did Fulton Bag lead southern textiles. Oscar Elsas stood at the forefront of the industry in his acceptance of child labor laws and movement toward a greater adult male labor force; in his advocacy of greater coordination among textile manufacturers, especially in fighting unions; in his employment of labor spies; and in his introduction of modern efficiency, management, and personnel measures. Indeed, many of the practices that Fulton management adopted in the teens anticipated textile industry developments of the 1920s, along with their attendant tensions. Obviously both Atlanta and Fulton Bag departed from regional norms in important ways. Yet, equally obviously, they set the tone for and were inextricably intertwined with larger currents in the New South.

White Fulton workers during the period of the strike did differ in certain respects from their Piedmont counterparts. They moved from job to job more readily and were less likely to live in company housing. They worked under a distinctive labor contract and fining system and in a place that employed African Americans in large numbers, though certainly strictly segregated. Men in Fulton households were much more likely to work outside the mill than other Piedmont workers, and Fulton workers in general had more connection to the larger urban environment and the white working class. And the personal ties between workers, managers, and owners ran less deep at Fulton Bag than elsewhere.

Yet Fulton workers also clearly belonged to the developing regionwide pool of mill hands. They overwhelmingly came to Fulton Bag from textile communities across the Piedmont, especially from Georgia and Alabama, and they overwhelmingly left Fulton Bag to work in other regional cotton mills. The Fulton baseball team and its fans traveled as much as sixty miles to play other mill teams from the Georgia Upcountry. Across the Piedmont, mill hands were knowledgeable about Fulton and constantly compared wages and working conditions at Fulton to those at other cotton mills. Workers from as far away as South Carolina knew of the Fulton labor contract, the altercations surrounding the strike, and the union-sponsored commissary.[6] Indeed, the very transience of the labor force contributed to the making of an informal communications network among textile workers by the early twentieth century that extended literally hundreds of miles across the region.

Piedmont textile manufacturers also belonged to a web of regional contacts and more formal associations, which generally expanded with the maturation of the industry in the teens and more specifically with the UTW and IWW campaigns. At the center was David Clark, Charlotte-based founder and editor of the *Southern Textile Bulletin*. With the advent of the organizing drives, the militantly antilabor Clark distributed to Oscar Elsas and other mill men "confidential circulars" detailing union activity and management's counterploys across the Piedmont, and he continued the practice through at least the fall of 1914. Clark thus served as a regional clearinghouse for the advancement of unified employer union-busting action.

The Fulton strike itself both reflected and influenced the growing interconnectedness of Piedmont mill owners. Elsas communicated with literally scores of other regional manufacturers during the course of the strike and its aftermath. He requested labor to help the mill resume full production, traded information about how to deal with "troublesome" workers, attended special meetings of Atlanta area mill owners and the Georgia Cotton Manufacturers Association, corresponded with *Mill News* and the *Textile Manufacturer* as well as the *Southern Textile Bulletin*, and solicited donations to the Joint Committee of Associated Employers for its assistance during the CIR hearing. While the strike did reveal divisions and differences among Piedmont mill men, which Elsas often took personally, on balance it accelerated coordination among southern manufacturers.

Elsas's communication with people outside the region was at least as extensive. When he felt the need, Elsas appealed to sectionalism, as when he asked his fellow Georgia manufacturers to send Charles Miles "back North where he came from, and let Georgia and the South alone." Yet at the same time, he regularly corresponded with New England textile executives, seeking recruits from their southern plants, inquiring about union activists and suspected radicals, and comparing antilabor strategies.[7] He communicated with representatives from three New York State espionage agencies, in addition to the Philadelphia-based Railway Audit and Inspection Company. He received news of the UTW's child labor photographs from Ohio, Texas, Arkansas, Massachusetts, and Florida. His campaign against the MRFM extended from Birmingham associates to New York business and banking executives to nationally prominent Jewish leaders in Chicago, as well as James Emery of the NAM. He was in touch with newspaper executives in Philadelphia and New York, including Adolph Ochs of the *Times* to discredit freelance writer Arthur St. George Joyce. He sought out information about the CIR from contacts in Denver and California, as well as from Claude Bennett of the Congressional Information Bureau.

Elsas's correspondence reflected the national dimension of the Fulton strike and the UTW's southern campaign more generally. While the workers themselves acted in a regional context, all other parties operated within a national framework. References to the New York "Protocol of Peace," the McNamara bombing, the Lawrence and Paterson strikes, Ludlow, and other contemporary American industrial flashpoints peppered the discourse surrounding the strike. The strike raised in high relief intersectional conflicts that ranged from tensions between northern and southern textile manufacturers to disputes in the halls of Congress. It was central to the AFL's southern strategy and one of only three beneficiaries of the AFL's 1914 national financial appeal. The strike figured in the final phase of the Commission on Industrial Relations. Thus, it could not be seen as merely an isolated local episode. What happened elsewhere in the nation as well as the region had an impact on the Fulton situation; what happened at Fulton Mills in turn influenced developments elsewhere.

The strike set in motion diverse trajectories for the people directly involved. Fiddlin' John Carson was one of the fortunate ones. After being evicted from his company house for joining the strike and forced to make a living, Carson played his fiddle on the streets of Atlanta, in particular for the crowds gathered at the time of the Frank case. Carson composed three songs about the case, including "The Ballad of Mary Phagan," which became a southern classic, and his popularity soared. As the first country music radio personality performing on Atlanta's WSB Radio almost from its inception and the first major recording artist of early country music, he became a musician with a largely nineteenth-century repertoire pioneering in two modern media.

Of course, Carson was exceptional. Many other strikers suffered greatly. Throughout the fall and winter of 1914–15, after the strike fell apart and full production resumed, numerous former strikers sought reemployment at Fulton Mills. Some of these workers wrote letters to mill management explaining their actions during the strike and revealing their often desperate circumstances as well as their disillusionment with the union. Although he did not take back most of these workers, Oscar Elsas still pointed to their letters as evidence that "even the worst of the strikers are anxious to get back."[8]

In September 1914, Sallie Wright wrote to company treasurer August Denk seeking reinstatement. Wright insisted that "i am not begging my job back" and stated that although she disagreed with the strike, she had already joined the union and was afraid to return to work when the walkout occurred. She also wrote, "I went to the [union] hall lots of times but i never don anything against the company but once i went to the vilidge tried to get some mill hands to leave here but i was afraid for them so i tried to get them off[.] i can give names of lots of folks that i beged to stay in there[.] some was scared out others was lazy to work and others was rebeling against the company[.] i joined [the union] last fall and was sorrow of it in a week."[9]

Wright's letter reveals the complex, often confused relationship many workers had with the strike and the union. It also provides a more or less accurate assessment of the diverse reasons why workers walked out. Some people undoubtedly did not go to work in part because of fear or coercion from strikers. In contrast, others joined the strike upon experiencing an accumulation of company-provoked grievances or after management violated unspoken codes of propriety, as when it fired union members and sympathizers or evicted strikers from company housing. Many strikers saw the strike and the union as potentially transforming industrial relations at Fulton Mills. Still other workers had more limited reasons for walking out, seeing the strike as an alluring alternative, a rare temporary respite from the long hours, onerous working conditions, tedium, and the dependency of textile work.

Despite her plea, Wright and her husband Robert were not rehired.[10] In addition to refusing to take back former strikers, management adopted various measures to ensure that labor unrest would not break out again at Fulton Mills. These initiatives attempted to address some recurrent worker grievances and included modern management techniques as well as a continued hard-line antilabor approach. These efforts also belied the company's repeated claims during the strike that the disturbance was inconsequential and merely instigated by outsiders. If nothing else, the strike illustrated that worker agitation could and did cause management to reconsider and significantly alter its industrial relations policies.

In December 1914, the company's employment contract was modified (though not discarded) and rewritten "in a rather plainer way," as Oscar Elsas stated, "with less legal phraseology, so that the average operative in reading would understand." In addition, the clause pertaining to management's right to charge workers for damage to machinery was eliminated. In 1916, the company waived portions of the contract "for any employees who may enlist in the militia under the Presidential call" and held those workers' positions for them until their return.[11]

To offset the criticism that the company had profited from the fines and the notice system, by March 1915 any "liquidations," including fines as well as the money left over from people who had not collected their withheld pay when they served their notices, were being turned over to the employees' mutual aid society. To further minimize adverse publicity about company profits, Oscar and Benjamin Elsas warned at the January 1916 stockholders meeting that "remarks to outsiders about the Company's affairs were inadvisable, and particularly that it was inadvisable this year to speak about the dividends that had been declared."[12]

On the night of 11 June 1915, Elsas gave an address to all the mill's second hands and overseers at Wesley House. The purpose of the "heart-to-heart talk" was to improve industrial relations at Fulton Mills, in particular to maintain a more steady and stable workforce and to dissipate the tensions that had accumulated before the strike. Management encouraged the overseers to control their tempers and "consider feelings of help [and] treat them civilly," especially since some workers were "hard of comprehension and don't understand." To help reduce the high turnover rate, overseers were to coordinate better with the company's time keepers, and more actively intervene to "hold" workers when they voiced their intention to leave. To cut down on the "friction between mill and office," they were asked to work more closely with paymaster T. S. Florence over hiring practices, to avoid criticizing their supervisors or office staff when fines had been reversed, and to show "apparent agreement" among themselves when workers were transferred from one department to another. In addition, Elsas ordered fifty subscriptions of *Skyland Magazine*, a new North Carolina–based publication highly favorable toward mill owners and managers, to be distributed to the overseers and second hands.[13]

This shift toward a somewhat more conciliatory approach likely also had consequences for general manager Gordon Johnstone. Following continued complaints about his performance and management style in the years after the strike, Johnstone left Fulton Mills. In 1927, he took a similar position with the Loray Mills of Gastonia, North Carolina. There, the modern efficiency measures that Johnstone introduced helped precipitate one of the most famous textile strikes in southern history, as they had done over a decade earlier at Fulton Mills.[14]

To further advance stability and loyalty among Fulton workers, in the strike's aftermath management significantly increased its welfare capitalism activities. In 1915, the company launched *The Fulton*, a monthly newspaper for employees, which contained social news, proverbs, and jokes; health tips; and photographs and articles promoting company-sponsored functions and services. By 1919, company-sponsored undertakings included a concert band, a new Men's Club building, a daily noonday volleyball game, a steam laundry in the mill district, housing improvements, a company basketball team, an upgraded cafeteria, girls' and boys' clubs, outings to parks and scenic places, the purchase of Liberty bonds for workers, and a cooperative store benefiting the Fulton Mutual Aid Society.[15] In addition to being a direct response to the strike and its attendant tensions, such initiatives were part of a broader movement among Piedmont mill owners during the late teens to advance welfare capitalism and thus better secure labor.[16]

Management's greater direct intervention in the personal lives of Fulton mill hands increasingly encroached on the work of Wesley House. In 1916, the company took over the health clinic, claiming the equipment and supplies that had belonged to the City Board of Missions. The Wesley House auditorium was used for the new cafeteria, and a room in the building was turned over to the mill for a kitchen. In 1918, Elsas criticized the day nursery for admitting the children of neighborhood residents who did not work at the mill. In addition, the company now fed the nursery children in the new cafeteria and deducted the cost from its monthly contribution to the settlement.[17]

As the company undermined their efforts, the Wesley House women reconsidered their association with Fulton Mills. In September 1919, Mrs. J. H. McCoy, from the Home Department of the Methodist Church South headquarters in Nashville, wrote the Board of Missions, "I am quite sure that the sooner you sever the ties with Mr. Elsas, the better it will be for all concerned." By January 1920, the women had moved out of the old textile workers' hotel to a small house in the adjoining community, where they redirected their social work efforts.[18]

Mill management also modified its personnel system and hiring practices after the strike. As of 1916, the company made out a card for each worker who entered the employ of Fulton Mills. Along with basic demographic and health information, the cards detailed a worker's employment history. In addition, drawing from the latest developments in personnel management, many of them contained a revealing list of polar characteristics that supervisors could check off:

healthy/unhealthy
quick/slow
energetic/lazy
punctual/tardy
steady/lies out
obedient/stubborn
efficient/incapable
content/shiftless
teachable/stupid

The cards also included space for additional comments by supervisors. Thus, it was reported that one worker was a "globe trotter"; another agreed to stay at the mill until Christmas; and a black yardman was going to leave at "cotton picking time." Another worker, rather improbably, "claimed to be able to cure pel[l]agra and was doing that when he was thought to be busy at something else."

Various comments made specific reference to the strike. For instance, a supervisor reported that one worker had "fought the union people." In contrast, on the card of an active striker who had testified for the union at the CIR hearing it was written, "never again . . . trouble maker in mill and village . . . rock thrower." Other former strikers did not even warrant comments. Interspersed among the personnel records were a number of cards that, along with the person's name, included only one piece of information stamped on them: "May 20, 1914." With a very few exceptions, the workers who walked out on that date, the first day of the strike, never returned to work at Fulton Mills.[19]

Workers associated with labor unrest elsewhere could not get hired at Fulton Mills either. In particular, at least for a while, management refused to employ workers from the Greenville, South Carolina, mills where the IWW had concentrated its efforts. "Under no circumstances will we hire Greenville help," Oscar Elsas declared.[20] The blacklist went the other way, too, as manufacturers across the South declined to take on former Fulton workers associated with the strike. H. P. Meikleham of Lindale even made a commitment not to hire any former Fulton workers at all, because they came from a "strike situation."[21]

Meikleham also helped Elsas track down a report that Will Fowler, the loom fixer whose dismissal in October 1913 had sparked the entire protest, was now working in a Greenville mill, and he alerted Fowler's new employer. The blacklist extended beyond textiles as well. When strike leaders W. C. Sweatt and Frank Odell applied for jobs on the Atlanta police force, Elsas asked A. R. Colcord of the Police Board to turn them down because they were unfit and there were "too many on the force of that sort already," a comment that reflected his outrage at the police during the strike.[22]

Even after the strike ended, the company continued to employ labor spies. "We still have that," Elsas declared at the CIR hearing, "and intend to continue [the] same the balance of our natural lives."[23] Into the 1920s, at least forty-one spies wrote some 2,700 daily reports for Fulton Mills, documenting not only incipient unionism but also shop-floor practices in need of improvement and questionable moral behavior among workers. Spearheading much of the company's espionage was none other than Harry Preston, who returned to Atlanta in 1916 as the southern vice president for the Railway Audit and Inspection Company, a position he had gained through his work during the Fulton strike.[24]

Elsas also encouraged the expansion of labor espionage throughout the region. With his endorsement, in 1915 labor spy Raymond W. Oglesby (Operative No. 16), who had reported on the tent colony and helped discredit the strike leaders, continued his work in various South Carolina and Tennessee textile communities. In addition, Elsas recommended the services of the Railway Audit and Inspection Company to other manufacturers and extended the company's labor espionage activities to its plants outside Atlanta.[25]

Management's sustained use and promotion of labor spies in part reflected the fact that the strike did have ripple effects across the region, even though it had finally been called off. The publicity and support generated by the Fulton strike, along with the comparatively flush times of World War I, helped sustain UTW activity and organization across the textile South through 1918. More specifically, Fulton strike leaders like W. E. Fleming and H. N. Mullinax continued to be active in this effort. Furthermore, despite all of management's anti-union measures and changes in industrial relations, Fulton Bag itself, like other Atlanta area mills, was not exempt from renewed organizing efforts.[26]

Elsas closely monitored this initiative. Through the teens, he secured copies of the UTW convention proceedings, the *Journal of Labor*, and additional union publications. He also provided antilabor advice and insights drawn from his own experience to other manufacturers.[27] In the aftermath of the strike, Elsas also accelerated his efforts on behalf of unified employer and anti-union organization at the local, state, and national levels. Following the CIR hearing in

Atlanta, he tried to recruit his fellow Georgia cotton manufacturers into the NAM and by April 1916 had become a member of the NAM board of directors, in essence serving as its southern point man. In addition, he drummed up support for the recently established Georgia Manufacturers Association, serving on its executive committee. Elsas recommended that the company join the American Anti-Boycott Association. He also played a leading role in another new open-shop organization, the Employers' Association of Atlanta, which he had initially proposed at the height of the strike and the MRFM's push for arbitration legislation.[28]

The strike continued to reverberate at the local level in other ways, at least for a while. It certainly informed Atlanta's next big industrial dispute, a dramatic streetcar strike in the fall of 1916. Agitation coming out of the Fulton strike seems to have directly contributed to embryonic organization among the city's motormen and conductors. Many of the elements of the Fulton strike—mass meetings, publicity campaigns, labor politics, community support, even a dictograph surveillance machine—were repeated during the streetcar strike.

In addition, the Fulton strike was specifically evoked at a sensational trial that accompanied the streetcar dispute. One of the character witnesses for organizer William Pollard, who was accused of placing dynamite on streetcar tracks, was former MRFM leader Marion Jackson. Rather than retreating from social concerns following the Fulton strike, Jackson now edited a Social Gospel publication titled *The Way*. Jackson's MRFM partner, John Eagan, continued his social activism, too. After World War I, Eagan established an employee ownership plan at his ACIPCO plant in Birmingham and was one of the early members of the Commission on Interracial Cooperation.[29]

On the stand at Pollard's trial, Jackson stated that he had made a special study of strikes, in which he concluded that corporations invariably "hocuspocus the public into believing that the strikers are a lot of ignorant, violent and lawless anarchists." He asserted it was "pretty well admitted" that in the Lawrence strike it had been the employers who had done the dynamiting. Jackson then brought up the Fulton strike, which precipitated "a brisk tilt" between defense and prosecution attorneys, after which Judge Ben H. Hill dismissed him from the stand for continuing to express his personal views.[30]

In addition, A. Cloyd Gill, news editor for *The Way*, testified that he had attended a meeting of the elite Citizens Committee on Law and Order, an organization formed to break the streetcar strike. During the meeting, Gill recounted, committee members had voiced their opinions about what to do with Pollard. Trust Company Bank vice president John Murphy, who in 1914 had chaired the Chamber of Commerce committee appointed at the behest of

Elsas to investigate the Fulton situation, suggested that Pollard be handled "in the same manner the Oscar Elsas strike was handled, which was to arrange for the agitator to vanish."[31]

It is unclear from his words alone whether Murphy was referring to Charles Miles or O. Delight Smith. In addition to ordering the discrediting campaign by Preston and others, company officials and attorneys had openly collaborated with Smith's husband during her divorce trial, shortly before her departure from Atlanta. Smith resurfaced in Portland, Oregon, where she continued her trade union activism, and was honored over thirty years later as the "first lady of the Oregon labor movement." In 1950, she still recalled the Fulton strike as arguably the pivotal event in her nearly half-century career of activism.[32]

Also in 1916, Paul Donehoo, a labor lawyer and union musician seeking re-election as county coroner, complained that because he had successfully handled the criminal cases of Fulton strikers and strike leaders, he now faced "a concerted effort on the part of the Fulton Bag and Cotton Mills officials and their friends to visit vengeance on me." Donehoo may have been right; it is certainly true that Elsas held grudges against his perceived enemies. For instance, in 1916 he refused to contribute to the King's Daughters based upon a spy report filed during the strike that members of the group had provided strike support. And over three-quarters of a century later, his son Norman still harbored resentment against the MRFM.

Yet most memories of the strike faded away. The scattering of union members and activists and the overall transience of textile workers certainly contributed to this amnesia, as did the sudden death in 1924 of Oscar Elsas, who had kept all of his voluminous strike-related documents locked up in a vault, not to be discovered until the property was sold in the mid-1980s. The company's efforts to stabilize its workforce and foster loyalty after the strike did have an effect, as such initiatives did in other textile communities, serving to mute expressions of discontent. Some Fulton workers in the early 1930s did formally protest to the National Recovery Administration about abuses of the NRA's textile code, and others joined the 1934 general textile strike.[33] Yet there is no evidence to suggest any direct linkage between the outbreaks of the thirties and of the teens.

In her novel *The Southerners*, published in 1953, Atlantan Edna Lee showed perhaps some awareness of the Fulton strike and its attendant issues in her depictions of unrest among local mill hands during the World War I era. But the connections to this earlier period of Fulton's history became yet more attenuated with the sale of the firm later in the 1950s, as the cloth bag industry went into decline, and with the cessation of all operations in the mid-1970s.

The 1970s marked a renewal of interest in the former mill district, now called Cabbagetown. Reflecting the revival in Appalachian culture marked by the *Foxfire* series and other works, community activists, newspaper reporters, and others repeatedly claimed that the neighborhood was an enclave of mountain people with a unique and traditional folklore transplanted in the heart of downtown Atlanta.[34] Such attention to the supposed mountain ways of Cabbagetown residents brought grants to neighborhood organizations, spawned songs, festivals, plays, and television programs about the community, aided in placing the neighborhood on the National Register of Historic Places, and helped encourage residential development.[35] Yet it also not only obscured the actual Upcountry origins of most Fulton workers but served to suppress accounts of labor unrest and worker dissatisfaction as well.

By the late 1970s, perhaps the only resident of Cabbagetown who remembered the 1914 strike was Horace Carson, son of Fiddlin' John, who included in his memoir a chapter titled "The Union That Never Was." It may also have been Carson who vividly recalled to author Pamela Durban about how company men on horseback had assisted in the evictions of workers from company housing during the strike. Durban later wove the tale into part of a short story. "To work, to live," she wrote, "you had to be angry, you had to fight—that much she remembered. Her father had fought for his life, for all of their lives, the time half the mill walked out, and the mill police came muscling into their house on fat horses. She could still see the door frame give, before her father's arm raised, all the veins standing up, before he brought the stick of cord wood down hard across the horse's nose. That was what life was for—fighting to keep it."[36]

At its core, this is what the Fulton strike signified for many of those who took part: a rare opportunity for people who were often despised and humiliated, marginalized, powerless, and subservient, to retaliate, to assert their dignity, independence, and self-respect, to challenge usual relationships of power, to claim their place, however precariously, in the volatile New South. In addition to everything else the Fulton strike influenced and revealed, this disruption of business as usual meant a great deal.

NOTES

ABBREVIATIONS

AC
Atlanta Constitution
ACCR
Atlanta Chamber of Commerce Records, Atlanta Chamber of Commerce, Atlanta, Ga.
AG
Atlanta Georgian
AHS
Atlanta Historical Society
AJ
Atlanta Journal
AJC
Atlanta Journal-Constitution
CCC
Christian Council Collection, Atlanta Historical Society, Atlanta, Ga.
CIR Microfilm
Dubofsky, Melvin, ed., U.S. Commission on Industrial Relations, 1912–15, Unpublished Records of the Division of Research and Investigation: Reports, Staff Studies, and Background Research Materials (Frederick, Md.: University Publications of America, 1985).
Daly, "Sworn Testimony"
Alexander M. Daly, "Sworn Testimony Taken before William C. Massey, Notary Public, in and for the City of Atlanta, and State of Georgia, of about Forty Witnesses," n.d. [1915], Records of the U.S. Commission on Industrial Relations, RG 174, National Archives, Washington, D.C.
Daly Report
Report by Alexander M. Daly, 1 September 1914, Records of the U.S. Commission on Industrial Relations, RG 174, National Archives, Washington, D.C.
Duke
Perkins Library, Duke University, Durham, N.C.
Dun Collection
R. G. Dun and Company Collection, Baker Library, Harvard Business School, Boston, Mass.
FBCM-Emory
Fulton Bag and Cotton Mills Collection, Special Collections, Woodruff Library, Emory University, Atlanta, Ga.

FBCM-GIT
> Fulton Bag and Cotton Mills Collection, Price Gilbert Memorial Library, Archives, Georgia Institute of Technology, Atlanta, Ga.

Husband-Robinson Report
> Report of W. W. Husband and Herman Robinson, 24 July 1914, Case File 33/41, Records of the Federal Mediation and Conciliation Service, RG 280, National Archives, Suitland, Md.

JOL
> *Journal of Labor*

LAC
> Living Atlanta Collection, Atlanta Historical Society, Atlanta, Ga.

McWade and Colpoys Report
> *In Re Strike of Employees of the Fulton Bag and Cotton Mills, Atlanta, Georgia*, by Robert M. McWade and John B. Colpoys, 21 July 1915, Case File 33/41, Records of the Federal Mediation and Conciliation Service, RG 280, National Archives, Suitland, Md.

Operative Reports
> Operative Reports, Fulton Bag and Cotton Mills Collection, Price Gilbert Memorial Library, Archives, Georgia Institute of Technology, Atlanta, Ga.

"Reports and Exhibits"
> Inis Weed and Alexander M. Daly, "Reports and Exhibits on the Fulton Bag and Cotton Mills Strike, Atlanta, Georgia, and on Conditions in Nearby Mill Towns," Records of the U.S. Commission on Industrial Relations, RG 174, National Archives, Washington, D.C.

RG 2
> Records of the National War Labor Board, National Archives, Suitland, Md.

RG 174
> Records of the United States Commission on Industrial Relations, National Archives, Washington, D.C.

RG 280
> Records of the Federal Mediation and Conciliation Service, National Archives, Suitland, Md.

SLA
> Southern Labor Archives, Special Collections, Georgia State University, Atlanta, Ga.

Strike Records
> Strike Records, Fulton Bag and Cotton Mills Collection, Price Gilbert Memorial Library, Archives, Georgia Institute of Technology, Atlanta, Ga.

"Testimony for the Complainants"
> "In the Matter of Fulton Bag and Cotton Mills, Atlanta, Georgia, before the United States Commission on Industrial Relations, Testimony Taken at Atlanta, Georgia," vol. 1, "Testimony for the Complainants," Box 6, Strike Records, Fulton Bag and Cotton Mills Collection, Price Gilbert Memorial Library, Archives, Georgia Institute of Technology, Atlanta, Ga.

"Testimony for the Defendants"
> "In the Matter of Fulton Bag and Cotton Mills, Atlanta, Georgia, before the United States Commission on Industrial Relations, Testimony Taken at Atlanta, Georgia," vol. 2, "Testimony for the Defendants," Box 7, Strike Records, Fulton Bag and Cotton Mills Collection, Price Gilbert Memorial Library Archives, Georgia Institute of Technology, Atlanta, Ga.

Walsh Papers
> Frank P. Walsh Papers, New York Public Library

Weed, "Preliminary Report"
Inis Weed, "Preliminary Report," 28 July 1914, Records of the U.S. Commission on Industrial Relations, RG 174, National Archives, Washington, D.C.
Weed Report, 12 September 1914
Report of Inis Weed, 12 September 1914, Records of the U.S. Commission on Industrial Relations, RG 174, National Archives, Washington, D.C.
Weed Report, 19 September 1914
Report of Inis Weed, 19 September 1914, Records of the U.S. Commission on Industrial Relations, RG 174, National Archives, Washington, D.C.
WHR
Wesley House Records, Wesley Community Centers, Atlanta, Ga.

INTRODUCTION

1. Cash, *Mind of the South*, 248. For discussions of Cash and his famous work, see Woodward, "Elusive Mind of the South," 261–84, and Clayton, *W. J. Cash*, especially 192–222.

2. Golin, *Fragile Bridge*; Tripp, *I.W.W. and the Paterson Silk Strike*; Cameron, *Radicals of the Worst Sort*. Quote from *New Bedford Morning Standard*, 21 October 1914.

3. Testimony of Mrs. R. H. [Sallie] Wright, 20–21, "Testimony for the Defendants."

4. Wiggins, *Fiddlin' Georgia Crazy*, 19–45.

5. Report of no. 115, 8 July 1914, Folder 7, Box 1, Operative Reports.

6. Testimony of R. H. Wright, 10–11, and Testimony of R. H. Wright (recalled), 2, both in "Testimony for the Defendants"; Reports of no. 115, 7–11, 14, 17, 27–29 July 1914, Folder 7, and Report of no. 115, 26 August 1914, Folder 8, all in Box 1, Operative Reports; Testimony of R. H. Wright, in Weed, "Preliminary Report," and Daly Report.

7. Testimony of R. H. Wright, 14, and Testimony by R. H. Wright (recalled), 3, 6, both in "Testimony for the Defendants"; Robert H. Wright to Harry G. Preston, 10 September 1914, Folder 9, Box 1, Operative Reports; Hall, "O. Delight Smith's Progressive Era."

8. Mercer G. Evans, "History of the Organized Labor Movement in Georgia," 82–86; Nesbitt, "Social Gospel in Atlanta," 133–39; Deaton, "Atlanta during the Progressive Era," 125–27; Brooks, "United Textile Workers of America," 301–2; George S. Mitchell, *Textile Unionism and the South*, 34–35; Marshall, *Labor in the South*, 86.

9. For instance, *AJC*, 15 December 1974, 19 May 1979, 29 August 1982, 17 September 1982, 6 March 1983; *AJ*, 9, 29 May 1980; *New York Times*, 30 October 1984; *AC*, 5 August 1988, 21 April 1991; "What's Cookin' in Cabbagetown"; Flowers and Putter, "Cabbagetown," 34.

10. For overviews of the recent historiography on southern textiles, see Zieger, "Textile Workers and Historians," 35–59; Zieger, Introduction to "Southern Textiles," 3–8; Beatty, "Gender Relations in Southern Textiles," 9–16; Carlton, "Paternalism and Southern Textile Labor," 17–26; McCurry, "Piedmont Mill Workers," 229–37.

11. Zieger, Introduction to "Southern Textiles," 7.

12. Gary Fink, *Fulton Bag and Cotton Mills Strike*, 7.

13. Ayers, *Promise of the New South*, 116.

14. Wiebe, *Search for Order*; Galambos, "Emerging Organizational Synthesis," 279–90; Cmiel, "Destiny and Amnesia," 352–56; Leon Fink, "Search for Order Reconsidered."

15. For instance, Hall, "Disorderly Women"; Gilmore, *Gender and Jim Crow*; Hunter, *To 'Joy My Freedom*; Ayers, *Promise of the New South*; Carlton, *Mill and Town*; and Flamming, *Creating the Modern South*.

1. Henderson, "Paupers, Pastors and Politicians," 42–60; Chaikin, "Jewish Sections of Oakland Cemetery," 55–64.

2. Elsas, interview by author, 5 October 1990.

3. Louis J. Elsas, "Data for Biography of Jacob Elsas," 19 April 1929, and Clarence E. Elsas, speech to Traffic Club, August 1935, both in FBCM-Emory; *America's Textile Reporter*, 21 May 1953; *Textile Industries* 132 (December 1968): 61–76; *Textile World*, 23 January 1968; Teel, "How a Yankee Brought Textiles to Georgia," 124–27.

4. "Auszug aus dem Kirchenregister."

5. Elsas, "Data for Biography of Jacob Elsas."

6. "Auszug aus dem Kirchenregister." Although fatherless, Jacob Elsas was not an orphan, as numerous accounts have claimed, including one in *Textile World*, 23 January 1968.

7. Elsas, "Data for Biography of Jacob Elsas."

8. Dannenbaum, *Drink and Disorder*, 27, 72; Ross, *Workers on the Edge*, xvi–xvii, 67, 71, 76.

9. Ross, *Workers on the Edge*, 131–34.

10. Georgia, 14:23, Fulton County, 1 April 1875, Dun Collection; Elsas, "Data for Biography of Jacob Elsas."

11. Elsas, "Data for Biography of Jacob Elsas"; Doyle, *New Men*, 23–24, 27.

12. Elsas, interview by McMath.

13. Elsas, "Data for Biography of Jacob Elsas"; Elsas, interview by McMath; Georgia, 14:23, 1 April 1875, Dun Collection; Payroll records, FBCM-GIT; Elsas, interview by author, 5 October 1990; Clarence E. Elsas speech; Segal, "Cabbagetown Community, 7.

14. *AC*, 3 April 1869. Dennett, *South as It Is*, 268; McLeod, *Workers and Workplace Dynamics*, 7–8. Of Atlanta's business elite in 1880, none was a native of the city (Doyle, *New Men*, 90).

15. Doyle, *New Men*, 34–41, 91–95, 99–103.

16. Wilson, *Atlanta as It Is*, 105.

17. Garrett, *Atlanta and Environs*, 1:808–9; Georgia, 13:240, 22 April 1870, Dun Collection.

18. Garrett, *Atlanta and Environs*, 1:808. It is unknown if the jeans sold in the store came from Elsas's uncle or other Cincinnati manufacturers. Perhaps Cincinnati connections helped Elsas meet his partners, since he had a relative there named Adler and had worked for the Cincinnati firm of Karlsruher and Adler. According to one source, Morris Adler supplied the financial backing for the new Atlanta concern. See Georgia, 13:217, 8 February 1869, Dun Collection.

19. Elsas, "Data for Biography of Jacob Elsas"; Clarence E. Elsas speech; *Textile World*, 23 January 1968; Elsas, interview by McMath.

20. Elsas, interview by McMath; Elsas, interview by author, 5 October 1990.

21. P. C. Schroeder [great-grandson of Isaac May] to author, 29 December 1992. May's influence has been overlooked in conventional accounts of the company. Yet the Fulton firm continued to be popularly known as Elsas, May well into the twentieth century (Kuhn et al., *Living Atlanta*, 263).

22. Georgia, 13:217, May 1871; Georgia, 13:240, 24 February 1872; Georgia, 13:240, 7 April 1874; Georgia, 14:23, 1 April 1875, all in Dun Collection.

23. Georgia, 13:240, 15 December 1874; Georgia, 14:23, 1 April 1875; Georgia, 14:22, 20 April 1878; Georgia, 14:234, 20 October 1879, all in Dun Collection.

24. Georgia, 13:217, May 1871; Georgia, 14:23, 1 April 1875; Georgia, 14:234, 25 April 1879; Georgia, 14:22, 20 April 1878, all in Dun Collection.

25. Georgia, 14:234, 20 October 1879; Georgia, 14:234, 24 April 1880, Dun Collection; Manuscript Census Schedules 1880, Special Census of Manufactures, Fulton County, Georgia, Georgia Department of Archives and History, Atlanta; McLeod, *Workers and Workplace Dynamics*, 11, 85; Hertzberg, *Strangers*, 40.

26. "Fulton Cotton Spinning Company and Its Successors," undated manuscript, FBCM-Emory.

27. Davis, *Henry Grady's New South*; Gaston, *New South Creed*, 18.

28. Doyle, *New Men*, 149; Reagan, "Hannibal I. Kimball," 112–13; Reagan, *Kimball*, 77.

29. Doyle, *New Men*, 38; Reagan, "Promoting the New South," 7–9; Duncan, *Entrepreneur for Equality*, 148–49; Arthur Reed Taylor, "From the Ashes," 113–14.

30. Arthur Reed Taylor, "From the Ashes," 12; Reagan, *Kimball*, 77–90; Reagan, "Hannibal I. Kimball," 119–20, 125, 127, 133; McLeod, *Workers and Workplace Dynamics*, 11; Duncan, *Entrepreneur for Equality*, 149; *AC*, 30 July, 20 November 1879, 2 January, 20 July 1880; *AJ*, 10 December 1884, 2 October 1885; Samuel P. Richards, Diary, 30 June 1879, 27 July 1879, Richards Papers, AHS.

31. Segal, "Cabbagetown Community," 8.

32. Carlton and Coclanis, "Capital Mobilization and Southern Industry," 73–94. For Seasongood, see Ross, *Workers on the Edge*, 134; Joblin, *Cincinnati Past and Present*, 243–46; and Minutes, Board of Directors, FBCM-Emory. A study of the role of Cincinnati-based finance in advancing New South industry might be fruitful. For the tax exemption, see *AC*, 25 January 1882.

33. Grable, "Other Side of the Tracks," 53–54; National Register of Historic Places, Inventory-Nomination Form: Cabbagetown District.

34. Coleman, *Short History of the Roswell Manufacturing Company*; Mrs. Fanny King Pratt to editor, *AJ*, 29 July 1948.

35. Doyle, *New Men*, 151–58; Davis, *Henry Grady's New South*, 168–73.

36. Blicksilver, "International Cotton Exposition of 1881," 5.

37. Clarence E. Elsas speech; "Fulton Cotton Spinning Company and Its Successors," FBCM-Emory; *AJ*, 11 March 1885; *Manufacturer's Record*, 11 January 1883, 398.

38. Doyle, *New Men*, 87, 100–103, 136–37, 189.

39. Cooper, "Origin and Early Years of the Atlanta Chamber of Commerce," 6.

40. Garrett, *Atlanta and Environs*, 2:71, 135; McMath et al., *Engineering the New South*, 33.

41. Garrett, *Atlanta and Environs*, 2:258; Clarence E. Elsas speech to Rotary Club, 7 April 1952, FBCM-Emory; *AC*, 5 March 1932.

42. Garrett, *Atlanta and Environs*, 2:170; McMath et al., *Engineering the New South*, ix, 9, 13, 33, 54, 85.

43. Doyle, *New Men*, 189–97, 208–11, 216–17, 222–23.

44. *AC*, 6 March 1932; Hertzberg, *Strangers*, 119, 120; Norman Elsas, interview by author, 6 March 1991.

45. Elsas, "Data for Biography of Jacob Elsas."

46. Elsas, interview by author, 6 March 1991; photograph of Oscar Elsas in Stuttgart, formerly in Norman Elsas's possession; Boston, 11:253, Dun Collection. On Jews at Harvard, see Solomon, *Ancestors and Immigrants*, and Brudno, *Tether*.

47. Elsas, interviews by author, 6 March 1991 and 5 October 1990; Hertzberg, *Strangers*, 125.

48. Handlin, *Adventure in Freedom*, 112, 146; Birmingham, *"Our Crowd"*; Gal, *Brandeis of Boston*, 32.

49. Elsas, interviews by author, 6 March 1991 and 5 October 1990.

50. Testimony of Alfred S. Guffin, 1, "Testimony for the Defendants." The literature on the

transformation of agriculture in the late-nineteenth-century South, and the Upper Piedmont more particularly, is quite rich. See, for example, Hahn, *Roots of Southern Populism*, 139–52, 163–73, 181–86; Wright, *Old South, New South*, 52–56, 65, 76; Carlton, *Mill and Town*, 18–19; Tullos, *Habits of Industry*, 135; Hall et al., *Like a Family*, 6, 10; and Flynt, *Poor but Proud*, 60–61, 63, 71–72, 84. For personal accounts of the Georgia Upcountry, see Saye, ed., *Walter McElreath*; Watkins and Watkins, *Yesterday in the Hills*; and Hosch, *Nevah Come Back No Mo'*.

51. *AC*, 20 November 1879; Maclachlan, "Women's Work," 28.

52. *AJ*, 13 May 1884.

53. McLaurin, *Paternalism and Protest*, 76; *AJ*, 20 November 1883, 19 November 1884, 9 April 1885. Of Atlanta's two daily newspapers in the 1880s, the *Journal* carried the most news about Atlanta's working-class population and organizations. The *Constitution* was the organ of Henry Grady, the New South's and Atlanta's foremost publicist, and he was not particularly inclined to write about labor organizations or working-class activity except in a derogatory manner. The paper also was struck by union printers and was later placed on the Knights of Labor boycott list until March 1886 (*AC*, 12 March 1886; McLaurin, *Knights of Labor in the South*, 64). Yet most chroniclers of nineteenth-century Atlanta have relied primarily upon the *Constitution*.

54. "Missionary Work among the Destitute Whites at Atlanta, Georgia," *Philadelphia Methodist*, 17 June 1880; Miss Stokes to John Emory Bryant, 13 November 1883, John Emory Bryant Papers, Duke.

55. *Working World*, 19 September 1885, AHS. Although references to the *Working World* exist in the *Atlanta Journal*, this is the only known extant issue.

56. H. P. Blount to Miss Loula, 10 March 1881, H. P. Blount Papers, Duke.

57. *AJ*, 19 July 1886.

58. *AC*, 8, 10, 11, 25, 26 January 1882; *AJ*, 19, 26 November 1884. For evidence that the property indeed was sold below value, see Fulton County Superior Court, Deed Book JJ, Atlanta, Ga., 759–63.

59. *AJ*, 20 November 1883, 1 May 1886.

60. *AJ*, 3 October 1883, 19 November 1884, 17 March 1885, 9 April 1885; *Atlanta Sunday Telegram*, 11 October 1885.

61. For a larger context, see Gutman, "Class, Status, and Community Power," and Leon Fink, "Class Conflict in the Gilded Age."

62. Kuhn, "Critique of the New South Creed."

63. Garlock, *Guide to the Local Assemblies*; McLaurin, *Knights of Labor in the South*, 92; Brooks, "United Textile Workers of America," 32.

64. *AJ*, 11 November 1885, 27 July 1886.

65. *AJ*, 7, 9, 11, 16 November 1885. Because of other historians' neglect of the *Journal*, there is no mention of this walkout in the historical literature.

66. *Proceedings of the Knights of Labor*, 1887, 1399; Mercer G. Evans, "History of the Organized Labor Movement in Georgia," 31.

67. P. C. Schroeder to author, 29 December 1992.

68. "Agreement between H. and L. Chase, Jacob Elsas, Bemis Bros. re territorial limits and regulations for offering bags," 13 February 1895, FBCM-Emory.

69. Clarence E. Elsas speech, August 1935.

70. *AJ*, 26 January 1899.

71. Weed, "Preliminary Report."

72. *Fulton Bag and Cotton Mills v. Wilson*, 318.

73. Contracts between Masters and Servants, 97.

74. *Gleaton v. Fulton Bag and Cotton Mills*; *Winn v. Fulton Bag and Cotton Mills*.

75. *AC*, 1 August 1889.

76. "Report of the Fulton Bag and Cotton Mills" (Atlanta, Ga., n.d. [March 1915]), Folder 6, Box 3, Strike Records; *AJ*, 7 August 1897.

77. *AJ*, 26 January 1899; "Report of the Fulton Bag and Cotton Mills"; U.S. Congress, U.S. Industrial Commission, "Report on . . . the Relations and Conditions of Capital and Labor," 569.

78. "Report of the Fulton Bag and Cotton Mills"; *AJ*, 7 August 1897.

79. Maclachlan, "Women's Work," 291–93.

80. U.S. Congress, U.S. Industrial Commission, "Report on . . . the Relations and Conditions of Capital and Labor," 572.

81. *AJ*, 26 January 1899.

82. U.S. Congress, U.S. Industrial Commission, "Report on . . . the Relations and Conditions of Capital and Labor," 572.

83. Newby, *Plain Folk*, 477, 480; George S. Mitchell, *Textile Unionism and the South*, 27.

84. Mercer G. Evans, "History of the Organized Labor Movement in Georgia," 264; Carter, "Jerome Jones," 13.

85. *AJ*, 6–7, 13–16 April, 19, 27 July 1897; Kuhn and Hough, *Generations of Sheet Metal Craftsmanship*, 6–8; Mercer G. Evans, "History of the Organized Labor Movement in Georgia," 103; *American Federationist* 4, no. 7 (September 1897): 163; no. 8 (October 1897): 198.

86. *AJ*, 6 July 1897. Unless otherwise noted, biographical information comes from Atlanta city directories, 1891–98.

87. Seretan, *Daniel DeLeon*, 101–3, 149–50; Rayback, *History of American Labor*, 226–28; Hillquit, *History of Socialism*, 235, 276–77; Herreshoff, "Daniel DeLeon," 205.

88. McLaurin, *Paternalism and Protest*, 129–34; *American Federationist* 3, no. 10 (December 1896): 220; no. 11 (January 1897): 254–55; 4, no. 5 (July 1897): 93; no. 7 (September 1897): 139–40.

89. *AC*, 7 July 1897; *AJ*, 7, 13, 19 July 1897.

90. Williamson, *Crucible of Race*, 128; Woodward, *Origins of the New South*, 321–95; Logan, *Betrayal of the Negro*; Whites, "Love, Hate, Rape, Lynching."

91. Gutman, "Negro and the United Mine Workers," 113–14, 119–24. While Gutman has been criticized for understating racism in the American white working class, his insistence on exploring the complexities of working-class race relations remains essential.

92. *AJ*, 13, 15, 22 July 1897; *AC*, 15, 17 July 1897.

93. Mercer G. Evans, "History of the Organized Labor Movement in Georgia," 89, 103; *AC*, 23 May 1896; Marshall, "Negro in Southern Unions," 135–39; Karson and Radosh, "AFL and the Negro Worker," 29–36, 80.

94. Figures for the number of black women hired vary widely in newspaper accounts, ranging from six to twenty-five, and there is no mention of their individual names in the company's payroll ledgers. "A dozen or so" comes from the following passage: "There were twelve of these women who had been the immediate cause of the trouble" (*AC*, 7 August 1897); Payroll book, 1896–98, FBCM-GIT.

95. *AJ*, 5 August 1897.

96. Newby, *Plain Folk*, 471–74, 481–86; McLaurin, *Paternalism and Protest*, 61–65.

97. *AJ*, 5–6 August 1897.

98. *AJ*, 4 August 1897; *AC*, 5 August 1897.

99. *AJ*, 4–5 August 1897; *AC*, 5 August 1897.

100. *AC*, 5 August 1897; *AJ*, 4–5, 7 August 1897.

101. "Story of Wesley Community House Inc. and of Some of the Peoples It Has Served," Book I, and Mrs. T. R. Kendall, "History of Atlanta City Mission Board," *Wesley House Bulletin*, 1903–7, both in "Old Records," WHR; Maclachlan, "Women's Work," 80.

102. *AJ*, 4–5 August 1897; *AC*, 5 August 1897.

103. Foner, *American Socialism and Black Americans*, 75.

104. Columbus *Enquirer-Sun*, 7 August 1897, cited in Newby, *Plain Folk*, 480.

105. *AC*, 6 August 1897.

106. *AC*, 7 August 1897. Payroll records indicate the black women *were* paid less than white women. The total outlay for the "colored help" in the folding department was $5.90. If twelve black women were employed for a day and a half, their pay was still 20 percent lower than the average wage for white workers in the bag mill, the lowest paid workers at Fulton Bag. Payroll book, 1896–98, FBCM-GIT.

107. *AJ*, 6 August 1897.

108. *AC*, 8 August 1897; *AJ*, 9 August 1897.

109. *AC*, 10 August 1897.

110. *American Federationist* 4, no. 12 (February 1898): 268–70.

111. McLaurin, *Paternalism and Protest*, 135–37; *American Federationist* 4, no. 7 (September 1897): 163; *AJ*, 9 August 1897.

112. *American Federationist* 4, no. 8 (October 1897): 188; *AC*, 2, 3, 5–7 September 1897; *AJ*, 4, 6 September 1897.

113. *American Federationist* 4, no. 7 (September 1897): 163; no. 11 (January 1898): 265.

114. Payroll book, 1896–98, FBCM-GIT; *AJ*, 16 December 1897. This account of the December 1897 strike draws from company payroll records, *AJ*, 6–22 December 1897, and *AC*, 7–16 December 1897.

115. Payroll book, 1896–98, FBCM-GIT.

116. *AJ*, 21 January 1899; *Augusta Chronicle*, 21 January 1899; Newby, *Plain Folk*, 102–3.

117. U.S. Congress, U.S. Industrial Commission, "Report on . . . the Relations and Conditions of Capital and Labor," 571; *AC*, 12 July 1899.

118. *AC*, 12 July 1899; Newby, *Plain Folk*, 103.

119. U.S. Congress, U.S. Industrial Commission, "Report on . . . the Relations and Conditions of Capital and Labor," 573.

120. Ibid., 569, 571.

CHAPTER TWO

1. James A. Greer to Oscar Elsas, 3 August 1914, Folder 15, Box 1, Strike Records; *Charlotte News*, 8 August 1914.

2. Collier, *Fire in the Sky*. Collier went on to be a well-known liberal journalist and New Dealer. He also was the father-in-law of Daniel Duke, who prosecuted the Ku Klux Klan in the 1940s (Egerton, *Speak Now against the Day*, 136, 226, 299, 417, 442, 462, 485, 614; Duke, interview).

3. *Brooklyn Daily Eagle*, 24 September 1906. For another description of early-twentieth-century Atlanta as a national city, see Inman, *Inman Diary*, 1:33.

4. Deaton, "Atlanta during the Progressive Era," 36, 74, 76, 99 102; Wrigley, "Triumph of Provincialism," 31–40.

5. Du Bois, "Negro Landholder of Georgia," 720.

6. U.S. Congress, Senate, Board of Trade of London, "Cost of Living in American Towns," 48. Emphasis in original.

7. Washington, "Golden Rule in Atlanta."

8. Godshalk, "In the Wake of Riot"; Mixon, "Atlanta Riot of 1906"; Crowe, "Racial Violence and Social Reform"; Crowe, "Racial Massacre in Atlanta."

9. Freeman, interview; Kuhn et al., *Living Atlanta*, 36; Baker, *Following the Color Line*, 30.

10. *AC*, 8 July 1906; Reports of no. 470, 3, 14 August 1914, Folder 20, Box 2, Operative Reports.

11. Oscar Elsas to J. T. Rose, 8 July 1914, and Elsas to Mell Wilkinson, 9 July 1914, both in Folder 49, Box 8, Strike Records; Elsas to Allen F. Johnson, 9 July 1914, Folder 1, Box 4, Strike Records.

12. Kuhn et al., *Living Atlanta*, 3; Carson, *Time and Changes*, 7.

13. U.S. Congress, Senate, Board of Trade of London, "Cost of Living in American Towns," xxxiv, xxxvi, 60.

14. Lyons, "Skyscrapers in Atlanta"; Lyons, "Business Buildings in Atlanta."

15. Elsas, interview by author, 6 March 1991; Bauman, "Centripetal and Centrifugal Forces," 26–27.

16. Interview with Carrie Goodwin by George Mitchell in George Mitchell, *Ponce de Leon*; *AJ*, 16 October 1969, 26 July 1974, 17 December 1981; *AJC*, 24 June 1977; *AC*, 5 October 1976, 21 June 1981, 18 March 1982; Elsas, interview by author, 6 March 1991.

17. U.S. Congress, Senate, Board of Trade of London, "Cost of Living in American Towns," 52; Baker, *Following the Color Line*, 64–65; Weed, "Preliminary Report"; Testimony of H. N. Mullinax, 28, "Testimony for the Complainants."

18. Kuhn et al., *Living Atlanta*, 284; Goodson, " 'South of the North,' " 235, 247–50.

19. Kuhn et al., *Living Atlanta*, 283; Wiggins, *Fiddlin' Georgia Crazy*, 46–61; Burrison, "Fiddlers in the Alley," 59–87; Goodson, " 'South of the North,' " 277–81; *AC*, 16 November 1919.

20. Quoted in Goodson, " 'South of the North,' " 279; Wiggins, *Fiddlin' Georgia Crazy*, 231–40, 256–72.

21. *Atlanta Georgian*, 30 April 1916, quoted in Goodson, " 'South of the North,' " 253.

22. Park, "National Negro Business League," 222; Deaton, "James G. Woodward," 11–23.

23. U.S. Congress, Senate, Board of Trade of London, "Cost of Living in American Towns," 55.

24. Hunter, *To 'Joy My Freedom*, 117; Mercer G. Evans, "History of the Organized Labor Movement in Georgia," 34; Gary Fink, "We Are City Builders, Too"; *JOL*, 6 February 1914; Atlanta Typographical Union Papers and Atlanta Labor Temple Association Papers, Southern Labor Archives, Special Collections, Georgia State University, Atlanta, Ga.

25. Mercer G. Evans, "History of the Organized Labor Movement in Georgia," 43; Deaton "Atlanta during the Progressive Era," 244; Bolden, "Political Structure of Charter Revision Movements; *JOL*, 23 December 1904; "To the Voters of Atlanta," flyer, 28 November 1908, Robert F. Maddox Collection, AHS.

26. Oscar Elsas to Hoke Smith, 11 February 1915, and Elsas to Thomas W. Hardwick, 11 February 1915, both in Folder 11, Box 4, Strike Records; Elsas to C. N. Daniels, 28 April 1915, Folder 16, Box 4, Strike Records; Folder 6, Elsas Collection, Ida Pearl and Joseph Cuba Archives and Genealogy Center, Atlanta Jewish Federation, Atlanta, Ga.

27. Elsas, interview by author, 6 March 1991; Henderson, *Atlanta Life Insurance Company*; Weed, "Preliminary Report."

28. Minutes, Advisory Committee on Smoke, 5 March 1912; Minutes, Smoke Ordinance Special Committee, 5 April 1912, and Minutes, Smoke Abatement Committee, 30 December 1912, ACCR.

29. Letter from Benjamin Elsas to Atlanta Chamber of Commerce, 28 April 1911; Minutes,

Joint Meeting of Committees on Commerce and Cotton, 6 May 1911; and Minutes, Directors, 8 May 1913, ACCR.

30. Minutes, Directors, 30 April 1913, ACCR. On the Sundry Civil Bill, see Wiebe, *Businessmen and Reform*, 174; Bates, *United States*, 143; and *JOL*, 29 April 1913.

31. Letter from Oscar Elsas and W. O. Foote to Wilmer L. Moore, 6 May 1913, ACCR.

32. Minutes, Directors, 8 May 1913, ACCR.

33. "Statistics of Cities," Bureau of Labor Statistics *Bulletin #330* (September 1900), 916–1014, and Annual Reports, Atlanta Police Department, AHS; Racine, "Atlanta's Schools," 193; Galishoff, "Atlanta."

34. Weed, "Preliminary Report"; Weed Report, 12 September 1914.

35. Kuhn et al., *Living Atlanta*, 233–34; Fulton County Health Department, Minutes; *AJ*, 21 October 1913; Schneider, "Survey of the Public Health Situation"; Deaton, "Atlanta during the Progressive Era," 255–56, 260, 263, 265, 270–73, 281–93; Dial, "Public Health in Atlanta"; Beardsley, *History of Neglect*, 45, 48, 56.

36. *JOL*, 7 November 1913.

37. *JOL*, 20 November, 11 December 1903, 1 July 1904; MacLean, "Leo Frank Case Reconsidered."

38. Ayers, *Promise of the New South*, 415–17; Grantham, *Southern Progressivism*; Link, *Paradox of Southern Progressivism*, 160–82; Carlton, *Mill and Town*, 169–74, 181–86, 199–203; Davidson, *Child Labor Legislation*.

39. Davidson, *Child Labor Legislation*, 70–71, 81, 194; *Children and Youth: Social Problems and Social Policy, Proceedings of the Annual Meeting of the National Child Labor Committee, 1905, 1906* (New York, 1974), 81–83, 153; McKelway, "Child Labor in the Southern Cotton Mills," 10, 80–83; *JOL*, 3 June 1904, 5, 19 May, 2 July, 11 August 1905, 13 July 1906; U.S. Congress, Senate, "Beginnings of Child Labor Legislation," 166–88; Jones, "Child Labor Reform Movement in Georgia," 396–412. One reporter who wrote about child labor was Don Marquis of the *Atlanta Journal*, who later became a famous American humorist (*AJ*, 25 August 1905).

40. Report of the Fulton Bag and Cotton Mills (Atlanta, Ga., n.d. [March 1915]), Folder 6, Box 3, and Oscar Elsas to Allen F. Johnson, 29 June 1914, Folder 15, Box 3, Strike Records; Daly Report; Payroll book, 1913–15, FBCM-GIT.

41. *JOL*, 5 January, 2, 9 February, 1 March, 12, 19, 26 April, 10, 31 May, 20 September 1912, 31 January, 14, 21, 28 February, 21, 28 March, 5, 19, 25 April 1913. All of these references to child labor took place before the celebrated murder of Mary Phagan in the Frank case, which greatly heightened public awareness of the issue.

42. Hall, "O. Delight Smith's Progressive Era," 172–73; Maclachlan, "Atlanta's Industrial Women," 16–23; Maclachlan, "Women's Work," 370; Hickey, "Visibility, Politics, and Urban Development"; Blackwelder, "Mop and Typewriter," 21–30.

43. Hall, "Private Eyes, Public Women."

44. For one portrait of traditional rural life and gender roles in Georgia during this period, see Le Guin, *Home-Concealed Woman*.

45. *AC*, 16 March 1913; Goodson, " 'South of the North,' " 106–9, 118, 120–21, 125, 128–31, 155, 180; Cohen, "Atlanta Scorned First Movie," *AJ* magazine, 11 September 1932.

46. *AJ* magazine, 18 May 1913, reprinted in Garrett, *Atlanta and Environs*, 2:607–9. For the idea of Decatur Street as a border zone, see Hickey, "Visibility, Politics, and Urban Development," 260–62, and Hickey, "Waging War," 781–84.

47. Hanchett, *Sorting Out the New South City*, 168.

48. Minutes, Women's Board of City Missions, March 1908, "Minutes and Records 1907–08," "Old Records," WHR; Wiggins, *Fiddlin' Georgia Crazy*, 22, 25; Minutes, Wesley House

Woman's Club, 8 December 1912, 20 December 1912, 10 January 1913, "Old Records," WHR; Dorothy L. Crim, "Wesley House No. 1," in Mrs. T. R. Kendall, "History of Atlanta City Mission Board," *Wesley House Bulletin*, 1903–7, "Old Records," WHR.

49. Report of no. 457, 9 January 1915, Folder 29, Box 2, Operative Reports.

50. Kuhn et al., *Living Atlanta*, 173, 177.

51. *JOL*, 14 June 1907; *AC*, 28 April 1912; Report of H. J. D., 6 June 1914, Folder 15, Box 2, Operative Reports; Cohen, "Atlanta Scorned First Movie"; Garrett, interview.

52. Minutes, Women's Board of City Missions, March 1908, "Minutes and Records 1907–08," "Old Records," WHR.

53. Minutes, Committee on Public Amusements, 29 April 1912, ACCR.

54. "Men and Religion Forward Movement in Atlanta"; Jackson, "Churches of Atlanta," 6–9; Lefever, "Prostitution, Politics, and Religion," 7–29; Nesbitt, "Social Gospel in Atlanta," 78–97.

55. Minutes, Committee on Public Amusements, 6 May 1912, ACCR.

56. Crim, "Wesley House No. 1."

57. Lefever, "Prostitution, Politics, and Religion."

58. Minutes, MRFM Executive Committee, 2 February, 24 March, 15 May 1913, CCC; Lefever, "Prostitution, Politics, and Religion."

59. Minutes, MRFM Executive Committee, 2 February, 16, 30 March 1914, and Minutes, Evangelical Ministers Association, 15 January, 2 February, 6 April 1914, CCC; *AJ*, 22, 29 May 1914. For the MRFM's participation in the 1914–15 Fulton strike, see Lefever, "Involvement of the Men and Religion Forward Movement." While useful, Lefever's account does not draw upon the various federal investigations of the strike or the company records.

60. Deposition of James I. Brush, 21 July 1914, Folder 6, Box 1, Strike Records; Maclachlan, "Women's Work," 218.

61. Minutes, Evangelical Ministers Association, 4 December 1911, Folder 8, Box 3, CCC; Daly, "Sworn Testimony"; Testimony of Marion M. Jackson, 4, "Testimony for the Complainants"; Affidavit of E. W. Hawkins, 26 June 1914, Folder 11, Box 1, Strike Records; Report of J. W. W., 18 June 1914, Folder 2, Box 1, Operative Reports; Memo from Gordon A. Johnstone, 24 July 1914, Folder 2, Box 2, and Memo from Johnstone, 24 July 1914, Folder 5, Box 2, both in Strike Records.

62. Hall, "Private Eyes, Public Women"; A. Elizabeth Taylor, "Woman Suffrage Activities in Atlanta."

63. For instance, see P. A. Smith to Gordon A. Johnstone, n.d. [June 1914?], Folder 12, Box 2, Strike Records; "Mr. J Police Court Witnesses," n.d. [October 1913], Folder 1, Box 1, Operative Reports; and Testimony of Jennie Clinton, 23, "Testimony for the Defendants." In its emphasis on a working-class sexuality that often trangressed Victorian norms, the following account differs somewhat from MacLean, "Leo Frank Case Reconsidered."

64. Testimony of Jennie Clinton, 23, and Testimony of Emma Burton, 8–9, both in "Testimony for the Defendants"; Daly, "Sworn Testimony." For evidence of venereal disease in the Exposition Cotton Mill district, see Kuhn et al., *Living Atlanta*, 150–51.

65. Daly Report.

66. *AC*, 11 November 1905.

67. Testimony of Jennie Clinton, 23, and Testimony of Emma Burton, 8–9, both in "Testimony for the Defendants."

68. See, for instance, Oscar Elsas's description of the "hereditary traits" and "moral laxity" of "this particular element of labor" in Oscar Elsas to Frank P. Walsh, 29 March 1915, Folder 6, Box 3, Strike Records.

69. James A. Greer to Oscar Elsas, 3 August 1914, Folder 15, Box 1, Strike Records. This letter was reprinted in the *Charlotte News*, 8 August 1914.

70. Rhodes, "Free Clinic," 14.

71. Mrs. T. R. Kendall, "History of Atlanta City Mission Board"; Crim, "Wesley House No. 1"; "A Methodist Work," 1906; and Mary Dickinson, "Reminiscences of Miss Rosa Lowe as a Settlement Worker," n.d., all in "Old Records," WHR.

72. Daly, "Sworn Testimony," 9; Testimony of G. R. Buford, 7, "Testimony for the Complainants."

73. "Draft of Report of the Fulton Bag and Cotton Mills" (Atlanta, Ga., n.d. [March 1915]), Folder 4, Box 3, Strike Records.

74. U.S. Congress, Senate, Board of Trade of London, "Cost of Living in American Towns," 52. For the best discussion of the evolving cultural conflict between "mill people" and "town people," see Carlton, *Mill and Town*, esp. 129–214.

75. James A. Greer to Oscar Elsas, 3 August 1914, Folder 15, Box 1, Strike Records.

76. Hall, "Private Eyes, Public Women."

77. On the Frank case, see Dinnerstein, *Leo Frank Case*; McLean, "Leo Frank Case Reconsidered"; and especially the forthcoming book by Steve Oney (New York: Pantheon, 2001).

78. *AC*, 24 August 1913.

79. Elsas, interview by Oney; Elsas, interview by author, 6 March 1991.

80. Reports of G. J. M., 8–10, 27–29 June 1914, Folder 11, Box 1, and Report of no. 470, 12 August 1914, Folder 20, Box 2, all in Operative Reports.

81. Weed, "Preliminary Report."

82. Daly Report; Memo, 24 June 1915, Box 5, Folder 5, and Memo, n.d. [June 1915], Box 4, Folder 19, both in Strike Records.

CHAPTER THREE

1. Dorothy L. Crim, "Wesley House No. 1," in Mrs. T. R. Kendall, "History of Atlanta City Mission Board," *Wesley House Bulletin*, 1903–7, "Old Records," WHR.

2. "Report of the Fulton Bag and Cotton Mills" (Atlanta, Ga., n.d. [March 1915]), Folder 6, Box 3, Strike Records.

3. See Daly Report: "The operatives are drawn from the mountain sections of the State of Georgia,"; Statement by H. C. McCord in Weed Report, 12 September 1914.

4. Unless otherwise mentioned, all references to the origins of Fulton workers are from a survey of 2,500 personnel cards in "Personnel Records—Old File," FBCM-GIT.

5. Wiggins, *Fiddlin' Georgia Crazy*, 3–7, 31, 48, 49, 51.

6. "Notes from the Textile Workers," *JOL*, 9 January–13 February 1914.

7. "Employment Applications 1913," Folders 1–5, FBCM-GIT.

8. Porter, ed., *Cabbagetown Families*, 9.

9. Federal investigator Inis Weed was struck by the significant presence of third-generation textile workers at Fulton Mills (Weed Report, 12 September 1914).

10. Carlton, *Mill and Town*, 90–97; Flynt, *Poor but Proud*, 94–97, 101, 105.

11. Hall et al., *Like a Family*, xvii, 56, 140; Tullos, *Habits of Industry*, 8, 10, 11, 76–77; Newby, *Plain Folk*, 107, 233.

12. Tullos, *Habits of Industry*, 57, 61, 69, 75–76; Hall et al., *Like a Family*, xviii, 13, 99, 145. The phrase "touchy independence" comes from *Habits of Industry*, 75.

13. "Report of Fulton Bag and Cotton Mills." On mill worker transience and labor

turnover, see Hall et al., *Like a Family*, 105–8; Newby, *Plain Folk*, 96, 172–73; Wiggins, *Fiddlin' Georgia Crazy*, 6; and Flynt, *Poor but Proud*, 98.

14. Weed, "Preliminary Report."

15. Washburn, interview.

16. Weed, "Preliminary Report."

17. Reports of G. J. M., 9, 29 June 1914, Folder 11, Box 1, Operative Reports.

18. Hall et al., *Like a Family*, 106–7; Newby, *Plain Folk*, 173; Washburn, interview.

19. Elsas, interview by author, 6 March 1991.

20. Housing Questionnaire, Industrial Service Division, Unpublished Survey Questionnaires, Industrial Survey, United States Housing Corporation, 1918, Records of the U.S. Housing Corp., RG 3, National Archives, Washington, D.C.

21. Daly, "Sworn Testimony."

22. Weed, "Preliminary Report."

23. Daly Report.

24. "Memorandum of Discussion Held with Mr. McWade and Mr. Colpoys," 27 November 1914, Folder 16, Box 1, Strike Records.

25. "Report of the Fulton Bag and Cotton Mills"; McHugh, *Mill Family*; Flamming, *Creating the Modern South*, 114–19.

26. "Report of the Fulton Bag and Cotton Mills"; Daly Report; Wright, *Old South, New South*, 130, 137, 138, 140, 142, 145; Tullos, *Habits of Industry*, 9, 15.

27. Daly, "Sworn Testimony."

28. On working-class housing in Atlanta, see Kuhn et al., *Living Atlanta*, 3–4.

29. Weed, "Preliminary Report"; Testimony of H. N. Mullinax, 28, "Testimony for the Defendants."

30. Mary Dickinson, "Reminiscences of Miss Rosa Lowe as a Settlement Worker," n.d., "Old Records," WHR.

31. E. M. Evans, *Living for Jesus*. Mary Dickinson, "Reminiscences of Miss Rosa Lowe as a Settlement Worker," n.d., "Old Records," WHR.

32. Kuhn et al., *Living Atlanta*, 33; Mrs. E. B. Smith, "'The Story Told in Pictures': Pictures Taken and Compiled by: Mrs. E. B. Smith," photo album, George Meany Memorial Archives, Silver Spring, Maryland, copy in Special Collections, Southern Labor Archives, Georgia State University, Atlanta, Ga.; Porter, ed., *Cabbagetown Families*, 44.

33. Weed Report, 12 September 1914.

34. U.S. Congress, U.S. Industrial Commission, "Report on . . . the Relations and Conditions of Capital and Labor," 572; "Report of the Fulton Bag and Cotton Mills"; Housing Questionnaire.

35. U.S. Congress, U.S. Industrial Commission, "Report on . . . the Relations and Conditions of Capital and Labor," 572; Daly Report.

36. "Report of the Fulton Bag and Cotton Mills."

37. Daly Report.

38. Weed Report, 12 September 1914.

39. On Fulton workers taking the streetcar to work, see Oscar Elsas to James L. Beavers, 29 June 1914, Folder 14, Box 3, and 29 July 1914, Folder 3, Box 4, Strike Records.

40. "Statement of Home Owners and Illiterates" in "Report of Fulton Bag and Cotton Mills." For other evidence of worker home ownership, see Crim, "Wesley House No. 1."

41. U.S. Congress, Senate, Board of Trade of London, "Cost of Living in American Towns," 52.

42. Daly, "Sworn Testimony"; Testimony of G. R. Buford, 3–4, "Testimony for the Complainants."

43. U.S. Congress, Senate, Board of Trade of London, "Cost of Living in American Towns," 52.

44. "Draft of Report of the Fulton Bag and Cotton Mills" (Atlanta, Ga., n.d. [March 1915]), Folder 4, Box 3, Strike Records.

45. U.S. Congress, U.S. Industrial Commission, "Report on . . . the Relations and Conditions of Capital and Labor," 573.

46. Daly Report; Weed Report, 12 September 1914; Testimony of Eugene Wallace Hawkins, 5, "Testimony for the Defendants."

47. "Draft of Report of the Fulton Bag and Cotton Mills."

48. Testimony of Jennie Clinton, 11, "Testimony for the Defendants."

49. "Draft of Report of the Fulton Bag and Cotton Mills"; Testimony of Emma Burton, 8–9, "Testimony for the Defendants."

50. "Memorandum of Discussion Held with Mr. McWade and Mr. Colpoys."

51. Maclachlan, "Woman's Place." Maclachlan emphasizes the dissonance between Wesley House and mill management, while I stress the harmony.

52. "Draft of Report of the Fulton Bag and Cotton Mills."

53. Dickinson, "Reminiscences of Miss Rosa Lowe."

54. Crim, "Wesley House No. 1."

55. Mrs. T. R. Kendall, "History of Atlanta City Mission Board," *Wesley House Bulletin*, 1903–7; "Story of Wesley Community House Inc. and of Some of the Peoples It Has Served," Book I; Dickinson, "Reminiscences of Miss Rosa Lowe"; and "History of Atlanta City Mission Board," *Wesley House Bulletin*, 1910–11, all in "Old Records," WHR.

56. Rhodes, "Free Clinic," 11–15; Rhodes, "Brief Report," 50–53.

57. Rhodes, "Brief Report," 50–53; Branch, "Atlanta and the American Settlement House Movement." In 1911, Lowe left Wesley House to direct the Atlanta Tuberculosis Association, and Dickinson eventually moved to the Red Cross.

58. Crim, "Wesley House No. 1"; Minutes, Women's Board of City Missions, December 1907, "Minutes and Records 1907–08"; and "History of Atlanta City Mission Board," *Wesley House Bulletin 1910–1911*, all in "Old Records," WHR; Carson, *Time and Changes*, 11.

59. Crim, "Wesley House No. 1."

60. Minutes, Women's Board of City Missions, November 1908, "Minutes and Records 1907–08," "Old Records," WHR.

61. "Story of Wesley Community House Inc. and of Some of the Peoples It Has Served," Book I; Crim, "Wesley House No. 1"; Minutes, Wesley House Woman's Club, 12 December 1913; and Minutes, Women's Board of City Missions, June 1908, "Minutes and Records 1907–08," all in "Old Records," WHR.

62. Kendall, "History of Atlanta City Mission Board," and Minutes, Women's Board of City Missions, August 1908, "Minutes and Records 1907–08," both in "Old Records," WHR.

63. Minutes, Women's Board of City Missions, 10 March 1908, April 1909, "Minutes and Records 1907–08," "Old Records," WHR; Testimony of Emma Burton, 14, "Testimony for the Defendants."

64. Crim, "Wesley House No. 1."

65. Minutes, Wesley House Women's Club, 18 November 1910, 21 April, 5 May 1911, 3 February 1912, all in "Old Records," WHR.

66. Crim, "Wesley House No. 1"; Carson, *Time and Changes*, 11, 13.

67. Kuhn et al., *Living Atlanta*, 234–37; Freeman, interview; Oscar Elsas to Frank P. Walsh, 29 March 1915, Folder 6, Box 3, Strike Records; Florrie Crim, "Day Nursery," in Kendall, "History of Atlanta City Mission Board"; Rhodes, "Free Clinic," 12, 14. For more on textile

worker resentment of doctors and modern medical practices, see Simon, *Fabric of Defeat*, 30–31.

68. Testimony of Josie Sisk and Dora Davis in Weed, "Preliminary Report"; Testimony of Addie Camp in Weed Report, 12 September 1914.

69. Minutes, Women's Board of City Missions, June 1908, "Minutes and Records 1907–08," "Old Records," WHR. For a reference to tacky parties, see Lewis and O'Donnell, eds., *Telling Our Stories*, 63.

70. Kendall, "History of Atlanta City Mission Board."

71. Ibid.; Carson, *Time and Changes*, 11; Testimony of Horace Carson in "Testimony of Child Workers in the Fulton Bag and Cotton Mills," in Weed, "Preliminary Report."

72. Minutes, Women's Board of City Missions, March 1908, January 1909, "Minutes and Records 1907–08," "Old Records," WHR.

73. Kendall, "History of Atlanta City Mission Board."

74. Minutes, Women's Board of City Missions, March 1908, "Minutes and Records 1907–08," "Old Records," WHR; Carson, *Time and Changes*, 11–12.

75. Minutes, Women's Board of City Missions, March 1908, "Minutes and Records 1907–08," "Old Records," WHR; Kendall, "History of Atlanta City Mission Board"; Carson, *Time and Changes*, 11–12.

76. Testimony of E. H. Rogers, 21, "Testimony for the Defendants"; Testimony of H. N. Mullinax, 52, "Testimony for the Complainants"; Oscar Elsas to Will Nally, 3 June 1914, Folder 7, Box 8, Strike Records.

77. Crim, "Wesley House No. 1."

78. Dickinson, "Reminiscences of Miss Rosa Lowe."

79. Daly Report; Alexander M. Daly to Dr. Charles McCarthy, RG 174. By the 1910s, Coca-Cola *was* widely consumed among Fulton workers. See Report of no. 457, 26 November 1914, Folder 27, Box 2, Operative Reports.

80. For MRFM members' opinions of the settlement house's work, see Daly Report.

81. Rhodes, "Free Clinic," 14; Kuhn et al., *Living Atlanta*, 3; Brookshire, interview; Roden, interview; Porter, ed., *Cabbagetown Families*.

82. Carlton, "Paternalism and Southern Textile Labor," 22.

83. Carson, *Time and Changes*, 10, 18, 19, 20. For another reference to the metaphor of slavery to describe mill work, see Simon, *Fabric of Defeat*, 23.

84. Porter, ed., *Cabbagetown Families*, 10, 12.

85. Rosser, Brandon, Slaton, and Phillips to Fulton Bag and Cotton Mills, 20 March 1915, Folder 5, Box 3, Strike Records; Daly Report.

86. Testimony of Bertie May Berry, Margaret Dempsey, Willie Anne Walker, Blanche Prince, Dorothy Pows, and unnamed weaver, in Weed, "Preliminary Report."

87. Testimony of Mrs. Nancy Sanders and Eva Stephens in Weed, "Preliminary Report"; Oscar Elsas to Rosser, Brandon, Slaton, and Phillips, 19 March 1915, and Rosser, Brandon, Slaton, and Phillips to Elsas, 20 March 1915, both in Folder 5, Box 3, Strike Records; "Report of the Fulton Bag and Cotton Mills"; Deposition of Hattie Peeler, "Reports and Exhibits."

88. Weed Report, 19 September 1914.

89. "Report of the Fulton Bag and Cotton Mills."

90. Weed, "Preliminary Report."

91. Testimony of Nancy Sanders in Weed, "Preliminary Report"; Depositions of Nancy Sanders and Hattie Peeler, "Reports and Exhibits"; Payroll book, 1913–15, FBCM-GIT.

92. Wright, *Old South, New South*, 132–33, 138–39, 145.

93. *Twelfth Census of the U.S., 1900* and *Thirteenth Census of the U.S., 1910*. My thanks to

Gretchen Maclachlan who tabulated these figures. Maclachlan, "Women's Work," 291, 309; Maclachlan, "Factory Lot in 1900."

94. Daly Report; "Comparative Statement of Wages, 1910–1914," Folder 4, Box 2, Strike Records; Payroll records for weeks ending 19 October 1913 and 16 May 1914, Payroll book, 1913–15, FBCM-GIT.

95. "Memorandum of Discussion Held with Mr. McWade and Mr. Colpoys."

96. Daly Report; Weed Report, 12 September 1914; "Comparative Statement of Wages, 1910–1914," Folder 4, Box 2, Strike Records; "Memorandum of Discussion Held with Mr. McWade and Mr. Colpoys."

97. "Memorandum of Discussion Held with Mr. McWade and Mr. Colpoys"; Payroll book, 1913–15, FBCM-GIT; "Report of Fulton Bag and Cotton Mills"; Weed Report, 12 September 1914.

98. The following discussion draws from the *Thirteenth Census of the U.S., 1910*.

99. U.S. Congress, Senate, Board of Trade of London, "Cost of Living in American Towns," 55; National War Labor Board Case Files, Case 159 [*Division No. 732, Amalgamated Association of Street and Electric Railway Employees of America v. Georgia Railway and Power Company, Atlanta, Ga.*], 1919, RG 2.

100. Daly Report; *AG*, 29 June 1914; "Draft of Report of Fulton Bag and Cotton Mills"; G. M. Brock to editor, 14 June 1914, Folder 64, Box 8, Strike Records. Evidence suggests that Brock did not author this letter; rather, it was at least written down by James Brush, head of the company's private security force, and sent to the paper under Brock's name.

101. "Memorandum of Discussion Held with Mr. McWade and Mr. Colpoys."

102. Payroll book, 1913–15, FBCM-GIT.

103. Testimony of Sarah Nations, 4, "Testimony for the Complainants."

104. U.S. Department of Labor, Bureau of Labor Statistics, Consumer Price Index, U.S. City Average.

105. Kuhn et al., *Living Atlanta*, 3; Testimony by C. C. Houston, U.S. Congress, U.S. Industrial Commission, "Report on . . . the Relations and Conditions of Capital and Labor," 552; Testimony of H. N. Mullinax, 52, "Testimony for the Complainants."

106. Weed Report, 12 September 1914; Testimony of Alfred S. Guffin, 8, "Testimony for the Defendants"; Testimony of William J. Allen, 5, "Testimony for the Complainants."

107. Daly Report; "Memorandum of Discussion Held with Mr. McWade and Mr. Colpoys"; Memorandum from Oscar Elsas, 3 March 1915, Folder 3, Box 3, Strike Records.

108. Daly Report; "Memorandum of Discussion Held with Mr. McWade and Mr. Colpoys."

109. "Record of Employee Fines," Folders 1 and 2, Box 2, Strike Records. This discussion is influenced by the arguments developed in Gutman and Sutch, "Sambo Makes Good."

110. Testimony of Samuel Wilson, 2, 8, "Testimony for the Complainants."

111. Testimony of C. H. Mundy, 23 July 1914, in Weed, "Preliminary Report"; Testimony of H. N. Mullinax, 49, 51, and Testimony of Rufus Odell, 23, both in "Testimony for the Complainants."

112. Weed, "Preliminary Report." Eva Stevens's last name is also spelled "Stephens" in various accounts.

113. Testimony of E. H. Rogers, 14, "Testimony for the Defendants."

114. Weed, "Preliminary Report"; "Memorandum of Discussion Held with Mr. McWade and Mr. Colpoys." Emphasis in original.

115. Daly Report.

116. "Digest of Two Interviews with the Rev. G. R. Buford" in Weed, "Preliminary Report."

117. Weed, "Preliminary Report."

118. Daly Report; Weed, "Preliminary Report"; Rhodes, "Free Clinic," 12, 14.

119. "Digest of Two Interviews with the Reverend G. R. Buford."

120. Weed, "Preliminary Report."

121. Ibid.; Daly Report; Testimony of H. N. Mullinax, 53–54, "Testimony for the Complainants."

122. Testimony of C. H. Mundy and Josie Sisk in Weed, "Preliminary Report"; Weed Report, 19 September 1914; McWade and Colpoys Report.

123. Weed, "Preliminary Report."

124. Ibid.

125. Ibid.

126. Testimony of Sarah Nations, 6, "Testimony for the Complainants"; Report of no. 457, 18 November 1914, Folder 26, Box 2, Operative Reports.

127. *AC*, 2 September 1903.

128. Reports of G. J. M., 18, 19 July 1914, Folder 13, Box 1, Operative Reports.

129. On the indiscriminate use of the word "dagoes," see Baker, *Following the Color Line*, 41.

130. Testimony of Bertie May Berry and C. H. Mundy in "Testimony of Child Workers in the Fulton Bag and Cotton Mills," in Weed, "Preliminary Report."

131. Payroll book, 1913–15, FBCM-GIT; Testimony of Gordon A. Johnstone, 1, 5–6, and Testimony of E. H. Rogers, 28, both in "Testimony for the Defendants."

132. Testimony of Gordon A. Johnstone, 17, 20, "Testimony for the Defendants."

133. Report of no. 457, 10 December 1914, Folder 27, Box 2, Operative Reports; Elsas, interview by author, 5 October 1990.

134. Testimony of Jennie Clinton, 2, "Testimony for the Defendants." Payroll ledgers, census records, spy and company police reports, federal investigations, and other sources all illustrate the bonds developed by Fulton workers. For instance, worker Si Prater and grocer Harris Gober, both identified with the same cluster of strikers and strike supporters during the 1914–15 strike, had boarded together in 1910; workers who testified together to federal investigators often worked side by side in the spinning room or weave shop. See also Porter, ed., *Cabbagetown Families*; Wiggins, *Fiddlin' Georgia Crazy*, 22–23; and Carson, *Time and Change*, 11–12, 20–23.

135. Reports of no. 470, 3, 4, 12 August 1914, Folder 20, Box 2, Operative Reports; *AC*, 20 September 1906; Testimony of C. H. Mundy in Weed, "Preliminary Report."

136. *AC*, 13 August 1904; Report of no. 457, 16 January 1915, Folder 30, Box 2, Operative Reports.

137. "Number of Looms Run—5-14-14 to 9-3-14," Folder 20, Box 1, Strike Records; Report of no. 457, 16 January 1915, Folder 30, Box 2, Operative Reports.

CHAPTER FOUR

1. Carson, *Time and Changes*, 15.

2. *AJ*, 20 October 1913.

3. Testimony of Alfred J. Wilson, 2, "Testimony for the Complainants"; Hall, "Private Eyes, Public Women," 248.

4. *AJ*, 20 October 1913.

5. "Record of Employee Fines," Folders 1–2, Box 2, Strike Records.

6. Testimony by H. N. Mullinax, 4–6, 9, "Testimony for the Complainants"; Testimony by

Gordon A. Johnstone, 7–8, "Testimony for the Defendants." For Metzger, who during World War I was accused of being a German spy, see Folder 19, Box 8, Strike Records.

7. Testimony by H. N. Mullinax, 5, "Testimony for the Complainants"; "Report of the Fulton Bag and Cotton Mills" (Atlanta, Ga., n.d. [March 1915]), Folder 6, Box 3, Strike Records; Memo from Oscar Elsas, 3 March 1915, Folder 5, Box 5, Strike Records; *JOL*, 9 January 1914; *AC*, 21 October 1913.

8. *JOL*, 24 October 1913.

9. *AC*, 21 October 1913; *AJ*, 20 October 1913; *JOL*, 31 October 1913; Memo from Oscar Elsas, 3 March 1915, Folder 5, Box 5, Strike Records.

10. "Report of the Fulton Bag and Cotton Mills"; *AJ*, 20 October 1913.

11. *AG*, 20 October 1913, quoted in *JOL*, 3 April 1914.

12. Note, n.d., "Mr. J Police Court witnesses," Folder 1, Box 1, Operative Reports; *AJ*, 20, 22 October 1913. The *Atlanta Journal*, along with the Hearst-owned *Georgian*, was still noticeably more sympathetic to organized labor than the *Constitution* (Gary Fink, "We Are City Builders, Too," 46–47). In addition to newspaper accounts, information about Fulton workers comes from Atlanta city directories and company payroll records.

13. *AJ*, 21 October 1913; *AC*, 22 October 1913.

14. *JOL*, 31 October, 7 November 1913.

15. *JOL*, 28 November 1913.

16. *AJ*, 22 October 1913; Unsigned Memo, 23 October 1913, Folder 1, Box 1, Operative Reports; Unsigned Memo, "accused Johnstone of carrying pistol," n.d. [16 December 1913?], Folder 8, Box 5, Strike Records; Testimony of Gordon A. Johnstone, 12, "Testimony for the Defendants."

17. "Draft of Report of the Fulton Bag and Cotton Mills" (Atlanta, Ga., n.d. [March 1915]), Folder 4, Box 3, Strike Records; Payroll book, 1913–15, FBCM-GIT; Memo, "Ask Johnstone about Wood, Fleming," 28 October 1914, Folder 1, Box 1, Operative Reports; Testimony of W. E. Fleming, 3–4, and Testimony of H. N. Mullinax, 9, both in "Testimony for the Complainants"; Testimony of Mrs. R. H. [Sallie] Wright, 6–7, Testimony of Oscar Elsas, 19, and Testimony of Gordon A. Johnstone, 8, 10, all in "Testimony for the Defendants." In addition to Fleming and Wood, workers who had left by the week of 25 October included identified strike leaders John Lewis, James Lewis, C. V. Chastien, William Barfield, and Mollie Black. See "these were the leaders," October 1913, Folder 1, Box 1, Strike Records.

18. "Draft of Report of the Fulton Bag and Cotton Mills."

19. Payroll book, 1913–15, FBCM-GIT.

20. C. McFarland et al. to Oscar Elsas, 30 October 1913, Folder 3, Box 3, Strike Records.

21. Gordon A. Johnstone to Oscar Elsas, 1 December 1913, Folder 3, Box 3, Strike Records. With European markets closed off at the outset of World War I, the southern textile industry was indeed in a depressed state.

22. Unsigned Memo, "those convicted," 22 October 1913; Unsigned Memo, "those who swore at court against GAJ," 23 October 1913; Unsigned Memo, n.d., "Mr. J Police Court witnesses"; and Unsigned Memo, 23 October 1913, all in Folder 1, Box 1, Operative Reports; Unsigned Memo from Gordon A. Johnstone, 24 October 1913, Folder 3, Box 1, Strike Records; Unsigned Memo, "union members 1913," n.d., Folder 8, Box 5, Strike Records.

23. List, "these were the leaders," October 1913, and List, "Beginning," 20 October 1913, both in Folder 1, Box 1, Strike Records.

24. Memo from Gordon A. Johnstone, 24 October 1913, and Unsigned Memo, 20 October 1913, both in Folder 1, Box 1, Operative Reports; Testimony of Gordon A. Johnstone, 13, "Testimony for the Defendants."

25. Payroll book, 1913–15, FBCM-GIT; Memo, Gordon A. Johnstone to Oscar Elsas, 24 October 1913, Folder 3, Box 1, Strike Records.

26. Weed, "Preliminary Report"; Testimony of E. H. Rogers, 13, and Testimony of P. A. Smith, 4–5, both in "Testimony for the Defendants."

27. Daly Report; Testimony of H. N. Mullinax, 13, "Testimony for the Complainants"; *JOL*, 13 February, 12 June 1914; Husband-Robinson Report.

28. Testimony of Rufus Odell, 5–6, "Testimony for the Complainants."

29. *Textile Worker* 2, no. 9 (February 1914): 18.

30. Gordon A. Johnstone memo, "these were the leaders," October 1913, Folder 1, Box 1, Strike Records; Payroll book, 1913–15, FBCM-GIT.

31. Daly, "Sworn Testimony"; Testimony of H. N. Mullinax, 25–27, "Testimony for the Complainants"; Payroll book, 1913–15, FBCM-GIT.

32. *Textile Worker* 2, no. 9 (February 1914): 18.

33. B. O. Fussell to Oscar Elsas, 22 October 1913; Elsas to Fussell, 24 October 1913; Elsas to Fussell, 26 November 1913; Fussell to Elsas, 1 December 1913; Elsas to Fussell, 3 December 1913; Fussell to Elsas, 8 December 1913; and Elsas to Fussell, 12 December 1913, all in Folder 9, Box 3, Strike Records; Gordon A. Johnstone to Fussell, 1 January 1914, Folder 8, Box 5, Strike Records; Oscar Elsas to Fussell, 19 January 1914, Folder 10, Box 3, Strike Records; Payroll book, 1913–15, FBCM-GIT.

34. *Textile Worker* 2, no. 10 (March 1914): 5; Testimony of Mrs. R. H. [Sallie] Wright, 19, and Testimony of W. C. Sweatt, 14, both in "Testimony for the Defendants"; Testimony of Rufus Odell, 7–8, "Testimony for the Complainants."

35. *JOL*, 2 January–13 February 1914.

36. *JOL*, 20 March 1914. For a response to the petition, see *JOL*, 3 April 1914.

37. Identified leaders of the October walkout who also signed the Mayo petition included Fleming, Wood, Fowler, Tumlin, Lucy Batchler (or Batchlor), J. A. Strickland, N. D. Autrey (or Awtrey), J. W. Rice, J. T. Hendrix, Georgia Moore, J. T. Allen, Fred Royal, W. H. Norris, and George Christian.

38. *JOL*, 26 September 1913, 24 April, 1 May 1914. For Mangum's self-defense against the charges of favoritism for Frank, see *JOL*, 26 September 1913. For a claim of favoritism awarded Jews by the criminal justice system, made by a supporter of Fulton strikers, see Unsigned Memo [P. A. Smith?] to Mr. Culberson, n.d. [13 July 1914?], Folder 14, Box 2, Strike Records.

39. To distinguish himself from Mangum's alleged preferential treatment of Leo Frank, Mayo made a point of including in his campaign platform the "humane but impartial treatment of prisoners." See *JOL*, 27 February 1914. Many people in Atlanta's Jewish community supported Mangum, a fact that also may have led to resentment among Fulton workers (Eplan, interview).

40. *JOL*, 24 April 1914.

41. Marshall, *Labor in the South*, 83; George S. Mitchell, *Textile Unionism and the South*, 32–33; Brooks, "United Textile Workers," 4.

42. Brooks, "United Textile Workers," 115–16, 331; *Textile Worker* 2 (November 1913): 10–11.

43. *Textile Worker* 2 (September 1913): 4–9.

44. George S. Mitchell, *Textile Unionism and the South*, 31; Brooks, "United Textile Workers," 114.

45. George S. Mitchell, *Textile Unionism and the South*, 9; Brooks, "United Textile Workers," 42, 114, 117, 130, 278; Tripp, *I.W.W. and the Paterson Silk Strike*, 20, 27, 113–14; Golin,

Fragile Bridge, 82–83. During the Lawrence strike, IWW songwriter Joe Hill wrote a derisive song about Golden to the tune of "A Little Talk with Jesus":

A little talk with Golden makes it right, all right;
He'll settle any strike, if there is coin in sight,
Just take him out to dine and ev'rything is fine
A little talk with Golden makes it right, all right.

(Renshaw, *Wobblies*).

46. For more on Miles, see *JOL*, 25 October 1912; Brooks, "United Textile Workers," 136; and Tripp, *I.W.W. and the Paterson Silk Strike*, 37, 38, 46–48.

47. *Augusta Chronicle*, 30 December 1913–18 January 1914; *Textile Worker* 2 (December 1913): 21.

48. *Columbus Ledger*, 24, 27 March 1914; *Rome Tribune Herald*, 21 March 1914; *Textile Worker* 2, no. 6 (November 1913): 18; no. 9 (February 1914): 17–18; no. 10 (March 1914): 5; Husband-Robinson Report.

49. On the IWW, see the following: "Visit to Houses of Elsas Mills" in Daly Report; Weed Report, 12 September 1914; Report of no. 115, 3 July 1914, Folder 6, Box 1, Operative Reports; Oscar Elsas to James A. Emery, 11 July 1914, and Elsas to Franklin W. Hobbs, 7 July 1914, both in Folder 16, Box 3, Strike Records; Frank Gregg to Elsas, 27 July 1914, Folder 17, Box 3; Franklin W. Hobbs to Elsas, 29 June 1914, Folder 15, Box 3; Elsas to *Southern Textile Bulletin*, 25 July 1914, Folder 12, Box 3; and Allen J. Graham to Elsas, 13 June 1914, Folder 12, Box 3, all in Strike Records; *Textile Manufacturer*, 26 November 1914; Oscar Elsas to Jacob Elsas, 17 July 1914, Folder 3, Box 4; Oscar Elsas to L. T. Plunkett, 19 December 1914, Folder 8, Box 4; and C. V. S. Remington to Oscar Elsas, 28 December 1914, Folder 10, Box 4, all in Strike Records; Carlton, *Mill and Town*, 251; *Greenville Daily Piedmont*, 10 July 1914; *Greenville Daily News*, 17 July 1914; "IWW and the Cotton Mills," *Skyland Magazine*, September 1915, 615–16.

50. For more on Clark, see Hall et al., *Like a Family*, 59, 112; Tullos, *Habits of Industry*, 294; and Simon, *Fabric of Defeat*, 50.

51. "Confidential Circulars" in Folder 5, Box 2, Strike Records; quote from Confidential Circular no. 4, 25 September 1914, ibid.

52. *Textile Worker* 2, no. 9 (February 1914): 17; no. 10 (March 1914): 5; Weed Report, 12 September 1914.

53. C. E. McLin to David Clark, 26 March 1914, Folder 5, Box 2, Strike Records.

54. Ibid.; Fidelity Secret Service Bureau to C. E. McLin, 1 April 1914, and I. A. Silverman to McLin, 25 April 1914, both in Folder 16, Box 3, Strike Records.

55. *JOL*, 27 March, 17 April 1914; *Rome Tribune Herald*, 21, 27 March 1914; George S. Mitchell, *Textile Unionism and the South*, 33–34; C. E. McLin to *Southern Textile Bulletin*, 6 June 1914, Folder 5, Box 2, Strike Records.

56. *Textile Worker* 2, no. 10 (March 1914): 5.

57. CDH [C. D. Honiker] to Mr. Florence, 23 March 1914, Folder 14, Box 2, Strike Records; Testimony of H. N. Mullinax, 28, in "Testimony for the Complainants"; Testimony of T. S. Florence, 14, in "Testimony for the Defendants."

58. Cleo Breedlove to Mr. Denk, 25 March 1914, Folder 1, Box 3, Strike Records; Payroll book, 1913–15, FBCM-GIT.

59. D. L. Miller, "A Statement of Facts," *Strikers' Journal*, 18 July 1914. The date may be significant; according to one account, the UTW required a six-month waiting period before a local could be formally chartered. See *AJ*, 20 May 1914.

60. J. H. Baker to Gordon A. Johnstone, 22 April 1914, Folder 11, Box 2, Strike Records; Payroll book, 1913–15, FBCM-GIT.

61. Handbill, n.d. [c. 1 May 1914], Folder 5, Box 1, Strike Records.

62. Testimony of Shuford B. Marks, 2–3, "Testimony for the Complainants"; *JOL*, 6 February 1914; *Party Builder*, 25 October 1913; Paul, "Making Gains in Old Dixie."

63. Bolling H. Jones to Oscar Elsas, 6 May 1914; W. W. Waits to Elsas, 8 May 1914; Elsas to Allen F. Johnson, 9 May 1914; Johnson to Elsas, 11 May 1914; and Johnson to Elsas, 21 May 1914, all in Folder 11, Box 3, Strike Records.

64. Ibid.

65. Handbill, n.d. [early May 1914], Folder 20, Box 1, and Anonymous letter, 5 May 1914, Folder 5, Box 5, Strike Records; Husband-Robinson Report.

66. Notice, 6 May 1914, Folder 1, Box 1, Strike Records. Emphasis in original.

67. Memo, Oscar Elsas to Mr. Florence, 9 May 1914, Folder 1, Box 1, Strike Records; Testimony of W. C. Sweatt, 14, in "Testimony for the Defendants."

68. For instance, see "Draft of Report of the Fulton Bag and Cotton Mills"; "Facts for James G. Woodward's information," 12 June 1914, Folder 1, Box 1, Operative Reports; Oscar Elsas to H. M. Stanley, 23 June 1914, Folder 15, Box 3, Strike Records; Elsas to James A. Emery, 2 July 1914, Folder 16, Box 3, Strike Records; and Testimony of Oscar Elsas, 26, "Testimony for the Defendants."

69. Oscar Elsas to *Southern Textile Bulletin*, 3 September 1914, Folder 3, Box 1, Strike Records.

70. *Textile Worker* 3, no. 2 (July 1914): 7.

71. Carson, *Time and Changes*, 15.

72. Husband-Robinson Report.

73. S. B. Marks to Oscar Elsas, 19 May 1914, Folder 11, Box 3, Strike Records.

74. Testimony of Louie Marquardt, 3–4, "Testimony for the Complainants."

75. *AG*, 24 May 1914.

76. Daly, "Sworn Testimony"; Oscar Elsas to H. M. Stanley, 23 June 1914, Folder 15, Box 3, Strike Records; Testimony of Shuford B. Marks, 3–4, 9–10, "Testimony for the Complainants"; Testimony by Jennie Clinton, 2, "Testimony for the Defendants."

77. *AJ*, 20 May 1914.

78. *AJ*, 20–21 May 1914; *AG*, 20 May 1914; *AC*, 21 May 1914.

79. Payroll book, 1913–15, FBCM-GIT. These figures include those working in the carding, spinning, and weaving departments of Mills No. 1 and No. 2, and those working in both the regular and second departments of the bag mill.

80. "No. Looms Run—5-4-14 to 9-3-14," Folder 20, Box 1, Strike Records.

81. *AG*, 24 May 1914.

82. *AJ*, 27 May 1914; *AG*, 27 May 1914; *AC*, 28 May 1914; Note from J. H. Evans, n.d., and Unsigned Report, 26 May 1914, both in Folder 12, Box 2, Strike Records.

83. Memo from J. H. Evans, n.d., Folder 12, Box 2, and R. F. Irwin to Gordon A. Johnstone, 26 May 1914, Folder 24, Box 2, both in Strike Records; Memo from James I. Brush, 28 May 1914, and Unsigned Memo, n.d., both in Folder 11, Box 2, Strike Records.

84. Hall, "O. Delight Smith's Progressive Era"; Hall, "Private Eyes, Public Women," 250–51, 254–55, 257–58.

85. Mrs. E. B. Smith, " 'The Story Told in Pictures': Pictures Taken and Compiled by: Mrs. E. B. Smith," photo album, George Meany Memorial Archives, Silver Spring, Maryland, copy in Special Collections, Southern Labor Archives, Georgia State University, Atlanta, Ga.; R. F. Irwin to Gordon A. Johnstone, 26 May 1914, Folder 24, Box 2, Operative Reports; Unsigned Memo, n.d. [28 May 1914], Folder 5, Box 1, Strike Records.

86. Oscar Elsas to Allen F. Johnson, 29 May 1914, Folder 11, Box 3, Strike Records; Report of Operative J. W. W., 30 May 1914, Folder 2, Box 1, Operative Reports; Unsigned Memo, 30 May 1914, Folder 11, Box 2, and Unsigned Note, n.d. [28 May 1914], both in Folder 5, Box 1, Strike Records; Minutes, MRFM Executive Committee, 1 June 1914, CCC; *JOL*, 5 June 1914.

87. Payroll book, 1913–15, FBCM-GIT; "No. Looms Run—5-14-14 to 9-3-14."

88. Unsigned notes for talk, 29 May 1914, Folder 5, Box 1, Strike Records. Emphasis in original.

89. *AC*, 1 June 1914; *JOL*, 5 June 1914; *Atlanta Georgian and News*, 1 June 1914.

90. *AC*, 1 June 1914.

91. The other mills were Whittier Mills, Martel Manufacturing, Gate City Cotton Mills, Scottdale Mills, and Exposition Cotton Mills. See Oscar Elsas to Scottdale Mills, 1 June 1914, and Elsas to Gate City Cotton Mills, 1 June 1914, both in Folder 12, Box 3, Strike Records.

92. Oscar Elsas to Georgia cotton manufacturers, 3 June 1914, Folder 12, Box 3, Strike Records.

93. Jeff Davis to Oscar Elsas, 4 June 1914; Elsas to Davis, 12 June 1914; Harry L. Williams to Elsas, 4 June 1914; Elsas to Williams, 12 June 1914; Elsas to James P. Verdery, 12 June 1914; W. M. McCafferty to Elsas, 4 June 1914; Elsas to McCafferty, 12 June 1914; R. T. Jones to Elsas, 5 June 1914; Jones to Elsas, 6 June 1914; Jones to Elsas, 8 June 1914; Elsas to Jones, 9 June 1914; Elsas to Jones, 12 June 1914; J. O. Nichols to Elsas, 5 June 1914; Elsas to Nichols, 12 June 1914, all in Folder 12, Box 3, Strike Records.

94. Payroll book, 1913–15, FBCM-GIT.

95. *JOL*, 5 January 1912.

96. Information obtained from Atlanta city directories and from payroll records. The actual number of company informants is probably higher, since many of the notes and reports to management were anonymous.

97. Memo from J. H. Baker to Gordon A. Johnstone and James I. Brush, 22 April 1914, Folder 11, Box 2, Strike Records.

98. Affidavit of Sarah F. Nix, 21 May 1914, and Affidavit of Hannah Taylor, 22 May 1914, both in "Affidavits gathered by James I. Brush, n.p.," Folder 8, Box 1, Strike Records; Affidavit of Ida Gunn, 12 June 1914, Folder 9, Box 1, Strike Records.

99. Memo to Oscar Elsas, 23 May 1914, Folder 4, Box 5, Strike Records.

100. Affidavit of Nettie Safford, 29 June 1914, and Affidavit of James I. Brush, 29 June 1914, both in Folder 7, Box 1, Strike Records; Two affidavits of Lum G. Neal, 7 July 1914, Folder 4, Box 5, Strike Records.

101. Back of card of Mrs. Carl Karston, 1 July 1914, Folder 5, Box 4, Strike Records; Dr. W. V. Garret[t], "Pellagra Follows Child Labor in Cotton Mills," *AG*, 21 July 1914; Garrett, "Poor Wages Endanger the Health of All Citizens" and "Cases of Pellagra in Vicinity of Fulton Bag and Cotton Mills," *Strikers' Journal*, 18 July 1914; Affidavit of Mrs. Lillie Priest, 16 July 1914, Folder 8, Box 1, and Affidavit of James I. Brush, 21 July 1914, Folder 6, Box 1, both in Strike Records.

102. *Atlanta Star*, 8 June 1914.

103. Two memoranda from James I. Brush, 28 May 1914, and Memo from James I. Brush, 29 May 1914, all in Folder 11, Box 2, Strike Records.

104. Four memoranda from James I. Brush, 2 June 1914, Folder 11, Box 2, Strike Records.

105. Memo from James I. Brush, 2 June 1914, Folder 11, Box 2, Strike Records; Atlanta City Directories.

106. *AJ*, 6 July 1897, 9 February 1899; *JOL*, 10 October 1913.

107. Unsigned Note, n.d. [29 May 1914?], Folder 5, Box 1; Unsigned Note, 2 June 1914, Folder 1, Box 3; Unsigned Note, "*Meyers*," 3 June 1914, Folder 11, Box 2; John Craig to Mr.

Oscar, n.d., Folder 11, Box 2; Craig to Mr. Oscar, 10, 30 June, 2, 11 July 1914, Folder 12, Box 2, Strike Records; T. W. Lipscomb to Ben Z. Phillips, 24 June 1914, Oscar Elsas to Rosser, Brandon, Slaton, and Phillips, 27 June 1914, Phillips to Elsas, 29 June 1914, Phillips to Elsas, 29 June 1914, Elsas to Rosser, Brandon, Slaton, and Phillips, 2, 13, 16 July 1914, all in Folder 34, Box 8, Strike Records; Elsas to Joseph M. Brown, 20 July 1914, Folder 2, Box 4, Strike Records.

108. Affidavit of E. W. Hawkins, 26 June 1914, Folder 11, Box 1, Strike Records. For more on Annie Green, see "Annie Carlton alias Annie Green," Unsigned Memo, 29 May 1914, Folder 8, Box 1, Strike Records.

109. For Nunnally, see John Golden to William B. Wilson, 24 July 1914, RG 280; Daly Report; "Augusta Mullinax" folder, Folder 11, Box 1, Strike Records; and Smith, " 'Story Told in Pictures.' "

110. AG, 2 June 1914; Reports of J. W. W. and A. E. W., 4–5 June 1914, Folder 2, Box 1, and Reports of no. 115, 29–30 June 1914, Folder 6, Box 1, both in Operative Reports.

111. Unsigned Memo, 3 June 1914, Folder 11, Box 2, Strike Records. For another reference to a strike organizer who was a "one-eyed man from Boston," see Report of no. 470, 17 August 1914, Folder 21, Box 2, Operative Reports.

112. Louis J. Elsas to Gordon A. Johnstone, 14 June 1914, Folder 1, Box 3, Strike Records. For another example of the strikers and others making up verses about their opponents, see Report from G. A. Stalnaker, 21 June 1914, and Report from H. L. Sargent, 21 June 1914, both in Folder 13, Box 2, Strike Records.

113. Unsigned Memo, n.d., Folder 3, Box 3, Strike Records.

114. H. N. Brown to Oscar Elsas, 22 October 1913, Folder 3, Box 1, Operative Reports.

115. H. N. Brown to Oscar Elsas, 13, 18, 19 May 1914, Folder 3, Box 1, Operative Reports.

116. Oscar Elsas to Allen F. Johnson, 29 May 1914, Folder 11, Box 3, Strike Records. For evidence that indicates, although does not conclusively prove, that no. 40 was a Pinkerton agent, see J. H. Kelley to Gordon A. Johnstone, 28 August 1914, Folder 3, Box 2, Strike Records, in conjunction with Folders 16–19, Box 2, Operative Reports. Kelley is "Supt. JHK," referred to in Report of no. 41, 1 August 1914, Folder 19, Box 2, Operative Reports. For additional evidence of Pinkertons used by the Exposition Cotton Mill during the World War I era, see Dennis et al., interview, and Report of no. 115, 28 October 1914, Folder 10, Box 1, Operative Reports.

117. Oscar Elsas to H. N. Brown, 15 May 1914; Elsas to Railway Audit and Inspection Co., 22 May 1914; Elsas to L. A. Thomas, 22 May 1914; Charles A. Wickersham to Elsas, 23 May 1914; Landon A. Thomas to Elsas, 23 May 1914; and T. S. Raworth to Elsas, 23 May 1914, all in Folder 3, Box 1, Operative Reports.

118. Anonymous Report, n.d., Folder 3, Box 1, and Report from J. W. W., 31 May 1914, Folder 2, Box 1, Operative Reports.

119. Reports of H. A. H., 1–5 June 1914, Folder 14, Box 2, and Report of H. J. D., 1 June 1914, Folder 15, Box 2, Operative Reports.

120. Reports from H. A. H., 2–5 June 1914, Folder 14, Box 2, and Reports from H. J. D., 3–4 June 1914, Folder 15, Box 2, Operative Reports.

121. Report from H. J. D., 3 June 1914, Folder 15, Box 2, Operative Reports.

122. List, "Dispossessed up to 6/13/14," Folder 2, Box 3, Strike Records; Daly, "Sworn Testimony."

123. Anonymous Memo, 9 June 1914, Folder 5, Box 1, Strike Records.

124. Testimony of Mrs. R. H. [Sallie] Wright, 20, "Testimony for the Defendants."

125. Payroll book, 1913–15, FBCM-GIT; "No. Looms Run—5-4-14 to 9-3-14."

126. Reports of H. A. H., 3–5 June 1914, Folder 14, Box 2; Report of H. J. D., 4 June 1914,

Folder 15, Box 2; and Report of J. W. W. and A. E. W., 5 June 1914, Folder 2, Box 1, Operative Reports.

127. Reports of H. A. H., 2, 3, 5 June 1914, Folder 14, Box 2, Operative Reports; Reports of J. W. W., 2, 4 June 1914, and Report of J. W. W. Inspector and A. E. W. no. 10, 3 June 1914, all in Folder 2, Box 1, Operative Reports.

128. Reports of H. A. H., 2–3 June, Folder 14, Box 2, and Reports of H. J. D., 2, 3, 5 June 1914, Folder 15, Box 2, Operative Reports; Notes of phone conversation between Oscar Elsas and H. W. Miller, 8 June 1914, and Elsas to H. W. Miller, 9 June 1914, both in Folder 13, Box 3, Strike Records; Unsigned Memo [P. A. Smith?], 9 June 1914, Folder 2, Box 1, and Report of no. 457, 1 December 1914, Folder 5, Box 1, Strike Records.

129. Report of H. A. H., 5 June 1914, Folder 14, Box 2, Operative Reports; Notes of phone conversation between Oscar Elsas and H. W. Miller, 8 June 1914; Elsas to Miller, 9 June 1914; Miller to Elsas, 11 June 1914; and Elsas to Miller, 12 June 1914, all in Folder 13, Box 3, Strike Records.

130. Reports of G. J. M., 8, 10, 28, 29 June 1914, Folder 11, Box 1, Operative Reports.

131. Report of H. A. H., 3 June 1914, Folder 14, Box 2, and Report of J. W. W. Inspector and A. E. W. no. 10, 3 June 1914, Folder 2, Box 1, Operative Reports; "A few of my family" from caption of photograph, RG 280. Except for the caption, this photo is identical to photo no. 72; see Smith, " 'Story Told in Pictures.' "

132. Reports of J. W. W. and A. E. W. no. 10, 6, 8 June 1914, Folder 2, Box 1, Operative Reports.

133. Report of H. J. D., 2 June 1914, Folder 15, Box 2, Operative Reports; Report of J. W. W. Inspector and A. E. W. no. 10, 3 June 1914, and Report of J. W. W. and A. E. W., 5 June 1914, both in Folder 2, Box 1, Operative Reports. The Atlanta police had already resented the involvement of private detectives in the Frank case.

134. Unsigned memo, "Mayers," 9 June 1914, Folder 12, Box 2, Strike Records; Report of H. A. H., 9 June 1914, Folder 14, Box 2, and Reports of H. J. D., 9–11 June 1914, Folder 15, Box 2, all in Operative Reports.

135. Oscar Elsas to C. E. McLin, 3 July 1914, Folder 16, Box 3, Strike Records.

136. Fidelity Secret Service Bureau of New York to C. E. McLin, 1 April 1914; I. A. Silverman to McLin, 29 April 1914; Oscar Elsas to McLin, 3 July 1914; and McLin to Elsas, 4 July 1914, all in Folder 16, Box 3, Strike Records; Oscar Elsas to Allen Johnson, 8 July 1914; Elsas to W. C. Martin, 14 July 1914; and Elsas to Martin, 20 July 1914, all in Folder 1, Box 4, Strike Records.

137. Frank Gregg to Oscar Elsas, 8 July 1914; Elsas to Gregg, 13 July 1914; Gregg to Elsas, 25 July 1914; and Gregg to Elsas, 27 July 1914, all in Folder 1, Box 4, Strike Records.

138. Reports from J. W. W., 1–2 June 1914, Folder 2, Box 1, Operative Reports. For other references to Detecto and other dictograph machines, see AJ, 1 September 1912, and advertisements in Atlanta city directories.

139. Report of H. J. D., 9 June 1914, Folder 15, Box 2, and Reports of H. A. H., 10–11 June 1914, Folder 14, Box 2, Operative Reports; Reports of J. W. W. and A. E. W. no. 10, 9–10 June, and Reports of J. W. W., 14–22 June 1914, all in Folder 2, Box 1, Operative Reports; Expense statement, 15 June 1914, Folder 3, Box 1, Operative Reports; P. A. Smith to Gordon A. Johnstone, 11 June 1914, Folder 12, Box 2, Strike Records.

140. Reports of J. W. W. Inspector and A. E. W. no. 10, 3–4 June 1914, Folder 2, Box 1, and Report of H. A. H., 3 June 1914, Folder 14, Box 2, Operative Reports.

141. Report of J. W. W. and A. E. W. no. 10, 4 June 1914, Folder 2, Box 1, and Report of H. J. D., 7 June 1914, Folder 15, Box 2, Operative Reports.

142. Report of J. W. W. and A. E. W. no. 10, 5 June 1914, Folder 2, Box 1, and Report of H. J. D., 5 June 1914, Folder 15, Box 2, Operative Reports.

143. Report of J. W. W. and A. E. W., 5 June 1914, and Report of J. W. W. and A. E. W. no. 10, 8 June 1914, both in Folder 2, Box 1, Operative Reports.

144. Report of J. W. W., 2 June 1914, Folder 2, Box 1; Report of H. A. H., 2 June 1914, Folder 14, Box 2; and Reports of H. J. D., 2–3 June 1914, Folder 15, Box 2, all in Operative Reports; "Reports and Exhibits."

CHAPTER FIVE

1. Elsas, interview by Oney; Elsas, interview by author, 6 March 1991.

2. On one occasion Elsas did allow that 210 workers quit work that first day; on another, he admitted that as many as 300 workers took part in the strike (*AJ*, 20 May 1914; *AC*, 21 May 1914; *AG*, 24 May 1914; Memo from Oscar Elsas, 21 July 1914, Folder 3, Box 4, Strike Records).

3. *AC*, 3 June 1914; Oscar Elsas to James G. Woodward, 12 June 1914, Folder 13, Box 3, Strike Records; Memo from Oscar Elsas, 12 June 1914, Folder 1, Box 1, Operative Reports; Unsigned Memo, "Chamber Commerce," n.d. [19 June 1914], Folder 2, Box 3; Oscar Elsas to H. M. Stanley, 23 June 1914, Folder 15, Box 3; Oscar Elsas to William Schley Howard, 1 July 1914, Folder 16, Box 3, all in Strike Records; Benjamin Elsas to Charles E. Perkins, 3 July 1914, and Benjamin Elsas to James S. Alexander, 3 July 1914, both in Folder 14, Box 5, Strike Records; Oscar Elsas to William Donald, 11 July 1914, Folder 13, Box 1; Memo, 27 August 1914, Folder 4, Box 4; and Oscar Elsas to Richard Sloss, 18 March 1915, Folder 5, Box 3, all in Strike Records; Husband-Robinson Report.

4. *AJ*, 20 May 1914; *AC*, 21 May 1914; *AG*, 24 May 1914; *Strikers' Journal*, 18 July 1914; *American Federationist* 21 (September 1914): 707; *Fall River Daily Globe*, 10 September 1914; U.S. Congress, House, Congressman William S. Greene speech; *Textile Worker* 3, no. 5 (October 1914); McWade and Colpoys Report.

5. Alexander M. Daly to Charles McCarthy, 31 July 1914, RG 174.

6. Oscar Elsas to Jacob Elsas, 17 July 1914, Folder 3, Box 4, Strike Records.

7. Ibid., 20 July 1914.

8. Two letters from C. A. Green to Gordon A. Johnstone, 5 June 1914, Folder 13, Box 5, and Memo, n.d., Folder 1, Box 3, all in Strike Records.

9. R. E. Hightown to Oscar Elsas, 5 June 1914, and Elsas to Hightown, 12 June 1914, both in Folder 13, Box 3, Strike Records; W. C. Vereen to Elsas, 9 July 1914, Folder 16, Box 3, and Darden Borders to Elsas, 28 July 1914, Folder 3, Box 4, both in Strike Records.

10. Oscar Elsas to Will Nally, 3 June 1914, Folder 7, Box 8, Strike Records. Emphasis in original.

11. Reports from H. J. D., 7, 10 June 1914, and Report from J. W. W. and A. E. W. no. 10, 9 June 1914, all in Folder 15, Box 2, Operative Reports; Report from J. W. W. and A. E. W. no. 10, 8 June 1914, Folder 2, Box 1, Operative Reports; Oscar Elsas to Charles A. Wickersham, 9 June 1914, Folder 13, Box 3, Strike Records; Reports from J. W. W., 19, 22 June 1914, Folder 2, Box 1, Operative Reports; Oscar Elsas to R. T. Pace, 22 June 1914, and Pace to Elsas, 25 June 1914, both in Folder 13, Box 3, Strike Records.

12. G. B. S. to Oscar Elsas, 1 July 1914, Folder 10, Box 1, Strike Records.

13. Oscar Elsas to Charles A. Wickersham, 9 June 1914; Elsas to R. T. Pace, 22 June 1914; and Pace to Elsas, 25 June 1914, all in Folder 13, Box 3, Strike Records.

14. Statement of Joe Wells, 8 June 1914, Folder 8, Box 1, and Memo from Joe Head, 11 June 1914, Folder 12, Box 2, both in Strike Records; Report of no. 115, 19 June 1914, Folder 6, Box 1, Operative Reports.

15. Report of James I. Brush, 28 May 1914, Folder 11, Box 2, and Oscar Elsas to James L. Beavers, 29 July 1914, Folder 3, Box 4, both in Strike Records.

16. Evidence that the commissary was on Tennelle Street comes from close investigation of strike photographs and maps of the area by photo archivist Peter Roberts of Georgia State University.

17. Anonymous Memo, n.d., Folder 14, Box 2, Strike Records.

18. *AJ*, 23 October 1913, 20 May 1914; CDH [Charles D. Honiker] to T. S. Florence, 23 March 1914, Folder 14, Box 2, Strike Records; Memo from James I. Brush, 23 May 1914, and Anonymous Memo [James I. Brush?], 29 May 1914, both in Folder 11, Box 2, Strike Records; Memo from J. H. Evans, n.d., and Memo from J. H. Evans, 5 June 1914, both in Folder 12, Box 2, Strike Records; Report of J. W. W., 19 June 1914, Folder 2, Box 1, Operative Reports; Affidavit of Nettie Safford, 29 June 1914, Folder 7, Box 1, Strike Records.

19. H. L. Sargent to P. A. Smith, 20 June 1914, Folder 13, Box 2, Strike Records; Anonymous report, 5–6 July 1914, and Report of Fowler, 18–19 July 1914, both in Folder 1, Box 1, Operative Reports; P. A. Smith to Culberson, 14 July 1914, Folder 12, Box 2, Strike Records.

20. For instance, see the following: Report of A. M. St. John, 29–30 May 1914, Folder 11, Box 2, Strike Records; Report of Hood and Fowler, 15 June 1914, Report of Fowler, 21–22 June 1914, Report of Hood, Neal, and Gill, 22 June 1914, Report of Hood and Kelly, 1 July 1914, Reports of Hood, Young, and Mathis, 6, 16 July 1914, and Reports of Fowler, 20–21, 21–22 July 1914, all in Folder 1, Box 1, Operative Reports; Report of Hood, Young, and Mathis, 7 July 1914, Report of Fowler, 7–8 July 1914, P. A. Smith to Culberson, 18 July 1914, and Memo from Gordon A. Johnstone, 5 June 1914, all in Folder 12, Box 2, Strike Records.

21. *AG*, 2 June 1914; Reports of H. A. H., 1–2 June 1914, Folder 14, Box 2, Operative Reports; Report of J. W. W. and A. E. W. no. 10, 4 June 1914, and Report of J. W. W. and A. E. W., 5 June 1914, both in Folder 2, Box 1, Operative Reports; Reports of H. J. D., 4, 6–7 June 1914, Folder 15, Box 2, Operative Reports; Memo from Joe Head, 11 June 1914, Folder 12, Box 2, Strike Records.

22. Reports of H. A. H., 1, 11 June 1914, Folder 14, Box 2; Report of J. W. W. and A. E. W., 5 June 1914, Folder 2, Box 1; and Report of H. J. D., 6 June 1914, Folder 15, Box 2, all in Operative Reports; Oscar Elsas to E. L. Jett, 17 June 1914, Folder 14, Box 3, Strike Records; Report of no. 115, 19 June 1914, Folder 6, Box 1, Operative Reports; Affidavit by Lum G. Neal, 7 July 1914, Folder 7, Box 1, Strike Records.

23. Memo from Joe Head, n.d., Folder 12, Box 2, and Oscar Elsas to E. L. Jett, 15 June 1914, Folder 14, Box 3, both in Strike Records.

24. P. A. Smith to Gordon A. Johnstone, 11 June 1914; Report of P. A. Smith, n.d.; Report of J. W. M. [*sic*?]; Report of Joe Head, 11 June 1914; Report of Aran-Barbar, 13 June 1914; Report from Tom McGuffy, Hyde, and Williams, 15 June 1914; Report of Hardy and Quick, 16 June 1914; P. A. Smith to Culberson, 27 June 1914; and Report of J. J. Cobb, 27 June 1914, all in Folder 12, Box 2, Strike Records; Report of G. J. M., 12 June 1914, Folder 11, Box 1, and Memo from Oscar Elsas, 13 June 1914, Folder 1, Box 1, both in Operative Reports; Report of G. A. Stalnaker, 21 June 1914, Folder 13, Box 2, Strike Records.

25. P. A. Smith to Culberson, 8 July 1914, Folder 12, Box 2, Strike Records.

26. Report of H. J. D., 2 June 1914, Folder 15, Box 2, Operative Reports; Anonymous memo, 8 June 1914, Folder 2, Box 1, Strike Records; Report of H. A. H., 9 June 1914, Folder 14, Box 2, Operative Reports; Oscar Elsas to E. L. Jett, 15 June 1914, Folder 14, Box 3, Strike Records.

27. Report from James I. Brush, 1 June 1914, Folder 11, Box 2, Strike Records; Report of G. J. M., 6 June 1914, Folder 11, Box 1, Operative Reports; Anonymous Memo, n.d., Folder 13, Box 2, Strike Records.

28. McWade and Colpoys Report.

29. Report from S. E. Purgason, 12 June 1914, and Report from P. A. Smith, n.d., both in Folder 12, Box 2, Strike Records; Oscar Elsas to E. L. Jett, 16 June 1914, Folder 14, Box 3, Strike Records.

30. Memo from J. W. McCuen, 12 June 1914; Memo from Joe Head, n.d.; and Memo from S. E. Purgason, 12 June 1914, all in Folder 12, Box 2, Strike Records; Oscar Elsas to E. L. Jett, 15 June 1914, Folder 14, Box 3, Strike Records; Affidavits of Sarah Dunn, Ida Gunn, Mary Davis, and Maggie Culberson, 12 June 1914, Folder 9, Box 1, Strike Records.

31. Ibid.; Reports of James I. Brush, 5, 13 June 1914, Folder 11, Box 2, and Jacob James to Oscar Elsas, 16 June 1914, Folder 10, Box 1, all in Strike Records; Affidavit of Claudia Fuller, 29 June 1914, and Affidavit of Henry Johnson, 22 July 1914, both in Folder 8, Box 1, Strike Records.

32. Notes to Walter Burdett, 20 June 1914 and n.d., Folder 10, Box 1, Strike Records.

33. *AJ*, 14 June 1914; *AC*, 16 June 1914; Oscar Elsas to E. L. Jett, 15 June 1914, Folder 14, Box 3, Strike Records.

34. *Atlanta Star*, 8 June 1914; Annual Report of Chief of Police for the year ending 31 December 1914, Atlanta Police Department Papers, AHS; Daly Report; Weed, "Preliminary Report"; P. A. Smith to Mr. Culberson, 8 July 1914, Folder 12, Box 2, Strike Records.

35. Memo from G. A. Stalnaker and Homer L. Sargent, 13 June 1914, Folder 12, Box 2, Strike Records.

36. Reports of G. J. M., 8–10, 27–29 June 1914, Folder 11, Box 1, and Report of no. 470, 12 August 1914, Folder 20, Box 2, all in Operative Reports.

37. Report of G. J. M., 9 June 1914, Folder 11, Box 1, Operative Reports; P. A. Smith to Gordon A. Johnstone, 11 June 1914, Folder 12, Box 2, Strike Records; Testimony of Mrs. R. H. [Sallie] Wright, 20, "Testimony for the Defendants."

38. Testimony of Mrs. R. H. [Sallie] Wright, 20; Testimony of R. H. Wright, 4–5; and Testimony of R. H. Wright (recalled, second time), 1, all in "Testimony for the Defendants."

39. Testimony of R. H. Wright, 10–11, and Testimony of R. H. Wright (recalled), 1–2, both in "Testimony for the Defendants"; Reports of no. 115, 7–11, 14, 17, 27–29 July 1914, Folder 7, Box 1, and Report of no. 115, 26 August 1914, Folder 8, Box 1, all in Operative Reports; Testimony of R. H. Wright in Weed, "Preliminary Report," and Daly Report.

40. Testimony of W. C. Sweatt, 1–5, "Testimony for the Defendants"; Report of James I. Brush, 3 June 1914, Folder 11, Box 2, Strike Records; P. A. Smith to Culberson, n.d., and Unsigned Memo, 23 June 1914, both in Folder 12, Box 2, Strike Records; Reports of no. 115, 23–24 June 1914, Folder 6, Box 1, Operative Reports.

41. Testimony of Mrs. R. H. [Sallie] Wright, 20, "Testimony for the Defendants." Existing family tensions and conflicts could inform one's position on the strike. For instance, during the 1934 general textile strike, Fulton worker Effie Dodd Gray's hostility toward the union clearly was influenced by her antagonistic relationship with her father, a union painter and strike sympathizer (Gray, interview).

42. P. A. Smith to Gordon A. Johnstone, 11 June 1914, Folder 12, Box 2, Strike Records.

43. Reports of G. J. M., 9–10 June 1914, Folder 11, Box 1, Operative Reports.

44. Carson, *Time and Changes*, 15.

45. Report of no. 470, 12 August 1914, Folder 20, Box 2, and Reports of G. J. M., 28–29 June 1914, Folder 11, Box 1, all in Operative Reports.

46. *AJ*, 9–11 June 1914.

47. Reports of G. J. M., 8, 10, 28, 29 June 1914, Folder 11, Box 1, Operative Reports.

48. Reports of G. J. M., 8, 10, 28 June 1914, Folder 11, Box 1, Operative Reports.

49. Report of G. J. M., 28 June 1914, Folder 11, Box 1, Operative Reports.

50. Two memoranda from G. A. Stalnaker and Homer Sargent, n.d., Folder 12, Box 2, Strike Records; Report of G. J. M., 12 June 1914, Folder 11, Box 1, Operative Reports.

51. Oscar Elsas to H. P. Meikleham, 9 June 1914; Meikleham to Elsas, 11 June 1914; and Elsas to Meikleham, 12 June 1914, all in Folder 13, Box 3, Strike Records; Testimony of E. H. Rogers, 15–17, and Testimony of H. P. Meikleham, 19, both in "Testimony for the Defendants"; Testimony of Arthur K. Wilson, 4, 6, and Testimony of Columbus L. Howell, 3–7, both in "Testimony for the Complainants"; Affidavit of Sam Womack, 5 August 1914, "Reports and Exhibits."

52. Payroll book, 1913–15, FBCM-GIT; Report from James I. Brush, 3 June 1914, Folder 11, Box 2, Strike Records; Reports from G. J. M., 7, 10, 12–13 June 1914, Folder 11, Box 1, Operative Reports; Oscar Elsas to H. P. Meikleham, 9 June 1914, and Meikleham to Elsas, 11 June 1914, both in Folder 13, Box 3, Strike Records.

53. "Number of Looms Run—5-14-14 to 9-3-14," Folder 20, Box 1, Strike Records.

54. Reports of G. J. M., 13–14 June 1914, Folder 11, Box 1, Operative Reports.

55. Report of G. J. M., 14 June 1914, Folder 11, Box 1, Operative Reports; Oscar Elsas to H. P. Meikleham, 12 June 1914, Folder 13, Box 3, Strike Records.

56. Memo from Oscar Elsas to E. G. Meyers, 9 June 1914, Folder 12, Box 2, and Elsas to H. P. Meikleham, 13 June 1914, Folder 13, Box 3, both in Strike Records; Report from G. J. M., 13 June 1914, Folder 11, Box 1, Operative Reports.

57. Oscar Elsas to H. P. Meikleham, 13 June 1914, Folder 13, Box 3, Strike Records.

58. Memo from Tom McGuffy, Hyde, and Williams, 15 June 1914, Folder 12, Box 2, Strike Records; Report from G. J. M., 15 June 1914, Folder 11, Box 1, Operative Reports.

59. Report from J. W. W., 16 June 1914, Folder 2, Box 1, and Report from G. J. M., 16 June 1914, Folder 11, Box 1, both in Operative Reports; two letters from Oscar Elsas to E. L. Jett, 17 June 1914, Folder 13, Box 3, Strike Records.

60. Report from G. J. M., 17 June 1914, Folder 11, Box 1; Report from no. 115, 18 June 1914, Folder 6, Box 1; and Reports from G. J. M., 20–21 June 1914, Folder 11, Box 1, all in Operative Reports; Oscar Elsas to H. P. Meikleham, 23 June 1914, Folder 15, Box 3, and two letters from Oscar Elsas to E. L. Jett, 17 June 1914, Folder 14, Box 3, all in Strike Records.

61. Report of G. J. M., 20 June 1914, and two reports of G. J. M., 21 June 1914, all in Folder 11, Box 1, Operative Reports; Oscar Elsas to H. P. Meikleham, 23 June 1914, Folder 15, Box 3, Strike Records.

62. Affidavit of Sam Womack, 5 August 1914, "Reports and Exhibits"; Testimony of Columbus L. Howell, 4, "Testimony for the Complainants."

63. Two reports from G. J. M., 21 June 1914, Folder 11, Box 1, and Report from no. 115, 22 June 1914, Folder 6, Box 1, all in Operative Reports; Oscar Elsas to H. P. Meikleham, 23 June 1914, Folder 15, Box 3, Strike Records.

64. For Conboy, see Fiedman, "Sara Agnes McLaughlin Conboy"; Johnson and Malone, *Dictionary of American Biography*, 338; *Who Was Who in America*, 249; Wertheimer, *We Were There*, 360–61; and Norwood, *Labor's Flaming Youth*, 97, 101–2.

65. Wiggins, *Fiddlin' Georgia Crazy*, 25; Reports of J. W. W., 18, 21 June 1914, Folder 2, Box 1, Operative Reports; Testimony of R. H. Wright, 17, 35, "Testimony for the Defendants."

66. Memo from T. S. Florence, 15 June 1914, Folder 8, Box 1; Memo from T. S. Florence, 29 June 1914, Folder 8, Box 5; Oscar Elsas to B. Z. Phillips, 16 June 1914, Folder 15, Box 3; C. B. Wilmer to Louis J. Elsas, 22 June 1914, Folder 13, Box 1, all in Strike Records; *AG*, 29 June 1914. For Logan, see Weisiger, "Joe Logan."

67. Reports of H. A. H., 1, 10 June 1914, Folder 14, Box 2; Report of G. J. M., 12 June 1914, Folder 11, Box 1; and Report of J. W. W., 17 June 1914, Folder 2, Box 1, all in Operative Reports.

68. P. A. Smith to Gordon A. Johnstone, 9 June 1914, Folder 12, Box 2, Strike Records; Report of no. 115, 26 June 1914, Folder 6, Box 1, Operative Reports.

69. Unsigned memo, 27 May 1914, Folder 4, Box 5, Strike Records.

70. Report of J. W. W. and A. E. W. no. 10, 8 June 1914, Folder 2, Box 1, Operative Reports; Memo from P. A. Smith to Gordon A. Johnstone, 9 June 1914, and Memo from J. W. M. [sic?], 12 June 1914, both in Folder 12, Box 2, Strike Records; Unsigned memo, 14 June 1914, Folder 14, Box 1, Strike Records.

71. Union attendance list, 15 July 1914, Folder 2, Box 1, Strike Records. When carefully used in conjunction with Atlanta city directories and other sources, attendance records give some sense of who actually attended union meetings and frequented the commissary. However, full identification of those in attendance cannot be obtained because of faulty or inconsistent spelling, poor handwriting, multiple listings in city directories under the same name, the transient nature of many working-class Atlantans, and the fact that quite a few people did come to the union and the commissary from outside Atlanta.

72. JOL, 7 November 1913; Survey, 8 August 1914.

73. Affidavit of C. H. Gartman, 26 June 1914, Folder 8, Box 1, Strike Records.

74. Memo from P. A. Smith to Gordon A. Johnstone, 9 June 1914, Folder 12, Box 2, and Affidavit of C. H. Gartman, 26 June 1914, Folder 8, Box 1, both in Strike Records; Testimony of R. H. Wright, 14, "Testimony for the Defendants."

75. Report of G. J. M., 7 June 1914, Folder 11, Box 1, Operative Reports; Memo from G. A. Stalnaker and Homer Sargent, 13 June 1914, Folder 12, Box 2, Strike Records.

76. Lola Petty to Oscar Elsas, n.d., Folder 3, Box 4, Strike Records.

77. Unsigned Memo, "Tune of Yankee Doodle," n.d., Folder 3, Box 3, and Louis J. Elsas to Gordon A. Johnstone, 14 June 1914, Folder 1, Box 3, both in Strike Records.

78. Testimony of Emma Burton, 14–15, "Testimony for the Defendants"; "Report of the Fulton Bag and Cotton Mills" (Atlanta, Ga., n.d. [March 1915]), Folder 6, Box 3, Strike Records.

79. Testimony of R. H. Wright (recalled), 13–14, 30, "Testimony for the Defendants."

80. Testimony of W. C. Sweatt, 15, and Testimony of R. H. Wright, 17, 35, both in "Testimony for the Defendants."

81. For more on Preston, see Gary Fink, "Labor Espionage," 10–35, and Hall, "Private Eyes, Public Women," 255–57.

82. Reports of no. 115, 29 June, 1 July 1914, Folder 6, Box 1, and Reports of no. 115, 16, 18, 19, 26 July 1914, Folder 7, Box 1, all in Operative Reports.

83. Reports of no. 115, 16, 18, 19, 22, 26 July 1914, Folder 7, Box 1, and Report of G. J. M., 18 July 1914, Folder 13, Box 1, all in Operative Reports.

84. Reports of G. J. M., 7, 9, 13, 20 June 1914, Folder 11, Box 1, and Report of G. J. M., 15 July 1914, Folder 12, Box 1, all in Operative Reports.

85. Report of G. J. M., 7 June 1914, Folder 11, Box 1, Operative Reports; P. A. Smith to Culberson, 26 June 1914, Folder 12, Box 2, Strike Records; Testimony of Jennie Clinton, 16, "Testimony for the Defendants."

86. Report from James I. Brush, 5 June 1914, Folder 11, Box 2, and P. A. Smith to Culberson, 14 July 1914, Folder 12, Box 2, both in Strike Records.

87. Report of J. W. W. and A. E. W. no. 10, 9 June 1914, Folder 2, Box 1, and Reports of no. 115, 25 June, 4 July 1914, Folder 6, Box 1, all in Operative Reports; Anonymous Memo, 29 June 1914, Folder 4, Box 5, Strike Records.

88. Report of Ed Thomason, 13 June 1914, Folder 12, Box 2, Strike Records; Two reports of G. J. M., 28 June 1914, Folder 11, Box 1, Operative Reports.

89. Reports from no. 115, 25 June, 1 July 1914, Folder 6, Box 1, and Reports from no. 115, 8,

14, 17, 25 July 1914, Folder 7, Box 1, all in Operative Reports; Unsigned to D. L. Miller, 11 July 1914, Folder 5, Box 1, Strike Records.

90. "Number of Looms Run—5-14-14 to 9-3-14," Folder 20, Box 1, Strike Records; Alexander M. Daly to Charles McCarthy, 31 July 1914, RG 174.

91. Reports of no. 115, 24–25 July 1914, Folder 7, Box 1, Operative Reports; Memo, 27 August 1914, Folder 4, Box 4, Strike Records.

92. Weed, "Preliminary Report"; Reports of no. 115, 27–28 July 1914, Folder 8, Box 1, Operative Reports. My emphasis on the continuity between Oscar and Jacob Elsas differs from the account given in Gary Fink, *Fulton Bag and Cotton Mills Strike*.

CHAPTER SIX

1. Elsas, interview by Oney; Elsas, interview by author, 6 March 1991.

2. *JOL*, 19 June 1914; *Textile Worker* 3, no. 3 (August 1914): 23–24; Arthur D. Lown to Oscar Elsas, 21 August 1914, and Fall River *Evening Herald*, n.d. [August 1914], both in Folder 13, Box 5, Strike Records.

3. For more on the engendered characteristics attributed to the Fulton Mills strikers, see Hall, "Private Eyes, Public Women."

4. Stott, *Documentary Expression and Thirties America*, 27–28. This is not to say that propagandistic motives were the sole or principal driving forces behind the actions of Progressive Era reformers or the Fulton strike organizers.

5. *AG*, 17 June 1914; *AJ*, 17 June 1914; *Atlanta Star*, 17 June 1914; Report of H. A. H., 3 June 1914, Folder 14, Box 2, and Report of H. J. D., 3 June 1914, Folder 15, Box 2, both in Operative Reports; flyer, "An Urgent Appeal to All Who Love Liberty," RG 174.

6. E. G. Myers to Oscar Elsas, 24 June 1914, Folder 3, Box 1, and Report of no. 115, 22 July 1914, Folder 7, Box 1, both in Operative Reports; *AG*, 17 June 1914; *AJ*, 17 June 1914; *Atlanta Star*, 17 June 1914; *AC*, 18 June 1914.

7. *AG*, 4, 7 June 1914; Report from H. J. D., 3 June 1914, Folder 15, Box 2, and Report from no. 115, 19 June 1914, Folder 6, Box 1, both in Operative Reports; Oscar Elsas to James G. Woodward, 12 June 1914, Folder 13, Box 3, Strike Records; E. G. Myers to Oscar Elsas, 24 June 1914, Folder 3, Box 1, Operative Reports.

8. Testimony of Shuford B. Marks, 12–13, "Testimony for the Complainants."

9. For Hine, see Trachtenberg, "Ever-the Human Document," esp. 129–33. For documentary and reform photography more generally, see Stange, *Symbols of Ideal Life*, 5.

10. *AJ*, 17 June 1914; Report from J. W. W., 17 June 1914, Folder 2, Box 1, Operative Reports.

11. *Atlanta Sunday-American*, 28 June, 2 August 1914.

12. Frank Gregg to Oscar Elsas, 25 July 1914, Folder 1, Box 3, Strike Records; *Survey*, 8 August 1914. For more on the Ludlow photographs and the decoding of historical photographs more generally, see Margolis, "Mining Photographs."

13. Letter from John Golden to William B. Wilson, 24 July 1914, RG 280; *Philadelphia Ledger*, n.d.; *Atlanta Sunday-American*, 28 June 1914; *Plumbers, Gas and Steam Fitters Journal* 18 (August 1914): 26; *Fort Smith Southwest American*, 4 October 1914; *Philadelphia Globe*, 17 November 1914; F. L. Mills to Oscar Elsas, 11 July 1914, Folder 14, Box 5, and Claude N. Bennett to Oscar Elsas, 18 August 1914, Folder 4, Box 4, both in Strike Records; Pittman and Harrison to Dave Elsas, 5 October 1914, and Dave Elsas to Oscar Elsas, 8 October 1914, both in Folder 4, Box 5, Strike Records.

14. Report on Milton Nunnally, 7 January 1914, Folder 8, Box 1, and Minor contract with Gusta Mullinax, Folder 11, Box 1, both in Strike Records.

15. Daly, "Sworn Testimony."

16. *AC*, 3 June 1914.

17. Report of H. A. H., 3 June 1914, Folder 14, Box 2; Report of J. W. W. and A. E. W. no. 10, 3 June 1914, Folder 2, Box 1; Report of J. W. W. Inspector and A. E. W. no. 10, 3 June 1914, Folder 2, Box 1; and Report of H. J. D., 3 June 1914, Folder 15, Box 2, all in Operative Reports; *AG*, 4 June 1914.

18. Reports of H. J. D., 4, 7 June 1914, Folder 15, Box 2, Operative Reports.

19. Stange, *Symbols of Ideal Life*, xiii, xiv, 51, 63, 147; *AC*, 23 April 1913; *AJ*, 4, 15–20 June 1914.

20. Report of J. W. W. Inspector and A. E. W. no. 10, 3 June 1914, Folder 2, Box 1, and Report of J. W. W. and A. E. W. no. 10, 3 June 1914, Folder 2, Box 1, both in Operative Reports.

21. List, "Dispossessed up to 6/13/14," Folder 2, Box 3, Strike Records; Daly, "Sworn Testimony."

22. Report of H. A. H., 3 June 1914, Folder 14, Box 2, and Report of H. J. D., 3 June 1914, Folder 15, Box 2, both in Operative Reports.

23. Images by Russell can be found at AHS.

24. Report from H. J. D., 4 June 1914, and Report from H. A. H., 5 June 1914, both in Folder 15, Box 2, Operative Reports; Memo from Gordon A. Johnstone to Oscar Elsas, 5 June 1914, Folder 12, Box 2, Strike Records.

25. Reports from H. A. H., 4–5 June 1914, Folder 14, Box 2, Operative Reports; Memo from Gordon A. Johnstone to Oscar Elsas, 5 June 1914, Folder 12, Box 2, Strike Records; Mrs. E. B. Smith, " 'The Story Told in Pictures': Pictures Taken and Compiled by: Mrs. E. B. Smith," photo album, George Meany Memorial Archives, Silver Spring, Maryland, copy in Special Collections, Southern Labor Archives, Georgia State University, Atlanta, Ga.

26. Memo from Gordon A. Johnstone to Oscar Elsas, 5 June 1914, Folder 12, Box 2, Strike Records; Report from H. A. H., 5 June 1914, Folder 14, Box 2, Operative Reports.

27. Report of H. A. H., 4 June 1914, Folder 14, Box 2, and Report of H. J. D., 4 June 1914, Folder 15, Box 2, both in Operative Reports.

28. Reports from H. J. D., 5–6 June 1914, Folder 15, Box 2; Reports from H. A. H., 5–6 June 1914, Folder 14, Box 2; and Report from J. W. W. and A. E. W. no. 10, 6 June 1914, Folder 2, Box 1, all in Operative Reports. On the custom of placing photographs in drugstore windows, see *AC*, 25 April 1913.

29. Report from H. J. D., 5 June 1914, Folder 15, Box 2, and Report from H. A. H., 5 June 1914, Folder 14, Box 2, both in Operative Reports.

30. *AG*, 7 June 1914; Report from H. J. D., 5 June 1914, Folder 15, Box 2, and Report from J. W. W. and A. E. W. no. 10, 6 June 1914, Folder 2, Box 1, both in Operative Reports. Later on during the strike, organizers screened such films as "The Factory Girl" as benefits for the strikers. For the use of film by labor and the Left during this period, see Ross, "Struggles for the Screen" and *Working-Class Hollywood*.

31. Sphinx Film Company to Oscar Elsas, Folder 3, Box 3, Strike Records; Report from H. J. D., 8 June 1914, Folder 15, Box 2, Operative Reports; Testimony of Margaret Dempsey in Weed, "Preliminary Report"; photo no. 83 in "Evictions," book 2 of Smith, " 'Story Told in Pictures' "; Inscription on back of photograph, RG 280.

32. Report from H. J. D., 8 June 1914, Folder 15, Box 2, and Report from H. A. H., 8 June 1914, Folder 14, Box 2, both in Operative Reports.

33. Sphinx Film Company to Oscar Elsas, Folder 13, Box 3, Strike Records.

34. Report from H. A. H., 8 June 1914, Folder 14, Box 2, Operative Reports; Photographs, RG 280. The numerous colorful newspaper articles about Carson frequently mentioned his faithful coon dog (Wiggins, *Fiddlin' Georgia Crazy*, 51).

35. Report of H. A. H., 8 June 1914, Folder 14, Box 2, Operative Reports.

36. Report of H. J. D., 5 June 1914, Folder 15, Box 2, and Report of H. A. H., 5 June 1914, Folder 14, Box 2, Operative Reports; photo nos. 55 and 86 in Smith, "'The Story Told in Pictures.'"

37. UTW flyer, "An Urgent Appeal for a Deserving Cause," RG 174; UTW flyer, "AN URGENT APPEAL TO ALL WHO LOVE LIBERTY TO ASSIST IN STAMPING OUT FOR ALL TIME INDUSTRIAL WHITE SLAVERY IN THE COTTON MILLS OF THE SOUTH," RG 280, reprinted in *JOL*, 24 July 1914.

38. Reports of no. 115, 17, 19 July 1914, Folder 7, Box 1, Operative Reports; Charles C. Thorn to Oscar Elsas, 29 July 1914, Folder 2, Box 4, Strike Records; *Strikers' Journal*, 18 July 1914.

39. Report of H. A. H., 9 June 1914, Folder 14, Box 2, and Reports of H. J. D., 9–10 June 1914, Folder 15, Box 2, all in Operative Reports.

40. Oscar Elsas to Allen F. Johnson, 24 June 1914, Folder 15, Box 3, Strike Records; Reports from no. 115, 22–23 June 1914, Folder 6, Box 1, Operative Reports.

41. Oscar Elsas to *Southern Textile Bulletin*, 9 June 1914, Folder 12, Box 3, Strike Records.

42. Jacob Elsas to Oscar Elsas, 15 June 1914, Folder 14, Box 3, Strike Records.

43. Oscar Elsas to J. M. Jarman, 12 June 1914, Folder 12, Box 3, and Elsas to Nym Hurt, 6 July 1914, Folder 16, Box 3, both in Strike Records.

44. Oscar Elsas to James G. Woodward, 12 June 1914, Folder 13, Box 3, Strike Records.

45. Oscar Elsas to E. L. Jett, 15 June 1914, and Elsas to Mell W. Wilkinson, 15 June 1914, both in Folder 14, Box 3, Strike Records.

46. E. L. Jett to Oscar Elsas, 17 June 1914, and Elsas to Jett, 17 June 1914, both in Folder 14, Box 3, Strike Records.

47. Oscar Elsas to Walter G. Cooper, 16 June 1914; Elsas to Allen F. Johnson, 16 June 1914; and Johnson to Elsas, 17 June 1914, all in Folder 15, Box 3, Strike Records.

48. Memo from Oscar Elsas, 16 March 1915, Folder 5, Box 5, Strike Records.

49. Unsigned Notes, "Chamber Commerce 6/19/14," Folder 15, Box 3, Strike Records.

50. Oscar Elsas to James G. Woodward, 22 June 1914; two letters from Elsas to James L. Beavers, 27 June 1914; and Elsas to Beavers, 29 June 1914, all in Folder 15, Box 3, Strike Records; Elsas to Mell R. Wilkinson, 3 July 1914, Folder 6, Box 3, and Elsas to Wilkinson, 14 July 1914, Folder 1, Box 4, both in Strike Records; Weed, "Preliminary Report"; *AC*, 30 November 1916.

51. Reports of J. W. W. and A. E. W. no. 10, 6, 8–9 June 1914, Folder 2, Box 1, and Report from no. 115, 22 June 1914, Folder 6, Box 1, all in Operative Reports.

52. Anonymous Memo, 9 June 1914, Folder 5, Box 1, Strike Records.

53. Daly, "Sworn Testimony."

54. Minutes, MRFM Executive Committee, 1 June 1914, CCC.

55. Report from J. W. W. and A. E. W., 5 June 1914, Folder 2, Box 1, Operative Reports.

56. *AG*, 5 June 1914; *AJ*, 5 June 1914; *AC*, 6 June 1914.

57. For the "Protocol of Peace," see Adams, *Age of Industrial Violence*, 101, 116–25.

58. Captions from photographs 33, 61, Smith, "'Story Told in Pictures'"; Report from J. W. W. and A. E. W. no. 10, 7 June 1914, Folder 2, Box 1, Operative Reports.

59. Report of J. W. W., 5 June 1914, Report of A. E. W. no. 10, 5 June 1914, and Report of J. W. W. and A. E. W. no. 10, 6 June 1914, all in Folder 2, Box 1, Operative Reports; Reports of H. J. D., 6–7 June 1914, Folder 15, Box 2, Operative Reports.

60. Minutes, MRFM Executive Committee, 8 June 1914, CCC.

61. Daly, "Sworn Testimony."

62. Minutes, MRFM Executive Committee, 15, 22 June 1914, CCC.

63. Grantham, *Hoke Smith*, 270–71.

64. Oscar Elsas to Allen Johnson, 16 June 1914, Folder 15, Box 3, and Unsigned Notes, "Chamber Commerce 6/19/14," Folder 2, Box 3, all in Strike Records.

65. Minutes, MRFM Executive Committee, 22 June 1914, CCC; *JOL*, 24 June 1914.

66. *JOL*, 19 June 1914.

67. E. G. Myers to Oscar Elsas, 24 June 1914, Folder 3, Box 1, Strike Records; Report of no. 115, 27 June 1914, Folder 3, Box 1, Operative Reports.

68. Joseph M. Brown to Oscar Elsas, 24 June 1914, and Elsas to Brown, 26 June 1914, both in Folder 15, Box 3, Strike Records.

69. Records of this meeting, including transcripts of the speeches, appear in Folder 9, Box 2, Strike Records.

70. Minutes, MRFM Executive Committee, 29 June 1914, CCC; Report from no. 115, 29 June 1914, Folder 6, Box 1, Operative Reports; Transcript of the 12 July mass meeting, Folder 10, Box 2, Strike Records.

71. Minutes, MRFM Executive Committee, 29 June, 13 July 1914, and Minutes, Evangelical Ministers Association, 6 July 1914, all in CCC; Oscar Elsas to C. B. Wilmer, 1 July 1914; Wilmer to Elsas, 7 July 1914; and Elsas to Wilmer, 11 July 1914, all in Folder 16, Box 3, Strike Records.

72. *JOL*, 3 July 1914; Minutes, MRFM Executive Committee, 29 June, 6, 13 July 1914, CCC.

73. A. F. Sherrill to Oscar Elsas, 1 July 1914, Folder 16, Box 3, Strike Records.

74. *AC*, 30 June 1914; Report of no. 115, 30 June 1914, Folder 6, Box 1, Operative Reports; C. E. McLin to Oscar Elsas, 2 July 1914, Folder 16, Box 3, Strike Records.

75. Louis J. Elsas to Oscar Elsas, 25 June 1914, Folder 13, Box 1, Strike Records; Louis J. Elsas to C. B. Wilmer, 11 July 1914, attached to Oscar Elsas to Frank P. Walsh, 29 March 1915, Folder 6, Box 3, Strike Records.

76. For another MRFM reference to Jacob as a crafty businessman, see MRFM bulletin, *AC*, 23 April 1913.

77. *AC*, 24 August 1913.

78. *AJ*, 29, 31 May 1914. The MRFM apparently saw fit to respond to Benjamin's letter, although the reply was not recorded. See Minutes, MRFM Executive Committee, 1 June 1914, CCC. For another example of MRFM anti-Jewish prejudice, see "Digest of Two Interviews with the Reverend G. R. Buford," in Weed, "Preliminary Report."

79. Minutes, MRFM Executive Committee, 6, 13 July 1914, 10 August 1914, CCC; Jacob Elsas to Marion M. Jackson, John J. Eagan, Jacob Patterson, and W. W. Orr, 7 August 1914, Folder 14, Box 5, Strike Records.

80. For more on Emery, NAM, and NCID, see Weinstein, *Corporate Ideal*, 14–15, 184; Wiebe, *Businessmen and Reform*, 29; Sklar, *Corporate Reconstruction*, 266; and especially Sarah Watts Lyon, *Order against Chaos*.

81. "No. Looms Run—5-14-14 to 9-3-14," Folder 20, Box 1, Strike Records.

82. Oscar Elsas to James A. Emery, 2 July 1914, Folder 16, Box 3, Strike Records.

83. Ibid., 6 July 1914.

84. Oscar Elsas to James A. Emery, 11 July 1914, and Emery to Elsas, 24 July 1914, both in Folder 3, Box 4, Strike Records.

85. *AG*, 17 June 1914; Weed Report, 12 September 1914; Frank Gregg to Oscar Elsas, 27 July 1914, Folder 1, Box 3, Strike Records.

86. Franklin W. Hobbs to Oscar Elsas, 29 June 1914, Folder 15, Box 3, Strike Records; Elsas to Hobbs, 7 July 1914, and Hobbs to Elsas, 9 July 1914, both in Folder 16, Box 3, Strike Records; Joseph Hamilton to Gordon A. Johnstone, Folder 14, Box 5, Strike Records.

87. Benjamin Elsas to Charles E. Perkins, 3 July 1914, and Elsas to James S. Alexander, 3 July 1914, both in Folder 14, Box 5, Strike Records. For Perkins's connection to Fulton Bag, see Private Ledger, 1889–1929, 72, FBCM-Emory.

88. J. S. Alexander to Benjamin Elsas, 7 July 1914, Folder 14, Box 5, Strike Records.

89. Charles E. Perkins to F. W. Lafrentz, 8 July 1914, Folder 14, Box 5, Strike Records.

90. F. W. Lafrentz to Charles E. Perkins, 10 July 1914, Folder 14, Box 5, Strike Records.

91. Charles E. Perkins to Benjamin Elsas, 7, 9, 11 July 1914; Elsas to Perkins, 11 July 1914; Perkins to Elsas, 13 July 1914; Elsas to Perkins, 14 July 1914; and Perkins to Elsas, 16 July 1914, all in Folder 14, Box 5, Strike Records; Private ledger, 1889–1929, 72–73, FBCM-Emory.

92. Benjamin Elsas to William Donald, 11 July 1914, Folder 13, Box 1, Strike Records.

93. Ibid.

94. Dinnerstein, *Leo Frank Case*, 92, 100, 104, 105, 134, 137, 172.

95. Benjamin Elsas to Adolph Elsas, 11 July 1914, and Benjamin Elsas to Adolph Ehrlich, 11 July 1914, both in Folder 14, Box 5, Strike Records.

96. Oscar Elsas to J. T. Rose, 8 July 1914, and Elsas to Mell Wilkinson, 9 July 1914, both in Folder 49, Box 8, Strike Records; Elsas to Allen F. Johnson, 9 July 1914, Folder 1, Box 4, Strike Records.

97. Oscar Mayer to Benjamin Elsas, 30 June 1914, Folder 66, Box 8, Strike Records.

98. Memo, 7 July 1914, Folder 66, Box 8, Strike Records; Atlanta City Directory [for Broome].

99. Report, "American Cast Iron Pipe Co," 11 July 1914, Folder 66, Box 8, Strike Records.

100. Oscar Mayer to Oscar Elsas, 13 July 1914; Elsas to the Bert G. Covell Co., 17, 21 July 1914; and M. T. Stratford to Elsas, 25 July 1914, all in Folder 66, Box 8, Strike Records.

101. Oscar Elsas to the Bert G. Covell Co., 17 July 1914, Folder 66, Box 8, Strike Records.

102. Folder 5, Box 3, Strike Records. A crossed-out reference in the statement, evidently a draft, to "The Real War," the title of the MRFM's Bulletin no. 132, which appeared 4 August 1914, helps date the statement.

103. Folder 5, Box 3, Strike Records.

104. James E. C. Pedder to Oscar Elsas, 29 July 1914, Folder 66, Box 8, Strike Records.

105. Elsas, interview by Oney; Elsas, interviews by author, 5 October 1990 and 6 March 1991.

106. For evidence that Fulton management in fact employed Pinkertons themselves in addition to Railway Audit and other labor spies, see J. H. Kelley to Gordon A. Johnstone, 28 August 1914, Folder 1, Box 2, Strike Records, as well as Folders 16–19, Box 2, Operative Reports.

107. Weed, "Preliminary Report"; Daly Report; Minutes, MRFM Executive Committee, CCC; Reports of no. 115, 12–13 September 1914, Folder 9, Box 1, Strike Records.

108. Reports of no. 115, 12, 19, 26 July 1914, Folder 7, Box 1, Operative Reports.

109. "Number of Looms Run—5-14-14 to 9-3-14," Folder 20, Box 1, Strike Records.

CHAPTER SEVEN

1. Mary Anderson to S. J. Gompers Jr., 3 June 1920, Case File 33/41, RG 280.

2. In the testimony presented before the War Labor Board in Atlanta, there was one brief reference to unionizing efforts in local cotton mills in the 1917–18 period. See Case 159, Case Files, RG 2, p. 853.

3. H. L. Kerwin to Mary Anderson, 4 June 1920, Case File 33/41, RG 280.

4. Minutes, MRFM Executive Committee, 6 July 1914, CCC. For the CIR, see Adams, *Age of Industrial Violence*; Weinstein, *Corporate Ideal*; and Leon Fink, "Monday Morning Quarterback."

5. Oscar Elsas to Hoke Smith, 9 July 1914, and Telegram from Elsas to Smith, 9 July 1914, both in Folder 1, Box 4, Strike Records; Confidential Circular, 15 July 1914, Folder 5, Box 2,

Strike Records; Adams, *Age of Industrial Violence*, 207; Grantham, *Hoke Smith*, 299–300; and U.S. Congress, Senate, Senator Hoke Smith speech, 11681–84, 11687–90.

6. Telegram from William Schley Howard to Oscar Elsas, 1 July 1914, and Elsas to Howard, 1 July 1914, both in Folder 16, Box 3, Strike Records; Telegram from Howard to S. B. Marks, 1 July 1914; Telegram from Charles A. Miles to Howard, 1 July 1914; Telegram from Marks and Jerome Jones to Howard, 1 July 1914; and Howard to Miles, 8 July 1914, all in *Congressional Record*, 64th Cong., 1st sess., 2 March 1915, 5841; *AJ*, 8 July 1914. The Division of Conciliation had been established under the enabling legislation of the DOL in 1913, then later became the Federal Mediation and Conciliation Service (Kolb, *Mediators*, 7–8).

7. Report of no. 115, 2 July 1914, Folder 6, Box 1, and Report of no. 115, 9 July 1914, Folder 7, Box 1, both in Operative Reports; Anonymous Report, 3 July 1914, Folder 12, Box 2, Strike Records.

8. Report of G. J. M., 13 July 1914, Folder 12, Box 2, Operative Reports; Oscar Elsas to Jacob Elsas, 14 July 1914, Folder 3, Box 4, Strike Records; *AJ*, 18 July 1914; *AG*, 12, 21 July 1914; Minutes, MRFM Executive Committee, 20 July 1914, CCC.

9. Report of G. J. M., 15 July 1914, Folder 12, Box 2, Operative Reports; Memoranda, 16, 21 July 1914, Folder 4, Box 3, Strike Records.

10. Husband-Robinson Report; Memo from Oscar Elsas, 16 July 1914, Folder 4, Box 3, Strike Records; Report of no. 115, 24 July 1914, Folder 7, Box 1, Operative Reports; Weed, "Preliminary Report."

11. *AJ*, 20 September 1905; Grantham, *Hoke Smith*, 147; Claude N. Bennett to Oscar Elsas, 19 September 1914, Folder 5, Box 4, Strike Records.

12. Oscar Elsas to Claude N. Bennett, 21, 25 July 1914, Folder 2, Box 4, Strike Records.

13. Claude N. Bennett to Oscar Elsas, 25, 27 July 1914, Folder 2, Box 4, Strike Records.

14. Claude N. Bennett to Oscar Elsas, 18 August 1914, Folder 2, Box 4, Strike Records; Jacob Elsas to William S. West, 20 August 1914, and West to Jacob Elsas, 24 August 1914, both in Folder 13, Box 5, Strike Records; J. S. Brand to West, 26 August 1914, Case File 33/41, RG 280; Oscar Elsas to Bennett, 9 October 1914, and Bennett to Oscar Elsas, 13 October 1914, both in Folder 6, Box 4, Strike Records; Oscar Elsas to Bennett, 21 November 1914, Folder 8, Box 4, Strike Records; Bennett to Oscar Elsas, 8, 24 December 1914, and Oscar Elsas to Bennett, 26 December 1914, both in Folder 9, Box 4, Strike Records.

15. Alexander M. Daly, "A Brief Survey of Textiles in Massachusetts and Rhode Island," Reel 4; Daly, "Strikes in the Bituminous Coal Fields of Ohio," Folder 575, Reel 7; and Daly, "Brief Inquiry into the Relations between Employer and Employee in the Textile Industry in the City of Philadelphia and State of Pennsylvania," Folder 574, Reel 12, all in CIR Microfilm.

16. Adams, *Age of Industrial Violence*, 210.

17. Alexander Daly to Oscar Elsas, 28 July 1914, Folder 5, Box 3, Strike Records.

18. Daly Report; Daly, "Welfare Work in Iron and Steel ACIPCO, Birmingham," Reel 6, and Daly, "Industrial Relations and Labor Conditions in the Birmingham Steel and Iron Industry," Reel 12, both in CIR Microfilm; Minutes, MRFM Executive Committee, 27 July 1914, CCC; Oscar Elsas to David Clark, 4 September 1914, Folder 4, Box 4, Strike Records.

19. Alexander M. Daly to Charles McCarthy, 31 July 1914, RG 174.

20. Weed, "Instead of Strikes"; Weed and Carey, "I Make Cheap Silk"; Golin, *Fragile Bridge*, 144. On *Masses*, see Leach, "Radicals of *The Masses*," and Fishbein, *Rebels in Bohemia*.

21. Weed, "Preliminary Report." Emphasis in original.

22. Testimony of Louie P. Marquardt, 7–8, "Testimony for the Complainants," Box 6, Strike Records; Mrs. E. B. Smith to Frank Morrison, 8 August 1914, Frank Morrison Letter-

books, Duke; Samuel Gompers to Mrs. E. B. Smith, 12 August 1914, Gompers Copybooks, Library of Congress, Washington, D.C.

23. Report of no. 115, 1 September 1914, Folder 8, Box 1, Operative Reports. A reference to the Atlanta tent colony as "A Second Ludlow" appeared in *Textile Worker* 3, no. 7 (December 1914): 21. Oscar Elsas also made the connection, stating that in establishing the tent colony, the UTW was "imitating the Colorado method" (Oscar Elsas to H. W. Butterworth, 17 December 1914, Folder 9, Box 4, Strike Records). MRFM members had also referred to Ludlow at the 12 July mass meeting (see *AC*, 13 July 1914).

24. Memo, 28 August 1914, Folder 16, Box 1, Strike Records. According to Claude Bennett, Colpoys was the editor of a Washington, D.C., labor paper; by early 1916, he was secretary of the Washington Central Labor Union (Claude N. Bennett to Oscar Elsas, 8 December 1914, Folder 9, Box 4, Strike Records; *JOL*, 28 January 1916).

25. Reports of no. 115, 28 August–2 September, 6 September 1914, Folder 8, Box 1, and Report of no. 115, 11 September 1914, Folder 9, Box 1, all in Operative Reports; Testimony of Mrs. R. H. [Sallie] Wright, 4, "Testimony for the Defendants."

26. Report of no. 115, 2 September 1914, Folder 8, Box 1, Operative Reports.

27. Report of no. 457, 28 October 1914, Folder 26, Box 2, and Reports of no. 457, 29 November, 4 December 1914, Folder 27, Box 2, all in Operative Reports; Draft of article by Arthur St. George Joyce, n.d. [16 December 1914], Folder 9, Box 4, Strike Records.

28. Reports of no. 115, 27 August, 1 September 1914, Folder 8, Box 1, Operative Reports.

29. *Textile Worker* 3, no. 8 (January 1915): 20; "Notes from the Strikers' Camp," *JOL*, 19 September–4 December 1914.

30. Report of W. L. Shields, 19 September 1914, and Memo from James I. Brush, 22 September 1914, both in Folder 11, Box 5, Strike Records.

31. Report of no. 115, 12 September 1914, Folder 8, Box 1, Operative Reports.

32. R. H. Wright to Harry G. Preston, 23 September 1914, Folder 9, Box 1, and Wright to Preston, 22 November, 21 December 1914, Folder 4, Box 1, all in Operative Reports.

33. For Calahan's occupation, see Kuhn and Hough, *Generations of Sheet Metal Craftsmanship*, 59–62.

34. Reports of no. 115, 2–3 September 1914, Folder 8, Box 1, and Report of no. 457, 6 December 1914, Folder 27, Box 2, all in Operative Reports; Testimony by H. N. Mullinax, 40, "Testimony for the Complainants"; Testimony by R. H. Wright (recalled), 6, "Testimony for the Defendants."

35. Reports of no. 115, 27–29 July 1914, Folder 8, Box 1, Operative Reports.

36. Reports of no. 115, 12, 14, 17–18 September 1914, Folder 9, Box 1, Operative Reports; Testimony by R. H. Wright (recalled), 2, "Testimony for the Defendants."

37. R. H. Wright to Harry G. Preston, 21 December 1914, Folder 4, Box 1, Operative Reports; Report of no. 115, 12 September 1914, Folder 8, Box 1, Operative Reports.

38. Report of no. 115, 10 September 1914, Folder 9, Box 1, Operative Reports; Testimony by R. H. Wright (recalled), 3, 6, "Testimony for the Defendants."

39. Report of no. 115, 14 September 1914, and R. H. Wright to Harry G. Preston, 23 September 1914, both in Folder 9, Box 1, Operative Reports; Report of no. 115, 17 October 1914, Folder 10, Box 1, Operative Reports; Report of no. 457, 11 December 1914, Folder 27, Box 2, Operative Reports; R. H. Wright to Harry G. Preston, 21 December 1914, Folder 4, Box 1, Operative Reports; Testimony by R. H. Wright (recalled), 4–5, "Testimony for the Defendants."

40. Report of no. 115, 19 September 1914, Folder 9, Box 1; Report of no. 457, 6 December 1914, Folder 27, Box 2; and Memo from Oscar Elsas, 12 January 1915, Folder 31, Box 2, all in Operative Reports; "Residents of Textile Camp 3-17-15," Folder 5, Box 3, Strike Records.

41. Report of no. 115, 10 September 1914, Folder 9, Box 1; Memo from Oscar Elsas, 20 January 1915, Folder 1, Box 1; and Reports of no. 16, 23 December 1914–20 January 1915, Folder 31, Box 2, all in Operative Reports.

42. Reports of no. 115, 11, 13, 25 September 1914, Folder 9, Box 1, and Report of no. 115, 23 October 1914, Folder 10, Box 1, all in Operative Reports.

43. Reports of no. 115, 1, 6 September 1914, Folder 8, Box 1, and Reports of no. 115, 7, 12 September 1914, Folder 9, Box 1, all in Operative Reports; Memoranda, 27 August, 8 October 1914, Folder 4, Box 5, Strike Records.

44. Report of no. 115, 12 September 1914, Folder 9, Box 1, Operative Reports.

45. Reports from no. 115, 19–23 September 1914, and Harry G. Preston to E. G. Myers, 24 September 1914, all in Folder 9, Box 1, Operative Reports. It is unclear whether Johnstone was in Boston on other business or specifically to meet with Preston.

46. Report of no. 115, 24 September 1914, Folder 9, Box 1, Operative Reports.

47. Ibid., 25 September 1914.

48. John B. Morgan to Oscar Elsas, 5 October 1914; Elsas to Morgan, 8 October 1914; Morgan to Elsas, 12 October 1914; and Elsas to Morgan, 14 October 1914, all in Folder 6, Box 4, Strike Records.

49. Memo of Oscar Elsas, 8 October 1914, Folder 8, Box 5; Flyer, n.d. [October 1914], Folder 3, Box 1; and Text of speech by John Golden, 11 October 1914, Folder 2, Box 3, all in Strike Records; R. H. Wright to Harry G. Preston, 14 October 1914, and Report of no. 115, 17 October 1914, both in Folder 10, Box 1, Operative Reports; Testimony of R. H. Wright, 33–34, and Testimony of R. H. Wright (recalled), 3, both in "Testimony for the Defendants."

50. Reports of no. 115, 19, 21–24, 27–28 October 1914, Folder 10, Box 1, Operative Reports.

51. Oscar Elsas to C. L. Denk, 26 October 1914; Denk to Elsas, 1 November 1914; and Elsas to Denk, 3 November 1914, all in Folder 7, Box 4, Strike Records. Denk, a salesman for Fulton Mills, was the son of company treasurer August Denk.

52. Report of no. 115, 24 June 1914, Folder 6, Box 1, and Reports of no. 115, 20, 22, 24 October 1914, Folder 10, Box 1, all in Operative Reports.

53. Reports of no. 115, 25, 28 October 1914, Folder 10, Box 1, and T. C. Cary to E. G. Myers, 28 October 1914, Folder 3, Box 1, all in Operative Reports; Sara Conboy to Harry G. Preston, n.d., and Preston to Oscar Elsas, 7 August 1916, both in Folder 4, Box 1, Operative Reports; List of witnesses to testify at CIR hearings, Folder 4, Box 3, Strike Records; Testimony of R. H. Wright (recalled), 1, 4, "Testimony for the Defendants."

54. "Golden's Talk," 1 November 1914, Folder 19, Box 1, Strike Records; Report of no. 457, 6 December 1914, Folder 27, Box 2, and Report of no. 457, 13 December 1914, Folder 28, Box 2, both in Operative Reports; "Rules for Camp," RG 174.

55. Mrs. E. B. Smith, " 'The Story Told in Pictures': Pictures Taken and Compiled by: Mrs. E. B. Smith," photo album, George Meany Memorial Archives, Silver Spring, Maryland, copy in Special Collections, Southern Labor Archives, Georgia State University, Atlanta, Ga.

56. Ibid.; Photographs, RG 280.

57. R. H. Wright to Harry G. Preston, 22 November 1914, Folder 4, Box 1, Operative Reports; Textile Worker 3, no. 8 (January 1915): 20.

58. Report of W. L. Shields, 11 November 1914, Folder 2, Box 3, Strike Records; Pittman and Harrison to David Elsas, 5 October 1914, and David Elsas to Oscar Elsas, 8 October 1914, both in Folder 4, Box 5, Strike Records.

59. Claude N. Bennett to Oscar Elsas, 19 September 1914, Folder 5, Box 4, Strike Records; Columbus Citizen, 30 September 1914; Fort Smith Southwest American, 4 October 1914.

60. Reports of no. 115, 19, 21, 28 October 1914, Folder 10, Box 1, Operative Reports; Textile Worker 3, no. 7 (December 1914): 21.

61. *Textile Worker* 3, no. 8 (January 1915): 12; Report of Proceedings of the Thirty-fourth Annual Convention of the American Federation of Labor, 1914, 341–42; *American Federationist* 22 (January 1915): 47–48.

62. Arthur St. George Joyce to Jacob Elsas, 14 December 1914; Statement, 15 December 1914; Draft of article by St. George Joyce, n.d. [16 December 1914]; Oscar Elsas to St. George Joyce, 16 December 1914; Oscar Elsas to Editor, *Philadelphia North American*, 16 December 1914; Oscar Elsas to Editor, *Philadelphia North American*, 17 December 1914; Oscar Elsas to H. W. Butterworth, 17 December 1914 [three letters]; Oscar Elsas to no. 154 [Adolph Elsas], 17 December 1914; Oscar Elsas to James A. Emery, 17 December 1914; Oscar Elsas to St. George Joyce, 17 December 1914; and St. George Joyce to Oscar Elsas, Thursday [17 December 1914], all in Folder 9, Box 4, Strike Records; Harry W. Butterworth to Oscar Elsas, 17 December 1914; Louis J. Elsas to Harry Poth, 17 December 1914; St. George Joyce to Oscar Elsas, 22 December 1914; Oscar Elsas to B. Z. Phillips, 22 December 1914; and James A. Emery to Oscar Elsas, 23 December 1914, all in Folder 10, Box 4, Strike Records.

63. Memorandum for Secretary Wilson by John B. Colpoys and Robert M. McWade, 18 August 1915, Case File 33/41, RG 280; Memo from Oscar Elsas, 20 November 1914, Folder 13, Box 5, and Oscar Elsas to Claude N. Bennett, 21 November 1914, Folder 8, Box 4, Strike Records.

64. Memo, 27 November 1914, Folder 16, Box 1, Strike Records; McWade and Colpoys Report.

65. F. A. Weiss to Oscar Elsas, 22 April 1915, Folder 16, Box 4, Strike Records.

66. U.S. Congress, House, 63rd Cong., 2nd sess., H.R. 621; Claude N. Bennett to Oscar Elsas, 16 September 1914, Folder 5, Box 4, Strike Records.

67. Oscar Elsas to Claude N. Bennett, 15 September 1914; Bennett to Elsas, 16 September 1914; and Elsas to William Schley Howard, 17 September 1914, all in Folder 5, Box 4, Strike Records.

68. Claude N. Bennett to Oscar Elsas, 16 September 1914, Folder 5, Box 4, Strike Records; William Schley Howard to Elsas, 2 October 1914, and Bennett to Elsas, 5 October 1914, both in Folder 6, Box 4, Strike Records.

69. James A. Emery to Oscar Elsas, 19 September 1914, Folder 5, Box 4, Strike Records.

70. Oscar Elsas to James A. Emery, 21 September 1914; Elsas to Claude N. Bennett, 21 September 1914; and Bennett to Elsas, 23 September 1914, all in Folder 5, Box 4, Strike Records.

71. *AG*, 1 October 1914; Oscar Elsas to Claude N. Bennett, 2 October 1914; Elsas to John S. Candler, 2 October 1914; Candler to Elsas, 3 October 1914; and Candler to Thomas W. Hardwick, 3 October 1914, all in Folder 6, Box 4, Strike Records.

72. John Golden to William S. Greene, 8 December 1914, in *Congressional Record*, 64th Cong., 1st sess., 5842.

73. J. F. Bradfield to William Schley Howard, 5 December 1914, and Howard to Bradfield, 9 December 1914, both reprinted in *Congressional Record*, 64th Cong., 1st sess., 5841.

74. Oscar Elsas to William Schley Howard, 23, 28 November, 7 December 1914, Folder 8, Box 4, Strike Records.

75. *Congressional Record*, 64th Cong., 1st sess., 5840–42.

76. Claude N. Bennett to Oscar Elsas, 16, 17, 19 September 1914, Folder 5, Box 4, Strike Records.

77. Claude N. Bennett to Oscar Elsas, 23 September 1914, Folder 5, Box 4, Strike Records. *Kansas City Journal*, 8 November 1914, in Volume 31, Box 34, Walsh Papers.

78. Oscar Elsas to Arthur D. Lown, 19 September 1914; Elsas to James A. Emery, 21 September 1914; and Elsas to Claude N. Bennett, 21 September 1914, all in Folder 5, Box 4, Strike

Records. The Joint Commission of Associated Employers included the NAM, the NCID, the National Metal Trades Association, and the National Erectors Association (Adams, *Age of Industrial Violence*, 210).

79. Oscar Elsas to Claude N. Bennett, 8 February 1915, Folder 12, Box 4; Bennett to Elsas, 11 February 1915, Folder 13, Box 4; Elsas to M. C. Sloss, 18 March 1915, Folder 5, Box 3; Sloss to Elsas, 15 April 1915, Folder 7, Box 3; and Elsas to Walter Drew, 12 April 1915, Folder 16, Box 4, all in Strike Records; Adams, *Age of Industrial Violence*, 63–64. On Weinstock, see Larsen, "A Progressive in Agriculture," and Weinstock, "Free Speech."

80. Oscar Elsas to Claude N. Bennett, 8 February 1915, and Bennett to Elsas, 11 February 1915, both in Folder 12, Box 4, Strike Records; Elsas to A. Mayer, 13 February 1915, Folder 13, Box 4, and Dave [Elsas] to Oscar [Elsas], 20 March 1915, Folder 14, Box 4, both in Strike Records.

81. Oscar Elsas to Edwards-Adams Studio, 27 March 1915, Folder 14, Box 4, Strike Records.

82. James A. Emery to Oscar Elsas, 15 February 1915, Folder 12, Box 4, and Emery to Elsas, 3 March 1915, Folder 14, Box 4, both in Strike Records.

83. James A. Emery to Oscar Elsas, 11 March 1915, Folder 14, Box 4, Strike Records.

84. Ibid.; Emery to Elsas, 15 February 1915, Folder 12, Box 4, and Walter Drew to Rosser, Brandon, Slaton, and Phillips, 11 March 1915, Folder 14, Box 4, both in Strike Records.

85. Oscar Elsas to Walter Drew, 3, 6 March 1915, Folder 14, Box 4, Strike Records.

86. Weed, "Preliminary Report"; Weed Report, 19 September 1914; McWade and Colpoys Report.

87. Oscar Elsas to Walter Drew, 9 March 1915, Folder 14, Box 4, Strike Records; McWade and Colpoys Report.

88. James A. Emery to Oscar Elsas, 11 March 1915, and Walter Drew to Rosser, Brandon, Slaton, and Phillips, 11 March 1915, both in Folder 14, Box 4, Strike Records.

89. Among his other activities, Macintyre helped Elsas track down a report that a local bread company was donating food to the tent city residents. Elsas was only mollified when it turned out that an Atlanta man was making a film to raise funds for Belgian hunger relief, and, in perhaps the most remarkable misrepresentation of the whole affair, had cast the strikers as starving Belgians! See Folder 53, Box 8, Strike Records.

90. Oscar Elsas to Walter Drew, 9, 17 March 1915, and Alexander M. Daly to Elsas, 17 March 1915, all in Folder 14, Box 4, Strike Records.

91. Alexander M. Daly to Oscar Elsas, 25 February 1915, Folder 13, Box 4, and Daly to Elsas, 17 March 1915, Folder 14, Box 4, both in Strike Records; Telegram from Basil M. Manly to Frank P. Walsh, 12 March 1915, Box 2, Folder 47, and Manly to Walsh, 23 April 1915, Box 2, Folder 49, both in Walsh Papers; Adams, *Age of Industrial Violence*, 208; *JOL*, 26 March 1915.

92. Oscar Elsas to H. P. Meikleham, 30 March 1915, Folder 14, Box 4, and Elsas to Meikleham, 14 May 1915, Folder 18, Box 4, both in Strike Records. The possibility does exist that Elsas was exaggerating the role of the Joint Committee of Associated Employers in his frustrating effort to seek a contribution from the GCMA to the organization and in his attempt to help organize a Georgia Manufacturers Association along the lines of the NAM.

93. In addition to that of Mullinax, see in particular testimony of A. K. Wilson, Minnie B. Ware, Sarah Nations, Lina McFarland, Rufus F. Odell, S. B. Marks, Louie P. Marquardt, Columbus L. Howell, G. R. Buford, Lucretia Briley, Marion M. Jackson, William J. Allen, W. E. Fleming, and Lee Turner, all in "Testimony for the Complainants."

94. In addition to that of Elsas and Johnstone, see testimony of T. S. Florence, E. H. Rogers, P. A. Smith, Mabel Emma Wheeler, and Emma Burton, all in "Testimony for the Defendants."

95. In addition to that of Sweatt (quote on 15) and Wright (recalled two times), see also

testimony of Mrs. R. H. [Sallie] Wright, Fannie Carter, Jennie Clinton, Andrew Jackson Clark, and Harris Gober, all in "Testimony for the Defendants."

96. Testimony of E. H. Rogers, 5–9, and Testimony of T. S. Florence, 5–7, both in "Testimony for the Defendants."

97. Testimony of Alfred S. Guffin, 8; Testimony of Mrs. R. H. [Sallie] Wright, 1–3, 30–31; Testimony of Harris Gober, 5–6; and Testimony of E. H. Rogers, 21, all in "Testimony for the Defendants"; A. S. Guffin to the public, 1 July 1914, Folder 64, Box 8, Strike Records.

98. Oscar Elsas to Walter Drew, 7 July 1915, Folder 20, Box 4, Strike Records. Emphasis in original.

99. *Congressional Record*, 17 April 1915, 64th Cong., 1st sess., 6275–77; *JOL*, 28 January, 24 March, 14 April 1916; Frank P. Walsh to Herbert S. Bigelow, 24 August 1915, Box 2, Folder 47, Walsh Papers. It is unclear whether any direct connection existed between the Fulton situation and Smith's leadership in opposition to the CIR.

CONCLUSION

1. Gary Fink, *Fulton Bag and Cotton Mills Strike*, 140–57.

2. Daly Report.

3. Report of no. 115, 8 July 1914, Folder 7, Box 1, Operative Reports.

4. Lippmann, *Public Opinion*.

5. De Graffenreid, "Georgia Cracker in the Cotton Mills"; Baker, *Following the Color Line*; U.S. Congress, Senate, "Family Budgets of Typical Cotton Mill Workers" and "Cotton Textile Industry."

6. E. Darden Borders to Oscar Elsas, 28 July 1914, Folder 3, Box 4, Strike Records; Testimony of E. H. Rogers, 21, "Testimony for the Defendants"; Testimony of H. N. Mullinax, 52, "Testimony for the Complainants"; Oscar Elsas to Will Nally, 3 June 1914, Folder 7, Box 8; Affidavit of C. H. Gartman, 26 June 1914, Folder 8, Box 1; and R. T. Jones to Elsas, 8 June 1914, Folder 12, Box 3, all in Strike Records; S. C. Smyly to Elsas, 15 June 1915, and Elsas to American Textile Company, 13 June 1914, both in Folder 13, Box 3, Strike Records; Memo, 15 January 1915, Folder 11, Box 4, Strike Records.

7. For instance, Oscar Elsas to Franklin W. Hobbs, 24 June 1914, Folder 15, Box 3, and Gordon A Johnstone to Roxbury Carpet, 22 July 1914, Folder 2, Box 4, both in Strike Records; J. Eugene Cochrane to Johnstone, 14 July 1914, and Elsas to Hobbs, both in Folder 3, Box 4, Strike Records; Elsas to A. D. Lown, 5 September, Folder 5, Box 4; C. J. H. Woodbury to Elsas, 27 November 1914, Folder 8, Box 4; and Elsas to Summit Silk Mills, 23 February 1915, Folder 13, Box 4, all in Strike Records.

8. Testimony of Mrs. R. H. [Sallie] Wright, 10, "Testimony for the Defendants"; Memo, 3 June 1915, Folder 64, Box 8; R. H. Wright to Fulton Bag and Cotton Mills, 22 January 1915, Folder 11, Box 4; and Dan Ellis to Thomas S. Florance [*sic*], 9 March 1915, Folder 14, Box 4, all in Strike Records. Another individual who had difficulty finding employment after the CIR was disbanded was Alexander Daly. See Charles McCarthy to Joe Davies, 8 April 1915, McCarthy Papers, State Historical Society of Wisconsin, Madison, Wisc.

9. Sallie Wright to August Denk, 27 September 1914, Folder 64, Box 8, Strike Records.

10. The Wrights remained in the neighborhood near Fulton Mills, where Robert Wright worked primarily as a carpenter.

11. Testimony of T. S. Florence, 3–4, and Testimony of Oscar Elsas, 7, 10, both in "Testimony for the Defendants"; Minutes, Executive Committee, 22 June 1916, Volume 8, Box 2, FBCM-Emory.

12. Minutes, Stockholders meeting, 10 January 1916, Volume 7, Box 2, FBCM-Emory; Testimony of Oscar Elsas, 10, "Testimony for the Defendants."

13. "Head Notes of talk at Wesley House night of 6/11/15," Folder 49, Box 8, and Oscar Elsas to Allen F. Johnson, 5 October 1914, Folder 6, Box 4, Strike Records.

14. Elsas, interview by author, 5 October 1990; Hall et al., *Like a Family*, 201, 209, 215, 393 (n. 57); Pope, *Millhands and Preachers*, 229–33; Salmond, *Gastonia 1929*, 14–16, 40.

15. *The Fulton* 4 (June 1918); 5 (July 1919), in OBV 7, FBCM-Emory; Minutes, Board of Directors, 8, 19 January, 16 May 1917, 2 January 1918, Box 3, and Minutes, Executive Committee, 18 January 1917, Volume 8, Box 2, all in FBCM-Emory.

16. Flamming, *Creating the Modern South*, 130–41.

17. Maclachlan, "Woman's Place," 7–9; Rhodes, "Brief Report."

18. Maclachlan, "Woman's Place," 8–9.

19. "Personnel records—Old File," FBCM-GIT.

20. Oscar Elsas to Jacob Elsas, 17 July 1914, Folder 3, Box 4, Strike Records.

21. H. P. Meikleham to Oscar Elsas, 28 October, 2 November 1914, Folder 6, Box 4, Strike Records.

22. Oscar Elsas to H. P. Meikleham, April 1915, Folder 15, Box 4, and Elsas to A. R. Colcord, 23 October, 5 December 1914, Folder 8, Box 4, all in Strike Records.

23. Testimony of Oscar Elsas, 26, in "Testimony for the Defendants."

24. Harry G. Preston to Oscar Elsas, 7 August, 20 October 1916, Folder 4, Box 1, Operative Reports; Gary Fink, "Efficiency and Control."

25. Fuller E. Callaway to Oscar Elsas, 27 November 1915; H. N. Brown to Elsas, 29 December 1915; Brown to Elsas, 17 May 1916; Harry G. Preston to Elsas, 7 August 1916; and Preston to Elsas, 20 October 1916, all in Folder 4, Box 1, Operative Reports; Elsas to Joseph B. Morgan, 8 October 1914, Folder 6, Box 4, and Ernest Koella to Elsas, 20 April 1915, Folder 16, Box 4, both in Strike Records.

26. George S. Mitchell, *Textile Unionism and the South*, 22; Two memoranda, 18 October 1915, Folder 5, Box 5, Strike Records; Oscar Elsas to Allen Johnson, 5 January 1916; Memo, 15 January 1916; and Elsas to F. B. Gordon, 14, 23 February 1916, all in Folder 2, Box 5, Strike Records; Flyer, 17 March 1917, Folder 1, Box 5; Report of Operative G. L. B., 6 June 1918, Folder 15, Box 5; and H. N. Mullinax to Chrystal Springs Bag Manufacturing Company, 17 February 1915, Folder 3, Box 1, all in Strike Records; Case 159, Case Files, RG 2, p. 853; Kuhn et al., *Living Atlanta*, 14.

27. F. A. Weiss to Oscar Elsas, 22 April 1915, and Elsas to Weiss, 21 May 1915, both in Folder 16, Box 4, Strike Records; George W. Robertson to Elsas, 14 October 1915, and Elsas to Riverside and Dan River Cotton Mills, 16 October 1915, both in Folder 5, Box 5, Strike Records; Oscar Elsas to F. B. Gordon, 5 March 1919, Folder 22, Box 8, Strike Records.

28. Oscar Elsas to Allen F. Johnson, 9 July 1914, Folder 1, Box 4, Strike Records; Elsas to Edward H. Inman, 28 April 1915, and Elsas to C. N. Daniels, 28 April 1915, both in Folder 16, Box 4, Strike Records; Elsas to F. B. Gordon, 14 May 1915, Folder 17, Box 4; Elsas to F. A. Weiss, 6 April 1916, Folder 2, Box 5; J. F. Trazzare to the members of the Employers' Association of Atlanta, 19 May 1919, Folder 59, Box 8; and Elsas to Ben Z. Phillips, 18 February 1915, Folder 11, Box 4, all in Strike Records; Photograph of "First Annual Meeting, Georgia Manufacturers Association," 10 February 1916, Folder 11, Box 1, FBCM-Emory.

29. Lefever, "Prostitution, Politics, and Religion," 28–29; Thomas, "John J. Eagan," 270–88. It is not clear whether there was any direct connection between Eagan's involvement in the Fulton strike and his subsequent industrial plan.

30. Union attendance list, 30 May 1914, Folder 11, Box 2, Strike Records; Reports of J. W.

W., 15–16 June 1914, Folder 2, Box 1, Operative Reports; *AJ*, 29 November 1916; *AC*, 30 November 1916. For more on the streetcar strike, see Kuhn et al., *Living Atlanta*, 14–20.

31. *AC*, 30 November 1916.

32. *JOL*, 7 April 1950.

33. Kuhn et al., *Living Atlanta*, 218–20; "The oppressed weavers of the Fulton Bag and Cotton Mills to Presedent [*sic*] Roosevelt," 21 March 1934, Records of the National Recovery Administration, RG 398, National Archives, Washington, D.C.

34. See, for instance, *AJC*, 15 December 1974, 19 May 1979; *AJ*, 9 May 1980; *AJC*, 6 March 1983; *New York Times*, 30 October 1984; *AC*, 5 August 1988, 21 April 1991; "What's Cookin' in Cabbagetown," AUDC [Atlanta Urban Design Commission] Newsletter, 1, no. 3 (September 1978): 34–38; and Flowers and Putter, "Cabbagetown," 34. In addition to uncritically assuming that Cabbagetown residents and Fulton workers came from the mountains, the authors of some of these articles resorted to stereotypes and condescension in their descriptions of the community and its residents. One reporter, for example, referred to Cabbagetown as "an island of Dogpatch in the shadow of urban America" (*AJC*, 29 August 1982).

35. See, for example, Porter, ed., *Cabbagetown Families*; Bynum, *Cabbagetown*; and "Cabbagetown Learning Center."

36. Durban, *All Set about with Fever Trees*, 12–13.

BIBLIOGRAPHY

MANUSCRIPT SOURCES

Athens, Georgia
    Hargrett Library, University of Georgia
        Atlanta Typographical Union Women's Auxiliary Collection
        Joseph M. Brown Papers
Atlanta, Georgia
    Atlanta Chamber of Commerce
        Atlanta Chamber of Commerce Records
    Atlanta Historical Society
        Atlanta Police Department Papers
        Christian Council Collection
        John Eagan Papers
        Living Atlanta Collection
        Robert F. Maddox Collection
        Samuel P. Richards Papers
    Atlanta Jewish Federation, Ida Pearl and Joseph Cuba Archives and Genealogy Center
        Elsas Collection
    Emory University, Woodruff Library, Special Collections
        Fulton Bag and Cotton Mills Collection
    Georgia Institute of Technology, Archives, Price Gilbert Memorial Library
        Fulton Bag and Cotton Mills Collection
    Georgia State University, Southern Labor Archives, Special Collections
        Al Kuettner Papers
        Mrs. E. B. Smith Collection
    Wesley Community Centers
        Wesley House Records
Boston, Massachusetts
    Harvard Business School, Baker Library
        R. G. Dun and Company Collection
Durham, North Carolina
    Duke University, Perkins Library
        H. P. Blount Papers
        John Emory Bryant Papers
        Frank Morrison Letterbooks

Madison, Wisconsin
  State Historical Society of Wisconsin
    Charles McCarthy Papers
New York, New York
  New York Public Library
    Frank P. Walsh Papers
Suitland, Maryland
  National Archives and Records Administration
    Records of the Federal Mediation and Conciliation Service, Record Group 280
    Records of the National War Labor Board, Record Group 2
Washington, D.C.
National Archives and Records Administration
    Records of the National Recovery Administration, Record Group 398
    Records of the United States Commission on Industrial Relations, Record Group 174
    Records of the United States Housing Corporation, Record Group 3

INTERVIEWS

Bratcher, Levie. Interview by Pam [Durban] Porter, n.d. [1976?]. Tape recording. Atlanta, Georgia. In possession of Pamela Durban.

Brookshire, Lila Brown. Interview by Pam [Durban] Porter, n.d. [1976?]. Tape recording. Atlanta, Georgia. In possession of Pamela Durban.

Brown, Marion. Interview by author, 26 January 1979, Atlanta, Georgia. Tape recording. Living Atlanta Collection, Atlanta Historical Society.

Dennis, Alec, et al. Interview by author, 29 January 1979, Atlanta, Georgia. Tape recording. Living Atlanta Collection, Atlanta Historical Society.

Duke, Daniel. Interview by author and Anne Larcom, 3 October 1990, Tyrone, Georgia. Georgia Government Documentation Project, Special Collections, Georgia State University.

Elsas, Norman. Interview by author, 5 October 1990, Atlanta, Georgia. Tape recording. In possession of author.

———. Interview by author, 6 March 1991, Atlanta, Georgia. Tape recording. In possession of author.

———. Interview by Robert C. McMath Jr. In "History by a Graveyard" television program, Prime Cable DeKalb, Atlanta, Georgia, 1989.

———. Interview by Steve Oney, December 1988, Atlanta, Georgia. Tape recording. In possession of Steve Oney.

Eplan, Samuel. Interview by author, 1981, Atlanta, Georgia. Tape recording. In possession of author.

Freeman, Calvin. Interview by author, 14 January 1979, Atlanta, Georgia. Tape recording. Living Atlanta Collection, Atlanta Historical Society.

Garrett, Franklin M. Interview by author, 10 October 1990, Atlanta, Georgia. Tape recording. Interview in possession of author.

Gray, Effie Dodd. Interview by author, 9 November 1978, Atlanta, Georgia. Tape recording. Living Atlanta Collection, Atlanta Historical Society.

Roden, Nancy. Interview by Pam [Durban] Porter, n.d. [1976?]. Atlanta, Georgia. Tape recording. In possession of Pamela Durban.

Washburn, Nanny. Interview by author, 8 December 1978, Atlanta, Georgia. Tape recording. Living Atlanta Collection, Atlanta Historical Society.

MICROFILM

Dubofsky, Melvin, ed. U.S. Commission on Industrial Relations, 1912–15. Unpublished Records of the Division of Research and Investigation: Reports, Staff Studies, and Background Research Materials. Frederick, Md.: University Publications of America, 1985.
American Federation of Labor Records: The Samuel Gompers Era. Sanford, N.C.: Microfilm Corporation of America, 1979.

GOVERNMENT DOCUMENTS

Census of Manufactures, 1880.
Fulton County Health Department, Minutes, 1910–15, Atlanta, Georgia.
Fulton County Superior Court. Deed Book JJ. Atlanta, Georgia.
National Register of Historic Places. Inventory-Nomination Form: Cabbagetown District. Unpublished survey, Georgia Department of Natural Resources, Historic Preservation Section, 1975.
Twelfth Census of the United States, 1900.
Thirteenth Census of the United States, 1910.
U.S. Congress. House. 63rd Cong., 2nd sess., H.R. 621. *Congressional Record* (15 September 1914).
——. Congressman William S. Greene of Massachusetts and others speaking before Committee of the Whole House considering appropriations to supply deficiencies in appropriations for the fiscal year 1915. H.R. 21546. 64th Cong., 1st sess. *Congressional Record* (26 February 1915).
——. Congressman William Schley Howard of Georgia speaking on a point of personal privilege. 64th Cong., 1st sess. *Congressional Record* (2 March 1915): 5840–42.
——. U.S. Industrial Commission, "Report on . . . the Relations and Conditions of Capital and Labor." House Record No. 184, vol. 7, 57th Cong., 1st sess. Washington, D.C.: Government Printing Office, 1900.
U.S. Congress. Senate. "Cotton Textile Industry." Vol. 1 of *Report on Condition of Woman and Child Wage-Earners in the United States*. Senate Document No. 645, 61st Cong., 2nd sess. Washington, D.C.: Government Printing Office, 1910.
——. "Family Budgets of Typical Cotton Workers." Vol. 16 of *Report on Condition of Woman and Child Wage-Earners in the United States*. Senate Document No. 645, 61st Cong., 2nd sess. Washington, D.C.: Government Printing Office, 1910.
——. "The Beginnings of Child Labor Legislation in Certain States: A Comparative Study." Vol. 6 of *Report on Condition of Woman and Child Wage-Earners in the United States*. Senate Document No. 645, 61st Cong., 2nd sess. Washington, D.C.: Government Printing Office, 1911.
——. Board of Trade of London, "Cost of Living in American Towns." Senate Document No. 22, 62nd Cong., 1st sess. Washington, D.C.: Government Printing Office, 1911.
——. Senator Hoke Smith of Georgia and others speaking on the U.S. Commission on Industrial Relations. 63rd Cong., 2nd sess. *Congressional Record* (7 July 1914): 11681–90.
——. Senator Hoke Smith of Georgia and others speaking about the printing of testimony

taken by the U.S. Commission on Industrial Relations. 64th Cong., 1st sess. *Congressional Record* (17 April 1915): 6275–77.

U.S. Department of Labor. Bureau of Labor Statistics. Consumer Price Index, U.S. City Average, 15 July 1990.

——. *Bulletin #330*, September 1900.

LEGAL SOURCES

Gleaton v. Fulton Bag and Cotton Mills, 5 *Georgia Appeals*, 420.

Fulton Bag and Cotton Mills v. Wilson, *Georgia Reports* 89 (March Term 1892), 318–19.

Masters and Servants, Contracts between, Exempting Master from Liability for Negligence, *Georgia Laws*, 1895, No. 184.

Mrs. O. L. Smith v. Edgar B. Smith, Divorce Suit, September Term, 1915, Fulton Superior Court.

Mrs. O. L. Smith v. E. B. Smith, Petition for Divorce, and Cross-bill by defendant and second verdict for defendant upon his Cross-bill in Fulton Superior Court, 7 June 1917.

Winn. v. Fulton Bag and Cotton Mills, 10 *Georgia Appeals*, (March Term 1914), 33–34.

PROCEEDINGS

American Federation of Labor
Annual Meeting of the National Child Labor Committee, 1905, 1906
Knights of Labor
United Textile Workers

NEWSPAPER AND PERIODICALS

American Federationist
America's Textile Reporter
Atlanta Constitution
Atlanta Georgian
Atlanta Journal
Atlanta Star
Atlanta Sunday-American
Atlanta Sunday Telegram
Augusta Chronicle
Charlotte News
Columbus Citizen
Columbus Ledger
Fall River Daily Globe
Fort Smith Southwest American
Greenville Daily News
Greenville Daily Piedmont
Journal of Labor
Kansas City Journal
Looking Glass
Manufacturer's Record
Mill News
New Bedford Morning Standard

Party Builder
Philadelphia Globe
Philadelphia Ledger
Plumbers, Gas and Steam Fitters Journal
Rome Tribune Herald
Skyland Magazine
Southern Textile Bulletin
Strikers Journal
Survey
Textile Industries
Textile Manufacturer
Textile Worker
Textile World
Working World

MISCELLANEOUS

Atlanta City Directories, Atlanta Historical Society.
"Auszug aus dem Kirchenregister der Gemeinde Aldingen am Neckar, Oberamts Ludwigs-
    burg, Wuerrttemburg Elsass" (Extract from the church register of the Aldingen and
    Neckar community, under the jurisdiction of Ludwigsburg, Wuerrttemburg Elsass). In
    possession of Dr. Louis Elsas.
"Cabbagetown Learning Center" grant proposal. The Patch Inc., n.d. [1978?].
"History by a Graveyard" television program. Prime Cable DeKalb, Atlanta, Georgia, 1989.
Promotional brochure. The Patch, Inc., n.d. [1976?].

BOOKS AND PAMPHLETS

Adams, Graham, Jr. *Age of Industrial Violence: The Activities and Findings of the United
    States Commission on Industrial Relations*. New York: Columbia University Press, 1966.
Ayers, Edward L. *The Promise of the New South: Life after Reconstruction*. New York:
    Oxford University Press, 1992.
Baker, Ray Stannard. *Following the Color Line: American Negro Citizenship in the Progressive
    Era*. New York: Harper and Row, 1964.
Bates, J. Leonard. *The United States, 1898–1928: Progressivism and a Society in Transition*.
    New York: McGraw-Hill, 1976.
Beardsley, Edward H. *A History of Neglect: Health Care for Blacks and Mill Workers in the
    Twentieth-Century South*. Knoxville: University of Tennessee Press, 1987.
Birmingham, Stephen. *"Our Crowd": The Great Jewish Families of New York*. New York:
    Harper and Row, 1967.
Brudno, Ezra S. *The Tether*. New York: J. P. Lippincott, 1908.
Bynum, R. Cary. *Cabbagetown: 3 Women: An Oral History Play with Music*. Adapted by
    R. Cary Bynum; music by Joyce Brookshire. Rabun Gap, Ga.: Foxfire Press, c. 1984.
Cameron, Ardis. *Radicals of the Worst Sort: Laboring Women in Lawrence, Massachusetts*.
    Urbana: University of Illinois Press, 1993.
Carlton, David L. *Mill and Town in South Carolina, 1880–1920*. Baton Rouge: Louisiana
    State University Press, 1982.
Carson, Horace. *Time and Changes in a City Called Atlanta: The Story of a Man, His
    Family, and a City as Seen by Horace Carson*. Atlanta: Published by Author, 1979.

Cash, W. J. *The Mind of the South*. New York: Knopf, 1941.

Clayton, Bruce. *W. J. Cash*. Baton Rouge: Louisiana State University Press, 1991.

Coleman, Richard G. *A Short History of the Roswell Manufacturing Company of Roswell, Georgia Home of "Roswell Grey."* 1 March 1982.

Collier, Tarleton. *Fire in the Sky*. Boston: Houghton Mifflin Company, 1941.

Dannenbaum, Jed. *Drink and Disorder: Temperance Reform in Cincinnati from the Washingtonian Revival to the WCTU*. Urbana: University of Illinois Press, 1984.

Davidson, Elizabeth H. *Child Labor Legislation in the Southern Textile States*. Chapel Hill: University of North Carolina Press, 1939.

Davis, Harold E. *Henry Grady's New South: Atlanta, a Brave and Beautiful City*. Athens: University of Georgia Press, 1990.

Dennett, John Richard. *The South as It Is: 1865–1866*. New York: Viking, 1965.

Dinnerstein, Leonard. *The Leo Frank Case*. New York: Columbia University Press, 1968.

Doyle, Don H. *New Men, New Cities, New South: Atlanta, Nashville, Charleston, Mobile, 1860–1910*. Chapel Hill: University of North Carolina Press, 1990.

Duncan, Russell. *Entrepreneur for Equality: Governor Rufus Bullock, Commerce, and Race in Post–Civil War Georgia*. Athens: University of Georgia Press, 1984.

Durban, Pam. *All Set about with Fever Trees*. Boston: David R. Godin, 1985.

Egerton, John. *Speak Now against the Day: The Generation before the Civil Rights Movement in the South*. New York: Knopf, 1994.

Evans, Mrs. E. M. *Living for Jesus or a Sketch of My City Mission Work in Atlanta, Georgia*. Atlanta: Evans Printing Company, c. 1900.

Fink, Gary M. *The Fulton Bag and Cotton Mills Strike of 1914–1915: Espionage, Labor Conflict, and New South Industrial Relations*. Ithaca: ILR Press, 1993.

Fink, Gary M, and Merl E. Reed, eds. *Race, Class, and Community in Southern Labor History*. Tuscaloosa: University of Alabama Press, 1994.

Fink, Leon. *Workingmen's Democracy: The Knights of Labor and American Politics*. Urbana: University of Illinois Press, 1983.

Fishbein, Leslie. *Rebels in Bohemia: The Radicals of the Masses, 1911–1917*. Chapel Hill: University of North Carolina Press, 1982.

Flamming, Douglas. *Creating the Modern South: Millhands and Managers in Dalton, Georgia, 1884–1984*. Chapel Hill: University of North Carolina Press, 1992.

Foner, Philip S. *American Socialism and Black Americans*. Westport, Conn.: Greenwood Press, 1977.

Flynt, Wayne. *Poor but Proud: Alabama's Poor Whites*. Tuscaloosa: University of Alabama Press, 1989.

Gal, Allon. *Brandeis of Boston*. Cambridge: Harvard University Press, 1980.

Garlock, Jonathan. *Guide to the Local Assemblies of the Knights of Labor*. Westport, Conn.: Greenwood Press, 1981.

Garrett, Franklin M. *Atlanta and Environs: A Chronicle of the People and Events*. 3 vols. Atlanta: Peachtree Publishers, 1954.

Gaston, Paul M. *The New South Creed: A Study in Southern Mythmaking*. New York: Knopf, 1973.

Gilmore, Glenda E. *Gender and Jim Crow*. Chapel Hill: University of North Carolina Press, 1996.

Glazer, Nathan. *American Judaism*. 2nd ed., rev. Chicago: University of Chicago Press, 1972.

Golin, Steve. *The Fragile Bridge: Paterson Silk Strike, 1913*. Philadelphia: Temple University Press, 1988.

Grantham, Dewey W., Jr. *Hoke Smith and the Politics of the New South*. Baton Rouge: Louisiana State University Press, 1958.

——. *Southern Progressivism: The Reconciliation of Progress and Tradition*. Knoxville: University of Tennessee Press, 1983.

Gutman, Herbert. *Work, Culture and Society in Industrializing America*. New York: Vintage, 1977.

Hahn, Steven. *The Roots of Southern Populism: Yeoman Farmers and the Transformation of the Georgia Upcountry, 1850–1900*. New York: Oxford University Press, 1983.

Hall, Jacquelyn Dowd, et al. *Like a Family: The Making of a Southern Cotton Mill World*. Chapel Hill: University of North Carolina Press, 1987.

Hanchett, Thomas. *Sorting Out the New South City*. Chapel Hill: University of North Carolina Press, 1998.

Handlin, Oscar. *Adventure in Freedom: Three Hundred Years of Jewish Life in America*. Port Washington, N.Y.: Kennikat Press, 1954.

Henderson, Alexa B. *The Atlanta Life Insurance Company*. Tuscaloosa: University of Alabama Press, 1990.

Hertzberg, Steven. *Strangers within the Gate City: The Jews of Atlanta, 1845–1915*. Philadelphia: Jewish Publication Society of America, 1978.

Hillquit, Morris. *History of Socialism in the United States*. New York: Funk and Wagnalls, 1910.

Hosch, Clarence Robert. *Nevah Come Back No Mo': Boyhood Memories of the Foothills of North Georgia*. New York: Exposition Press, 1968.

Hunter, Tera. *To 'Joy My Freedom: Southern Black Women's Lives and Labors after the Civil War*. Cambridge: Harvard University Press, 1997.

Inman, Arthur Crew. *The Inman Diary: A Public and Private Confession*. 2 vols. Edited by Daniel Aaron. Cambridge: Harvard University Press, 1985.

Jacobson, Julius, ed. *The Negro and the American Labor Movement*. Garden City, N.Y.: Anchor Books, 1968.

Joblin, M. *Cincinnati Past and Present*. Cincinnati: M. Joblin and Co., 1872.

Johnson, Allen, and Dumas Malone. *Dictionary of American Biography*. New York: Scribner, 1948.

Kolb, Deborah M. *The Mediators*. Cambridge: MIT Press, 1983.

Kuhn, Cliff, and Les Hough. *Generations of Sheet Metal Craftsmanship: A History of the Unionized Industry in Georgia*. Atlanta: Sheet Metal Workers International Association Local No. 85 and Central Georgia Sheet Metal Contractors Association, 1988.

Kuhn, Clifford M., Harlon E. Joye, and E. Bernard West. *Living Atlanta: An Oral History of the City, 1914–1948*. Athens: University of Georgia Press, 1990.

Lee, Edna. *The Southerners*. New York: Appleton-Century-Crofts, 1953.

Le Guin, Magnolia Wynn. *A Home-Concealed Woman: The Diaries of Magnolia Wynn Le Guin*. Athens: University of Georgia Press, 1990.

Lewis, Helen M., and Suzanna O'Donnell, eds. *Telling Our Stories, Sharing Our Lives*. Ivanhoe, Va.: Ivanhoe Civic League, 1990.

Link, William A. *The Paradox of Southern Progressivism, 1880–1930*. Chapel Hill: University of North Carolina Press, 1992.

Lippmann, Walter. *Public Opinion*. New York: Macmillan, 1922.

Logan, Rayford G. *The Betrayal of the Negro, from Rutherford B. Hayes to Woodrow Wilson*. New York: Collier Books, 1965.

Lyon, Sarah Watts. *Order against Chaos: Business Culture and Labor Ideology in America, 1880–1915*. Westport, Conn.: Greenwood Press, 1991.

McHugh, Cathy L. *Mill Family: The Labor System in the Southern Cotton Textile Industry.* New York: Oxford University Press, 1988.

McLaurin, Melton A. *The Knights of Labor in the South.* Westport, Conn.: Greenwood Press, 1978.

———. *Paternalism and Protest: Southern Cotton Mill Workers Organized Labor, 1875–1905.* Westport, Conn.: Greenwood Press, 1971.

McLeod, Jonathan W. *Workers and Workplace Dynamics in Reconstruction-Era Atlanta.* Los Angeles: Center for Afro-American Studies [and] Institute of Industrial Relations, University of California, 1989.

McMath, Robert C., Jr., et al. *Engineering the New South: Georgia Tech, 1885–1985.* Athens: University of Georgia Press, 1985.

Marshall, F. Ray. *Labor in the South.* Cambridge: Harvard University Press, 1967.

"The Men and Religion Forward Movement in Atlanta." Atlanta: Men and Religion Forward Movement, 1913.

Mitchell, George. *Ponce de Leon: An Intimate Portrait of Atlanta's Most Famous Avenue.* Atlanta: Argonne Books, 1983.

Mitchell, George S. *Textile Unionism and the South.* Chapel Hill: University of North Carolina Press, 1931.

Newby, I. A. *Plain Folk in the New South: Social Change and Cultural Persistence, 1880–1915.* Baton Rouge: Louisiana State University Press, 1989.

Norwood, Stephen H. *Labor's Flaming Youth: Telephone Operators and Worker Militancy, 1878–1923.* Urbana: University of Illinois Press, 1990.

Pope, Liston. *Millhands and Preachers: A Study of Gastonia.* New Haven: Yale University Press, 1942.

Portelli, Alessandro. *The Death of Luigi Trastulli and Other Stories: Form and Meaning in Oral History.* Albany: State University of New York Press, 1991.

Porter, Pam Durban, ed. *Cabbagetown Families, Cabbagetown Food.* Atlanta: Patch Publications, 1976.

Rayback, Joseph G. *A History of American Labor.* New York: Free Press, 1966.

Reagan, Alice E. *H. I. Kimball, Entrepreneur.* Atlanta: Cherokee Publishing Company, 1983.

Renshaw, Patrick. *The Wobblies: The Story of Syndicalism in the United States.* Garden City, N.Y.: Anchor Books, 1967.

Ross, Steven J. *Workers on the Edge: Work, Leisure, and Politics in Industrializing Cincinnati, 1788–1890.* New York: Columbia University Press, 1985.

———. *Working-Class Hollywood: Silent Film and the Shaping of Class.* Princeton: Princeton University Press, 1998.

Russell, James M. *Atlanta, 1847–1890: City Building in the Old South and the New.* Baton Rouge: Louisiana State University Press, 1988.

Salmond, John A. *Gastonia 1929: The Story of the Loray Mill Strike.* Chapel Hill: University of North Carolina Press, 1995.

Saye, Albert B., ed. *Walter McElreath: An Autobiography.* Macon: Mercer University Press, 1984.

Schneider, Franz, Jr. "Survey of the Public Health Situation, Atlanta, Georgia." New York: Russell Sage Foundation, 1913.

Seretan, L. Glen. *Daniel DeLeon: The Odyssey of an American Marxist.* Cambridge: Harvard University Press, 1979.

Simon, Bryant. *A Fabric of Defeat: The Politics of South Carolina Millhands, 1910–1948.* Chapel Hill: University of North Carolina Press, 1998.

Sklar, Martin J. *The Corporate Reconstruction of American Capitalism, 1890–1916.* Cambridge: Harvard University Press, 1988.

Solomon, Barbara. *Ancestors and Immigrants: A Changing New England Tradition.* Chicago: University of Chicago Press, 1972.

Stange, Maren. *Symbols of Ideal Life: Social Documentary in America, 1890–1950.* Cambridge: Cambridge University Press, 1989.

Stott, William. *Documentary Expression and Thirties America.* New York: Oxford University Press, 1973.

Thernstrom, Stephan. *The Other Bostonians: Poverty and Progress in the American Metropolis, 1880–1970.* Cambridge: Harvard University Press, 1973.

Tripp, Anne Huber. *The I.W.W. and the Paterson Silk Strike of 1913.* Urbana: University of Illinois Press, 1987.

Tullos, Alan. *Habits of Industry: White Culture and the Transformation of the Carolina Piedmont.* Chapel Hill: University of North Carolina Press, 1989.

Watkins, Floyd C., and Charles Hubert Watkins. *Yesterday in the Hills.* Athens: University of Georgia Press, 1973.

Weinstein, James. *The Corporate Ideal in the Liberal State: 1900–1918.* Boston: Beacon Press, 1968.

Wertheimer, Barbara Meyer. *We Were There: The Story of Working Women in America.* New York: Pantheon, 1977.

Who Was Who in America. Chicago: Marquis, 1943.

Wiebe, Robert H. *Businessmen and Reform: A Study of the Progressive Movement.* Cambridge: Harvard University Press, 1962.

——. *The Search for Order, 1877–1920.* New York: Hill and Wang, 1967.

Wiggins, Gene. *Fiddlin' Georgia Crazy: Fiddlin' John Carson, His Real World, and the World of His Songs.* Urbana: University of Illinois Press, 1987.

Williamson, Joel. *The Crucible of Race: Black-White Relations in the American South since Emancipation.* New York: Free Press, 1984.

Wilson, John Stainbeck. *Atlanta as It Is.* New York: Little, Rennie & Co., 1871. Reprinted as Atlanta Historical Bulletin no. 6 (January–April 1941).

Woodward, C. Vann. *Origins of the New South, 1877–1913.* Baton Rouge: Louisiana State University Press, 1951.

Wright, Gavin. *Old South, New South: Revolutions in the Southern Economy since the Civil War.* New York: Basic Books, 1986.

Zieger, Robert H., ed. *Organized Labor in the Twentieth-Century South.* Knoxville: University of Tennessee Press, 1991.

ARTICLES

Bauman, Mark K. "Centripetal and Centrifugal Forces Facing the People of Many Communities: Atlanta Jewry from the Frank Case to the Great Depression." *Atlanta Historical Journal* 23 (Fall 1979): 26–27.

Beatty, Bess. "Gender Relations in Southern Textiles: A Historiographical Overview." In *Race, Class, and Community in Southern Labor History*, edited by Gary M Fink and Merl E. Reed, 9–16. Tuscaloosa: University of Alabama Press, 1994.

Blackwelder, Julia Kirk. "Mop and Typewriter: Women's Work in Early-Twentieth-Century Atlanta." *Atlanta Historical Journal* 27 (1983): 21–30.

Blicksilver, Jack. "The International Cotton Exposition of 1881 and Its Impact upon the Economic Development of Georgia." *Atlanta Economic Review* 7, no. 5 (May 1957): 1–5.

———. "The International Cotton Exposition of 1881 and Its Impact upon the Economic Development of Georgia." *Atlanta Economic Review* 7, no. 6 (June 1957): 1–5.

Boyte, Harry. "The Textile Industry: Keel of Southern Industrialization." *Radical America* 6 (March–April 1972): 4–49.

Branch, Anne Lavinia. "Atlanta and the American Settlement House Movement." *Atlanta Historical Journal* 12 (June 1967): 37–51.

Burrison, John A. "Fiddlers in the Alley: Atlanta as an Early Country Music Center." *Atlanta Historical Bulletin* 21 (Summer 1977): 59–87.

Carlton, David L. "Paternalism and the Southern Textile Labor: A Historiographical Review." In *Race, Class, and Community in Southern Labor History*, edited by Gary M Fink and Merl E. Reed, 17–26. Tuscaloosa: University of Alabama Press, 1994.

Carlton, David L., and Peter A. Coclanis. "Capital Mobilization and Southern Industry: 1880–1945." *Journal of Economic History* 64 (March 1989): 73–94.

Chaikin, Ellen. "The Jewish Sections of Oakland Cemetery." *Atlanta Historical Journal* 23 (Fall 1979): 55–64.

Cmiel, Kenneth. "Destiny and Amnesia: The Vision of Modernity in Robert H. Wiebe's *Search for Order*." *Reviews in American History* 21 (1993): 352–56.

Cohen, Nathan. "Atlanta Scorned First Movie." *Atlanta Journal* magazine, 11 September 1932.

Cooper, Walter G. "Origin and Early Years of the Atlanta Chamber of Commerce." *The City Builder* 13 (March 1929): 6.

Crowe, Charles. "Racial Massacre in Atlanta, September 22, 1906." *Journal of Negro History* 54 (April 1969): 150–73.

———. "Racial Violence and Social Reform: Origins of the Atlanta Riot of 1906." *Journal of Negro History* 53 (July 1968): 234–56.

Deaton, Thomas M. "James G. Woodward: The Working Man's Mayor." *Atlanta History* 31 (Fall 1987): 11–23.

De Graffenreid, Clare. "The Georgia Cracker in the Cotton Mills." *Century* 41 (February 1891): 483–98.

Du Bois, W. E. B. "The Negro Landholder of Georgia." *Bureau of Labor Statistics Bulletin* 35 (July 1901): 720.

Durban, Pam. "This Heat." In *All Set About with Fever Trees*, by Pam Durban, 3–34. Boston: David R. Godine, 1985.

Fiedman, Harvey L. "Sara Agnes McLaughlin Conboy." In *Encyclopedia Americana*, 7:497. Danbury, Conn.: Grolier, 1988.

Fink, Gary M. "Efficiency and Control: Labor Espionage in Southern Textiles." In *Organized Labor in the Twentieth-Century South*, edited by Robert H. Zieger, 13–34. Knoxville: University of Tennessee Press, 1991.

———. "Labor Espionage and the Organization of Southern Textiles: The Fulton Bag and Cotton Mill Company Strike of 1914–15." *Labor's Heritage* 1 (1989): 10–35.

———. "We Are City Builders, Too: Atlanta Typographers and New South Boosterism, Atlanta Style." *Atlanta History* 36, no. 4 (Winter 1993): 4053.

Fink, Leon. "Class Conflict in the Gilded Age: The Figure and the Phantom." *Radical History Review* 3 (Fall–Winter 1975): 56–73.

Flowers, Sabrina, and Richard Putter. "Cabbagetown." *Mind and Nature: A Journal of Interdisciplinary Studies* 6 (Fall 1986): 34–43.

Frederickson, Mary. "Four Decades of Change: Black Workers in Southern Textiles, 1941–1981." *Radical America* 16 (November–December 1982): 27–44.

"From the Front Line to the Color Line." *Southern Exposure* 11 (January–February 1983): 72.

Galambos, Louis. "The Emerging Organizational Synthesis in Modern American History." *Business History Review* 44, no. 3 (1970): 279–90.

Grable, Stephen W. "The Other Side of the Tracks: Cabbagetown—A Working-Class Neighborhood in Transition during the Early Twentieth Century." *Atlanta Historical Journal* 26 (Summer–Fall 1982): 51–66.

Gutman, Herbert. "Class, Status, and Community Power in Nineteenth-Century American Industrial Cities: Paterson, New Jersey: A Case Study." In *Work, Culture and Society in Industrializing America*, by Herbert Gutman, 234–59. New York: Vintage, 1977.

———. "The Negro and the United Mine Workers of America." In *The Negro and the American Labor Movement*, edited by Julius Jacobson, 49–127. Garden City, N.Y.: Anchor Books, 1968.

Gutman, Herbert, and Richard Sutch. "Sambo Makes Good, or Were Slaves Imbued with the Protestant Work Ethic?" In *Reckoning with Slavery: A Critical Study in the Quantitative History of American Negro Slavery*, by Paul A. David et al., 55–94. New York: Oxford University Press, 1976.

Hall, Jacquelyn Dowd. "Disorderly Women: Gender and Labor Militancy in the Appalachian South." *Journal of American History* 73 (September 1986): 354–82.

———. "O. Delight Smith's Progressive Era: Labor, Feminism, and Reform in the Urban South." In *Visible Women: An Anthology*, edited by Nancy Hewitt and Suzanne Lebsock, 166–98. Urbana: University of Illinois Press, 1993.

———. "Private Eyes, Public Women: Images of Sex and Class in the Urban South, Atlanta, Georgia, 1913–1915." In *Work Engendered: Toward a New History of American Labor*, edited by Ava Baron, 243–72. Ithaca: Cornell University Press, 1991.

Henderson, Alexa Benson. "Paupers, Pastors and Politicians: Reflections upon Afro-Americans Buried in Oakland Cemetery." *Atlanta Historical Bulletin* 20 (Summer 1976): 42–60.

Herreshoff, David. "Daniel DeLeon: The Rise of Marxist Politics." In *American Radicals: Some Problems and Personalities*, edited by Harvey Goldberg, 199–218. New York: Modern Reader Paperbacks, 1969.

Hickey, Georgina. "Waging War on 'Loose Living Hotels' and 'Cheap Soda Joints': The Criminalization of Working-Class Women in Atlanta's Public Sphere." *Georgia Historical Quarterly* 82 (Winter 1998): 775–800.

Jackson, Marion M. "The Churches of Atlanta." *The City Builder* (February 1927): 6–9.

Jones, Alton Dumar. "The Child Labor Reform Movement in Georgia." *Georgia Historical Quarterly* 49 (December 1965): 396–412.

Karson, Marc, and Ronald Radosh. "The AFL and the Negro Worker, 1894–1949." In *The Negro and the American Labor Movement*, edited by Julius Jacobson, 155–87. Garden City, N.Y.: Anchor Books, 1968.

Kazin, Michael, and Steven J. Ross. "America's Labor Day: The Dilemmas of a Workers' Celebration." *Journal of American History* 78 (March 1992): 1294–1323.

Leach, Eugene E. "The Radicals of *The Masses*." In *1915, The Cultural Moment*, edited by Adele Heller and Lois Rudnick, 27–47. New Brunswick: Rutgers University Press, 1991.

Lefever, Harry G. "The Involvement of the Men and Religion Forward Movement in the Cause of Labor Justice, Atlanta, Georgia, 1912–1916." *Labor History* 14 (Fall 1973): 521–35.

———. "Prostitution, Politics, and Religion: The Crusade against Vice in Atlanta in 1912." *Atlanta Historical Journal* 24 (Spring 1980): 7–29.

McCurry, Stephanie. "Piedmont Mill Workers and the Politics of History." *Labour/Le Travail* 29 (Spring 1992): 229–37.

McKelway, Alexander J. "Child Labor in the Southern Cotton Mills." *Annals of the American Academy of Political and Social Sciences* 27 (March 1906): 10, 80–83.

Maclachlan, Gretchen E. "Atlanta's Industrial Women, 1879–1920." *Atlanta History* 36 (Winter 1993): 16–23.

MacLean, Nancy. "The Leo Frank Case Reconsidered: Gender and Sexual Politics in the Making of Reactionary Populism." *Journal of American History* 78 (December 1991): 917–48.

McMath, Robert C., Jr. "History by a Graveyard: The Fulton Bag and Cotton Mill Records." *Labor's Heritage* 1 (1989): 4–9.

Margolis, Eric. "Mining Photographs: Unearthing the Meanings of Historical Photos." *Radical History Review* 40 (January 1988): 32–50.

Marshall, F. Ray. "The Negro in Southern Unions." In *The Negro and the American Labor Movement*, edited by Julius Jacobson, 128–54. Garden City, N.Y.: Anchor Books, 1968.

"Missionary Work among the Destitute Whites at Atlanta, Georgia." *Philadelphia Methodist*, 17 June 1880.

Park, Robert E. "The National Negro Business League." *The Colored American Magazine* 11 (October 1906): 222.

Reagan, Alice E. "Promoting the New South: Hannibal I. Kimball and Henry W. Grady." *Atlanta Historical Journal* 27 (Fall 1983): 7–9.

Rhodes, Clarence A. "A Brief Report on the Year's Work and Progress of the Wesley House Clinic." *Atlanta Journal-Record of Medicine* 63, no. 2 (May 1916): 50–53.

——. "A Free Clinic and Does It Pay?" *Atlanta Journal-Record of Medicine* 61, no. 1 (April 1914): 11–15.

Ross, Steven J. "Struggles for the Screen: Workers, Radicals, and the Political Uses of Silent Film." *American Historical Review* 96 (April 1991): 333–67.

Taylor, A. Elizabeth. "Woman Suffrage Activities in Atlanta." *Atlanta Historical Journal* 23 (Winter 1979–80): 45–54.

Teel, Leonard Ray. "How a Yankee Brought Textiles to Georgia." *Georgia Trend* 1 (January 1986): 124–27.

Thomas, Rebecca L. "John J. Eagan and Industrial Democracy." *Alabama Review* 43 (Fall 1990): 270–88.

Trachtenberg, Alan, "Ever-the Human Document." Essay in *America and Lewis Hine*, by Lewis Wickes Hine, 118–37. New York: Aperture, Inc., 1977.

Washington, Booker T. "Golden Rule in Atlanta." *Outlook* 84 (1906): 913–16.

Weed, Inis. "Instead of Strikes." *Everybody's* 29 (July 1913): 131–32.

Weed, Inis, and Louise Carey. "I Make Cheap Silk." *The Masses* 5 (November 1913): 7.

Weinstock, Harris. "Free Speech: To Forbid a Man to Speak, on the Assumption That He Will Say Something Important, Endangers the Republic." *Twentieth Century Magazine* 6 (August 1912): 76–82.

Weisiger, Kendall. "Joe Logan, Genius of Social Work in the South." *Atlanta Historical Bulletin* 4 (January 1939): 5–22.

"What's Cookin' in Cabbagetown." Atlanta Urban Design Commission *Newsletter* 1 (September 1978): 34–38.

Whites, LeeAnn. "Love, Hate, Rape, Lynching: Rebecca Latimer Felton and the Gender Politics of Racial Violence." In *Democracy Betrayed: The Wilmington Race Riot of 1898 and Its Legacy*, edited by David S. Cecelski and Timothy B. Tyson, 143–62. Chapel Hill: University of North Carolina Press, 1998.

Woodward, C. Vann. "The Elusive Mind of the South." In *American Counterpoint*. Boston: Little, Brown, 1971.

Zieger, Robert H. Introduction to "Southern Textiles: Toward a New Historiographical Synthesis." In *Race, Class, and Community in Southern Labor History*, edited by Gary M Fink and Merl E. Reed, 3–8. Tuscaloosa: University of Alabama Press, 1994.

———. "Textile Workers and Historians." In *Organized Labor in the Twentieth-Century South*, edited by Robert H. Zieger, 35–59. Knoxville: University of Tennessee Press, 1991.

DISSERTATIONS, THESES, AND UNPUBLISHED PAPERS

Bolden, Willie Miller. "The Political Structure of Charter Revision Movements in Atlanta during the Progressive Era." Ph.D. dissertation, Emory University, 1978.

Brooks, Robert R. "The United Textile Workers of America." Ph.D. dissertation, Yale University, 1935.

Carter, Raymond Douglas. "Jerome Jones and the Journal of Labor." Ph.D. dissertation, Georgia State University, 1996.

Deaton, Thomas M. "Atlanta during the Progressive Era." Ph.D. dissertation, University of Georgia, 1969.

Dial, Alton Timothy. "Public Health in Atlanta during the Progressive Era." M.A. thesis, Georgia State University, 1970.

Evans, Mercer Griffin. "The History of the Organized Labor Movement in Georgia." Ph.D. dissertation, University of Chicago, 1929.

Fink, Leon R. "The Monday Morning Quarterback: Charles McCarthy and the Debacle of the Commission on Industrial Relations." Unpublished paper in possession of author.

———. "The Search for Order Reconsidered." Paper delivered at American Historical Association meeting, 3 January 1997.

Galishoff, Stuart. "Atlanta: A Pioneer in Wastewater Technology, 1890–1918." Paper delivered at American Society for Environmental History meeting, 2 March 1991.

Godshalk, David Fort. "In the Wake of Riot: Atlanta's Struggle for Order, 1899–1919." Ph.D. dissertation, Yale University, 1992.

Goodson, Howard Steven. " 'South of the North, North of the South': Public Entertainment in Atlanta, 1880–1930." Ph.D. dissertation, Emory University, 1995.

Hickey, Georgina Susan. "Visibility, Politics, and Urban Development: Working-Class Women in Early-Twentieth-Century Atlanta." Ph.D. dissertation, University of Michigan, 1995.

Kuhn, Clifford. "A Critique of the New South Creed: Artisans and Politics in 1880s Atlanta." Paper delivered at Southern Labor Studies Conference, October 1982.

———. "Images of Dissent: The Pictorial Record of the 1914–1915 Strike at Atlanta's Fulton Bag and Cotton Mills." Paper delivered at Organization of American Historians meeting, 1989.

Lyons, Elizabeth Mack. "Business Buildings in Atlanta: A Study in Urban Growth and Form." Ph.D. dissertation, Emory University, 1975.

———. "Skyscrapers in Atlanta, 1890–1915." M.A. thesis, Emory University, 1962.

McCallum, Brenda. "Manipulating Culture and Managing Workers: A Case Study of Invented Tradition." Paper delivered at the Oral History Association annual meeting, 13 October 1988.

Maclachlan, Gretchen Ehrmann. "The Factory Lot in 1900: Urban or Rural." Unpublished seminar paper, Emory University, 1986.

——. "A Woman's Place: The Methodist Women's Settlement House in Atlanta." Paper delivered at Southern Conference on Women's History, 1988.

——. "Women's Work: Atlanta's Industrialization and Urbanization, 1879–1929." Ph.D. dissertation, Emory University, 1992.

Mixon, Gregory Lamont. "The Atlanta Riot of 1906." Ph.D. dissertation, University of Cincinnati, 1989.

Nesbitt, Martha. "The Social Gospel in Atlanta: 1900–1920." Ph.D. dissertation, Georgia State University, 1975.

Paul, Brad. "Making Gains in Old Dixie: The Socialist Party of Georgia, 1903–1917." Unpublished seminar paper, Georgia State University, 1992.

Racine, Philip Noel. "Atlanta's Schools: A History of the Public School System, 1869–1955." Ph.D. dissertation, Emory University, 1969.

Reagan, Alice E. "Hannibal I. Kimball: Northern Entrepreneur in Reconstruction Atlanta." Ph.D. dissertation, North Carolina State University, 1981.

Scott, Thomas A. "Cobb County, Georgia, 1880–1900: A Socio-Economic Study of an Upper Piedmont County." Ph.D. dissertation, University of Tennessee, 1978.

Segal, Scott Howard. "The Cabbagetown Community in Atlanta, Georgia: A Rural Fixture in the Urban Landscape." Honors thesis, Emory University, 1986.

Taylor, Arthur Reed. "From the Ashes: Atlanta during Reconstruction." Ph.D. dissertation, Emory University, 1973.

Wrigley, Steven Wayne. "The Triumph of Provincialism: Public Life in Georgia, 1898–1917." Ph.D. dissertation, Northwestern University, 1986.

Social Gospel, 46, 64, 229
Socialist Labor Party, 24, 27
Socialist Party, 102, 118, 216
Socialist Trade and Labor Alliance, 24
Sociological Society, 66
Southern Bag Factory, 11
The Southerners, 230
Southern Labor Congress, 41
Southern Railroad, 118
Southern Textile Bulletin, 99, 105, 163, 185,
    222
Sphinx Film Company, 158–59
Stahl, Clara, 15
Stalnaker, G. A., 77, 131, 135, 142
Stanley, H. M., 123
Star Theater, 49
Steel, Samuel, 202
Stephenson, Jason, 73
Stevens, Cliff, 127
Stevens, Eva, 80, 85
Stevens, Nannie May, 85
Strike of 1914–15, 1, 88; celebrity of, 1; central
    to southern organizing campaign, 2, 6,
    190, 196; significance of, 2, 196, 205, 223,
    231; October 1913 walkout and aftermath,
    89, 90–94, 133; increased worker self-
    activity, 93, 95–97; harassment and dis-
    missal of activists, 95–96, 133, 212–13;
    meetings in early May 1914, 104; issue of
    discrimination against union members,
    104, 106; commencement of, 106; esti-
    mates of number of participants in, 106;
    original issues of, 106; strike vote, 106;
    minimized by Oscar Elsas, 106, 117, 123–
    24, 174, 195, 201–2, 219; impact on produc-
    tion, 106–7, 108, 117, 137, 139, 140, 147, 176,
    208; support for, 107, 108, 112, 117–18, 140–
    41; women workers and, 107, 112; picket-
    ing, 107, 112, 116, 123, 125–29, 131, 144–47,
    192; Oscar Elsas speech, 108; strike meet-
    ings, 108–9, 121, 134, 138, 139; meeting of
    Atlanta area manufacturers about, 109;
    union commissary, 109, 112, 163; company
    surveillance operation, 110–15, 128, 137–
    38; role of police in, 111, 128, 163–65;
    encounters between strikers and non-
    strikers, 111–12, 125–29, 137–38; and effort
    to organize black workers, 113; linkage of
    strikers to immoral practices, 113–14;

prostrike songs, 114–15; employment of
    labor spies, 115–16, 119–21; gathering
    steam, 116; evictions of strikers, 116–17,
    132–33, 139; importance of publicity to,
    117, 122, 150; use of photographs in, 117,
    151–58, 160–63; use of motion pictures in,
    117, 158–60; retaliation against strike sup-
    porters, 118; key role of Smith and Miles
    in, 118–19; organizers' appeal to anti-
    Semitism, 121; appeals to racism, 121, 160–
    62; Detecto incident, 121, 163; documenta-
    tion of company abuses, 122; memories
    of, 123, 149, 182, 230–31; misrepresenta-
    tions of, 124; recruitment of strike
    breakers, 124–27; threats and violence,
    127–31; use of labor contract to keep
    workers on job, 129–30; families divided
    over, 134–35; and Lindale recruits, 136–39;
    UTW resources taxed after evictions, 139;
    problems with commissary, 141–43, 193;
    growing worker dissatisfaction with, 142,
    145, 191–94; gradual return of strikers, 145;
    decline of picketing, 145–46; return to full
    production, 147; expansion of strike
    demands, 150; connected to child labor
    issue, 151–54, 187; involvement of MRFM
    in, 167–74; call for independent investiga-
    tion of, 168; removal of control from
    workers involved, 171; MRFM mass meet-
    ing, 171–74; MRFM call for arbitration of,
    173–74; in national labor-related debates,
    184; Division of Conciliation involvement
    in, 185–87; CIR investigation of, 187–90;
    tent colony, 190–93, 194; discrediting of
    strike leadership, 193–95; as symbol of
    southern mills, 198; discussed in Con-
    gress, 203–6; as reflection of tensions in
    Atlanta and New South, 214–15; described
    as involving mainly women and children,
    217; modern character of, 220–21;
    reflected growing interconnectedness of
    mill owners, 222; national dimension of,
    223; complex relationship of workers to,
    224; impact of on industrial relations, 225;
    mentioned in personnel records, 227; role
    of in sustaining UTW southern cam-
    paign, 228; influence on 1916 streetcar
    strike, 229–30
Strikers' Journal, 163

Wesley House Athletic Club, 69
Wesley House Boys Club, 69
Wesley House Woman's Club, 48, 66, 67, 68
West, William S., 187
West Point, Georgia, 115
White, John E., 170, 171–72, 174, 221
White, Mose, 10
White, Samuel, 25, 27
White City Park, 48, 108
White supremacy, 25–26, 27, 34; among
    Fulton workers, 35–36, 217–18; and
    Fulton management, 36, 217–19
Wickersham, Charles A., 127
Wiggins, R. W., 96
Wilk, Max, 118
Wilkinson, Mell W., 165, 179
Williams, J. W., 116, 119, 121, 152
Wilmer, C. B., 140, 172, 175
Wilson, Samuel, 80
Wilson, William B., 122, 153, 184, 185, 187
Wilson, Woodrow, 184
Winn, W. H., 29
Winyard, A. E., 116, 119, 121
Womack, Sam, 137–38
Woman's Building, 26
Women, 18; in Factory Lot, 23; growing pub-
    lic visibility, 26–27, 52, 216; concern over
    working, 45, 46–47, 51, 54, 150; challeng-
    ing gender norms, 52; in mill district, 70;
    portrayal of strikers as, 150, 217
Women's Bureau, Department of Labor, 184
Women's League of Atlanta, 117
Women suffrage, 52
Women workers: in early cotton mills, 17; in
    1897 race strike, 26–27; in Labor Day
    parade, 29; increase of white women in
    Atlanta workforce, 46–47; MRFM inter-
    ested in, 51; in Fulton bag mill, 74; sexual
    harassment of, 85–86; in October 1913
    walkout, 93; affidavits from, 107; and
    Fulton strike, 107, 112, 122; conditions of
    investigated by Inis Weed, 189
Wood, R. L., 91, 92, 94, 97
Woodward, James G., 40, 42, 47, 91, 123, 164,
    166
Workers, Fulton Mills: and broader com-
    munity, 5, 24; number in workforce, 11, 21;
    Upcountry origins of, 17, 58–59, 231;
    resistance, 19–20; and ties to broader

working class, 24; compared to other
    Piedmont textile workers, 24, 221–22;
    grievances of, 31, 60, 64, 132; anti-
    Semitism of, 55; origins of, 56–59; pre-
    vious jobs in Atlanta, 57–58; from Pied-
    mont textile communities, 59–60; tran-
    sience of, 60–61, 88, 89; and company
    housing, 62–63; and alternatives to com-
    pany housing, 63; distrust of manage-
    ment, 64–65; and Wesley House, 68–70;
    compared to slaves, 71, 134; resentment of
    company rules, 84; loom fixers, 84, 88,
    89–90; bag mill workers, 86; interactions
    with work situation, 87–88; increased
    self-activity after October 1913 walkout,
    93, 95–97; surveillance of by manage-
    ment, 93–95; reprisals against, 94–96;
    reaction to dismissals, 95–96, 105–6;
    growing connection with organized
    labor, 96–98; reaction to evictions, 117,
    132–33, 213; portrayals of, 124, 150; com-
    plex relationship to strike, 124, 224; alien-
    ation of, 132, 135–36; reasons for leaving
    or staying during strike, 132–36; dissatis-
    faction with strike leadership, 142, 145,
    191–95; reasons for returning to work, 145;
    former strikers seek reemployment, 224
Working conditions, 19, 31, 72–90, 208, 212;
    hours, 19, 72; cotton dust, 72; child labor,
    72–74, 208; supervisors, 73, 80, 84–85;
    wages, 77–78, 208; piecework, 77–78, 80;
    fines, 78–81, 208, 212; rules and regula-
    tions, 84–87, 89–90
Working World, 18
Working World Publishing Company, 20
Wright, Robert, 2, 3, 6, 213, 217; active union
    member, 2, 133–34; and fines, 80; and
    rules, 83; and evictions, 133; speeches of,
    134; helped by son-in-law, 140; on new-
    comers at commissary, 142; critical of
    strike leadership, 143, 191–94; and Harry
    Preston, 145, 196; and tent colony, 192–93;
    expelled from union, 198; at CIR hearing,
    212; not rehired, 224
Wright, Sallie, 2, 6, 133, 134, 213; discharged,
    2, 133; seeks reinstatement, 224

Young, M. D., 135